MW01056330

THE CAMPAIGN
FOR
NORTH AFRICA

Also by Jack Coggins

THE CAMPAIGN FOR GUADALCANAL

SHIPS AND SEAMEN OF THE AMERICAN REVOLUTION

ARMS AND EQUIPMENT OF THE CIVIL WAR

THE FIGHTING MAN

THE HORSEMAN'S BIBLE

THE CAMPAIGN
FOR
NORTH AFRICA

WRITTEN AND ILLUSTRATED BY

JACK COGGINS

DOUBLEDAY & COMPANY, INC. | *Garden City, New York* | 1980

This book is dedicated to my wife, Alma, who gave up months of her painting time to help in researching, typing, proofreading, layout, and preparation for maps and drawings for this project—which would not have been attempted without her.

Library of Congress Cataloging in Publication Data

Coggins, Jack.
The campaign for North Africa.

Includes index.
1. World War, 1939–1945—Campaigns—Africa,
North. I. Title.
D766.82.C57   940.54′23
ISBN: 0-385-04351-1
Library of Congress Catalog Card Number 79–3179

CONTENTS

I

Prelude

SETTING THE STAGE

The Allied invasion of French Morocco and Algeria, code name "Torch," was for the American forces the beginning of a campaign. For the British it was the end of one. Allied forces went ashore in French-held North Africa on November 8, 1942, and the final Axis surrender in Tunisia came on May 13, 1943—just over six months later. But for the British the war in North Africa had begun almost three years earlier, on June 11, 1940. Operation "Torch," therefore, was only the final phase of a series of operations designed first to contain and then defeat the Axis forces on the African continent.

In many respects the campaign for North Africa was incidental to the grand strategy of World War II as a whole. For the German High Command it was a sideshow—often an annoyance—sidetracking men and materiel desperately needed for the all-out battle with the Soviets. Hitler appears never to have grasped the potentials of a victory in the Middle East. Unlike Napoleon, Egypt did not lure the German dictator, who preferred to batter his way eastward the hard way through the Soviet armies in the Caucasus.

The American military leaders in general also regarded the North African involvement with disfavor. It was a diversion from the basic plan of attacking across the Channel and ultimately defeating the Germans on their own soil. To drive straight at the enemy's main forces, regardless of other considerations, political or otherwise, may be a laudable precept, but given the expertise and equipment available in 1942, a cross-Channel drive could only have ended in disaster—a second Dunkirk.

The British approach was more realistic. A mountain climber, when asked why he climbed a lofty peak, replied "Because it is there." The British fought the Italians in North Africa for somewhat the same reason—because they were there. Churchill was not a mountain climber, but he was a fighter. And after Dunkirk, with the Continent closed to him, the only place he would get to grips with his enemies was in Africa.

Later in the war, many American leaders, political and military, were apt to see in Britain's concern for the Mediterranean some Machiavellian scheme for the advancement of British imperialism. It is true that the British, better versed in Continental diplomacy, saw long-range advantages in what Americans were prone to dismiss as Balkan and Middle Eastern "adventures"—adventures that, if pursued, might have ultimately resulted in a somewhat contracted base for the "Iron Curtain." But in 1940 the spread of Soviet power was not the issue. And while the Mediterranean Sea itself might be written off by the British as an open sea lane (as with Italy's entry into the war it actually was), what could not be written off was the Middle East and its approaches. For the Middle East meant oil—and without oil no ship could steam, no plane could fly, and no vehicle could roll. Loss of the Mediterranean "lifeline" meant only a grave inconvenience; loss of the oil fields meant disaster. It was not for love of Egypt or the Egyptians that the British finally stood with their backs to the wall at El Alamein. In general the British despised the "Gyppos" and were well hated in return. But Egypt was the key to the Levant, and as long as that door remained closed the vital fields were safe. And not only safe in Allied hands, but also denied to the oil-starved enemy.

At the outbreak of World War II Libya (Tripolitania and Cyrenaica), Eritrea, Italian Somaliland, and newly (1935–36) conquered Ethiopia were garrisoned by some five hundred thousand men, both Italian and native troops. It was not to be expected that the bellicose Mussolini would allow his vaunted legions to sit idle while his ally Hitler disposed of the French and the (supposedly) collapsing British. Soon after the fall of France the Italian armies in Africa were on the march. Poor Duce. By the time our narrative begins he had been defeated in the Western Desert, his East African empire was in ruins, and hundreds of thousands of his unhappy warriors were dead or prisoners. But his German allies had succeeded where his own troops had failed, and as Rommel pounded down the dusty road toward Alamein, Mussolini was in Africa (complete with white horse) for his triumphal entry into Cairo.

The fall of that ancient city seemed very close in June of 1942, but the latter-day Caesar was not to celebrate his triumph. Instead, the narrative recounts the check and defeat of the Axis forces in the Western Desert, the invasion by U.S. and British forces of French North Africa, and the subsequent annihilation of the enemy in Tunisia. But before beginning this history of the final Allied victories in North Africa, a brief résumé of the events preceding Alamein and the "Torch" operation is necessary. And as geography has a great deal to do with any military operation, a short description of the terrain (and climate) of North Africa is included in this opening chapter.

The fighting on land cannot be logically separated from the war at sea. Though the war was fought over part (a very small part) of a huge continent, control of the sea routes was vital. For excluding the minimal cargoes transported by air, nearly every man, tank, truck, gun, bullet, and shell came to Africa by sea, and the arrival of a convoy of merchant ships or the sinking of a tanker often had a direct and measurable impact on the fighting ashore.

The Axis supply routes were comparatively short, though at times exceedingly dangerous. Men and supplies for "Torch" came across the Atlantic or from British ports, with either route open to attack by U boats. The difficulties of supplying the forces in the Western Desert can best be appreciated by the realization that (the Mediterranean could be ruled out as a practical route) the distance from the United Kingdom to Suez via the Cape of Good Hope is some 12,800 miles.

Special convoys of fast ships could make the journey in less than five weeks. But fifteen-knot freighters were scarce, and most vessels had to break the journey at Freetown (Sierra Leone) and at the Cape to replenish with fuel, stores, and water. The average voyage took six weeks, but turnaround was often slow as the Egyptian ports were not geared for high-capacity cargo handling. The shortage of shipping made it uneconomical to send vessels back to Britain in ballast, so they were usually routed elsewhere—India or Australia, perhaps, to pick up cargo. As it is more than 3,000 miles from Port Said to Bombay, another 5,800-odd miles from Bombay to Melbourne and from there some 12,000 miles back to England, it is understandable that the round trip could take an average freighter five months or more.

Losses, particularly in the Mediterranean, were high, and only a percentage of the war materiel and fuel shipped reached its destination. Often the success or failure of an operation depended on how large this percentage might be. The passage or interdiction of these supplies called for the deployment of large numbers of warships, both surface craft and undersea, and thousands of aircraft. Almost the entire Italian merchant marine was ultimately involved in this supply struggle, as were a large number of British and Allied merchant and transport vessels.

But the landing of Allied fuel and materiel in Egypt and North Africa and Axis supplies in Libya, time-consuming and/or hazardous as this might be, was only the beginning. There was the desert to contend with, mile after mile of it—rough routes on which sand and rocks, dust and mud, heat and cold, and mines and enemy aircraft took their toll of vehicles and drivers.

One other factor must always be borne in mind when studying the campaign in North Africa. That is the effect of the other operations undertaken by the opposing forces in other and not necessarily adjacent theaters. Thus the Italian invasion of Greece on October 28, 1940, led ultimately to the disastrous British intervention, which drained the cream of their desert forces, fresh from victories over the Italians. The absence of these battle-tested troops laid the way open for the sweeping counteroffensive by the newly arrived Afrika Korps. And a fraction of the men and materiel absorbed by Operation "Barbarossa," the German invasion of the Soviet Union (June 22, 1941), might well have resulted in victory for Rommel and the subsequent loss to the British of Egypt and the Suez Canal.

THINGS GEOGRAPHICAL . . .

American troops who imagined that all North Africa was a sea of sand, dotted with oases and *Beau Geste*-type forts, were in for a surprise when they reached their destination, but the Western Desert was real enough. It stretched over five hundred miles—from the Nile to the Tripolitanian uplands—and covered some two million square miles. Except for a few small streams in the hills of Cyrenaica, there were no rivers. Along the coast it might rain several times a year. Deeper in the desert it might not rain at all for years. There were a few wells and farther south an oasis or two, but in general the area was completely arid, and providing water for tens of thousands of thirsty men and machines proved one of the major supply headaches of the campaign.

A coastal plain fringed the Mediterranean shore of Egypt and Cyrenaica, a distance, from Alamein to Benghazi, of some 575 miles. This plain varied in width from a few miles to a few feet and was bordered more or less continuously by an escarpment several hundred feet high, which was in most places impassable to wheeled transport. A few gaps, as at Halfaya, gave access for all types of vehicles to the desert plateau above. This scorching area was composed of vast stretches of stony waste and loose sand, spread more or less thinly over rock —so thinly in places that digging a shallow trench or gun pit was often impossible. In some spots the underlying rock pushed up to form low ridges. In others there were depressions—some mere saucer-like hollows, others steep-sided and rugged. South of El Alamein lay the largest, the Qattara Depression—several thousand square miles in extent and in places some 400 feet below sea level. West and south of Qattara lay the Great Sand Sea and the Kalansho and Rebiana sand seas. The Arabs called it "the Devil's Country."

The sand of the Western Desert was not really sand at all but fine gritty dust. This rose in great clouds behind any moving vehicles, covered and penetrated everything, made living a misery, and maintenance a mechanic's nightmare. A breeze covered the desert with a fog of dust, while strong winds raised the *khamsin*, which sometimes blew for days, rolling dust clouds that turned day into a dun-colored twilight. Naturally there was almost no vegetation, only scattered bushes of prickly "camel thorn," and on the coast an occasional palm.

These desolate plains appeared to be flat, but there were frequent dips and swells. These undulations were often only a few feet high, so gentle that only a trained man with an "eye for ground" could discern them. A "valley" two miles wide might be only ten or fifteen feet deep, and a "commanding" ridge only a hundred feet high. This featureless terrain, while affording almost unlimited mobility to tracked and wheeled vehicles, made navigation and the pinpointing of objectives extremely difficult.

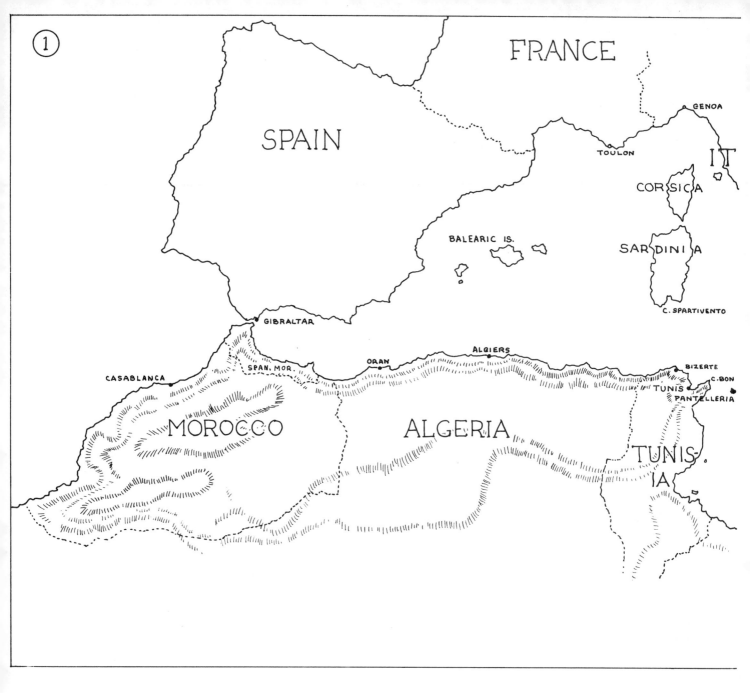

FRANCE

SPAIN

GENOA

TOULON

IT

CORSICA

BALEARIC IS.

SARDINIA

C. SPARTIVENTO

GIBRALTAR

CASABLANCA

SPAN. MOR.

ORAN

ALGIERS

BIZERTE

C. BON

TUNIS

PANTELLERIA

MOROCCO

ALGERIA

TUNIS-
IA

Where one stony hillock or depression looked like any other, maps meant little. Occasionally small cairns of stones were placed at known locations as reference points, but in the open desert, navigation was by compass and dead reckoning. It was easy to lose one's way. The monotonous and slightly rolling landscape was generally devoid of any landmark, and the horizon, dancing in heat haze or veiled in dust, appeared now near, now far—robbing the newcomer of sense both of direction and distance. It was over this terrain that the British, Italians, and Germans fought their seesaw battles. Rommel wrote, "It was only in the desert that the principles of armored warfare as they were taught in theory before the war could be fully applied and fully developed." And certainly no finer battleground could have been devised. There was ample room for tactical maneuver, generally fine and predictable weather, and a terrain over which, with a few limitations, even wheeled vehicles could travel regardless of roads. One of Rommel's officers, Von Ravenstein, made the now famous remark that the desert was the tactician's paradise and the quartermaster's nightmare.

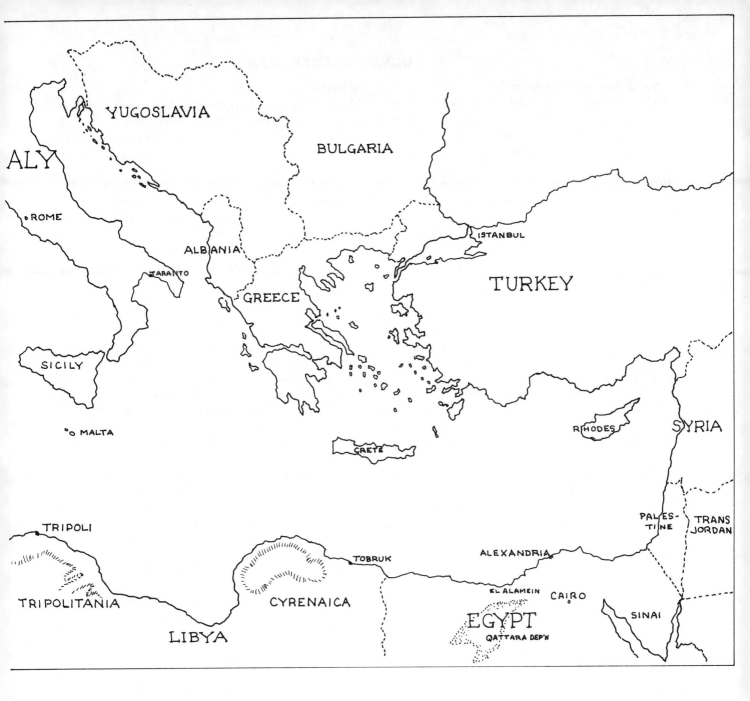

To the west of Cyrenaica the coast of Tripolitania trended slightly north. The coastal plains, which included areas of marsh, rose inland, at times sharply to a series of northward-facing scarps, or steep-faced hills. These scarps were cut in places by valleys or dried-up watercourses (*wadis*). Such obstacles played a considerable part in Rommel's fighting retreat to Tunisia.

In contrast to the generally low-lying area of Tripolitania and eastern Tunisia, much of the northern part of Algeria (and almost all of Morocco) was rugged hill country dominated by the lofty Atlas Mountains. A few low plains hugged the coast, closely hemmed in by steep ranges of hills. Here the climate varied from a mild but sometimes humid seventy-five to seventy-nine degrees Fahrenheit along the Mediterranean in summer to fifty to fifty-four degrees in the winter. Inland in the hills, temperatures were lower and frosts were common. September to December were the wettest months— winter gales from the Atlantic bringing cold rain, sleet, and occasional snow. In many areas where the fighting took place the use of armor was difficult or impossible, and pack mules took the place of motorized transport.

The Mediterranean itself, Homer's "wine-dark sea," was the scene of incessant action. As stated, across it came every man and weapon of the Axis armies in North Africa. In desperate attempts to cut off this flow of supplies the Allies, principally Britain, expended men by the thousands, planes by the hundreds, and warships by the score.

It might have been supposed that, as the world's greatest naval power, Britain would have no problem denying the sea to the enemy. And in the old days this would have been true. At the turn of the century "Britannia Rules the Waves" was more than a patriotic ditty—it was a statement of fact, as true in the Mediterranean as anywhere else. The Russian Black Sea Fleet, bottled up north of the Bosphorus, posed no threat; the Turkish Navy was a joke, and the Spanish, Italian, and Austrian fleets combined (a most unlikely combination, to say the least) would have been swept from the seas in short order. France with her bases at Toulon and in North Africa was the only possible challenger, and with the Anglo-French Entente of 1904 the "lifeline" seemed secure.

All this was in the days when the submarine was in its infancy and the airplane a dream. The First World War changed the picture somewhat, and the U boat became a recognized menace. But it was in the late 1920s and early 1930s that the winds of change really began to blow. World War I had eliminated the minor menace of the Austrian and Turkish navies, but the rise of the Fascist state in Italy presented a new danger. Mussolini's saber rattling was accompanied by the building of a modern navy and, even more disturbing, the creation of a powerful air force. The combination of a surface fleet of exceptionally fast and well-armed vessels, a large force of submarines, and numerous squadrons of bombers based on strategically located airfields drastically changed the power balance in the Mediterranean area.

A glance at the map of the Mediterranean shows Sicily cutting the 2,400-odd miles of that landlocked sea almost in two. It is less than 100 miles from Cape Bon in Tunisia to the southwestern tip of Sicily, while the distance between Bizerte and Cape Spartivento, Sardinia, is only about 120 miles. Almost square in the middle of the eastern end of the Strait of Sicily is the island of Pantelleria, while partially obstructing the western end is an area of shallows known as the Skerki Bank. The narrow waters exposed squadrons of larger vessels to attacks by aircraft, submarines, and motor torpedo boats.

Despite the often exaggerated claims of the exponents of aerial warfare, naval opinion was, in general, skeptical about the effectiveness of the bomber vs. large naval vessels. Increase in range, accuracy, and numbers of ship-mounted antiaircraft weapons would, it was thought, provide a squadron with an impenetrable "umbrella" of fire. The torpedo, however, was a weapon whose deadliness had been proved all too often in World War I, and naval authorities had deep respect for it. In a conflict with Britain, the geography of the central Mediterranean area was therefore all to the Italians' advantage. With the soon-to-be-proven success of the bomber against the surface vessel, this advantage would be materially increased.

The fact that the British naval base at Malta was only some 60 miles from the Sicilian airfields led some authorities to believe that, in a war with Italy, the base would be rendered untenable. Therefore, the British hold on the central Mediterranean appeared by no means secure, and passage of troops and supplies in wartime could be considered to be impractical.

The authorities were almost 100 per cent right—but not quite. Malta survived, though only just, and the strategic location of that tiny island proved a vital factor in the North African campaign.

. . . AND POLITICAL

Equally important to an understanding of the campaign was the political status of the states bordering the Mediterranean. When Hitler invaded Poland (September 1, 1939) the setup, reading clockwise, was as follows:

Spain: A Fascist state, beholden greatly both to Hitler and Mussolini for aid in the recent Civil War. The same Civil War had devastated the country, but left dictator Franco with a sizable army of veterans, well equipped by his Fascist allies. Uppermost in Spanish minds has always been the desire to win back Gibraltar (held by the British since 1704), and this factor entered into any calculations as to the Spanish leader's intentions.

Gibraltar: Occupying only 2.12 square miles of territory, the Crown Colony had long been a symbol of impregnability. Just how impregnable it really was against modern weapons was open to question. One thing was certain: In event of war with Spain, while the Rock itself might hold against attack from land or sea, the vital naval facilities and the one small airfield would be promptly rendered useless.

France: French strength in the Mediterranean area on September 1, 1939, was represented by a powerful naval force (the French Navy was the second strongest in Europe) based primarily at Toulon, Oran, and Bizerte—3 predreadnaught battleships, 6 heavy cruisers, 3 light cruisers, a seaplane carrier, 33 destroyers (19 of them so-called superdestroyers), 45 submarines, and many lesser warships and auxiliaries. Besides the armed forces in Metropolitan France, there were large numbers of troops in French North Africa.

Italy: Axis partner, but neutral as war broke out. Mussolini had grandiose dreams of creating anew the past glories of the Roman Empire. Unfortunately, he could not re-create the tough, disciplined legions of the Caesars, and the majority of Italian troops had little taste for war or glory. A one-sided campaign—tanks and planes against barefoot tribesmen—had won him Ethiopia, no great asset when the sea routes to his new conquest lay through British-dominated waters. The Italian Navy was a formidable force, at least on paper. In June 1940 it consisted of 4 modernized battleships (two new 35,000-tonners were to be ready in August), 7 heavy cruisers, 12 light cruisers, 61 fleet destroyers, 69 escort-type destroyers, and 115 submarines, plus numerous auxiliaries and fast MTBs.

The main Italian base was at Taranto, with other squadrons based at Naples, Brindisi, Bari, Spezia, Messina, Augusta, Syracuse, Palermo, Cagliari (Sardinia), Tobruk (Libya), Tripoli, at Leros, in the Dodecanese, in the Adriatic, and in the Red Sea. On land numerous squadrons of the Reggia Aeronautica posed a threat to any vessels within striking distance of the airfields in Sicily, southern Italy, and Italian North Africa.

Yugoslavia: Across the Adriatic, Yugoslavia was neutral—her land forces strong in numbers, rated good fighters but poorly furnished with modern weapons. Her navy was small and her air force of little account in a modern war. Bordering her to the south lay Italian-occupied (April 1939) Albania, an Italian bridgehead for a possible invasion of the Balkans—more specifically of Albania's southern neighbor, Greece.

Greece: At the outbreak of World War II, Greece was neutral but wary of an attack by Mussolini. As her frontiers had been guaranteed by Britain (in answer to Italy's annexation of Albania), it was assumed that Metaxas, the Greek dictator, leaned somewhat toward the Allies. The

Greek Army was small and ill-equipped, as was the Greek Navy—an ancient heavy cruiser, a cruiser-minelayer, some dozen assorted destroyers, and 7 submarines—and her air force was negligible. The Greek islands held considerable strategic value, as did the Italian Dodecanese.

Turkey: Also neutral. But while her navy consisted only of a reconstructed pre-World War I battle cruiser, 4 modern destroyers, 7 submarines, and auxiliaries of various ages and sizes (one was launched in 1886), her army was both sizable and tough, and her strategic position astride the Dardanelles made her a key figure in the Middle East.

Cyprus: A large island lying off the southern coast of Turkey. Occupied and administered by Britain since 1878 and a Crown Colony since 1925, it had some value strategically, especially during the brief campaign against the Vichy forces in Syria, June–July 1941.

Syria and Lebanon: At the outbreak of war, these were under French control. General Weygand was in command of the French forces, consisting of three divisions plus frontier troops, some 40,000 men, (Syria had been in a state of almost continuous internal unrest since 1920), and there was a naval squadron based at Beirut.

Palestine: A British mandate since 1923. British forces (some 27,500 troops plus R.A.F. in June 1940) were, like the French in Syria, partly engaged in policing an unruly population—in this case, trying to keep peace between Jew and Arab.

Egypt: Long under British influence. It officially was neutral but was tied to Britain by treaty. Anti-British sentiments were balanced by fear of Italian aggression. Alexandria was a British naval base, and Port Said was the Mediterranean entrance to the Suez Canal. There were some 36,000 British troops in the country, divided among the Western Desert, Cairo, Suez, and the Sudan.

Libya: Consisted then of the Italian colonies of Cyrenaica and Tripolitania. Italian troop strength in the two colonies amounted to some 215,000 men—9 divisions in Tripolitania and 6 in Cyrenaica. Tripoli was the main naval base, but there was a useful harbor at Tobruk and at Benghazi. The Reggia Aeronautica was represented by some 285 planes, many obsolete.

Abyssinia: A recently conquered territory not adjacent to the Mediterranean, but a major factor in any campaign in the North African area. Italian and native troops here and in Eritrea and Italian Somaliland numbered close to 300,000, with some 400 guns, 200 light tanks, and 100 armored cars.

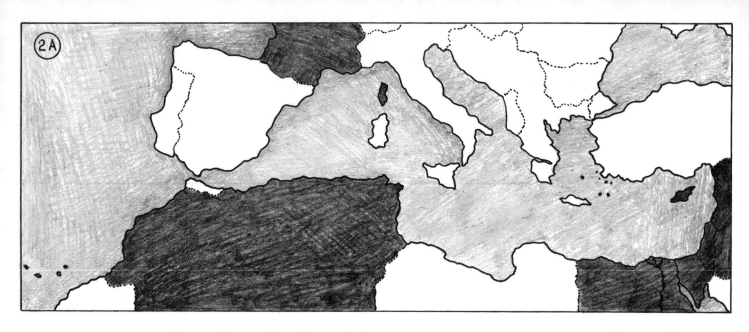

The two maps show the drastic change in the Mediterranean occasioned by the Italian declaration of war and the French capitulation. Franco-British territories shown in dark gray, neutral in white, and Axis in black.

Massawa, on the Red Sea, was the main port, the base for the Red Sea squadron of 8 submarines, 7 destroyers, and 11 escort vessels and MTBs.

French North Africa: Tunisia, Algeria, and French Morocco, French forces here were strong— 11 infantry divisions, a light cavalry division, and 2 cavalry brigades—and there were naval bases at Mers-el-Kebir, at nearby Oran, Algiers, Casablanca (Morocco), and Dakar (French West Africa). The coastal part of the border between Tunisia and Tripolitania was fortified (the Mareth Line).

Malta: Centrally located, just south of Sicily, Malta was held by the British. Acquired 1802–14, the island became a major naval base and coaling station. So important is Malta to the story of the campaign for North Africa that it deserves a chapter to itself.

Such was the line-up on the outbreak of war with Germany. The Mediterranean sea lanes were open, the Italian Fleet matched by the combined Anglo-French squadrons, and the Middle East as quiet as that unquiet part of the world ever was. On June 10, 1940, the Italian dictator shattered that quiet (and incidentally his empire).

Plunging his dagger (as President Roosevelt picturesquely put it) into the back of his neighbor, Mussolini declared war on dying France and supposedly doomed Britain. Twelve days later, France and Germany concluded an armistice (the feeble Italian thrust across the Italo-French border had little to do with this), and the scene in the Mediterranean underwent a drastic change.

The powerful French Navy lay—or so it seemed —at the disposal of the Germans and the Italians. The shattered French Army was now neutral (the few who elected to follow De Gaulle and fight on were but a drop in the bucket). The Italians were now a real, rather than an impending, menace, and the British position in Egypt and the Middle East appeared precarious, to say the least.

There may have been those among the Axis high command that June who doubted that total victory would be achieved easily. There were few, if any, who would have predicted that three years later the last Italo-German forces in North Africa would have surrendered and that Anglo-American armies would be preparing to storm ashore across the Sicilian beaches.

The series of maps and the chronology that follow at the end of this chapter represent over two years bitter fighting. In June of 1940 few people had even heard of the Western Desert. Two years later the public knew much about such places as Tobruk and Halfaya Pass, while the names of many of the commanders—Wavell, Rommel, Auchinleck —had become equally familiar.

The details of the desert war were hard for the general public to follow. With one or two exceptions, it was a fluid war, one where territory meant little and where vast acreages of "real estate" changed hands overnight. Tank columns circled and clashed at points marked only by a desert track or a pile of stones. And armored infantry fought desperately to take or hold some featureless ridge,

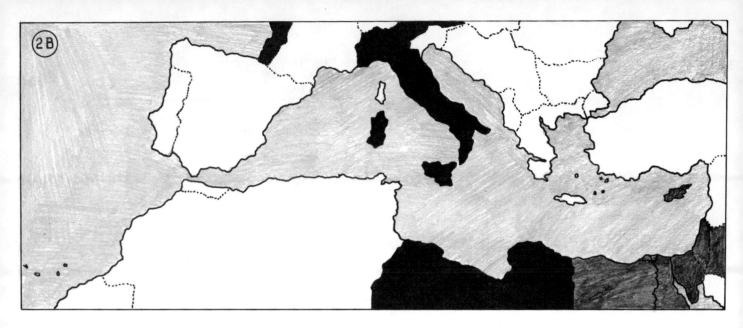

nameless a month before and forgotten a few weeks later.

The maps are therefore general in character and the descriptions of the actions brief. The chronology, after following the seesaw battles across Cyrenaica and the desert, ends with Rommel's first check before Alamein, Auchinleck's replacement by Montgomery, the repulse of the Afrika Korps at Alam el Halfa, and the preliminaries to the final victory at Alamein in October.

The weapons, illustrations of which are scattered throughout the text, are compared where possible. Comparison between the combatants is more difficult. Leadership, morale, motivation, *esprit de corps*, even the amount of food in a man's belly all play their part. These factors are not constants—they vary from day to day, and yesterday's heroes may run like rabbits tomorrow.

In general the Italians fought poorly. This was probably due to inferior leadership, as some units fought very well indeed. Their artillery was rated highly; some of their armored units performed well, especially so considering the death traps they fought in. And none can deny the courage of the seamen, merchant and navy, who ran the gauntlet of attacks by submarines, surface ships, and aircraft to deliver their cargoes from the Italian ports to Tunisia and Tripolitania. But on the whole the Italian soldier behaved as if his heart were not in the battle, and most definitely preferred the discomforts of a prison camp to the chances of death or glory on the battlefield.

The performance of British and German troops could be classed as equal. Training, equipment, and, above all, leadership proved the decisive factors. And so with the Americans, suffering at first from the teething troubles of a vast, hastily raised citizen army, they swiftly became battleworthy. Leadership was improved by drastic pruning, while the equipment, most of it first-rate, was supplied in lavish quantities, not only to their own combatants but in many cases to their Allies as well.

The French at first suffered from antiquated equipment and lacked training in the more sophisticated weapons developed since the fall of France. Properly supplied (mainly with American weapons) and retrained, they more than upheld the traditions of the French Army.

Statistics are sometimes confusing—official accounts do not always agree. Where quoted, figures for combatants, materiel, losses, etc., can be taken as giving a fair estimate. Tables showing comparative data on Allied and German equipment are in general from the Official British *History of the Second World War: the Mediterranean and Middle East.* For much of the information in this book I have relied on the above and on *The U. S. Army in World II: Mediterranean Theater of Operations.*

The following maps and their captions will, hopefully, provide a brief introduction to the story of the final defeat of the Axis forces in North Africa.

NORTH AFRICA	MEDITERRANEAN AND MALTA	EAST AFRICA AND MIDDLE EAST	EUROPE
1940—JUNE		*1940—JUNE*	
11—Italian columns ambushed at Sidi Omar 12—R.A.F. attacks Tobruk for first time. Patrol actions 21–22—First attack on Alexandria by Italian aircraft	11—First air raid on Malta R.N. makes first sweep in eastern Mediterranean 23—Force "H" assembles at Gibraltar Minor naval actions Severe losses of submarines on both sides	19—Trawler *Moonstone* captures sub *Galileo Galilei* in Red Sea R.A.F. begins attacks on Italian bases in East Africa	5—Dunkirk falls to Germans 10—Italy declares war on United Kingdom 14—Germans enter Paris 22—Franco-German Armistice 24—Franco-Italian Armistice 28—His Majesty's Government recognizes De Gaulle
1940—JULY		*1940—JULY*	
Frontier skirmishes	3—Action against French at Oran 4—French squadron at Alexandria demilitarized 9—Action off Calabria 19—Action off Cape Spada	3—Emperor Haile Selassie arrives at Khartoum 4—Italians take Kassala and Gallabat in Sudan 15—Italians take Moyale in Kenya	Battle of Britain begins
1940—AUGUST		*1940—AUGUST*	
Frontier skirmishes French Equatorial Africa declares for De Gaulle	2—H.M.S. *Argus* flies off Hurricanes to Malta	5–19—Italians invade and and take British Somaliland	15—Italians torpedo Greek cruiser *Helle*
1940—SEPTEMBER		*1940—SEPTEMBER*	
13–18—Italians invade Egypt Long-range Desert Group begin patrols 20—First Aircraft leaves Takoradi for Egypt 23–25—De Gaulle's unsuccessful attack on Dakar	2—Operation "Hats"— convoy to Malta 28—Mediterranean Fleet puts to sea 30—Cruisers land troops, airmen, and stores at Malta		22—In Far East, Japanese forces begin occupation of French Indo-China 27—Germany, Italy, Japan sign ten-year pact
1940—OCTOBER		*1940—OCTOBER*	
Frontier skirmishes	Convoy sails Alexandria to Malta under escort of Mediterranean Fleet; *Ajax* and *York* sink two TBDs and one destroyer		28—German forces enter Romania. Italians invade Greece 29—British advance parties land on Crete
1940—NOVEMBER		*1940—NOVEMBER*	
Wavell prepares a limited offensive	9–10—Operation "Coat"; ships to and from Malta 11—Fleet Air Arm attack on Taranto 18—Attempt to fly Hurricanes to Malta by *Argus* 26–27—Operation "Collar"; convoys to Malta and Crete. Action off Cape Spartivento	6–9—Action at Gallabat	4—R.A.F. begins operations in Greece 8—Italian offensive in Greece collapses 18—Greeks counterattack 20—Hungarians join Axis 23—Romania joins Axis

NORTH AFRICA	MEDITERRANEAN AND MALTA	EAST AFRICA AND MIDDLE EAST	EUROPE
1940—DECEMBER		**1940—DECEMBER**	
9—First British offensive—Operation "Compass" 16—British take Sollum and Capuzzo	10—Hitler orders Fliegerkorps X to Sicily 20—Cunningham escorts four supply ships into Malta	British raid El Wak on Kenya-Ethiopian frontier	6—Marshal Badoglio resigns as Italian Chief of State 18—Hitler issues directive for invasion of Soviet Union
1941—JANUARY		**1941—JANUARY**	
4—British capture Bardia 22—British take Tobruk	5—Inshore Squadron formed by R.N. 10—First attack by German aircraft from Sicily; *Illustrious* badly damaged, reaches Malta 16—First heavy attacks on Valetta 16–23—*Illustrious* target of many attacks 23—*Illustrious* sails for Alexandria	British begin offensives in Sudan and East Africa 18—Mega, Kenya captured 19—Kassala captured 22—Moyale falls	13—Greeks decline offer of British troops 29—General Metaxas dies
1941—FEBRUARY		**1941—FEBRUARY**	
5–7—Battle of Beda Fomm 6—Capture of Benghazi 12—General Rommel arrives at Tripoli 14—First of Afrika Korps disembarks at Tripoli	9—Bombardment of Genoa 12—First Me 109s over Malta	1—Actions at Agordat and (2) Barentu 3—Battle of Keren begins 19—British cross River Juba into Italian Somaliland 23—Emperor enters Ethiopia 25—British take Mogadishu	Eden mission in Athens
1941—MARCH		**1941—MARCH**	
1—Free French capture Kufra 30—Rommel begins offensive 31—Afrika Korps makes contact with British at Mersa Brega	28—Battle of Cape Matapan—three Italian cruisers and two destroyers sunk	27—British capture Keren	1—Bulgaria joins Axis 5—First British forces sail for Greece
1941—APRIL		**1941—APRIL**	
6—Generals O'Connor, Neame captured in desert 10—Tobruk cut off 14–17—Heavy German attack on Tobruk repulsed 25—Germans take Halfaya Pass	16—Four destroyers from Malta attack convoy, sink all five merchantmen and their three destroyer escorts 21—Bombardment of Tripoli	1—Asmara captured 3—*Coup d'état* in Iraq by pro-Axis Rashid Ali 6—British enter Addis Ababa 8—British enter Massawa 11—Red Sea opened to U.S. shipping	6—Germans invade Greece, Yugoslavia 17—Yugoslavian Government capitulates 23—Greeks sign armistice 24–25—British forces begin evacuation 27—Germans enter Athens
1941—MAY		**1941—MAY**	
15–16—Operation "Brevity" 19—Longmore replaced by Tedder	5–12—"Tiger" convoy to Egypt 9—Convoy from Egypt arrives at Malta	2—Iraqis attack R.A.F. base at Habbaniya 13—Habforce enters Iraq 16—Duke of Aosta	20—Germans invade Crete 21—Loss of Meleme airfield 24—*Bismarck* sinks *Hood*

NORTH AFRICA	MEDITERRANEAN AND MALTA	EAST AFRICA AND MIDDLE EAST	EUROPE
26—Germans retake Halfaya Pass	Axis air attacks on Malta lessen Fliegerkorps X transferred to Balkans	surrenders at Amba Alagi 19—British decide to invade Syria 23—Capture of Soddu Axis uses Syria to support Iraq revolt 27–30—Habforce advances on Baghdad 31—Armistice signed with Iraqis	27—*Bismarck* sunk 28–31—British evacuate Crete
1941—JUNE		**1941—JUNE**	
Siege of Tobruk 15–17—"Battleaxe" (British attack on Sollum-Capuzzo-Halfaya area fails) 28—Lytrelton appointed Minister of State, ME	Malta reinforced with aircraft	3—German intrigues in Persia; British occupy Mosul 8—British and Free French enter Syria 20—Capture of Damascus 20—Capture of Jimma (Ethiopia)	22—Germans invade Soviet Union 29—Germans reach Grodno, Brest-Litovsk, Vilna
1941—JULY		**1941—JULY**	
Siege of Tobruk 5—Wavell replaced by Auchinleck 12—Basties replaces Garibaldi	20–24—"Substance" convoy to Malta 25–26—Italian EMBs attack Grand Harbor, Malta 31–August 2—"Style" convoy to Malta	Fighting in Syria and East Africa continues 6—General Gazera surrenders in Gallo-Sidamo area (Ethiopia) 14—Convention signed ending hostilities in Syria Most of South African troops leave East Africa	1–2—Germans take Riga (Latvia) 13—Mutual-aid pact between Great Britain and Soviet Union 16—Germans capture Smolensk
1941—AUGUST		**1941—AUGUST**	
Siege of Tobruk 19–29—First-stage relief of Australians in Tobruk Begin plans for "Crusader"	2—"Style" convoy reaches Malta	17—Anglo-Russian note to Persia 25—British forces enter Persia 28—Persian Government falls, resistance ends	19—Germans claim almost all Ukraine west of Dneiper
1941—SEPTEMBER		**1941—SEPTEMBER**	
Siege of Tobruk 2—Auchinleck's preliminary orders for "Crusader." 18—Eighth Army formed 19–27—Second-stage relief of Australians	24–28—"Halberd" convoy to Malta Malta strike forces reinforced 28 per cent of Axis cargoes to North Africa lost	17—British and Soviet forces enter Teheran Development of supply route to Soviet Union begun	4—Germans begin siege of Leningrad 19—Kiev and Poltava taken by Germans
1941—OCTOBER			
Siege of Tobruk 12–15—Third-stage relief of Australians	21—Force "K" arrives at Malta		German advance in Soviet Union continues: Orel (8), Bryansk (12), Vyasma (13), Odessa (16), Taganrog (19), Kharkov (24) Moscow threatened.

NORTH AFRICA	MEDITERRANEAN AND MALTA	EAST AFRICA AND MIDDLE EAST	EUROPE
1941—NOVEMBER		*1941—NOVEMBER*	
18—"Crusader" offensive begins 26—Auchinleck replaces General Cunningham with Ritchie	German submarines ordered to Mediterranean 8–9—Force "K" destroys Axis convoy 13—Loss of *Ark Royal* 24—Force "K" destroys Axis convoy 25—Loss of *Barham* 62 per cent of Axis cargo to North Africa lost	Fighting in Gondar region 27—General Nasi surrenders at Gondar; end of campaign in East Africa FAR EAST	Germans invade Crimea 15—Siege of Sevastopol begun 16—Germans take Kerch 22–28—Soviets lose and retake Rostov
1941—DECEMBER		*1941—DECEMBER*	
First attempt to relieve Tobruk fails 5—British advance resumed 10—Relief of Tobruk 16—Enemy retreats from Gazala 25—British enter Benghazi	1—Hitler orders Fliegerkorps II from Soviet Union to Sicily 13—Action off Cape Bon; two Italian cruisers sunk 17—First Battle of Sirte 19—Force "K" meets disaster in mine field 19—*Valiant* and *Queen Elizabeth* damaged in Alexandria	7—Japanese attack Pearl Harbor, land in Malaya 9—Japanese occupy Bangkok 10—Japanese sink *Repulse* and *Prince of Wales* 12—Japanese invade Philippines 22—First Washington Conference 25—Japanese take Hong Kong	2—Some German units reach Moscow suburbs 6—Soviets begin counterattack near Moscow 11—Germany and Italy declare war on U.S.A.
1942—JANUARY		*1942—JANUARY*	
2—Bardia surrenders to British 17—Sollum and Halfaya surrender to British 21—Rommel counterattacks 28—British evacuate Benghazi, retreat toward Gazala	Three small convoys from Alexandria to Malta	2—Manila falls to Japanese 7—U.S., Philippine troops retreat to Bataan Peninsula 11—Japanese invade Netherlands East Indies 16—Japanese invade Burma 31—British retreat to Singapore Island	Soviets continue winter offensive
1942—FEBRUARY		*1942—FEBRUARY*	
Eighth Army stabilizes Gazala–Bir Hacheim line	12–15—Convoy from Alexandria fails to reach Malta	15—Singapore falls 19—Destructive air raid on Darwin, Australia 19—Night action in Badoeing Straits 27—Battle of Java Sea	Soviets continue winter offensive
1942—MARCH		*1942—MARCH*	
Lull in desert fighting	Air attacks on Malta 7, 21, 29—Reinforcements of aircraft to Malta 22—Second Battle of Sirte 23—Three ships of convoy reach Malta 26–27—The three ships bombed before finished unloading and sunk	1—Battle of Sunda Straits 7—Japanese capture Rangoon 9—Java surrenders to Japanese	Soviets continue counterattacks

NORTH AFRICA	MEDITERRANEAN AND MALTA	FAR EAST	EUROPE
1942—APRIL		**1942—APRIL**	
Both sides reorganize for Battle of Gazala	Air attacks on Malta reach peak 10th Submarine Flotilla withdrawn from Malta 15—George Cross awarded to Malta 20—U.S.S. *Wasp* flies Spitfires to Malta Admiral Cunningham leaves, temporarily succeeded by Pridham-Whippell	9—Bataan surrenders 20—Japanese take Cebu and Panay 30—Japanese complete conquest of central Burma	Soviet counteroffensive begins to taper off Germans begin to plan offensive in South
1942—MAY		**1942—MAY**	
26—Rommel attacks Gazala–Bir Hacheim line	Air attacks on Malta begin to decrease Fliegerkorps II weakened by losses and withdrawals	3—Japanese land at Tulagi in Solomons 4–8—Battle of Coral Sea 20—Japanese occupy rest of Burma	12—Soviets begin offensive toward Kharkov
1942—JUNE		**1942—JUNE**	
5–6—British armor defeated in "Cauldron" 10—Bir Hacheim evacuated 14—Ritchie decides to withdraw from Gazala 21—Tobruk falls 25—Auchinleck relieves Ritchie	3, 9—Operations to fly Spitfires to Malta 12–16—"Harpoon" convoy reaches Malta from west; "Vigorous," from east, turned back	4—Battle of Midway 7—Japanese invade Aleutians 9—Japanese conquest of Philippines complete	3—German assault on Sevastopol begins 10—Germans force passage of the Donetz 28—Germans launch main offensive
1942—JULY		**1942—JULY**	
1–5—Rommel's attempt to break through at El Alamein defeated 10–26—British counterattacks end indecisively	1–14—Heavy air attacks on Malta 15, 21—Two operations reinforce Malta Spitfires 10th Submarine Flotilla returns to Malta	Americans plan offensive in Solomons 21—Japanese occupy Buna, New Guinea 31—Solomons Expeditionary Force sails from Fiji	7—Germans reach Veronezh 15—Germans reach Millerovo 24—Germans re-enter Rostov
1942—AUGUST		**1942—AUGUST**	
4–10—Churchill visit to Cairo 7—Gott killed. Was to have taken command of Eighth Army 13—Montgomery takes command of Eighth Army 15—Alexander succeeds Auchinleck as Commander-in-Chief 30–31—Axis offensive begins: Battle of Alam el Halfa	10–15—"Pedestal" convoy to Malta—heavy losses 11—Loss of *Eagle* 11, 17—Malta reinforced with Spitfires 33 per cent of Axis shipments to North Africa lost	7—U.S. Marines land on Guadalcanal 8–9—Battle of Savo Island 21—Battle of Tenaru River 24—Battle of Eastern Solomons	9—Germans take Maikop, reach foothills of Caucasus Germans begin offensive at Stalingrad 24—Allied headquarters set up in London for "Torch."

NORTH AFRICA	MEDITERRANEAN AND MALTA	FAR EAST	EUROPE
1942—SEPTEMBER		*1942—SEPTEMBER*	
2—Rommel begins withdrawal 7—Lines stabilized; British begin preparations for offensive	Supplies on Malta very short but air strikes and submarines continue to harass Axis supply routes 20 per cent of Axis shipments lost	Heavy fighting on and around Guadalcanal 12—Battle of Bloody Ridge begins 17—On New Guinea, Japanese stopped thirty-two miles from Port Moresby	1—Germans cross Kerch Straits, capture Novorossisk Mid-September—continuous heavy fighting at Stalingrad 21—Soviets counterattack northeast of Stalingrad
1942—OCTOBER		*1942—OCTOBER*	
13–14—Abortive raid on Tobruk Germans continue to perfect defenses on El Alamein line 23—Battle of El Alamein begins—Operation "Lightfoot"	Submarines run supplies in to Malta 11—Germans begin last air assault on island 20—Luftwaffe raids begin to taper off; little effect on island's strike capacity—Axis losses in month, 44 per cent	Continued heavy fighting on and around Guadalcanal 11, 12—Battle of Cape Esperance 26—Battle of Santa Cruz	1—Russians counterattack southeast of Stalingrad 4—Fierce battle in heart of Stalingrad

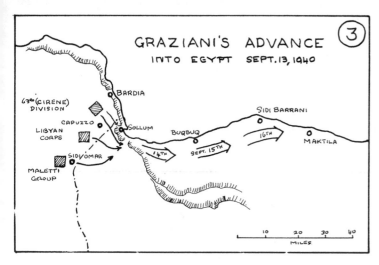

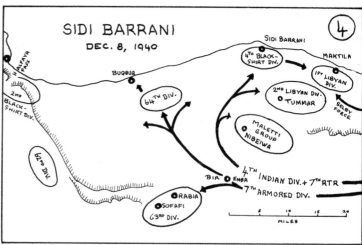

Urged on by Mussolini, Graziani—who considered his forces (5 divisions and 7 tank battalions) lacking in equipment and transport—began his advance.

Graziani's offensive soon stalled. Wavell, prodded in turn by Churchill, then ordered General O'Connor to launch a large-scale raid on the frontier. (Operation "Compass")

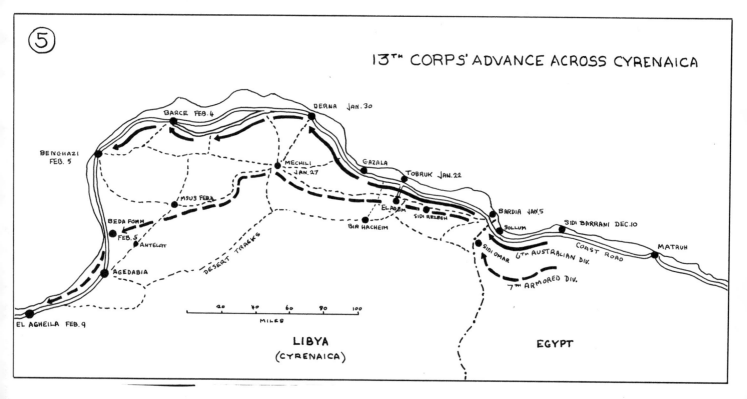

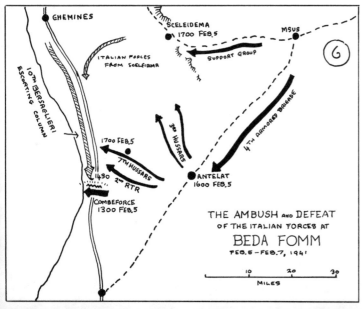

THE AMBUSH and DEFEAT
OF THE ITALIAN FORCES AT
BEDA FOMM
FEB. 5 - FEB. 7, 1941

As the above map shows, the main Italian retreat was along the coast road. Despite worn-out vehicles and a shortage of fuel, General O'Connor sent 7th Armored Division across the desert toward the coast well south of Benghazi. At Msus a small group of wheeled vehicles and guns under Colonel Combe (Combeforce) was sent ahead—reaching the coast road near Beda Fomm on February 5 only some ninety minutes before the head of a huge column of retreating Italians appeared (map left). Fourth Armored Brigade hurried in support; desperate Italian efforts to break through failed, and by noon of February 7 the Italians surrendered, over 25,000 with more than 100 tanks, 216 guns, and 1,500 vehicles. The British had advanced 500 miles since December with losses of less than 2,000. Italian losses: over 130,000 prisoners, nearly 400 tanks, and 845 guns.

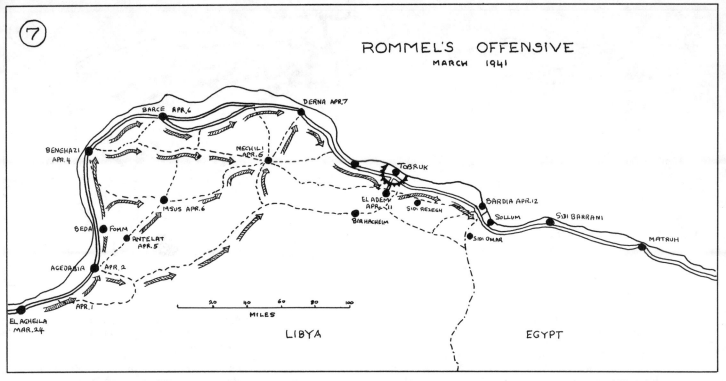

ROMMEL'S OFFENSIVE
MARCH 1941

⑦

To bolster the defeated Italians, Rommel and Afrika Korps landed at Tripoli on February 14, 1941. The best British units had been sent to Greece or Egypt. The untried units could not check the assault Rommel launched on March 31. By April 12, some British forces were shut up in Tobruk, and Axis forces had reached the frontier.

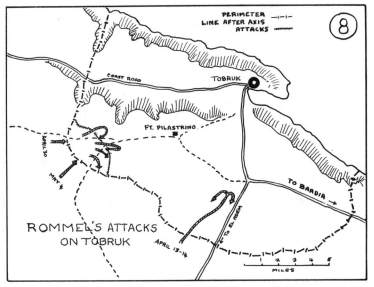

⑧ ROMMEL'S ATTACKS ON TOBRUK

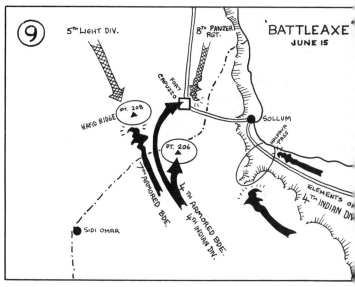

⑨ "BATTLEAXE" JUNE 15

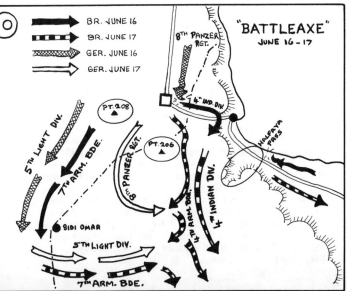

⑩ "BATTLEAXE" JUNE 16-17

Operation "Battleaxe," planned to free the frontier area, failed. Fort Capuzzo was taken on the fifteenth and Sollum next day, but mine fields and strong anti-tank defenses checked efforts to take Halfaya, and 7th Armored Brigade made no headway at Hafid Ridge and Pt. 208. A flanking movement on June 16 by 5th Light Division forced 7th Armored Brigade south, and danger of encirclement forced a British withdrawal on the seventeenth. German anti-tank guns (including 88s) proved too much for the undergunned British cruiser (Crusaders) and I tanks.

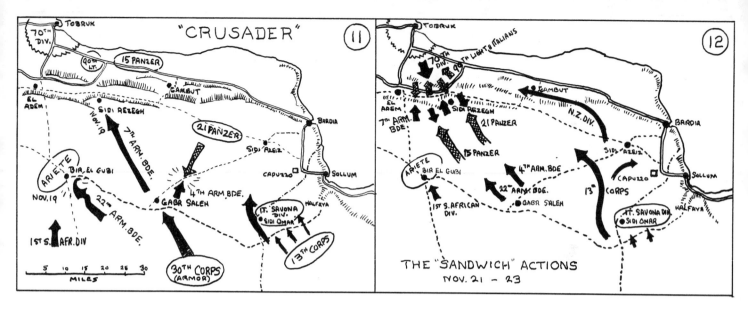

Crusader plan: Starting November 18, XXX Corps to engage and defeat Axis armor; XIII Corps to contain forces at Sidi Omar–Halfaya and advance on Tobruk, while 70th Division broke out. Three days' fighting saw D.A.K.'s (Deutsches Afrika Korps) 2 armored divisions in the area west of Capuzzo; XXX Corps' 7th Armored Brigade around Sidi Rezegh; New Zealand Division near Gambut; 70th Division beginning its sortie; and the 1st South African Division moving on Bir el Gubi.

The operation developed into a series of furious actions involving thousands of vehicles—often too confusing for even the commanders to follow. Training exercises never envisioned a situation like that shown in the much-simplified diagram above. Axis besiegers of Tobruk are battling both 70th Division and 7th Armored Brigade, which in turn is attacked from the southeast by D.A.K., which is followed closely by the rest of 7th Armored Division. Better tanks and tactics and intelligent use of powerful anti-tank guns helped Rommel inflict great damage on the British armor.

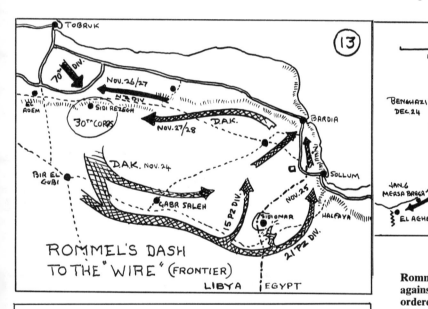

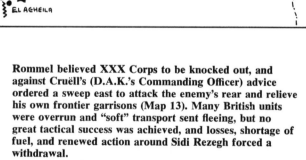

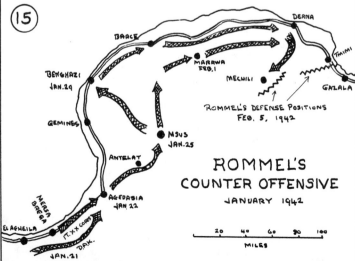

Rommel believed XXX Corps to be knocked out, and against Cruëll's (D.A.K.'s Commanding Officer) advice ordered a sweep east to attack the enemy's rear and relieve his own frontier garrisons (Map 13). Many British units were overrun and "soft" transport sent fleeing, but no great tactical success was achieved, and losses, shortage of fuel, and renewed action around Sidi Rezegh forced a withdrawal.

Reinforced frequently, Eighth Army wore down the Axis forces in seesaw fighting. Finally (December 7) Rommel decided to retreat to positions at Gazala. The long siege of Tobruk was over. A threat to his flank induced Rommel to abandon Cyrenaica and regroup at El Agheila. An orderly retreat began on December 17 (Map 14). Pursuit was slow and cautious and there was no second Beda Fomm. Axis garrisons at Halfaya and Bardia surrendered January 12, 1942.

Now the pendulum swung back. Rapid buildup enabled Rommel to stage a raid (January 21) which smashed into newly arrived and inexperienced 1st Armored Division. Exploiting his success, Rommel, by swift advances, kept Eighth Army's Ritchie off balance (Map 15) and by February 6 was at Tmimi.

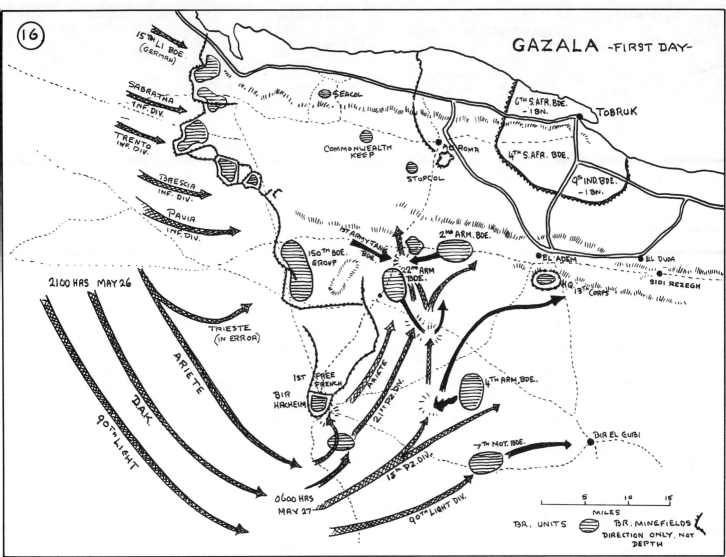

16

GAZALA -FIRST DAY-

15TH LI BDE. (GERMAN)

SABRATHA INF. DIV.

TRENTO INF. DIV.

BRESCIA INF. DIV.

PAVIA INF. DIV.

SEACOL

COMMONWEALTH KEEP

STUPCOL

HQ ROMA

6TH S.AFR. BDE. - 1 BN.

TOBRUK

4TH S.AFR. BDE.

9TH IND. BDE. - 1 BN.

151 ARMY TANK BDE.

2ND ARM. BDE.

150TH BDE. GROUP

22ND ARM BDE.

EL ADEM

EL DUDA

HQ 13TH CORPS

SIDI REZEGH

2100 HRS MAY 26

TRIESTE (IN ERROR)

ARIETE

D.A.K.

90TH LIGHT

1ST FREE FRENCH

BIR HACHEIM

ARIETE

21ST PZ. DIV.

4TH ARM. BDE.

15TH PZ. DIV.

7TH MOT. BDE.

BIR EL GUBI

0600 HRS MAY 27

90TH LIGHT DIV.

5   10   15
MILES

BR. UNITS   BR. MINEFIELDS

DIRECTION ONLY, NOT DEPTH

Forestalling an attack by Eighth Army, Rommel struck on May 26. The British defenses consisted of a series of "boxes" protected and linked by mine fields, supported by armored brigades. Rommel's plan was for a diversion in the north while his armor swept south around Bir Hacheim. Some units were overrun or scattered (Map 16) but Rommel lost many tanks. Two days' fighting brought further losses, and supplies of all kinds were almost exhausted. British armored car units disrupted the supply route south of Bir Hacheim, and unless the mine fields could be breached Rommel was in serious trouble. May 30 he attacked west,

concentrating on 150th Brigade box, while a screen of anti-tank guns held off the British armor. No concerted efforts were made to relieve 150th Brigade (a fatal error) and on June 1 it was overwhelmed. The same fate befell the Free French in Bir Hacheim. An attempt (Map 17) to smash the German armor in the so-called Cauldron ended in disaster, and the loss of nearly 200 tanks, 6,000 men, and 7 regiments of artillery. With no relief possible Bir Hacheim was evacuated the night of June 10/11, after a heroic resistance. With the final destruction of the British armor on June 11–12 (Map 18) the battle came to an end, units retreating as they could.

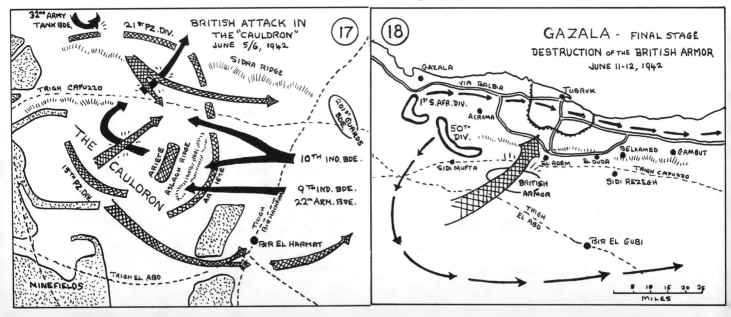

17   BRITISH ATTACK IN THE "CAULDRON" JUNE 5/6, 1942

32ND ARMY TANK BDE.

21ST PZ. DIV.

SIDRA RIDGE

TRIGH CAPUZZO

201ST GUARDS

THE CAULDRON

ARIETE

ASLAGH RIDGE

ARIETE

10TH IND. BDE.

9TH IND. BDE.

22ND ARM. BDE.

15TH PZ. DIV.

TRIGH BIR HACHEIM

BIR EL HARMAT

TRIGH EL ABD

MINEFIELDS

18   GAZALA - FINAL STAGE

DESTRUCTION OF THE BRITISH ARMOR JUNE 11-12, 1942

GAZALA

VIA BALBIA

TOBRUK

1ST S.AFR. DIV.

ACROMA

50TH DIV.

SIDI MUFTA

BELHAMED

GAMBUT

EL ADEM

EL DUDA

TRIGH CAPUZZO

SIDI REZEGH

BRITISH ARMOR

TRIGH EL ABD

BIR EL GUBI

5 10 15 20 25
MILES

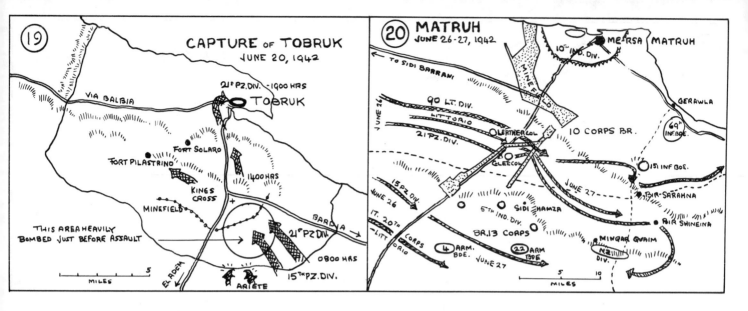

(19) CAPTURE of TOBRUK JUNE 20, 1942

(20) MATRUH JUNE 26-27, 1942

While the British were deciding whether to hold Tobruk (loaded with supplies for Eighth Army) or abandon it and consolidate farther east, Rommel struck. Heavy air raids began early, June 20, then, infantry preparing the way, D.A.K. burst through the outer lines. The original defenses were now almost nonexistent (Klopper, the South African in command, was inexperienced), and D.A.K.'s attacks were met by isolated units. Capture of King's Cross brought the harbor under fire and the town soon fell. Klopper ordered surviving units to break out and surrendered next morning.

Eighth Army, disorganized, attempted a stand at Matruh. The defenses had not been maintained since 1940. The mine fields were sketchy and the southern defenses were incomplete. The center (see Map 20) was weak. Plan: hold enemy at Matruh or Sidi Hamza. If he penetrated between or south of the southern escarpment, he would be hit by XIII Corps. Enemy penetration was deep but losses were high and the Axis center columns were in danger between X and XIII Corps. Overestimating enemy strength and fearing encirclement, the British retreated fighting, toward Alamein.

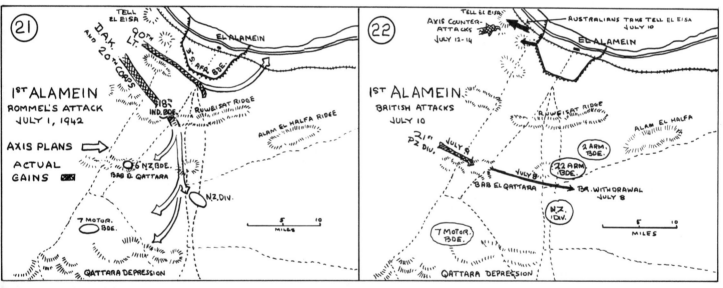

(21) 1st ALAMEIN ROMMEL'S ATTACK JULY 1, 1942

(22) 1st ALAMEIN BRITISH ATTACKS JULY 10

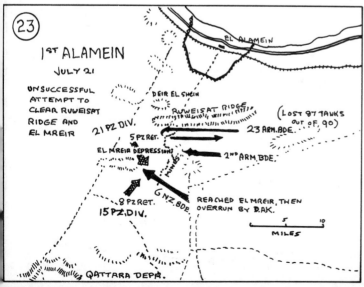

(23) 1st ALAMEIN JULY 21

Alamein, long recognized as a natural defense position (the impassable Qattara Depression was only thirty miles south) was Eighth Army's next stand. Physical defenses were almost nil, some hastily strung wire and scattered mines. Attackers and defenders arrived almost simultaneously. Rommel's assault was poorly planned, without proper reconnaissance. Map 21 shows his projected advance and what his exhausted forces attained the first day. Heavy air attacks and prolonged and unexpected resistance by 18th Indian Brigade at Deir el Shein disrupted Rommel's timetable. July 2–5 saw some Axis gains north of Ruweisat, some by Eighth Army south of it. July 10, Eighth Army took Tell el Eisa (Map 22). The last phase—July 14–27 (Map 23)—brought heavy fighting as Eighth Army tried to take Miteriya Ridge and El Mreir Depression. These attacks, although costly to the Axis, failed—partly because of poor co-operation between infantry and armor.

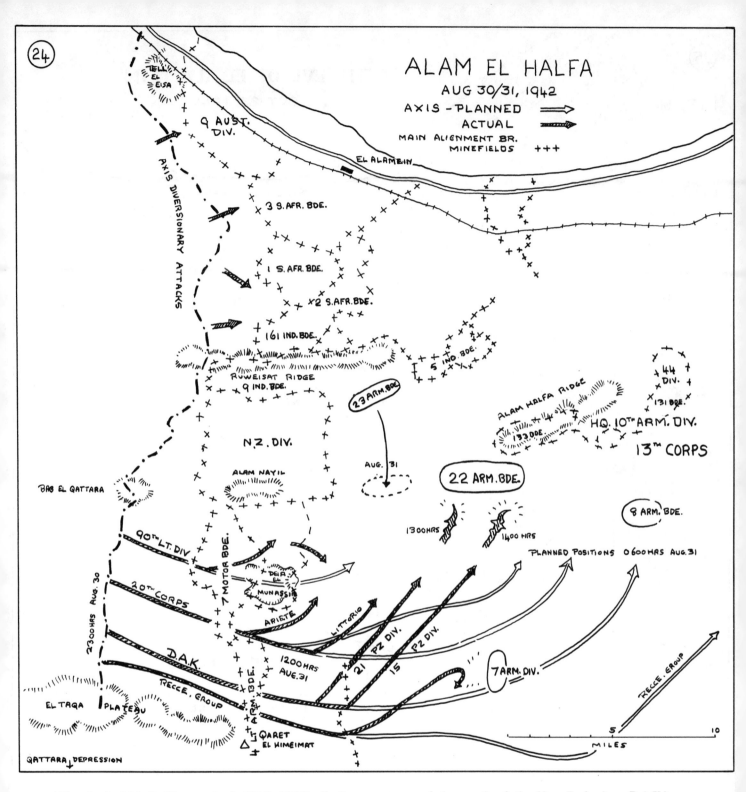

ALAM EL HALFA
AUG 30/31, 1942
AXIS - PLANNED ⟹
ACTUAL
MAIN ALIGNMENT BR.
MINEFIELDS +++

TELL EL EISA

9 AUST. DIV.

EL ALAMEIN

AXIS DIVERSIONARY ATTACKS

3 S. AFR. BDE.

1 S. AFR. BDE.

2 S. AFR. BDE.

161 IND. BDE.

5 IND. BDE.

RUWEISAT RIDGE
9 IND. BDE.

23 ARM. BDE.

44 DIV.
131 BDE.

ALAM HALFA RIDGE
133 BDE.
HQ. 10TH ARM. DIV.
13TH CORPS

N.Z. DIV.

AUG. 31

22 ARM. BDE.

BAB EL QATTARA

ALAM NAYIL

8 ARM. BDE.

1300 HRS

1400 HRS

90TH LT. DIV.

7 MOTOR BDE.

DEIR EL MUNASSIB

PLANNED POSITIONS 0600 HRS AUG. 31

20TH CORPS

ARIETE

LITTORIO

21 PZ DIV.

15 PZ DIV.

7 ARM. DIV.

2300 HRS AUG. 30

D.A.K.

RECCE. GROUP

1200 HRS AUG. 31

RECCE. GROUP

EL TAQA PLATEAU

QARET EL HIMEIMAT

5   10

MILES

QATTARA DEPRESSION

Although Auchinleck (Commander-in-Chief, Middle East) had checked Rommel at 1st Alamein, Churchill had lost confidence in him and sent out Alexander as Commander-in-Chief and Montgomery as Commanding Officer, Eighth Army. As supplies and reinforcements were coming in far quicker to Eighth Army than to D.A.K., Rommel decided to attack the weakly held southern flank. His plan (Map 24) called for surprise, swift passage of the mine fields (extent unknown), and overcoming opposition (strength unknown). A risky plan, especially against a cautious enemy. Air reconnaissance betrayed Axis movements and aerial attacks, and unexpected resistance by 7th Armored Division (4th Light Armored Brigade and 7th Motorized Brigade) and difficulties in the mine fields upset Rommel's timetable. Ninetieth Light and the Italian armor were in some confusion south of the New Zealanders. D.A.K.'s Commanding Officer, General Nehring, had been wounded and 21st Panzer's Commanding Officer killed, and not until 1 p.m. August 31 did 15th Panzer Division attack, followed one hour later by 21st Panzer Division. Some fierce fighting followed but despite losses the British positions were never seriously threatened and at nightfall D.A.K. withdrew. There was some action near Tell el Eisa on September 1, and on September 2, short of fuel, Rommel ordered a gradual retreat. An attempt to move south by the New Zealanders to close the mine field gaps behind the Axis forces failed (September 3/4), and over the next few days Rommel retired (under round-the-clock air attacks) behind the westernmost British mine fields, leaving 49 wrecked tanks behind.

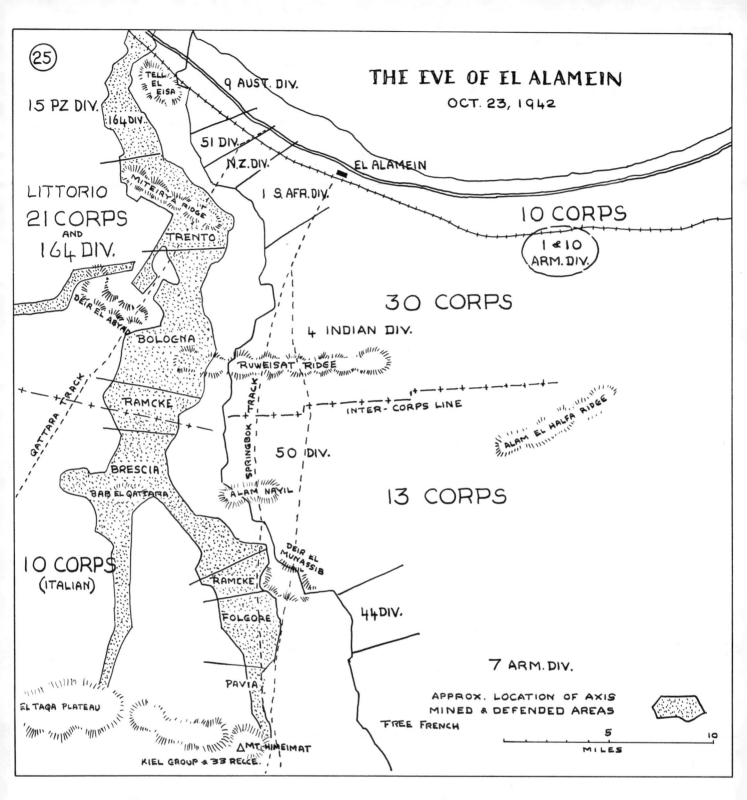

THE EVE OF EL ALAMEIN
OCT. 23, 1942

(25)

15 PZ DIV.

TELL EL EISA

164 DIV.

9 AUST. DIV.

51 DIV.

N.Z. DIV.

EL ALAMEIN

1 S. AFR. DIV.

LITTORIO
21 CORPS
AND
164 DIV.

MTEIRYA RIDGE

TRENTO

10 CORPS

1 & 10 ARM. DIV.

30 CORPS

DEIR EL ABYAD

BOLOGNA

4 INDIAN DIV.

RUWEISAT RIDGE

QATTARA TRACK

RAMCKE

SPRINGBOK TRACK

INTER-CORPS LINE

ALAM EL HALFA RIDGE

BRESCIA

50 DIV.

BAB EL QATTARA

ALAM NAYIL

13 CORPS

DEIR EL MUNASSIB

10 CORPS
(ITALIAN)

RAMCKE

44 DIV.

FOLGORE

7 ARM. DIV.

PAVIA

APPROX. LOCATION OF AXIS
MINED & DEFENDED AREAS

EL TAQA PLATEAU

FREE FRENCH

5   10

MILES

△ MT. HIMEIMAT

KIEL GROUP & 33 RECCE.

Deir—depression
Dahar—plateau
Alam—cairn or rock
Naqb, Bab—pass or cutting
Sanyet—deep well
Hagiag—barrier or escarpment
Maabus—steep cliff
Minqar—promontory or cliff

Qaret—low hill
Ras—cape
Tell—mound
Bir—cistern. Often from Roman times. Marked by pile of
excavated rock
Trigh—track
Wadi—ravine

II

Turning Point:

THE BATTLE OF EL ALAMEIN

The men of the Eighth Army were undoubtedly disheartened. After two years of fighting they seemed to be no nearer to a victory in the desert. Generals had come and gone—Wavell, Cunningham, Ritchie, Auchinleck—and now here were new men fresh from home, Montgomery and Alexander. Morale was still good, despite heavy losses. Given effective weapons, the troops knew they could more than hold their own, but there was a general feeling that leadership at the top was lacking. In contrast to the élan of Rommel, the wily and celebrated Desert Fox, their own commanders seemed dull, hesitant, and unsure. Not since General O'Connor's dashing campaign that drove the Italians out of Cyrenaica in 1940 had there been brilliant victories on a large scale. But O'Connor was in an Italian prison camp, and the battle still dragged on.

The new Eighth Army Commander, Lieutenant General Bernard Law Montgomery, was anything but dull. Unlike Auchinleck, whom he succeeded,

Montgomery was a showman ("showoff," some of his detractors said). He visited unit after unit, and soon his face, and his collection of cap badges, were well known to thousands of his men, most of whom had never set eyes on "top brass" before. More, wherever he went, he managed to instill a new combative spirit in all branches of the Army.

Not impressive in looks or stature, his brisk, confident manner speedily convinced the veteran desert hands (who were prone to look down on "tenderfeet" from home) that here was a no-nonsense professional who really meant business. The confidence he exuded soon spread and took hold. Troops, bewildered and disgusted by frequent retreats, began to think in terms of successful attack and ultimate victory. Under instructions from Alexander, Montgomery made it clear to all ("We stay here alive or we stay here dead") that there were to be no more retreats. His frequent appearances among the troops, his Australian slouch hat (later exchanged for the black Royal Tank Regiment beret), his tank named *Monty,* all helped make him familiar throughout his command. They also helped (as they were intended to do) to combat the "Rommel complex." Admiration for the German commander was widespread in the Eighth Army. Carried to extremes, it led to a defeatist attitude. Obviously the answer was to beat Rommel, and Montgomery made it very plain to all ranks that that was precisely what they were about to do.

While publicly playing down the myth of Rommel's invincibility, the British commander certainly did not underrate his opponent. Montgomery intended to make the coming battle a decisive one, with enough strength behind the battle units to ensure a powerful and continuous follow-up. To this end, reorganization, reinforcement, resupply, and retraining were the watchwords in the Eighth Army. Montgomery had very definite ideas about just how his battle was to be fought. A meticulous planner and one careful to leave little to chance, the Army commander was insistent that everyone, from divisional general to noncom, be thoroughly drilled in the particular part he was to play.

Montgomery was also insistent that the coming offensive be postponed long enough to allow time to build up the preponderance of weapons and supplies he considered as a minimum requirement for an all-out assault on a carefully prepared position.

The last of the series of map diagrams shown in Chapter I left the two armies of the desert facing each other at El Alamein, both badly mauled after the summer's fighting. But while reinforcements in men and materiel flowed almost uninterruptedly into the British camp, the situation in the Axis lines was not so bright. German reinforcements came in a trickle—the Soviet campaign saw to that—while redoubled efforts by the Royal Navy, R.A.F., and, increasingly, the U.S.A.A.F. took a heavy toll of Axis supply ships en route to Libya, as the following table shows.

Tankers were given high priority as targets, and by the time of the battle, Rommel's fuel reserves were perilously low.

It was obvious that a major thrust by the Eighth Army was only a matter of time, and Rommel wisely used the period between the end of the Alam el Halfa battle and the beginning of Montgomery's offensive on October 23 in creating a formidable defensive system of mines, wire, anti-tank guns, and automatic weapons. The mine belts were laid in irregular shapes, usually a few hundred yards deep, with expanses of open ground between. This ground was in turn laced with transverse belts, to trap vehicles piercing the first field. Scattered along these "Devil's Gardens," as the Germans called them, were hundreds of mutually supporting fire posts. These, wired and dug in or walled about with rock, contained machine guns, mortars, and/or anti-tank guns. Narrow lanes through the mine belts gave access to these strong points, whose function was to destroy or delay forces attempting to advance through the mine fields, leaving the main units of the army free to deliver the *coup de grâce* to any enemy who might succeed in breaking through.

These defenses were in great depth, and behind them ran another line, mainly of dug-in positions for tanks and anti-tank guns, and farther to the rear than assaulting infantry could reach in one night.

By the end of October nearly 500,000 mines had been laid—96 per cent of them anti-tank. The remainder were anti-personnel mines of various types. The former were mostly the round, shallow German Teller mine, which contained 12 pounds of TNT and required pressure of some 240 to 400 pounds to set it off. It could cripple a tank, usually by blowing off a tread, and destroy or badly damage any wheeled vehicle running over it. The anti-personnel mines were mostly the "S" type. This was a small cylinder with a neck from which three little prongs projected. When one of these was trodden on an ejector charge threw the cylinder some seven feet in the air where the main charge exploded, scattering pieces of mine and steel balls. This mine had a lethal radius of some 60 feet and did great execution at El Alamein. The "S" mine could also be activated by trip wires. Trip wires were also fastened to large aerial bombs. One of

AXIS SHIPS OF OVER 500 TONS

SUNK BY	R.N. SUBS	R.A.F.-U.S.A.A.F. F.A.A.	SURFACE SHIPS NAVAL, AIR CO-OP. MINES, ETC.	TOTAL	PER CENT SUNK OF TONNAGE SHIPPED
Aug.	7 ships—40,036 T.	3 ships—12,020 T.	2 ships—13,220 T.	65,276 T.	33
Sept.	5 ships—13,249 T.	5 ships—20,948 T.	2 ships—2,737 T.	36,934 T.	20
Oct.	11 ships—30,524 T.	4 ships—18,276 T.	2 ships—8,144 T.	56,944 T.	44

A. Teller mine 35

Diameter: c. 12½".
Height: 3".
Weight: 21 lbs. 8 oz.
Charge: c. 12 lbs. of TNT. Pressure needed
to activate: c. 240–400 lbs. Standard
German anti-tank mine until late 1942,
when it was supplemented by slightly
different Tmi 42.

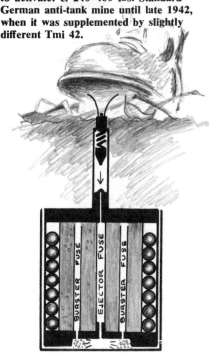

B. SIMPLIFIED DIAGRAM OF GERMAN "S" MINE 35

Three-pronged igniter at ground level
concealed by dirt, leaves, twigs, etc. Pressure
of 21 lbs. was sufficient to release spring-
loaded plunger, which fired fuse. After
3–6 second delay, ejector charge threw
mine about 7 feet in air, when a fuse-
detonated burster charge of TNT, scattering
bits of casing and ball bearings. Lethal
range—c. 60'. Pull igniters could be fixed
to most types of mines for use with trip
wires and booby traps.

these 250-pounders wiped out a whole platoon of the Black Watch on the night of October 23–24.

These defenses formed a deadly barrier, one that grew more impenetrable every week, and while engineers on one side were putting the finishing touches to their "Devil's Gardens," engineers on the other were working desperately on methods to uproot them and clear safe paths through which armor and vehicles could pass. There would be heroes in plenty at El Alamein, but none deserved more glory (and probably got less) than the men whose job it was to probe and prod their way across these death traps, usually under fire and nearly always at night. No one realized the importance of mine clearance more than Montgomery, and under his chief engineer, Brigadier F. K. Kisch,

the Eighth Army School of Mine Clearance was set up and a drill worked out.

The old method was to look for disturbed earth or other signs of a mine, probe carefully with a bayonet, search with fingers around and beneath the weapon to be sure it was not booby-trapped, then carefully unscrew the igniter, or in the case of the "S" mine, put a nail into the hole from which the safety pin had been removed by the enemy minelayer. All engineers were taught to disarm any known type of mine blindfolded—but finding them was another matter. The searching method above worked in daylight. This not only exposed the engineers to accurate fire but also tipped off the enemy as to the location of the breakthrough. Fortunately, an electronic type of detector, perfected by two officers of the Polish Free Forces, was available in limited quantities by the late summer. The device, which looked much like an electric floor waxer, had, unfortunately, to be operated from a standing position—the user walking slowly and swinging the instrument back and forth a few inches above the ground. Needless to say, casualties among mine-detecting personnel were high. The initial Alamein operation was not named "Lightfoot" for nothing.

The drill involved a party led by an officer with a compass, passing through a mine field and feeling gently for "S" mines and trip wires, unreeling a white tape as they went. A small blue light facing away from the enemy marked the beginning of the tape—another was put down when the reconnaissance party reached the other side of the mine field. This tape marked the center of the proposed lane. Next, three trios under an NCO moved along the tape. The first trio each carried a mine detector, and swept a path for "S" mines (which the NCO disarmed while everyone lay prone) 8 feet wide—

24 feet being enough for two tanks to pass. The second trio laid tapes marking the 24-foot path, which tapes the third trio pinned down. Once through, the party reversed course. The second trio now marked the anti-tank mines as they were located, and the last trio disarmed them and stacked them at the edge of the path. Another party of ten were working their way forward from the rear, and when they met, the path was ready for vehicles. MPs then drove in in a truck with stakes, pinpoint lamps, and route markers and finished the job.

This was the general practice. There were variations due to unusual circumstances—most circumstances in a battle are—and where detectors were in short supply, the old prodding method had to be used. All this was, of course, slow and methodical and liable to lead to heavy casualties among the engineers. Under ideal conditions (no enemy opposition), 200 yards per hour with detectors and half that distance with the probing method was expected.

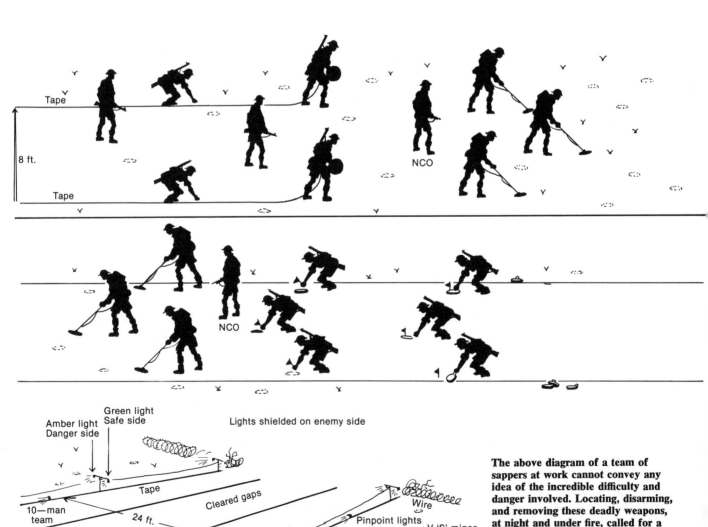

The above diagram of a team of sappers at work cannot convey any idea of the incredible difficulty and danger involved. Locating, disarming, and removing these deadly weapons, at night and under fire, called for a special kind of courage.

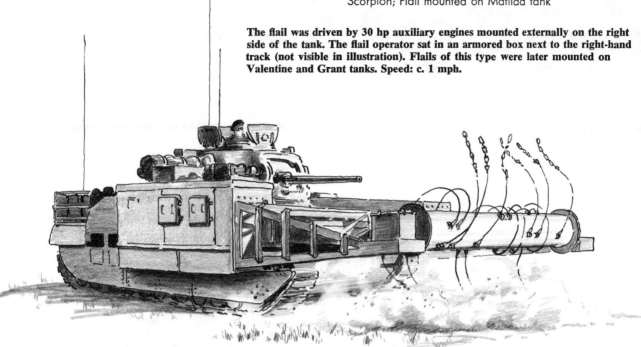

Scorpion; Flail mounted on Matilda tank

The flail was driven by 30 hp auxiliary engines mounted externally on the right side of the tank. The flail operator sat in an armored box next to the right-hand track (not visible in illustration). Flails of this type were later mounted on Valentine and Grant tanks. Speed: c. 1 mph.

An entirely different approach was the Scorpion, proposed by a South African engineer, Major A. S. du Toit—a Matilda tank with two projecting arms, between which a drum revolved, bearing short lengths of heavy chain. The whirling chains thrashed the ground (incidently raising great clouds of dust, which drew the enemy's attention— and fire) and exploded any mines they hit. Speed was little more than one mile per hour. Teller mines could be exploded to a depth of 4 or 5 inches. After about 15 mines the chains had to be replaced. Only 24 Scorpion tanks were ready by October 23. The early models, which were driven by a separate engine, were unreliable as well as being difficult to steer due to the dust, stones, scrub, and debris kicked up by the device. It was a good idea and was later seen in an improved version as the Sherman "Crab," but almost all mines at El Alamein had to be cleared by hand.

The Eighth Army received an important addition to its armory in the shape of the Sherman tank, 252 of which were ready for action on October 23. This well-armored and mechanically reliable vehicle mounted a long 75mm gun in a revolving turret and was considered a match for the Pz Kw IV Specials. There were also 78 of the new Crusader IIIs

U.S. M4 Medium Tank (Sherman)

For the greater part of World War II the standard U.S. medium tank. Sturdy and mechanically reliable, it was also used in quantity by both British and French. Often outgunned and outarmored by later German models, the Sherman triumphed by sheer weight of numbers. By the war's end almost 50,000 had been produced. Weight: c. 30 tons. Armament: one 75mm gun with 360° traverse, two hull-mounted .30 cal. machine guns (a .50 cal. machine gun could be mounted on turret). Armor: turret front 76 mm, sides 38–50 mm. Speed: max. 25 mph. Crew: 5.

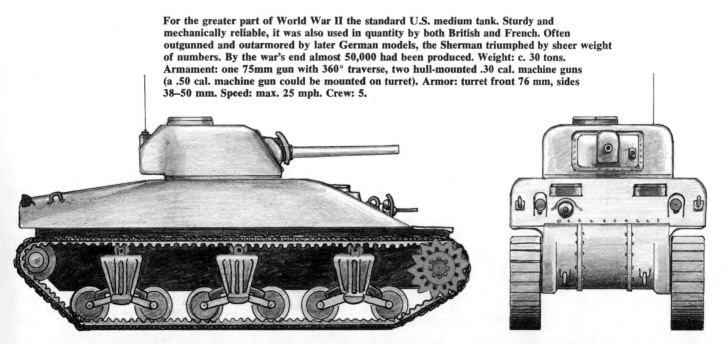

—mounting the high-velocity 6-pounder anti-tank gun. There were as well a number of American SP (self-propelled) 105mm howitzers—the Priest (so-called for the pulpitlike mounting for the .50-cal. machine gun). There were also a few SP 25-pounders on Valentine chassis—the Bishop, and 6-pounder anti-tank guns on a 4-wheeled chassis—the Deacon.

Carrier, Valentine, 25-pounder gun, MK1 (Bishop)

Produced in 1942 in limited quantity (about 100), in response to the urgent need for a self-propelled (SP) weapon with high explosive (HE) capacity. Until the arrival in the desert of Grants and Shermans with their 75mm guns, British armor had no weapon with HE capability. In the Bishop the weapon was mounted in a simple lightly armored box mounted on a Valentine II chassis. The ammunition was carried in a towed limber.

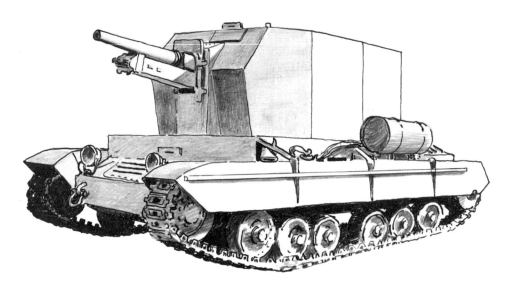

Unlike the Bishop, which was a hasty improvisation, the Priest (so called for the pulpitlike position for the .50 cal. machine gun) was a well-designed SP with a standard U.S. 105mm gun-howitzer mounted in a lightly armored structure on a Grant chassis. Weight: 50,000 lbs. Armament: one 105mm howitzer, one .50 cal. Browning machine gun. Armor: front plate ½". Crew: 7. A 500 Ford V-8 engine gave a speed of 26 mph on the road and a range of 150 miles. Began to arrive in the Middle East in September 1942.

R. Truck-mounted (Portée) British 6-pounder Anti-tank Gun
American M7 105mm Howitzer Motor Carriage (Priest)

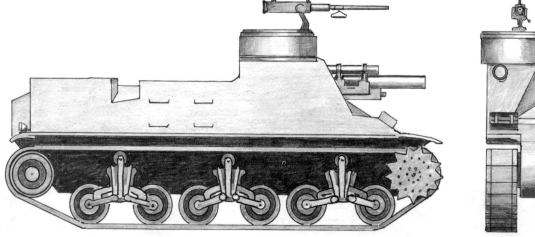

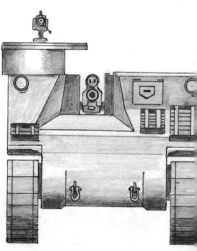

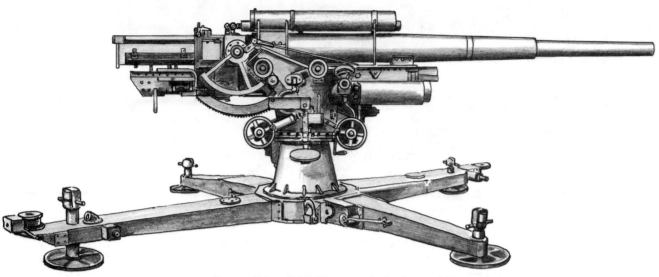

German 8.8cm FLAK (Flugzeugabwherkanone) 18

Used most effectively in the desert as an anti-tank weapon. Caliber: 88 mm. Length overall: 25'. Crew: 6. Rate of fire: max. 8 rounds per minute. Effective horizontal range (max.): 11,500 yds. Weight of shell: 21 lbs. Muzzle velocity: 2,600 fps. Penetration of armor (vertical) at 2,000 yds.: 159 mm. Naturally, the more the armor sloped from the vertical, the less the penetration. Even so, this meant that at battle ranges, the 88 could smash through the armor of any tank including the Sherman.

The 88 was furnished with three types of ammunition: time-fused (HE) for anti-aircraft use, percussion-fused for ground targets, and base-fused armor piercing (AP) with steel cap (C) ballistic cap (BC).

Perhaps as important as the new weapons was the abolishing of the mobile columns of all arms and brigade groups and the return to the division as the main tactical unit. Further—Montgomery meant to hold his armored commanders on a tight rein—no more "swanning" around in wild cavalry-type sweeps and charges. There was at last a sufficiency of effective anti-tank guns—849 6-pounders as well as 554 2-pounders. And it was hoped that those assigned to the armored brigades would work in close co-operation with the tankers. Rommel's success had depended in part on the effective use of his anti-tank guns—deploying them to combat tanks while the Panzers overwhelmed the infantry; now the Eighth Army planned to profit from past experience.

Montgomery's original plan for his offensive, Operation "Lightfoot," called for the infantry of XXX Corps to break through in the North, following a great artillery barrage. X Corps would then push its armor through the gap and take up position on the enemy supply lines, where the Axis armor would have to attack it. XIII Corps would meanwhile launch a secondary but heavy attack in the South, pinning down enemy units and forcing passage for light mobile units to move through and swing north. However, by the beginning of October, Montgomery had decided to alter his battle plan. After the breakthrough and passage of the breach by the armor, the infantry were to widen the gaps north and south, destroying the enemy troops holding the line—"crumbling" the defenses, as he put it. The Axis armor would be forced to move to the help of its infantry, when it would be met by the British armor and anti-tank guns, fighting in a defensive role as at Alam el Halfa.

The plan for breaching the enemy's defenses on a broad front and the clearing of two "corridors" for the passage of the armor before daylight were causes for concern among some of Montgomery's generals. Gatehouse and Lumsden feared that, even if the corridors were cleared in time, congestion was inevitable as large numbers of tanks, guns, and support vehicles bottlenecked in the narrow lanes whose western ends would at once be the target for concentrated enemy fire. Freyberg flatly predicted that the tanks would not get through. Morshead and Pienaar were doubtful.

Montgomery insisted that the armor *must* get through, even if it had to fight its way in daylight regardless of loss—and his commanders loyally prepared to see that it did.

"Sun shield" camouflages Crusader. To deceive enemy reconnaissance, frames of tubing were covered with burlap so that at a distance a tank resembled a truck.

In any case, much depended on surprise. The Axis commanders knew an offensive was coming; the exact time and location they did not know, and elaborate precautions were taken to ensure their not finding out. Forward ammunition and supply dumps were carefully concealed, and gun pits and trenches for the assaulting infantry were dug ahead of time so that, failing concealment (always difficult in the desert), they might be finally ignored as being part of the landscape. Tanks were covered with canvas covers ("sun shields") to resemble trucks, and dummy tanks and vehicles were also used freely.

As masses of vehicles could not be concealed, the above devices were used to mask their identities. For instance, enemy aerial photos might show numbers of supply vehicles in a certain area. Over a period of time this amount of traffic would be accepted as normal. But on some night prior to the attack tanks with sun shields would be substituted for the same number of trucks, so that nothing unusual would be noted from the air. Part of the deception plan was to fool the Axis commanders into thinking that the main attack was to come in the South. To this end a dummy water pipeline was laid, but at a rate that suggested it would not be finished until mid-November. To further the southern-attack concept, 10th Armored moved up behind XIII Corps without any attempt at concealment. Then at night 10th Armored moved to its proper position north of Alam el Halfa, and its position was taken by dummies. At the same time, normal but fictitious radio traffic was maintained in the southern area, while strict radio discipline was observed by the division in its assigned assembly position. This even included Gatehouse, whose voice on R/T was familiar to Afrika Korps monitors, making trips back to "go on the air" from his original position. The idea was to keep the enemy guessing until the moment of attack, and this it did—preventing any buildup by the Axis of supporting forces opposite the points of attack at the expense of part of the line not threatened.

On the Axis side of the mine fields the Panzerarmee had a new, though temporary commander. Rommel was to go to Germany on a long-deferred sick leave, and on September 22 he handed over his command to an armor expert from the Russian Front, General Georg Stumme. The work on the defense positions as laid down by Rommel went on under the new commander. The whole system, from the "battle outposts" at the eastern edge of the mine fields to the main defense lines west of the second mine belt, covered from 2½ to 4½ miles from front to rear. As noted, some of the artillery and heavy anti-tank guns were even farther back.

The weeks before the battle saw intensive patrolling and air reconnaissance by the Allied single-engine squadrons, as well as unrelenting attacks on ports, convoys, and airfields by the night bombers. Only Liberators could reach Benghazi, but many tons of bombs went down there, sinking an 8,000-ton ship and damaging others, while Tobruk continued to receive attention from all types. Until October 19, fighter-bomber and day-bomber activities were curtailed. Enemy air activity was also light. Nevertheless, between September 8 and October 8 the R.A.F. flew 8,806 sorties, and the U.S.A.A.F. flew 444. Losses for the period were: British, 54; U.S., 7; German, 50; Italian, 27 (these last included aircraft lost and on the ground). It was this growing intensity of the Allied air offensive that prompted Rommel to write: "The strength of the Anglo-American Air Force was, in all the battles to come, the deciding factor."

On the eve of the El Alamein battle, the Eighth

Army consisted of 3 corps.

XXX CORPS (Lieutenant General Sir Oliver Leese)

23rd Armored Brigade Group—194 2-pounder Valentines (one regiment each was attached to 51st, 9th Australian and 1st S.A. Divisions. One was in Corps Reserve)

51st (Highland) Division (Major General D. N. Wimberley)—3 infantry brigades

4th Indian Division (Major General F. Tuker)—3 infantry brigades

9th Australian Division (Lieutenant General Sir Leslie Morshead)—3 infantry brigades

1st South African Division (Major General D. Pienaar)—3 infantry brigades

New Zealand Division (Lieutenant General Sir Bernard Freyberg, V.C.)—2 infantry brigades

9th Armored Brigade (under command New Zealand Division)—36 Shermans, 37 Grants, 37 Crusaders, 12 Crusader IIIs

XIII CORPS (Lieutenant General B. G. Horrocks)

7th Armored Division (Major General A. F. Harding)—Div. H.Q.: 7 Crusaders

4th Light Armored Brigade: 14 Grants, 67 Stuarts

22nd Armored Brigade: 57 Grants, 42 Crusaders, 8 Crusader IIIs, 19 Stuarts

1st Fighting French Brigade Group (under command)

50th Division (Major General J. S. Nichols)—2 infantry brigades, and 1 French and 1 Greek Brigade Group

44th Division (Major General I. Hughes)—2 infantry brigades

X CORPS (Lieutenant General H. Lumsden)—Corps H.Q.: 2 Grants

1st Armored Division (Major General R. Briggs)—Div. H.Q.: 8 Crusaders

2nd Armored Brigade: 39 Crusaders, 29 Crusader IIIs, 92 Shermans, 1 Grant

7th Motor Brigade

A15, Cruiser Mark VI, Crusader II

An update of an earlier cruiser, the A13 MK II, the Crusader (I) was itself updated while in production to carry 50 mm of armor instead of 40. The need for a more powerful gun than the 2-pounder was also realized, but due to retooling and production problems following the losses of all armor and artillery in France in 1940 (nearly 700 tanks and 850 anti-tank guns) production of the 2-pounder tank and anti-tank gun was continued, delaying manufacture of the 6-pounder.

Hastily produced, before adequate testing, the Crusader was mechanically unreliable and undergunned. It was all that was available, however, and 4,350 gun tanks were built plus over 1,300 "Specials" (command vehicles, anti-aircraft tanks, bulldozers, gun tractors, etc.). The auxiliary machine gun turret was found impractical and was removed from many Is and IIs and eliminated in Crusader III. This carried the 6-pounder and began to arrive in the desert in the summer of 1942. Weight: 19¾ tons. Length: 19′8″. Height: 7′4″. Armament: I & II—one 2-pounder; III—one 6-pounder. Armor: 50 mm max. Hp: 340. Speed: road 27 mph, cross-country c. 12 mph. Crew: 4.

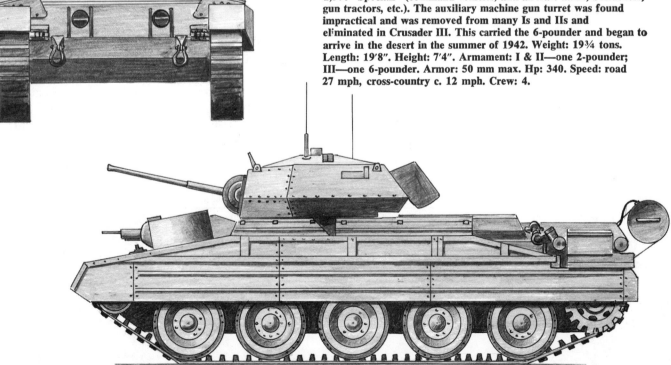

10th Armored Division (Major General A. H. Gate-house)—Div. H.Q.: 7 Crusaders
8th Armored Brigade: 31 Shermans, 57 Grants, 33 Crusaders, 12 Crusader IIIs
24th Armored Brigade: 93 Shermans, 2 Grants, 28 Crusaders, 17 Crusader IIIs
1 motorized infantry brigade

In addition to the tanks listed above, the New Zealand Division's Cavalry unit had 29 Stuarts, and the 9th Australian Cavalry had 15 Crusaders and 4 Stuarts. In all, the armor totaled 1,029 ready for action, with some 1,200 more in reserve or in the shops being repaired or modified for desert use.

Panzergruppe Afrika
Panzer General Georg Stumme

Army Troops Kampstaffel Kiel (Major General Krause)
221st RHQ (medium and heavy batteries), 612th and 617th Anti-Aircraft Bns.
19th Anti-Aircraft Division (Lieutenant General Burckhardt)
66th, 102nd, and 135th AA RHQs

Deutsches Afrika Korps (D.A.K.)

Lieutenant General Wilhelm Ritter von Thoma
15th Armored Division (Major General Gustav von Vaerst)
8th Tank Regiment, 113th Panzer Grenadier Regiment, 33rd Artillery Regiment, 33rd Anti-Tank Battalion, 33rd Engineer Battalion
21st Armored Division (Major General Heinz von Randow)
5th Tank Battalion, 104th Panzer Grenadier Regiment, 155th Artillery Regiment, 39th Anti-Tank Battalion, 200th Engineer Battalion
90th Light Division (Major General Theodor Graf von Sponeck)
155th Panzer Grenadier Regiment (with 707th Heavy Infantry Gun Company under command), 200th Panzer Grenadier Regiment (708th Heavy Infantry Gun Company under command), 346th Panzer Grenadier Regiment, 190th Artillery Regiment, 190th Anti-tank Battalion
Under command: Force 288, composed of: 605th Anti-tank Battalion, 109th and 606th Battalions
164th Light Division (Major General Carl-Hans Lungershausen)
125th Infantry Regiment, 382nd Infantry Regiment, 433rd Infantry Regiment, 220th Artillery Regiment, 220th Engineers Battalion, 220th Cyclist Unit, 609th AA Battalion
Reconnaissance Group: HQ 15th Lorried Infantry Brigade, 3rd, 33rd and 580th Recce Units
Ramcke (Parachute) Brigade (Major General Bernhard Ramcke)
3 battalions of 2nd, 3rd, and another parachute rifle regiment, Lehrbataillon Burckhardt, Parachute Battery, Parachute Anti-tank Battalion

Italian Corps

Marshal Ettore Bastico

X CORPS (Lieutenant General Edoardo Nebba)
Brescia Division (Major General Brunetto Brunetti)
19th and 20th Infantry Regiments, 1st Mobile Artillery Regiment, 27th Mixed Engineer Regiment
Folgore Division (Major General Enrico Frattini)
185th, 186th, and 187th Infantry Regiments
Pavia Division (Brigadier General N. Scattaglia)
27th and 28th Infantry Regiments, 26th Artillery Regiment, 17th Mixed Engineer Battalion
Corps Troops: 9th Bersagliere Regiment, XVI Corps Artillery Group, Eighth Army Artillery Group
XX CORPS (Lieutenant General Giuseppe de Stephanis)
Ariete Armored Division (Brigadier General Francesco Arena)
132nd Tank Regiment, 8th Bersagliere Regiment, 132nd Artillery Regiment, 3rd Armored Cavalry Group, 132nd Mixed Engineer Battalion (129 medium tanks)

GERMAN TANKS IN THE D.A.K.

Pz Kw	II	III 5-cm short	III Sp 5-cm long	IV 7.5-cm short	IV Sp 7.5-cm long	Comd
Fit	31	85	88	8	30	7
Under repair	2	17	1	2	—	1

Divided almost equally between 15th and 21st Panzer divisions

Littorio Armored Division (Major General G. Bitossi)

133rd Tank Regiment, 12th Bersagliere Regiment, 3rd Armored Cavalry Group (part), 3rd and part 133rd Artillery Regiments (115 medium tanks)

Trieste Motorized Division (Brigadier General Francesco La Ferla)

11th Tank Battalion, 65th and 6th Infantry Regiments, 21st Artillery Regiment, 8th Armored Bersagliere Regiment, 52nd Mixed Engineer Battalion (34 medium tanks)

Corps Troops: Part Eighth Army Artillery Group, 90th Engineer Company

XXI CORPS (Lieutenant General Enea Navarini)

Trento Division (Brigadier General Giorgio Masina)

61st and 62nd Infantry Regiments, 46th Artillery Regiment

Bologna Division (Major General Alessandro Gloria)

39th and 40th Infantry Regiments, 205th Artillery Regiment, 25th Engineer Battalion

Corps Troops: 7th Bersagliere Regiment, 24th Corps Artillery Group, Eighth Army Artillery Group

Army Reserve: Pistoia Division (35th and 36th Infantry Regiments, 3rd Motorized Artillery Regiment, Bersagliere Battalion); GGFF (young Fascists) Division (2 or 3 battalions)

The *Official History* gives the following comparison of weapons and vehicles:

	ALLIED	AXIS
Tanks (light excluded)	1029	496
Armored cars	435	192
Guns (field and medium)	908	about 480 plus 18 heavy
Anti-tank	1451	about 850
Serviceable aircraft, about	530	about 350

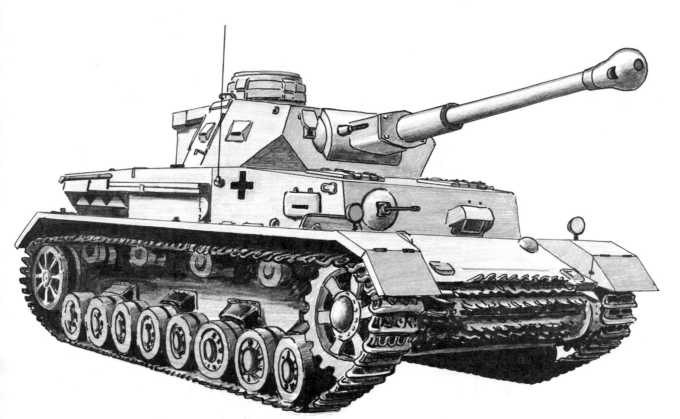

Pz Kw IV Ausf F2 MIT 7.5 Cm KWK L/43

(Pz Kw=*Panzerkampfwagen*=armored fighting vehicle. Ausf=*ausführung*=model or mark. MIT=with. KWK=*Kampfwagenkanone*=tank gun. L/43=length of barrel in calibers.) Known to the British as the Pz IV Special. The mounting of the long-barreled 75mm gun in place of the short L/24 changed the Pz Kw IV from a close-support vehicle to a formidable vehicle capable of destroying the heaviest Allied tanks.
Weight: 23.6 tons. Length: 19'6". Armament: one 75mm long barrel (3.23 meters) gun, firing a 15 lb. shell (APCBC), capacity 87 rounds; two 7.92 machine gun 34s. Armor: front 50 mm, sides 30 mm. Engine: 300 hp Maybach. Speed: road 24 mph, cross-country c. 10 mph. Range: 130 miles. Crew: 5.

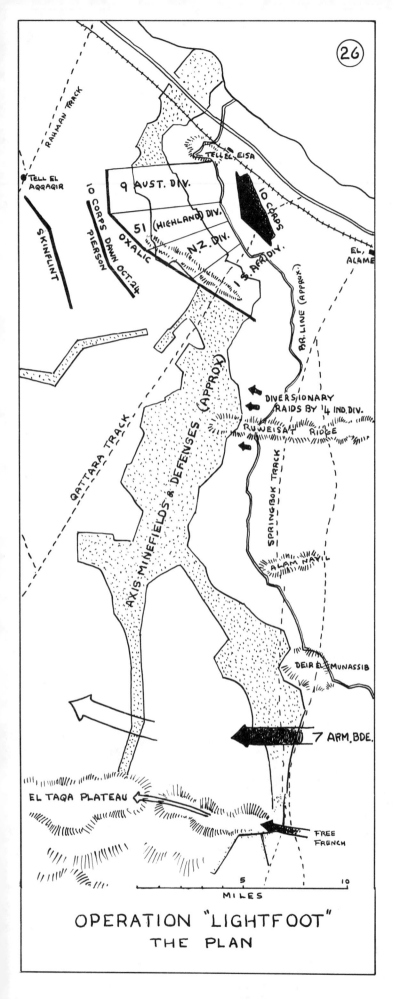

OPERATION "LIGHTFOOT"
THE PLAN

To partially offset this superiority of British strength there were with the Panzerarmee on October 1 (though not all deployed as anti-tank weapons) 86 of the deadly 88s.

Exact figures for comparison of the two armies are not available, but the Allied forces can be estimated at close to 200,000, and those of the Axis at about 50,000 Germans and 54,000 Italians.

The Allies' preponderance in supplies was even greater. Due to ship sinkings, Axis fuel supplies were low—about enough for eleven days at normal consumption, with sufficient ammunition for about nine days' fighting. In the Allied camp there was an ample supply of both fuel and ammunition, with a large number of transport vehicles—of which the Axis was also short.

The question remained whether a superiority of roughly two to one in all categories was a sufficient margin for an army to break through a series of strong defenses and, once through, do battle with the main enemy forces. As it turned out, it was, as Wellington said of Waterloo, "a near run thing."

OPERATION "LIGHTFOOT"

To reduce the chances of the Axis air forces interfering with the last-minute deployment of the Eighth Army for the coming battle, on October 19, Air Vice-Marshal Coningham began his own offensive by ordering constant and heavy attacks on the forward German fighter fields—mainly those near El Daba and Buka. Other attacks were made on transport and troop concentrations. From dawn on October 19 to dark on October 23, the British flew 2,209 sorties and the Americans 260. Seventeen British aircraft were lost, one American and thirteen German; Italian losses are not known. It was not an all-out effort—that was being saved for the battle itself—but enemy air attacks, and more important, reconnaissance were prevented while British reconnaissance flights went almost unhindered. On the night of October 23–24, Coningham's forces were to illuminate and bomb enemy troop and gun positions, attack them with night fighters, jam the enemy's wireless transmission, and generally create confusion—including dropping dummy parachutists. At daylight day bombers and fighter-bombers would attack selected targets, then be on call for support as requested.

The map shows the main objective of XXX Corps was the "Oxalic" line (to be reached before dawn of October 24) and X Corps' first and second positions after its breakthrough—"Pierson" and

"Skinflint."

To the south XIII Corps was to break through the two old British mine fields "January" and "February" (in Axis hands since Alam el Halfa) and pass 7th Armored Division through, while Koenig's French were to attack the commanding Himeimat high point.

On October 19 and 20, Montgomery explained his plan to all officers down to lieutenant colonel. His talk, according to reports of some of those participating, left the majority of his hearers completely convinced of the ultimate and complete success of the operation. It was not a pre-battle pep talk, but a professional exposition of his tactical thinking. He promised no quick victory but told his listeners to be prepared for a "dogfight of a week. Whole affair about twelve days." In many cases skepticism changed to enthusiasm—an enthusiasm passed on to the troops, who were all thoroughly briefed (with the exception of those front-line units exposed to possible capture) by their commanding officers on October 21. All leaves were stopped, and the Army began the long wait until the opening blast of the barrage signaled the beginning of its greatest battle.

On the night of October 22–23 the assault troops, engineers, and forward observing officers moved quietly into their previously dug and concealed positions. There they stayed all the next day roasted and flycovered, movement for any purpose forbidden, most thinking no doubt of the tons of potential death and mutilation hidden a few inches beneath the scorched sand ahead.

As sunset gave way to darkness, the waiting lines came alive—white tapes were run out and pinpoint lamps lit to guide men and vehicles through the British mine fields. A little to the rear, the tanks assigned to the infantry (their camouflage sun shields now discarded) and the infantry's own anti-tank guns, carriers, and vehicles moved up into position. Farther back still, the tanks and guns of the armored divisions also cast off their camouflage and moved to their final positions—and in the tensely waiting batteries, gun crews readied their pieces for the appointed second. They were to work hard that night—5½ hours of continuous fire, with only time out to cool the tubes. We will call it a barrage although it was not a barrage in the World War I sense. The number of guns per yard of front was much too small. First would come 15 minutes of counter-battery fire, concentrated on gun positions carefully plotted by air reconnaissance, ground observation, sound ranging, and flash spotting. Then

after 5 minutes' pause, at zero hour (2200), 7 minutes of fire would be poured on the enemy front-line positions while the infantry moved up close to the bursting shells; then the fire would lift and move forward ahead of the infantry.

At exactly 2140 hours on October 23, 1942, the crash of hundreds of guns heralded the opening of the battle. As a deluge of shells rained down on the enemy gun positions, Wellingtons roared overhead, dumping a further 125 tons of bombs on the targets. It was the biggest bombardment of the North African campaign and impressed friend and foe alike. Besides spreading death and destruction in the enemy's gun pits, the bombardment, plus the jamming by specially equipped Wellingtons, disrupted Axis communications so that for several hours response by their field and medium guns was sporadic.

At 2200 the hail of projectiles began to fall on the forward posts. "It stunned even our own troops," wrote an Australian. As the shells struck the enemy's front lines, thousands of infantrymen, engineers, signalmen, and medics moved out, following the tapes unreeled behind the navigating officers. These, compass in hand, led the advancing units. In minutes a haze of dust and smoke covered the battleground, and even with tapes, pinpoint lamps, and Bofors AA guns firing bursts of colored tracer along the boundaries between each brigade and division, keeping speed and direction was difficult.

As the rifle companies advanced through the smother, those near the 51st (Highland) Division could hear the wild music of the bagpipes above the crash of explosions and the crack of bullets. One Black Watch piper, hit twice, kept going until a third bullet brought him down, mortally wounded but still playing. Ahead through the murk rose a frantic display of pyrotechnics from the enemy forward positions, calling for Axis counter-barrage fire. But for a considerable time the major Axis response was from mortar and machine guns, firing from positions not knocked out by the barrage.

XXX Corps' four divisions attacked in line on two-brigade fronts—a total width of about six miles. Distances from the start line to "Oxalic" varied from some five miles on the right to three on the left. The leading troops of the eight attacking brigades met no great opposition from the easternmost battle-outposts, but as they progressed, resistance stiffened and casualties mounted. The

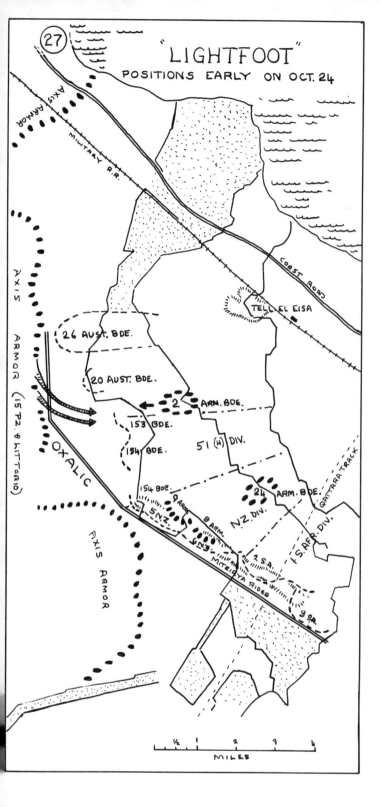

As expected, mines proved the greatest obstacle, but time needed to clear gaps had been underestimated. Pockets of enemy resistance slowed the infantry while the tanks were far behind schedule. Gaps, made (with considerable loss) by the engineers, were narrow and easily blocked by damaged vehicles.

brunt of the attack fell on the three battalions of the 382nd Panzer Grenadier Regiment. The majority of the Italian units incorporated in the defense system abandoned their positions, running rearward in panic or forward in surrender. The Panzer Grenadiers were of sterner stuff, and, though suffering heavy losses, held the remnants of a line at daybreak.

In only a few cases did the infantry reach "Oxalic" (see map), while mines had in most instances checked the accompanying "I" tanks and 9th Armored Brigade. The task of clearing the mines from the two corridors went more slowly than expected (one of the objections to Montgomery's plan had been the small margin of time allowed for this operation before daylight), and by dawn only one lane of 1st Armored's corridor had been cleared to the Australians' front (still some 1,000 yards short of "Oxalic"), while in 10th Armored's path four lanes had been cleared up to but not over Miteirya Ridge.

At dark X Corps' two armored divisions had moved from their assembly areas to the Springbok track, where they topped up with fuel, and at 0200 moved forward into the battle area. The head of 1st Armored Division, slowed to some three miles per hour by the dense clouds of dust, reached the old German front line at 0400 but was then brought to a halt by scattered mines and bypassed outposts. This meant that the tail of the long procession of tanks, guns, and trucks was still on the Springbok track. To the south, 10th Armored Division's 8th Armored Brigade reached the Miteirya Ridge, but by then it was getting light, and the brigade lost 18 tanks to mines and anti-tank guns and settled into hull-down position behind the ridge.

Thus at dawn of October 24 the advance had stalled all along the front and the armor was far short of Pierson, its first objective.

In the South, XIII Corps had breached the easternmost ("January") field against determined resistance (mainly by Ramcke and Folgore), but failed to get through "February" before daylight and spent the day in the ground between the two under incessant fire. This fire would have been less severe if the high ground at Himeimat had been taken by the French, who, while they made initial gains, were unable to bring up supporting weapons and lost most of their ground to a counter-attack by a German armored column (Kiel Group).

The sun rose on a scene of mixed devastation and activity. Through a thick fog of dust, white-sleeved MPs directed traffic as great columns of ve-

American M3 Medium Tank (General Grant)

First U.S. medium tank to reach the desert, where its 75mm gun helped bolster undergunned British armored forces. Original design (General Lee) had a cupola above the 37mm turret, mounting a .30 cal. Browning machine gun. The Grant had a British-designed turret without the cupola. A reliable, well-armed and -armored tank. A major defect was the sponson-mounted 75, which had a limited traverse.

Weight: 28.5 tons. Length: 18′6″. Height: 10′4″. Armament: one 75mm M2 L/31, rounds carried 41; one 37 mm M5 L/50, with 179 rounds; one, two, or three Browning .30 cal. machine guns. Armor: 57 mm front, sides and upper rear 38 mm. Engine: 340 hp air-cooled radial. Speed: road 26 mph, cross-country 10 mph. Range: 144 miles. Crew: 6.

hicles moved slowly through the narrow lanes, while salvage crews removed the damaged and still-smoldering vehicles, ambulances moved their cargoes to the rear, engineers worked to widen the existing corridors, and signal parties strung their web of lines. The generals were up on their fronts by now, the large figure of Gatehouse, in white poshteen and black beret, sitting nonchalantly on the top of his command tank. Currie visited his 9th Armored, oblivious of the enemy fire. Lumsden, Leese, and Montgomery himself came up to confer with Gatehouse and Freyberg. Miteirya Ridge was no picnic ground that morning as the shells came in and 10th Armored Division's tanks, hull down on the ridge thickly crowded with the vehicles of three armored brigades, traded shots with the tanks of 15th Panzer.

Montgomery held a brief conference, then gave orders that the attack should continue and that 1st Armored must push forward at once "at all costs," while 10th Armored renewed its attack that night.

Early in the morning tanks of 15th Panzer appeared in front of 1st Armored and were engaged at long range. The German armor sheered off, leaving some burning tanks behind, probably surprised by their first encounter with Shermans. As the morning wore on, 2nd Armored Brigade, with help from 51st Division and the Mine Field Task Force, gradually worked its way westward through multiple mine fields. At noon came word that Montgomery was not satisfied with the 51st's progress, reiterating the "at all costs" order. With the Scottish infantry attacking ahead and the engineers close behind, the last field was finally gapped, but not without heavy casualties. The British armor now began to pass through—losing tanks to mines and guns as they did so—and by 1600 were deploying in front of the low rise called Kidney Ridge. Tanks of 15th Panzer and Littorio advanced slowly on the British armor, and a brisk tank battle ensued until dark. When the panzers finally retired, they left 26 burning or wrecked tanks behind. British losses were about the same but could be more easily afforded.

After the first surprise the enemy had reacted swiftly, the infantry resisting fiercely on their individual fronts and the artillery bringing their guns to bear on preselected fields of fire. But severed communications had left headquarters in some doubt as to what was going on, and early in the morning Stumme drove out to see for himself. His car was caught in a barrage, his aide was killed, and Stumme suffered a fatal heart attack. General Ritter von Thoma, commanding D.A.K., took command pending Rommel's return (he arrived from Germany via Rome on October 25). Von Thoma appears to have seen little immediate cause for alarm. His front, though badly battered, was still holding, and his reserves, such as they were, were intact. He may have worried about the damage done by the incessant R.A.F. attacks (almost 1,000 sorties on the twenty-fourth), but Afrika Korps was getting used to being pounded from the air, while the Luftwaffe was seldom to be seen.

Two actions were scheduled for the night of October 24–25: an advance over Miteirya Ridge by 10th Armored, preceded by a barrage, to the Pierson line (which was its previous objective); and a breakthrough of the "February" barrier by XIII Corps. Neither succeeded. More mines were found on and beyond the ridge than expected, and flares, shellfire, and an air attack caught an armored brigade formed up for movement through a lane. Many vehicles were hit, including several carrying fuel and ammunition, and the fires attracted shelling and more bombing. This threw the neighboring brigades into some confusion, and the covering barrage passed well ahead. One lane was now blocked with burning and wrecked vehicles, and another was enfiladed by 88s. Part of the force managed to reach the Pierson line. But Gatehouse, who was up with his armor, foresaw that at daylight they would be dangerously exposed on open ground, and he wanted authority to withdraw them behind the ridge. He returned to his headquarters and talked via telephone to Montgomery, who "discovered to my horror that he himself was some 16,000 yards behind his leading armored brigades. I spoke to him in no uncertain voice and ordered him to go forward at once and take charge of his battle. . . ." This implied slur did not sit well with Gatehouse, but the upshot was that only the regiment already on Pierson should hold its ground— the others to stay on the ridge. The others had in fact already gone forward but, as Gatehouse had

predicted, at daylight the regiment on the Pierson line, the Staffordshire Yeomanry, came under devastating fire from 88s and dug-in tanks and went up, as an onlooker described, "in sheets of flame one by one, just as if someone had lit candles on a birthday cake." Gatehouse agreed to the regiment's withdrawal (it had lost 27 of 43 tanks in two nights' fighting), and all three regiments were back where they started.

Farther to the left, 9th Armored Brigade had almost reached Pierson, where they stayed all day, knocking out 13 enemy tanks and 10 guns and losing several tanks in the process. They returned to the ridge that night (October 25–26). The attack by XIII Corps saw two lanes cleared, but attempts to push the armor through failed, with the loss of 31 tanks.

With the attack at Miteirya Ridge stalled, Montgomery now switched his blow to the north. The orders to XXX Corps were now to hold Miteirya Ridge and strike north with the 9th Australian Division. X Corps was to move north and northwest as opportunity offered. While making no headway, 1st Armored Division was carrying out its function of holding off the Axis armor, which it did during the day of October 25 at the cost of 24 tanks, at the same time inflicting severe losses on the enemy.

On the night of October 25–26, the Australians gained ground and prisoners in a neatly carried-out attack. XIII Corps again failed to break through in the south, and the R.A.F. continued its own offensive, dropping 175 tons of bombs—some of them on D.A.K.'s headquarters. Rommel was concerned about the heavy losses. He had lost many tanks in the clashes with the British armor, and his infantry had also suffered heavily. Trento, for example, had lost over half its infantry and almost all its guns. Nevertheless, on the twenty-sixth he ordered a strong counter-attack to regain the ground around Point 29 lost to the Australians. The great concentration of men and vehicles drew down a storm of shells from the artillery and showers of bombs and bullets from the Allied air squadrons. Axis bombers and fighters also were out in some strength, and furious air combats occurred. Rommel remarked in his *Papers* on the "tremendous British artillery fire" and "inferno of fire" put up by the British Bofors and the "rivers of blood [he was always prone to exaggeration—especially when things were not going well] poured out" by his troops. That the seizure of a relatively minor point should induce Rommel to launch such a large and disastrous counter-attack proved that Montgomery's "crum-

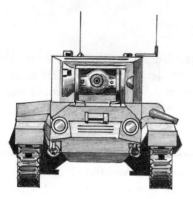

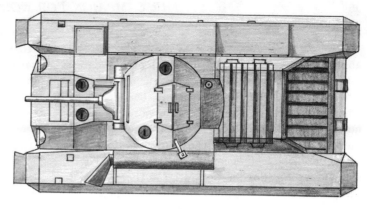

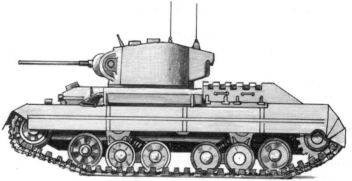

Tank, Infantry, MK III, Valentine II

More Valentines were built (6,855 in the U.K. and 1,420 in Canada) than any other British tank. Of these, some 2,700 were sent to Russia (not all got there), and the Soviets liked them, despite the inevitable 2-pounder gun. British crews liked them too. They were tough and mechanically reliable. Marks VIII–X mounted a 6-pounder, and the final XI a 75 mm.

Weight: 16 tons. Length: 17′9″. Width: 8′7½″. Height: 7′5½″. Armament: one 2-pounder with 60 rounds of ammo, one Besa machine gun, one Bren machine gun (could be mounted on turret). Armor: turret—front 65 mm, sides 60 mm; nose and sides 60 mm. Hp: 131 (later increased) Diesel. Speed: max. road 15 mph. Range: 90 miles.

bling" process was working to his advantage.

In another significant move, Rommel ordered 21st Panzer, followed by part of Ariete, and much of the artillery up from the South. The move began at midnight October 26–27 and was slowed by bombing attacks during its march.

Montgomery's battle had certainly not developed as speedily as he had hoped. On the other hand, the "crumbling" process had begun, and enemy losses in armor had been considerable. Records show that some 127 Axis tanks had been lost, while 1,700 Germans and 1,955 Italians were casualties. Eighth Army casualties to dawn of October 26 had amounted to 6,140, and some 300 tanks had been knocked out, many even then in the process of being repaired. For a force attacking against formidable defenses, the ratio of loss was not bad—and Montgomery may have felt in private some of the confidence he exuded publicly, especially as he could still muster some 900 "runners." His orders for the day were for XXX Corps to hold and consolidate; 51st Division to gain the rest of its objectives near Kidney Ridge; and XIII Corps to hold up its attacks. In the meantime, there would be some regrouping—with the ultimate result of creating a reserve of the New Zealand Division, 10th Armored Division, and possibly 7th Armored Division. With this reserve he would be able to restore some of the impetus of his offensive, which had

obviously lost momentum. The word "regroup" caused some alarm in London, where it had usually preceded announcement of a withdrawal, but Montgomery had his battle well in hand, and pressure was not relaxed.

On either side of "Kidney Ridge" (which was merely a kidney-shaped contour line on the map and indistinguishable from the rest of the featureless desert) were two equally vague points on the map—christened "Snipe" and "Woodcock." Opinions differed as to their exact positions by as much as a mile. These areas were to be cleared and occupied by two battalions of 7th Motor Brigade, after which 2nd Armored Brigade would pass north of "Woodcock" and 24th Armored Brigade would pass south of "Snipe." Second Battalion, King's Royal Rifle Corps dug in at daylight just short of "Woodcock," and 2nd Rifle Brigade, as near as they could judge, at "Snipe," where they prepared to hold on until the armor came up. Daylight showed the position near "Snipe" to be a shallow oval depression, dotted with scrub, some 900 yards long by 300 wide. The battalion, under Lieutenant Colonel V. B. Turner, consisted of 3 motor companies (reduced by casualties to 76 men), 22 Bren carriers of the scout platoons, machine-gun and mortar platoons, a few engineers, and the anti-tank company with 13 6-pounders as well as 6 6-pounders of 76th Anti-tank Regiment, R.A., less than 300 men all told.

Daylight also showed enemy tank leaguers all about, and a Mark IV and an SP that blundered into the position just before dawn were both destroyed. At dawn a number of enemy tanks emerged from dead ground near the position, and 8 tanks and SPs were destroyed on the north, and 3 more, with 5 damaged, on the southwest. The 24th Armored Brigade then appeared, after mistakenly shelling the position, and 3 Mark IVs that attacked them were knocked out by the "Snipe" guns. The 24th Armored Brigade drew heavy fire from German tanks, anti-tank guns, and medium artillery, and before the brigade withdrew, 7 Shermans were burning in Turner's position. The intense shellfire caused many casualties among the defenders, but an attack by Italian infantry was repelled with heavy loss. An attack by Italian tanks cost the Italians 4 tanks, while an assault by some 30 German tanks on "Snipe" and 24th Armored was beaten off. Eight Panzers were set on fire and several damaged. The position, however, was now all but surrounded and subjected to heavy fire. It was a scene of chaos, with burning tanks, carriers, wrecked guns, and bodies all half hidden by clouds of dust and smoke.

Another attack on "Snipe," by 8 Italian medium tanks and a self-propelled gun, occurred at 1300. It came at a point where only a single gun would bear, served by Sergeant Charles Calistan. He was alone, but Turner and another officer, Lieutenant Jack Toms, joined him as crew. Calistan had "brewed up" 5 of the tanks and the SP when he ran out of ammunition. Toms made a mad dash in a nearby Jeep to a disabled gun, loaded up some boxes, and drove back through a hail of machine-gun bullets from the remaining tanks, now only some 300 yards away. The Jeep, riddled, burst into flames, but Toms and 2 others lugged the ammunition clear, and Calistan, the bullets beating on the gun shield, finished off the remaining 3 tanks with a shot apiece.

By now many of the garrison had been killed, and others, including Turner and Toms, had been wounded by the almost ceaseless shelling and mortaring. At 1700 some 40 tanks of 21st Panzer rashly advanced northeast of the "Snipe" position to attack 2nd Armored Brigade. Waiting until the enemy were within 300 to 400 yards, the 4 remaining guns in that sector of "Snipe" crippled or set on fire a dozen of them. Some of the rest then made a frontal attack on Turner's position. More tanks were hit, and the German commander, under fire now by 2nd Armored Brigade, called off his attack. A second column now detached 15 MK IIIs to assault the northern end of the position. Dead ground (where they were out of sight of Turner's gunners) allowed them to approach to within some 200 yards. Then the 3 guns able to bear opened up and despite torrents of machine-gun fire, the 6 leading tanks were set on fire and the others retired to a hull-down position 800 yards away. This was the last assault, although a final shoot (the 6-pounders were almost out of ammunition) hit a tank silhouetted against the evening sky at 1,200 yards.

Late that night—the relieving troops having missed the position—the survivors of the garrison withdrew with their wounded and towed out one of the remaining guns. Scattered around the perimeter, like Indian dead after an attack on a wagon train, were some 56 Axis tanks or self-propelled guns. Inside the defense area lay the wrecks of 7 British and 1 German tank, 16 Bren carriers, several Jeeps, and ten 6-pounders. Five others of the original 19 AT guns were damaged.

This exploit has been recorded at some length, as an example of what determined troops with anti-tank guns of reasonable power could do. It gave heart to the infantry who were at last equipped with a weapon they could rely on, and delighted Montgomery. In one minor action more damage had been inflicted on Rommel's Panzers than in some previous armored battles, and a major Axis counter-attack, mainly by 21st Panzer, had been crippled. A well-merited V.C. for Turner and numerous other decorations were proofs of the Army commander's appreciation.

In conjunction with the assault by Axis armor near "Snipe," 90th Light was to attack at Point 29. This was beaten down by heavy shelling and concentrated bombing by R.A.F. and U.S.A.A.F. day bombers. So while the British armor had not made any of the hoped-for gains, their good shooting and that of the "Snipe" defenders had cost the Axis dearly in armor, and 90th Light had received a severe setback in the North. Rommel now ordered all positions held and settled down to await Montgomery's next move.

Fighting on October 28 followed much the same pattern. British infantry attempted to take over the Woodcock-Snipe area, with partial success, while the D.A.K.'s attempt to push back the British armor supporting them was halted by tank, anti-tank, and artillery fire. A second Axis effort later in the day was disrupted by heavy attacks by day

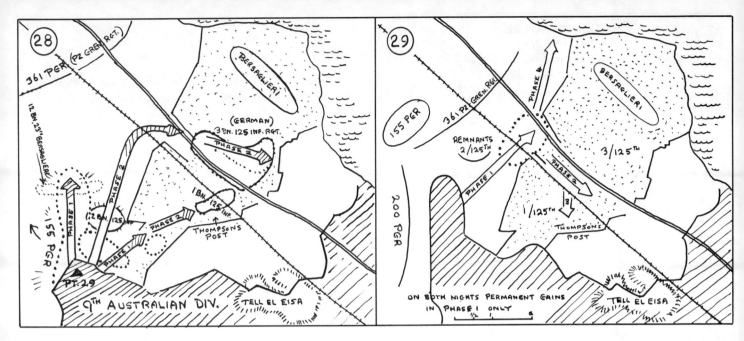

bombers.

Montgomery now decided to switch the weight of his attack to the northern flank. The Australians were to attack along the coast, strengthened by two infantry brigades.

On the night of October 28–29, Australian 9th Division made a second set-piece attack, with massive artillery support. The plan—to gain ground around Point 29, thrust northeast over the railroad to the main road, then along both to get behind the enemy in the coastal salient, was elaborate and ambitious. In the confusion of a night battle it failed, but it practically destroyed 2nd Battalion, 125th Panzer Grenadier Regiment, and overran a battalion of Bersagliere, and such was Montgomery's superiority in men and equipment that a drawn engagement with anywhere near even losses could be considered a success.

Rommel was by now considering a withdrawal, but with both armies at close grips and grave shortage of fuel (the tanker *Luisiano,* with 1,459 tons of gasoline, was sunk on October 28 by a Wellington off Greece), this would probably have meant abandoning the non-motorized units. The 21st Panzer, with 60 "runners" remaining, was to go in reserve north of Tell el Aqqaqir, relieved by Trieste. Part of 90th Light was withdrawn southeast of Sidi Abd el Rahman. This would help counter an expected thrust along the coast.

On hearing that 90th Light had been committed —thus indicating that Rommel had no fresh reserves—Montgomery again switched the thrust of his offensive. On the night of October 31/November 1, in an attack labeled "Supercharge," Freyberg's New Zealanders were to drive west on a

front of 4,000 yards. The objective—"to bring about the disintegration of the whole enemy army."

Hoping to keep Rommel's attention centered on the coastal flank, Montgomery ordered the Australians to make a third attack northward on the night of October 30–31. The attack was a many-pronged affair—in general a follow-up of the unsuccessful assault of October 28–29, with other phases calling for a drive east, cutting the Axis forces in two, and another southwest to capture a strong point known as Thompson's Post. As usual the attack was to be preceded by a great artillery concentration and preliminary bombing by fighter-bombers—Bostons and Baltimores. Again the program proved too ambitious, but again the Axis forces had taken heavy casualties and lost some 500 prisoners. The Australians now were astride both the main road and the railway, and to reach the remnants of 125th Panzer Grenadier Regiment, Rommel had again to attack. A battle group of about half 21st Panzer's remaining tanks, self-propelled guns, and artillery pushed down the railway, and there was seesaw fighting, continuing on the morning of November 1, in which ground changed hands several times and 40th Battalion, Royal Tank Regiment lost 21 Valentines. The Australians managed to hold most of their gains, while Rommel regained touch with 125th Panzer Grenadier Regiment. (Rommel's armor in this sector was now in a bad way. On November 1, D.A.K. had a total of 102, there were some 20 under 90th Light near the coast, and the two Italian divisions, Litterio and Trieste, had some 65 between them.)

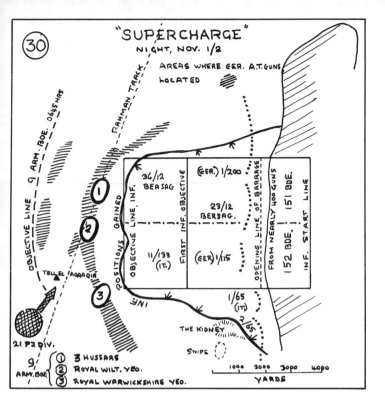

"SUPERCHARGE"
NIGHT, NOV. 1/2

AREAS WHERE GER. A.T. GUNS
LOCATED

RAHMAN TRACK

9 ARM. BDE. 0645 HRS

OBJECTIVE LINE

POSITIONS GAINED

OBJECTIVE LINE. INF.

FIRST INF. OBJECTIVE

OPENING LINE OF BARRAGE

FROM NEARLY 400 GUNS

152 BDE.

INF. START LINE

151 BDE.

36/12
BERSAG.

(GER.) 1/200

23/12
BERSAG.

11/133
(IT.)

(GER.) 1/15

1/65
(IT.)

2/65

INF.

THE KIDNEY

SNIPE

TELL EL AQQAQIR

21 PZ DIV.

9/ ARM. BDE.

① 3 HUSSARS
② ROYAL WILT. YEO.
③ ROYAL WARWICKSHIRE YEO.

1000 2000 3000 4000
YARDS

OPERATION "SUPERCHARGE"

To give Freyberg's tired troops more time to organize, the "Supercharge" attack was postponed until November 1–2. Sixty-eight Wellingtons plastered the rear areas, among other things wrecking D.A.K.'s advanced headquarters' signal system.

"Supercharge" was to be a major effort. The New Zealand Division's attack was to be led by two British brigades on loan (Freyberg had refused to use his weakened New Zealand troops in another assault, especially as they were earmarked for an important role in the pursuit). There would be a real barrage this time, close to 400 guns firing on a 4,000-yard front—a moving screen of 25-pounder shells bursting 20 yards apart. Ahead would fall another curtain 40 yards apart, and beyond that the mediums and heavies, the 4.5s and 5.5s, would search out known targets. As before, Bofors firing tracer would mark directions and boundaries. The ground once taken and cleared, 9th Armored Brigade (79 Shermans and Grants and 53 Crusaders) was to move through and smash the enemy gun line on the Rahman track and establish itself on the low Aqqaqir Ridge. That done, 1st Armored Division was to pass through and begin the inevitable and it hoped final, tank battle. The critical part was 9th Armored's smashing of the gun line, and to accomplish it, Montgomery told Freyberg that if necessary every tank in the brigade might have to be sacrificed.

As the guns crashed out, the infantry, supported by "I" tanks, began their advance at 0105, November 2. ["I" (infantry support) tanks (Valentines at the time of El Alamein.)] Resistance varied, and in places casualties were heavy. Dug-in tanks were encountered and destroyed and strong points and gun positions cleared, but in general the enemy had been badly hurt and much shaken by the barrage, and by 0530 word finally went back that the infantry had fulfilled their task. The barrage that was to precede 9th Armored's attack was scheduled for 0540, but Brigadier J. Currie asked for a half-hour delay to enable all his squadrons to get up. Some had already fallen casualty to mines and shellfire, and the approach march, in darkness and a fog of dust, had taken longer than expected.

At 0615 the barrage began, and the tanks, down to 94 now, surged ahead in line formation—churning over enemy positions, smashing anti-tank guns and automatic-weapons posts, and machine-gunning the dazed enemy who appeared in their path. But the timetable had been cut too fine. As the sky lightened in the east, silhouetting the British armor, a deadly sleet of armor-piercing shot screamed in from the heavy 88s and 7.62 cms dug in to the west and the numbers of smaller weapons on the flanks. Tank after tank went up in flames. The survivors pushed on, engaging anti-tank guns from as little as 10 yards before themselves being knocked out. To add to the destruction, Panzers of 21st and 15th Divisions loomed up through the haze of dust and smoke. Currie, sitting on top of the turret of his tank in the van, taking no notice of the flying shot, watched anxiously for 2nd Armored Brigade and the rest of 1st Armored Division.

Currie's brigade had not broken through the enemy line—not quite—but at a fearful price they had smashed into it and done much execution and enabled 1st Armored Division, the passage of whose vehicles (well over 2,000 all told) from the start line had been slower than anticipated, to deploy. Seventy out of 94 tanks had been wrecked. Within 100 yards of the smoking hulls were 35 knocked-out enemy anti-tank guns.

Under a smear of smoke and dust—lit by the glow of Currie's burning tanks—2nd Armored Group got itself into position, followed by the 8th, and aided by Currie's remaining 19 tanks. They were not on Aqqaqir Ridge, but the enemy armor was giving battle, and that was what the Army commander wanted. As some 120 Axis tanks clanked in to the attack, a vicious armored engagement began, made more deadly by concentrations

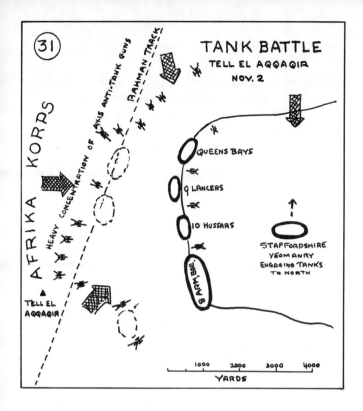

31

TANK BATTLE
TELL EL AQQAQIR
NOV. 2

AFRIKA KORPS

HEAVY CONCENTRATION OF AXIS ANTI-TANK GUNS

RAHMAN TRACK

QUEENS BAYS

9 LANCERS

10 HUSSARS

8 ARM'D BDE.

STAFFORDSHIRE YEOMANRY ENGAGING TANKS TO NORTH

TELL EL AQQAQIR

1000   2000   3000   4000
YARDS

of field artillery and anti-tank guns.

"For hours," wrote a regimental historian, "the whack of armor-piercing shot on armor plate was unceasing." R.A.F. and American fliers made repeated attacks on a great concentration of vehicles southeast of the mosque that marks Sidi Abd el Rahman, dropping 163 tons of bombs, while fighters fought off raiding Stukas, some of which

jettisoned their loads on their own troops. As the afternoon wore on, ammunition trucks dashed repeatedly across the open desert to replenish the empty shell racks as the tanks blazed away.

There was no breakthrough—but when the enemy drew off at nightfall more than 70 German and many Italian tanks had been destroyed or damaged. "The terrible British artillery" had also done great execution. Entire Axis batteries had been destroyed, the gunners dead, and the weapons smashed. Von Thoma estimated that a third of the infantry, field artillery, and anti-tank guns that began the battle had been lost.

It was this tank battle of Tell el Aqqaqir, the biggest of the campaign, that convinced Rommel that the time had come for a retreat to Fuka, where defensive positions had been reconnoitered. But the retirement was to be a "fighting withdrawal," the Italian infantry divisions first and D.A.K., the Italian armored divisions and the other mobile units following.

The 51st Division had meanwhile pushed forward on its front—taking prisoners from the battered Trieste Division—but an attempt in the early morning of November 3 failed to clear the Rahman track. Remnants of 21st and 15th Panzer and Littorio covered the track, helped by three troops of 88s. The day's fighting cost the British at least 26 tanks. The armored-car regiment, which had broken out on November 1–2 was still creating a disturbance behind the Axis lines, shooting up softskinned vehicles and disrupting things generally.

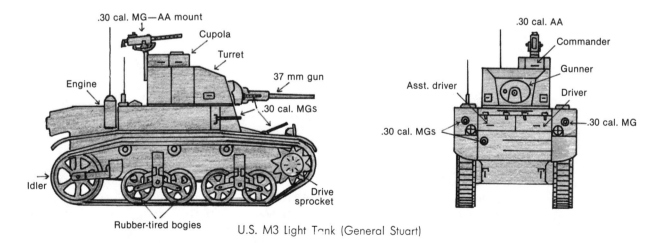

.30 cal. MG—AA mount
Cupola
Turret
37 mm gun
.30 cal. MGs
Engine
Idler
Drive sprocket
Rubber-tired bogies

.30 cal. AA
Commander
Gunner
Driver
.30 cal. MG
Asst. driver
.30 cal. MGs

U.S. M3 Light Tank (General Stuart)

Christened the "Honey" by the British. A good light tank and much used in the desert.
Length: 14′10″. Height: 7′4″. Width: 7′6″. Weight: 12.9 tons. Engine: one 250 hp radial.
Speed: max. road 36 mph. Range: 60 miles. Armament: one 37mm gun with a coaxially mounted 130 cal. machine gun; three .30 cal. machine guns mounted in hull; one .30 cal. machine gun on anti-aircraft mount on cupola. Armor: turret face and lower front 2″; driver's front, rest of turret 1½″; rest 1–1⅜″. Crew: 4.

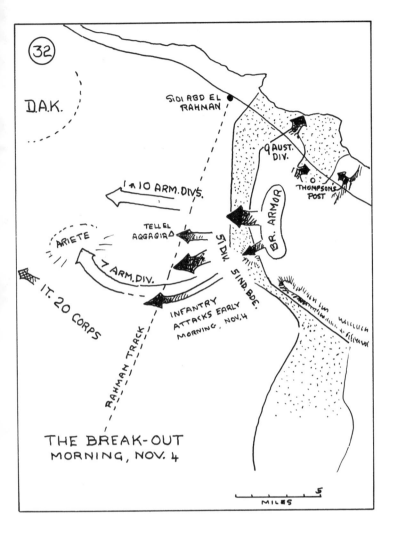

The Allied air forces continued to pound away; their targets were truck convoys, leaguers, and airfields.

Then, on the night of November 2–3, the Australians noted signs that the enemy was withdrawing, and in the morning XIII Corps reported the same thing. Rommel had in fact begun his withdrawal according to plan, and had hopes of occupying the Fuka positions during the pause given by Eighth Army's regrouping. At 1530 on November 3, a bombshell arrived in the form of a directive from Hitler, followed by one from Mussolini, that the Panzerarmee was to hold and "not to yield a step." Compliance meant the destruction of the Afrika Korps and their allies and the speedy loss of both Cyrenaica and Tripolitania. Rommel, torn between obeying orders and saving at least part of his army, compromised. The 90th Light Division and X and XXI Italian Corps were to hold where they were. D.A.K. was to withdraw some six miles west of Tell el Aqqaqir with Ariete and 20th Italian stationed on D.A.K.'s right.

With the approach of the climax of the battle, the Allied air forces redoubled their efforts. On November 3, the Desert Air Force flew 1,094 sorties, and the U.S.A.A.F. flew 125. Two Stuka raids were broken up and the Ju 87s forced to jettison their bombs on their own lines. That night Wellingtons bombed masses of vehicles around El Daba and Fuka.

THE BREAKOUT

The long-held enemy front was now beginning to crack wide open. Sensing this, and still thrusting and probing for the enemy's weakest spot (although the ranks of the rifle companies who bore the brunt of the thrusting were thinning rapidly), Montgomery planned another, and final, blow. To the 51st Division, with 5th Indian Brigade under command, went the task of spearheading the breakthrough. Driving generally southwest, they were to take Tell el Aqqaqir and the ground farther south on the Rahman track. Behind them the motorized New Zealanders, with 9th and 4th Armored Brigades under command, and the armored divisions close behind were to surge forward and (hopefully) wheel behind the Axis forces and cut their retreat. Down in the South the Italians were beginning to drift away, and XIII Corps was preparing to follow.

One of 51st Division's brigades' attacks on the evening of November 3 came to grief—erroneous reports of enemy withdrawal led to the canceling of artillery and air support, with consequent losses in men and "I" tanks. The other two, launched in the early hours of November 4, were completely successful. Opposition, such as it was, was brushed aside, and the gate through the defenses was open at last. Through it poured the armor, 7th Armored Division in the van. As they swung northwest, armored-car squadrons fanned out into the desert. In the two years of bitter desert fighting, British armor had surged forward hopefully many times before, only to blunt its spearheads on the guns of the Afrika Korps and its allies. And perhaps the Eighth Army had come subconsciously to expect the inevitable checks and counter-attacks and retreats. That morning, men said, *felt* different. Apart from the tangible signs—the columns of prisoners heading east, the wrecked and scattered vehicles and equipment—there was victory in the air, and the veterans of Alamein could sense it.

Square in the path of 7th Armored lay the Italian XX Motorized Corps, ordered up as bastion for the southern end of Rommel's new line. The heart of

XX Corps' defense was Ariete—fresh and backed by plentiful anti-tank guns and artillery. And Ariete held—for a while. But soon the Italian armored division disintegrated in a welter of flaming tanks and wrecked guns, and the survivors of XX Corps melted away west. Von Thoma reported the destruction of the Axis right—and the ominous dust clouds rising to the south. Rommel refused at first to believe it, convinced that all available British armor was committed to his front and that 7th Armored was still far away to the south. Von Thoma headed in the direction of the rout, and amid the smoke and dust of battle his tank was set afire and the commander of the Afrika Korps taken prisoner.

Axis losses by now were very heavy. Less than 36 tanks remained of the German armor. On the morning of November 4, about half of the Italians' original 278 tanks were fit to fight, but most of those were lost that afternoon in the destruction of XX Corps. Close to 3,000 Germans and 4,000 Italians had been captured, while casualties had been high.

Rommel had by now wrung agreement to a retreat from a reluctant Führer, and at 1730, November 4, the order went out. The X and XXI Italian Corps and Ramcke Brigade were to break off at once. The 90th Light Division, D.A.K., and XX Corps (long since dissolved in ruin), were to follow after dark.

The withdrawal was handled with Rommel's usual skill. Nor did the British press their advance with any unusual vigor. The battle had cost the Eighth Army some 13,560 men, almost 500 tanks (over 300 of which had already been repaired), and more than 100 guns. After 12 days of heavy fighting, there was no mobile force fresh and ready to dash in pursuit. Many units were scattered, and there had been considerable confusion as large columns of armor, motorized infantry, and transport converged on the narrow passages through the mine fields. Delays at these bottlenecks, coupled with the vigorous covering actions of Rommel's badly battered but still game Germans, held up the Eighth Army's thrust so that by nightfall even the farthest advance (of the New Zealand Division)

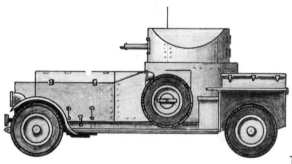

Types of Armored Cars

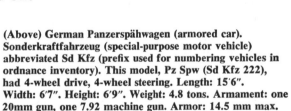

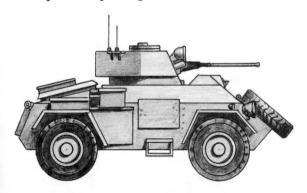

(Above) British Vintage Rolls-Royce, 1924 pattern. Little changed from 1914 model but some still in service in desert in World War II. Length: 17′. Width: 6′3″. Height: 7′8″. Weight: 3.8 tons. Armament: one .303 cal. machine gun. Armor: 9 mm max. Hp: 50. Speed: 60 mph. Crew: 3.

British. Humber Mark II. Length: 15′. Width: 7′2″. Height: 7′10″. Weight: 7.1 tons. Armament: one 15 mm, one 7.92 machine gun. Armor: 15 mm max. Hp: 90. Speed: 45 mph. Range: 250 miles. Crew: 3.

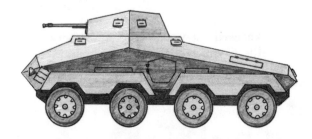

(Above) German Panzerspähwagen (armored car). Sonderkraftfahrzeug (special-purpose motor vehicle) abbreviated Sd Kfz (prefix used for numbering vehicles in ordnance inventory). This model, Pz Spw (Sd Kfz 222), had 4-wheel drive, 4-wheel steering. Length: 15′6″. Width: 6′7″. Height: 6′9″. Weight: 4.8 tons. Armament: one 20mm gun, one 7.92 machine gun. Armor: 14.5 mm max. Hp: 75. Speed: road 50 mph. Range: 200 miles. Crew: 3.

Pz Spw (Sd Kfz 231)
8-wheel drive and steering. Length: 19′. Width: 7′3″. Height: 7′7″. Weight: 8.2 tons. Armament: one 20mm gun, one 7.92 machine gun. Armor: 14.5 mm max. Hp: 150. Speed: road 53 mph. Range: 186 miles. Crew: 4.

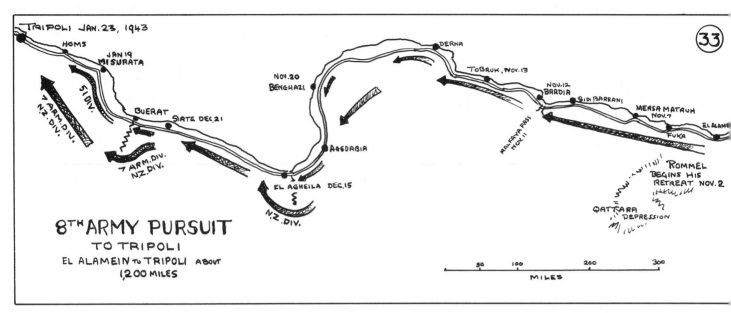

8TH ARMY PURSUIT
TO TRIPOLI
EL ALAMEIN TO TRIPOLI ABOUT
1,200 MILES

was only some 15 miles west of the Rahman track.

In contrast, the night of November 5–6 saw the New Zealand Division some 15 miles southwest of Fuka after covering about 35 miles; the 7th Armored, also southwest of Fuka, covered some 50 miles. The 8th Armored Brigade reached Galal about 1000 hours, scattering enemy columns as it went, then pushed on up the coast against the retreating 90th Light Division to within a few miles of Fuka. After measuring gains in hundreds of yards, these advances appear impressive. Actually they were disappointingly slow. While the bag of prisoners and materiel continued to mount, no great encirclement had been made, and the remnants of the Afrika Korps, far from being trapped, withdrew hastily but in fairly good order. The only long "end run" was by 1st Armored Division. El Daba was reached early on November 5. From the coast west of there the division began a night march toward Bir Khalda. At dawn of November 6 they were 16 miles east of it; then fuel ran low. "B" Echelon (a unit's own first-line transport, carrying gas, ammunition, food, water, etc.; these were replenished by Royal Army Service Corps convoys, 2nd line, who then refilled at a field maintenance center) accompanying the division had lost touch in the darkness and bad going, and did not come up until 1100. Worn-out tanks were using up to 3 gallons per mile, and some 20 miles west of Charing Cross the advance wheezed to a halt.

Some 20 miles to the northeast, 21st Panzer was also having fuel problems, and 22nd Armored Brigade caught up with it south of Qasaba and knocked out 16 tanks and a number of guns before the Germans managed to withdraw. Only four of the 30 tanks which had survived Alamein were un-

damaged. The weather had now broken, and 8th Armored, taking prisoners as it went, climbed the escarpment west of Fuka in torrents of rain, which turned the dusty tracks into a quagmire.

Progress on November 7 was slow; mud and shortage of fuel halted many units. The 10th Armored Division's 8th Armored Brigade, with full fuel tanks, pushed up to the Matruh defenses, where anti-tank weapons halted it until the rest of the division came up. When the position was probed next morning the 90th Light had slipped west in the night.

All this time the Desert Air Force, hampered by the uncertainty of a bomb line in the rapidly changing front and by bad weather, kept up its hammering of the fleeing enemy convoys. The enemy fields and ports came in for their share— and on November 6, American Flying Fortresses sank a vessel of over 2,000 tons at Tobruk, while Liberators sank a small ship and set the 6,400-ton tanker *Portofino* on fire at Benghazi. German air attacks were limited, thanks to the numerous attacks on their airfields. Ju 52s were in evidence, ferrying fuel to the front, and several were shot down.

On the southern front XIII Corps, stripped of much of its transport to serve the active fronts to the north, was busy rounding up prisoners, many of them in desperate plight for lack of water and provisions. So scattered were they that a Tactical Reconnaissance Squadron was called in to help locate them. In all, some 17,000 Italians were taken— "rescued" is a better word in most cases.

Rommel's intention was to fight a rear-guard action to give time for a more or less orderly withdrawal up the escarpment at Halfaya and Sollum. On November 8 came the news of the Allied landings in Morocco and Algeria, which, to Rommel's mind, made the necessity for a long retreat past El Agheila to Sirte (where he thought a stand might be made) all the more urgent. Mussolini and the Italian High Command at first wanted the Sollum-Halfaya area defended as long as possible, while reinforcements would be gathered on the El Agheila-Marada line. This they insisted must be held. Hitler also agreed that the El Agheila position must be held "to the last." By this time the disgusted Rommel had realized that to save anything of his army he must act as he thought fit regardless of pronunciamentos from Rome and Berlin.

As things turned out, the loss of Sidi Barrani on November 9 and the taking of Halfaya Pass early on the morning of November 11 sent the remainder of the Axis forces hurrying out of Egypt on their way to El Agheila regardless of any plans for a lengthy holding action. The Afrika Korps was too weak to do more than delay their pursuers by hastily placed mines and by demolitions (reports as of November 10 show 15th and 21st Panzer and 90th Light down to a combined strength of 3,186 men, 11 tanks, 20 anti-tank guns, and a few field guns; other units were in similar shape).

The British took Bardia on November 12. Tobruk fell the next day and Benghazi on November 20.

Montgomery had no doubt that Rommel planned to retreat at least as far as El Agheila. But this time Montgomery was determined that the position should not be the springboard for another of Rommel's lightning-like counter-attacks. Sufficient weight in armor and ample supplies must be brought forward and grouped to guard against any such thrust, while light columns of armored cars, stiffened with artillery and anti-tank guns, were to harass the retreating enemy and cut the main line of retreat if possible. But the logistics of maintaining a heavy armored force in a sweep across the neck of Cyrenaica—coupled with bad weather and the Army commander's natural caution—precluded any all-out effort to trap the Axis forces. And so with, figuratively speaking, "drums beating and colors flying"—but with very little else—the remnants of the Afrika Korps reached the El Agheila position on the night of November 23–24.

To those judging the battle at a later date the failure of the Eighth Army to produce another Beda Fomm was disappointing, to say the least. But Montgomery's forte was not the daring hell-for-leather dash across country. He was a "set-piece battle" general—willing to take chances only

after careful planning and preparation. And many of his commanders knew only too well the consequences of recklessness in the presence of the "Desert Fox." To the soldiers who had just won a hard-fought battle—smashed an army and driven its remnants some 800 miles in three weeks—their victory seemed complete enough. The final tally of Axis loss for the battle after the breakthrough and pursuit, showed, by November 11, some 25,000 killed and wounded and 30,000 prisoners—over a third of them German. More than 1,000 guns had been destroyed or captured. Some 320 tanks had been totally wrecked and many more put out of action. More than the damage inflicted on the enemy, the battle had marked a turning point. The seesaw of advances and retreats was over. As Churchill put it ". . . after Alamein we never had a defeat."

The whole Alamein offensive had shown a marked improvement in ground-air co-operation. In Montgomery's Introduction to his *El Alamein to the River Sangro* he wrote, "The part played by the Royal Air Force in these campaigns was truly tremendous. . . . The Desert Air Force and the Eighth Army formed one close integrated family. . . ." The cost in aircraft for the battle was 77 British aircraft, 20 American. Axis losses were 85—high in proportion to the number of sorties: R.A.F., 10,405; U.S.A.A.F., 1,181; German, 1,550; Italian (estimated), 1,570.

EL AGHEILA—AND ON TO TRIPOLI

The advance to the borders of Tripolitania had created a problem in logistics that strained the British supply services to the utmost. The Middle East base itself had increased in size and complexity at an astounding rate—handling tonnages that two years before would have been considered unbelievable.

Total military stores from overseas received in October, for instance: 253,000 tons. Vehicles received in September and October: 18,480. Ammunition in base installations in October: 272,000 tons; and so on. But to distribute these stores—fuel, ammunition, food, and water—across hundreds of miles of desert track was a colossal task. The railroad, which the British had extended in the spring of 1942 to Belhamed and which German additions had brought close to the harbor at Tobruk, was soon repaired and cleared of obstructions. The first supply trains reached El Alamein on November 5; El Daba (captured November 5) on November 9; Capuzzo (captured November 12) on November

Douglas DC-3 (known to the R.A.F. as the Dakota)

Span: 95'. Length: 64'5½". Height: 16'11". Weight empty: 16,976 lbs. Speed: max. 230 mph at 8,800'. Range: 1,350 miles. Power: two 1,200 hp Pratt & Whitney Twin Wasp radials. Armament: none. Crew: 4.

20, and Tobruk (captured November 13) on December 1. This, of course, was of no use during the pursuit, and even though the ports—such as they were—of Matruh and Bardia, and finally Tobruk, were opened on November 15, 19, and 20, respectively, they could only bring a portion of the required tonnage a little closer. The front at El Agheila was over 300 miles as the crow flies from Tobruk, and it is hard to equate the flight of the crow and the movement cross country of a convoy of trucks, sometimes axle-deep in soft sand or mud, or grinding in low gear over hilly, stony track. But the trucks of the Royal Army Service Corps did the job, and the buildup proceeded.

The opening of Benghazi on November 26 (there were 86 wrecks in Benghazi Harbor and 101 in Tobruk, ranging from lighters to large merchantmen and warships) soon took much of the burden from the railheads and from Tobruk. This shortened the truck run considerably (it was less than 200 miles from Benghazi to El Agheila). Even so, the problem of supply was formidable. The fuel for the transport alone amounted to a huge tonnage—a dead loss as far as useful payload was concerned. The sea route was both long and exposed to attack by air and submarine. From Alexandria to Tobruk is 300 nautical miles, some 1½ days' voyage. Alexandria to Benghazi—540 nautical miles—takes 2½ days.

The fuel problem was accentuated by the inefficiency of the 4-gallon container. This flimsy contraption was such a disaster—not to mention fire hazard—that it was estimated that on a long haul some 30 per cent of the contents might be lost. The German "jerrican" was treasured when obtainable—as were the 44-gallon drums. Why the "flimsy" was perpetuated in service in spite of its obvious shortcomings is one of the war's mysteries.

The air forces had by now managed to augment their fuel deliveries by means of airlifts. While the R.A.F. Hudsons could not load the 44-gallon drums (and a cargo of "flimsies" full of high octane was too dangerous), the U.S.A.A.F. Dakotas could—and on one occasion alone, 39 of these planes lifted over 130,000 gallons for the Desert Air Force from El Adem to the forward bases.

The Axis position at El Agheila was naturally strong, protected by salt marshes, soft sand, and/or broken ground—denying tracked or wheeled vehicles room to maneuver. To these obstacles had been added strong points and mine fields. The main line of defense (although not continuous) ran from the anchorage at Mersa Brega southwest to Maaten Giofer, then south for some 10 miles. There was an outpost at Marada, 45 miles farther south. Some 17 miles west of El Agheila (itself defended by a ring of mine fields) there was a large salt marsh. Between this and the sea was an anti-tank ditch protected by mine fields—called by the Germans the El Mugtaa Narrows.

Rommel considered that his troops were too few to hold the position in depth, while fuel and transport were lacking for a battle of maneuver. Mussolini was reluctant to give more ground without a fight—more as a matter of prestige than with any hope of stopping the Eighth Army. Hitler also demanded a stand, to give more time for the Axis buildup in Tunisia. On November 24, Cavallero, Chief of Staff of the Italian armed forces, and Field Marshal Kesselring, Commander Luftflotte 2 and Commander-in-Chief, South, met Rommel at Marble Arch. Rommel's position was that he could withdraw and save at least part of his army intact or stand and fight and risk total disaster. As a result Cavallero allowed that, while the position at El Agheila be held as long as possible, a retreat to

Buerat might be proposed.

Realizing that, first, the condition of his army called for drastic remedy and that, second, the one sensible thing was to evacuate North Africa altogether, Rommel flew off on November 28 to see Hitler. Hitler railed against the retreat, again demanded a "to the last man" defense and, in a tantrum, accused the men of the Afrika Korps of cowardice. Rommel's feeling of dismay and disgust was not altered by subsequent visits with Göring and Mussolini. There were the usual empty promises of supply and troops—but also a complete lack of understanding of the North African situation. Too late, troops and equipment were being poured into Tunisia, which Rommel was realistic enough to foresee could not be held indefinitely. It must have maddened him to know that with half the forces earmarked for Tunisia—and ultimately for capture—he could have taken Cairo and the Canal and most probably cleared the Middle East up to the Turkish border. It was a somber Rommel who returned to his troops. The only slight ray of sunshine in the otherwise gloomy picture was the fact that the Italian dictator had finally agreed that preparations for a retirement to Buerat might be made.

Montgomery had no intention that his assault on the El Agheila position and subsequent drive toward Tripoli should go off half cocked. His original estimate was that no move could be made before the end of December, but offloading at Benghazi was ahead of estimates, and increased efficiency in handling the truck convoys allowed the date to be set at December 16–17. Signs that Rommel was contemplating a withdrawal caused the date to be moved up to December 14–15.

Meanwhile, the Eighth Army had been reorganized into two corps—X and XXX. The XIII Corps was broken up and part of its components distributed among other units.

The XXX Corps was to spearhead the attack,

with X Corps in reserve. A frontal assault near the coast was to pin down the defenders, while a long left hook of over 200 miles by the New Zealand Division was to cut the coast road, the Via Balbia, some 55 miles west of El Agheila. The Desert Air Force meantime kept up its raids on Axis ports and supply lines and intensified its attacks on the Axis forward airfields. Tripoli was heavily attacked, and a ship of over 5,000 tons was sunk and another badly damaged.

Because of the length of their approach march, the New Zealand Division started out on December 11, so that by December 14 they should be in position to co-ordinate their attack with the forces to the north. However, by December 12–13 it was apparent that Rommel had ordered a retirement, and on December 13 the two divisions to the north began their advance—51st Highland on Mersa Brega and 7th Armored at Bir es Suera. Freyberg was ordered to hurry his division forward.

The Via Balbia had been efficiently mined and booby-trapped, and 51st Division advanced at a snail's pace. The 7th Armored, delayed by mines and a sharp rear-guard action by Ariete, entered El Agheila on December 15. Rommel's reconnaissance aircraft had spotted the New Zealanders' columns, and orders were at once given for all troops to withdraw behind the El Mugtaa Narrows.

Freyberg had made good time, but there had been just enough delay, chiefly caused by fuel problems and mechanical difficulties of his few accompanying tanks, so that his two infantry brigades did not reach the broken ground near the coast road until after midnight of December 15–16. Traffic could be heard moving west, and at daylight the few last enemy units managed to escape through gaps between the New Zealand formations. The bag was disappointingly small—450 prisoners, 18 tanks, and 25 guns. The Desert Fox had slipped away again.

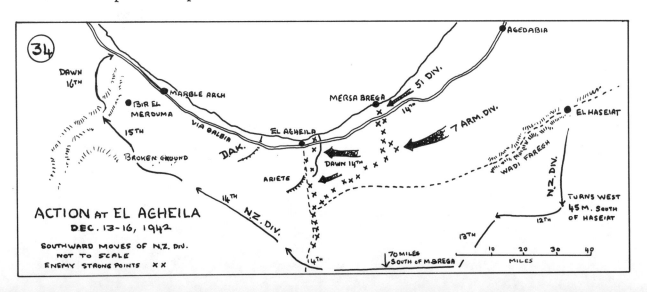

ACTION at EL AGHEILA
DEC. 13-16, 1942

SOUTHWARD MOVES OF N.Z. DIV.
NOT TO SCALE
ENEMY STRONG POINTS X X

The next objective for the Eighth Army was Tripoli, and Montgomery halted short of the Buerat line to gather his forces for the new advance. Supply was by now the major problem and, once the offensive began, it was imperative that Tripoli be won as speedily as possible and the work of reopening the vital port begun. A great storm on January 3 did extensive damage to the mole at Benghazi (5 merchant ships and 3 landing craft were sunk in the harbor, many more were damaged, and another ship sank outside the port). For two days not a ton of supplies was landed, and there was danger that the advance, planned for January 15, might have to be postponed. Heroic work at the port (2,000 tons were landed on January 8) and the elimination of X Corps' part in the operation—all its vehicles were used in the emergency to ferry supplies—allowed the timetable to be kept, and XXX Corps advanced on January 15 on schedule.

There was little opposition. Rommel decided he was not strong enough to give battle, and commenced a withdrawal. Liberal use of mines and demolitions slowed the British advance, but 1st Division was at Homs by December 19, and 7th Armored was approaching Tarhuna. Fearing another encircling movement, Rommel abandoned the temporary line—Homs-Tarhuna—and ordered demolitions begun in Tripoli, while 90th Light and D.A.K. fought rear-guard actions. All other units were ordered west—which upset the Italian High Command, who had demanded a stand.

Rear-guard actions, mines, and huge craters on the Via Balbia (one was 240 feet by 45 feet by 16 feet) stopped any rapid advance, but the situation was hopeless, and British troops entered Tripoli early on the morning of January 23, 1943. It was fitting that the first troops were "B" Squadron of the 11th Hussar, whose "A" and "B" Squadrons fired the first shots of the desert war June 11–12 at Sidi Omar. At noon the Italian Vice-Governor of Tripolitania formally surrendered the city to General Montgomery. The Desert Air Force and the heavy bombers of R.A.F. and U.S.A.A.F. had contributed mightily to the success of the operation—between January 12 and January 23, the R.A.F. flew over 3,000 sorties, and the Ninth Air Force flew more than 600.

The Royal Navy had, of course, done its share by the convoying of the ships of the Inshore Squadron, which from the beginning of November until January 23 had landed 157,000 tons of stores at various ports or beaches. In addition, minor raids were made on Tripoli and, in one, MTBs attacked the mole and sank an Italian submarine. Surface ships also sank several vessels attempting to flee the port before it fell. The war at sea went on uninterrupted, and between the Navy and the Allied air forces, 117,896 tons of Axis shipping were sunk in the Mediterranean in January alone.

The fall of Tripoli—so long the goal—brings to an end one phase of the African campaign. From now on the action in Tunisia became so inter-related with the efforts of the Eighth Army that it is time to turn back to the events leading up to the great Allied invasion of French North Africa, which burst ashore on November 8, 1942.

III

"Torch":

THE WESTERN TASK FORCE

THE AMERICAN LANDINGS IN FRENCH MOROCCO

The decision to invade French North Africa was not arrived at unanimously by the political and military chiefs of Great Britain and the United States. Rather it was hammered out after many months of discussion—often bitter—and never wholeheartedly received by all the heads of the two American services. It was at best considered by many a stopgap—almost a lesser of two evils—and as such it required a vast amount of tact and diplomacy to mount. Considering this (added to the normal friction to be expected in a joint operation conducted by two nations as different in many ways as are the two great English-speaking ones), it is astonishing that the enterprise, the largest and most complex amphibious landing in history to that date, succeeded as well as it did.

The plan had several antecedents. When it was hoped that "Crusader" might have led to the destruction of the Axis armies in Cyrenaica and an advance to the Tunisian border ("Acrobat"), the British prepared plans ("Gymnast") to enter French North Africa—with, hopefully, French consent and assistance. When the United States entered the war in December 1941, the plan was enlarged into an Anglo-American venture—"Super Gymnast." The failure of "Crusader" to give decisive results and the consequent German advance to Gazala, plus a shortage of shipping and a desire by the Americans to strike directly at the enemy in Europe, put an end to planning in the spring of 1942.

The Combined Chiefs of Staff—that is, the Chiefs of Staff of the three British services (in practice the British Chiefs of Staff were usually represented in Washington by the Joint Staff Mission) and the U. S. Army, Navy, U. S. Army Air Force, and the Chief of Staff to the President—then concentrated on a plan for the invasion of northwestern France in 1943 ("Round Up"). Things were going badly for the Allies in early 1942, but it was considered desirable to attempt something to take pressure off the Soviets, who had suffered staggering losses in men, materiel, and territory. With commendable pugnacity, the U. S. Chiefs of Staff wanted to strike at the Germans in 1942—in a series of raids at first, but this plan merged into one for a super-raid ("Sledgehammer"), which in turn developed into the idea of establishing a firm bridgehead, preferably on the Cherbourg or Brittany peninsulas, from which to launch "Round Up" in 1943.

The British Chiefs of Staff disagreed. Sir Alan Brooke (chairman of the British Chiefs of Staff) once replied to a remark of General George C. Marshall's that the best way to end the war in 1942 or 1943 was to invade Europe: "Yes, but not the way we want to end it!" They were willing to expand the small commando raids they were already making, but they felt that an attempt to establish a beachhead in 1942 would be disastrous. It was doubtful if many Germans would be drawn from the Russian Front, while the effects of a failure would probably deal the French Resistance movement a deathblow. The Americans, eager but inexperienced, began to doubt that the British were even keen to attempt "Round Up" at all (they were not). Suspicions grew that the British were more concerned with sea communications to the Middle East and its oil fields than in an immediate frontal attack on Occupied Europe (they were). Also that they were, by Machiavellian scheming, attempting to use American forces for forwarding plans for postwar imperialistic gains.

On the contrary, the British were only being realistic. The submarine menace notwithstanding, Allied control of the sea was a fact. To ignore the advantages it gave was to throw away one of the Allies' most potent weapons. To drive the Axis out of Africa was to reopen the Mediterranean, thus shortening the route to India, the Middle East, and the land route to the Soviet Union via Iran. And elimination of the long voyage around the Cape of Good Hope would, it was estimated, free over 1 million tons of shipping, at a time when the U-boat campaign was causing great concern.

To go direct for the enemy's throat was commendable, but when there was little chance of success it seemed the height of folly to forego the opportunity of striking at the enemy's more vulnerable extremities. The British realized that when the time came, the deathblow must be dealt by an invasion across Europe. To those of us who saw the immense preparations and preponderance of arms and equipment deemed necessary for a successful invasion in 1944 (by which time the Germans had taken a terrific battering on land and by air) the idea of a cross-Channel invasion even in 1943 seems fantastic. Yet there were many American leaders who advocated it—as well as countless civilians on both sides of the Atlantic who, egged on by the press, believed that Stalin's demands for a second front must be met, whatever the cost.

Molotov, the Soviet Foreign Minister, went to Washington in May and asked for a public commitment to a cross-Channel invasion that year. After some hedging he secured American approval for release of a communiqué stating in part, ". . . in the course of the conversations full understanding was reached with regard to the urgent task of creating a second front in Europe in 1942." In London, Churchill told Molotov privately that Britain could not guarantee a second front in 1942. This was repeated in an *aide-mémoire*, but the issuance of the unfortunate "Molotov Communiqué" was taken as a definite promise by the Soviets, and also by the American and British publics at large.

This pressure to "do something" was a factor in considering a 1942 offensive—the political and military leaders realizing that the psychological reaction to a "do nothing" policy would be unfortunate, to say the least.

So it will be seen that there was an urgent necessity to set some scheme in operation as soon as possible. "Sledgehammer" was definitely out—but not without a final American effort. General Marshall, Admiral Ernest J. King, Chief of U. S. Naval Operations and Harry Hopkins (Roosevelt's personal representative) arrived in London on July 18 for top-level conferences. Talks with the British Chiefs of Staff ended in deadlock, broken by Roosevelt's acceptance of the fact that the British military and Prime Minister were unalterably opposed. So on July 22, which date Eisenhower thought should well go down as the "blackest day in history," "Sledgehammer" was finally rejected (less than a month later, the disastrous Dieppe raid gave some idea of what could be expected of any large-scale landing on the French coast without overwhelming and continuous air support, and not backed by a massive and speedy buildup). After the war Eisenhower wrote: "Those who held the 'Sledgehammer' operation to be unwise at the moment were correct in their evaluation of the problem"—a masterpiece of understatement!

With a cross-Channel attempt in 1942 ruled out, there was little option but to revert to "Super Gymnast." Plans for the operation, re-christened "Torch," were begun at once. Time was short. Roosevelt (who had been veering toward a North African course for some time) cabled Hopkins on July 25 that plans for a landing in North Africa "not later than October 30 should be begun immediately."

One of the first things to be done was to decide on the commanders. It had been agreed on beforehand that, although the major part of the forces then available would be British, the Supreme Command of the Allied efforts, for political reasons, should go to an American (had the invasion been launched under British control the French were almost sure to fight). Marshall was the obvious choice, with Lieutenant General Dwight D. Eisenhower, Commanding General of the European Theater, as his deputy. But Marshall was needed in Washington, and on August 6 Eisenhower was appointed Commander-in-Chief, Allied Expeditionary Force. His deputy was Major General Mark Clark, and his Chief of Staff was Brigadier General Walter Bedell Smith. Command of the British land forces went first to Lieutenant General Alexander. On his leaving for Cairo to succeed Auchinleck, his place was taken by Lieutenant General Montgomery. When Lieutenant General Gott—who was to take over the Eighth Army—was killed, Montgomery took *his* place. The command was finally given to Lieutenant General K. A. N. Anderson. The Allied naval commander was Admiral Cunningham, returning to the Mediterranean after a seven-month absence. Vice-Admiral Sir Bertram Ramsey was his deputy. Allied Air Command was split—a rather awkward arrangement, terminated in February 1943 when Air Chief Marshal Sir Arthur Tedder was appointed Air Officer Commanding in Chief, Mediterranean Air Command. Brigadier General James H. Doolittle commanded the U.S.A.A.F. contingent, while Air Marshal Sir William Welsh headed the R.A.F. assigned to the expedition.

The planners of "Torch" were faced with a number of unknowns. First and foremost was the reaction of the French. British relations with the Vichy regime were very bad, and since Oran, the abortive attempt at Dakar, the campaign in Syria, and the seizure (May 5, 1942) of Diego Suarez and ultimately the whole island of Madagascar, many French military leaders echoed the sentiments of their Vichy superiors. The United States, on the other hand, had maintained relations with the Pétain government, and could also count to a certain extent on the traditional friendship between the two countries. Even so, it was a far cry from Pershing's proud, "Lafayette, we are here!" to Clark's sneaking ashore at night in a rubber boat and asking, in effect, "When we come, will you shoot?"

France itself was divided by political and geographical boundaries into the Occupied Zone and so-called Vichy France—while the African possessions were in a slightly different category, yet under Vichy control. Limited by the armistice agreement as to the size and composition of armed forces, they were far enough from Vichy to feel some small degree of independence. The divisions within the nation as a whole were varied and bitter. There were those who never accepted the armistice and still worked against the Germans—actively, in the Resistance groups, or in quiet preparation for the return of the Allies to the Continent. On the other extreme were the collaborationists—those convinced that fascism offered the only hope against communism, and the opportunists—those who wanted to be on the winning side, for political and/or monetary gain. In between were the many who merely desired to go their way in peace—any kind of peace. They, or most of them, cordially detested the Germans (fortunately, the Germans, when in a position of power, have a faculty for getting themselves detested), but had the normal French distrust of perfidious Albion. The military were in like case. To begin with, there was an undercurrent of Anglophobia (always noticeable in naval circles), added to the rather natural resentment of those who, having given up the fight, witnessed the growing strength of their erstwhile ally. There

were those who, swallowing this, worked wholeheartedly and at risk of life and limb to destroy the
enemy by one way or another. There were others,
many of them, who sympathized with the Allied
cause yet felt their duty lay in strict adherence to
the orders of their commander-in-chief. There were
those who would have liked nothing better than to
see a renascent France take her place in a Fascist-
dominated Europe—and still others, like De Gaulle
and his followers, who, often under sentence of
death for treason, fled France and continued the
war with whatever means at their disposal. And, of
course, among the rank and file, there were those
professionals and mercenaries (of which there
were many in the French forces of North Africa)
whose loyalties were regimental rather than national and who would follow any orders of their
immediate superiors.

From this hodgepodge of patriots, politicals,
professional militarists, and opportunists it was imperative to pick key men in North Africa, both best
able to assure the minimum resistance to an Allied
landing and willing to stake their careers (and perhaps their lives) on its success. It was also necessary that those men should, for security reasons, be
kept in the dark as to the date and projected landing places. Perhaps most important of all was the
necessity of choosing a nominal leader for the
French—one who could rally behind him men of
varied opinions and interests.

This was no small task—nor was it carried out to
a uniformly successful conclusion. But the attempt
was made with all the thrills and spills of a first-
class cloak-and-dagger spy production, complete to
lights blinking out to sea, rubber boats, secret rendezvous, et al. As the cast of players was a large
one, a program may be helpful:

Admiral Jean François Darlan: Commander-in-
Chief French Armed Forces (in North Africa more
or less by accident), Anglophobe, and committed
to the Axis (and hence mistrusted by the Allies).
However, he was now thought to be wavering, and,
if faced with an Allied *fait accompli*, might throw
his weight on the winning side. His position assured him of the loyalty of the majority of French
military leaders and therefore made his attitude all-
important to the success of an Allied invasion.

General Alphonse Juin: Commander-in-Chief of
French military forces in North Africa. Anti-Axis.
Had prepared undercover plans for resisting any
Axis invasion of French North Africa but was un-
willing to defy Vichy. Could be labeled as cau-

tiously pro-Allies.

General Auguste Paul Noguès: Resident General
of Morocco, at Rabat. Had the reputation of being
pro-Vichy, which had earned him the hostility of
the anti-Vichy French. Very influential among the
natives in Morocco, and for that reason more useful to the Americans in office than if removed (as
many demanded). Not to be counted as pro-Allies.

Vice-Admiral Jean Pierre Estéva: Resident General of Tunisia, at Tunis. Pro-Vichy.

Lieutenant General G. Barré: commander of
forces in Tunisia. Happy to work against the Germans, but not likely to act on his own initiative.

M. Yves Châtel: Governor General of Algeria.
One of the few civilians in a high administrative
post. Pro-Vichy.

Lieutenant General L.-M. Koeltz: commander of
the Algiers region. His leanings similar to Barré's.

Major General Charles Mast: Commanding
Officer, Algerian Division. Pro-Allies and in touch
with Robert D. Murphy and Henri Giraud.

General George Lascroux: Commander-in-Chief
of Moroccan troops (Rabat).

Vice-Admiral François Michelier: commander of
Moroccan naval forces commanding Casablanca
sector (Casablanca).

General Lahoulle: Commanding Officer, French
Air Forces in Morocco.

Major General Henri Martin: commanding Safi-
Mogador sector (Marrakech).

Major General André Dody: Meknès Division,
commanding North Morocco sector (Meknès).

Major General Emile Bèthouart: Commanding
Officer, Casablanca Division (pro-Allies and in
touch with Murphy).

With the exception of Bèthouart all these men
took their orders from Pétain via Darlan and down
the chain of command. They were not about to
welcome the Americans with open arms, but were
willing to co-operate on orders from above.

Robert D. Murphy: U. S. Consul General in Algiers. Had been in charge of arrangements for shipping food and supplies to North Africa under the
U. S. Government's agreement with Vichy. He
knew all the leaders and he (and his vice-consuls)
were in touch with those he knew to be pro-Allies.
After a visit to Washington in September 1942 he
was designated personal representative of the U. S.
President to deal with French officials in North
Africa. He was in charge of negotiations with
French leaders prior to the invasion.

There was one Frenchman who could not be ignored in any Allied planning even if he was deliberately denied any prior knowledge and was left out of active participation. This was General Charles de Gaulle, dynamic and controversial leader of the "Free French." While he had acquired a few devoted followers, in general he was highly unpopular in French military circles. These men had obeyed their government's orders to end the fighting in 1940 (whatever they might personally have thought about such a course). De Gaulle's action in carrying on the fight from overseas made him, in their eyes, a deserter. In a narrow, legalistic sense they were probably right—but the times called for more than a legalistic approach. The call to arms, and the Cross of Lorraine (the Free French emblem) waving on numerous battlefields, while it aroused the ire of the majority of the conservative officer corps, appealed to an ever-growing number of Frenchmen in France and the colonies.

"Le Grand Charles" was a prickly customer (Churchill once said that the heaviest cross he had to bear during the war was the Cross of Lorraine). Touchy as to French honor and his own dignity, there was no question of excluding him from North Africa, but the feeling against him in official circles was so strong (and the resistance movement in North Africa so weak) that he would obviously be more of a liability than an asset.

The man the Allies picked as the French soldier most likely to rally the military in North Africa behind him was General Henri Giraud. A full general (a hero of World War I and commander of the Seventh Army in 1940), Giraud had made a much-publicized escape from a castle prison in Saxony in 1942 and since then had been living in unoccupied France. While ostensibly recognizing Pétain's leadership, he had been secretly in touch with dissident groups and with the anti-German, anti-Vichy patriots in Algiers, including General Mast, his principle adherent, and General Bèthouart.

Murphy felt that some co-operation between the wavering Darlan and Giraud was desirable, but Mast believed that the general could win support from the French military and naval commanders in North Africa and preferred to do so without any help from the devious admiral. A letter was then sent to Giraud stating Allied terms (France to be considered an ally—her 1939 boundaries restored, overall command in North Africa returned to the French authorities at the proper time, and French troops rearmed with modern equipment) and arranging that he be brought out of France by submarine. To this Giraud agreed, with the results detailed below.

Of great concern was the attitude of Franco. The desirability of landings as far east in the Mediterranean as possible seemed obvious—Tunis was the goal, and the sooner the Allies got there, the better. Eisenhower, among others, favored landings at Oran, Algiers, and Bône (there were not enough troops or vessels for more). However, the American Chiefs of Staff, who had been so bold in planning to throw troops across the Channel in the teeth of the Luftwaffe and the Wehrmacht, now got cold feet. The reason: Spain. They feared an attack on their flank by German forces advancing through Spain at Franco's invitation (or possibly without it) and felt that by advancing into the Mediterranean they were running into a trap. They favored landings at Casablanca (which would secure the flank bordering Spanish Morocco) and perhaps one at Oran.

The British, on the other hand, felt that if Franco had been going to climb on the Axis bandwagon he would have done so before, when France had been newly defeated and Britain lay under the threat of invasion. So they tended to discount Spain—and also any attempt on Hitler's part to move German troops through to attack Gibraltar.

This Casablanca-landing "bombshell" from Washington caused confusion and dismay among the Allied planners. Churchill called it "the shattering memorandum" and protested at once to Roosevelt. Looking back over the years it seems a strange decision for Marshall to have made and perhaps bears out Brooke's opinion that his opposite number, while a great organizer, was not a great strategist. As Roosevelt (who, unlike Churchill, made no pretense of being a military expert) leaned heavily on Marshall for advice, it followed that the President echoed his military chief's opinion—and it took some persuasion on Churchill's part to convince Roosevelt that a landing on the Atlantic coast alone would in all probability only open the way for German intervention and the occupation of not only Tunisia but much of Algeria as well. It was a rare tangle—with Eisenhower, Churchill, and most of the British favoring landings as far east as fighter cover would allow; Brooke, the Chief of the Imperial General Staff, wanting Algiers and at the same time feeling that a threat-free port such as Casablanca was a necessity; and the American President and his staff fearful of venturing within the Pillars of Hercules at all.

After much delay, proposals, and counter pro-

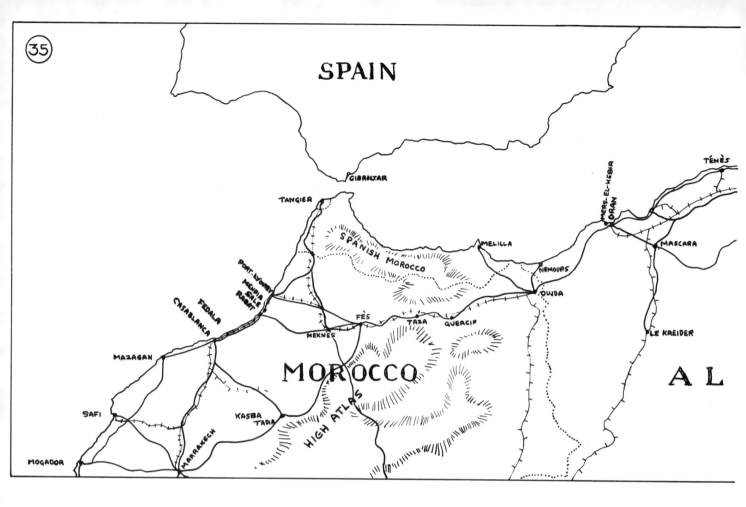

posals, what Eisenhower called the "transatlantic essay competition" ended with agreement on simultaneous landings at Casablanca, Oran, and Algiers —to be headed by American troops to lessen the chance of French resistance. The makeup of the forces—its commanders and its objectives—are listed below.

It was a mammoth undertaking, involving the movement of large numbers of troops and vast quantities of vehicles and supplies from the U.K. and the U.S.A. across submarine-infested waters— to rendezvous in secret and descend with precise timing at widely separate points on a possibly hostile shore. Altogether, counting the reinforcing convoys and escorts, some 370 merchant vessels were to be employed, and over 300 naval vessels. The assault forces from the U.S.A. would be 16 days at sea—those from the U.K. 13, and supply convoys, 17. To assemble such an armada necessitated suspending regular convoys and pulling in transports and escort vessels from other areas. Naval support vessels were scraped together from the British Home Fleet and from whatever U.S. warships could be wrung from a grudging Admiral King.

Even the smaller types of landing craft were in short supply, and the lack of vessels capable of landing medium tanks directly onto the beach made the speedy capture of ports with harbor facilities a necessity (the first of the familiar LSTs was not finished until November—too late for "Torch").

Despite the size of the invasion force there was a large element of risk. There were some 120,000 French troops in North Africa (about 55,000 in Morocco, 50,000 in Algeria, and 15,000 in Tunisia). They were mostly native units, with French officers —good soldiers and well led, although their arms and equipment were not the most modern. Along with the native troops were Chasseurs d'Afrique and Zouaves—mostly African-born Frenchmen, and, of course, some battalions of the ubiquitous Foreign Legion. There was some field artillery, but the terms of the armistice had allowed almost no medium or heavy artillery, and the tanks (some 250) were obsolete. The air force could put up some 500 planes—not the latest types but still a force to be reckoned with. While the main French Fleet lay at Toulon, there were a number of vessels

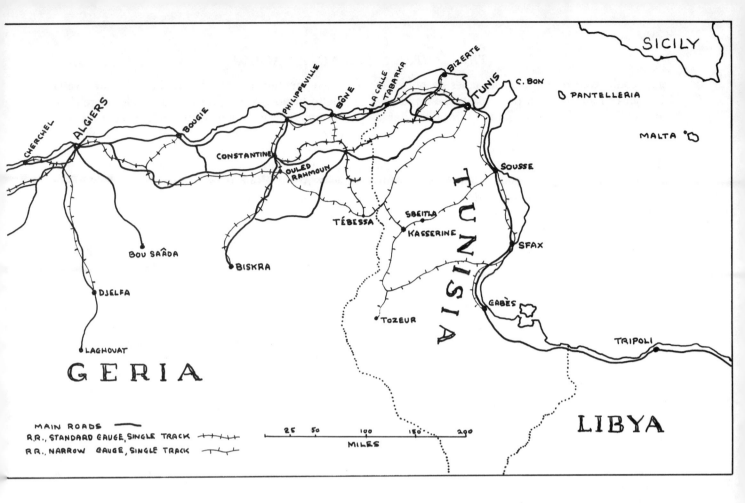

in North African ports. Thus, though it was hoped that the French would not resist an Allied landing —or at least an American one—should they do so they could muster enough force to make its success problematical.

As for the Germans, it was assumed that they would attempt to intervene in Tunisia (hence the need for landings as close to Tunis as possible), but the immediate threat was from submarines and the Luftwaffe. Allied fighter cover, until fields could be seized in Algeria, would depend on aircraft from carriers and from the overcrowded field at Gibraltar. But the die was cast and the innumerable preparations begun that would set the Allied force ashore on November 8, 1942.

Getting ashore was only one problem. French North Africa was large, and communications were poor. Only one standard-gauge railroad ran from Casablanca to Oran—a distance of over 500 miles. From Oran to Algiers by rail is another 250 miles, and to Tunis close to 500 more. The few branch lines in the interior were mostly narrow-gauge. By motor road it is nearly 1,300 miles from Casablanca to Tunis. A few main roads were in good condition,

surfaced and with bridges capable of bearing at least 25 tons; some were mere tracks over the mountains. But even the main highways (see map) were not entirely two-way affairs—single-lane bridges and tunnels and tight curves on mountain slopes created bottlenecks. The secondary roads, unsurfaced and lacking drainage, could not stand up to heavy traffic in wet weather. Poor road conditions notwithstanding, it was obvious that for the invading forces to press forward rapidly into Tunisia a large number of vehicles would be needed, as well as equipment for road maintenance.

The terrain is dominated by the Atlas Mountains, which stretch in almost continuous ranges for over 1,000 miles from the Atlantic, across Morocco and Algeria and into central Tunisia. On the Mediterranean coast of Algeria the rugged high ground runs in roughly parallel bands of ridges and valleys, in many places almost to the water's edge. On the Atlantic coast, flatter and more open, the Atlantic rollers break, even in relatively calm weather, in roaring surf (often 15 feet high in winter)—dangerous for landing craft at most times of the year. In October and November, reports showed that craft could land on the open beaches on only one day out of four. Thus on both coasts the rapid seizure of sheltered ports capable of handling large tonnage was essential. It was also essential to seize suitable airfields—within the first 24 hours, if possible. Carrier planes would be too few to support an invasion, and the one airfield at Gibraltar—hastily enlarged to a length of 1,800 yards with rubble excavated from the new tunnels that honeycombed the Rock—would be jammed to its utmost capacity with over 350 aircraft, parked wingtip to wingtip, ready to be flown in as soon as captured fields were available.

The weather was also a factor. In the late fall and winter northern and westerly winds bring heavy rains and comparatively cold weather, averaging 50 to 54 degrees Fahrenheit along the coast and near-freezing temperatures with snow and frost in the higher country inland (much of northern Algeria lies between 2,000 and 5,000 feet). During the rainy season, dry or almost dry water courses become raging torrents, and in places the low-lying country turns into seas of mud. Although considerable areas of northern Algeria and Tunisia are under cultivation (cereals, olives, grapes, citrus orchards, and vegetables), much stock is raised, chiefly sheep and goats.

The terrain is generally unfavorable for tank warfare. In many places vehicles are confined to the roads, and in some of the rugged mountain areas where even the Jeeps could not go, ammunition and supplies would have to be carried on muleback.

As noted above, airfields were of primary importance. In Algeria the three main fields were at La Senia (near Oran), Maison Blanche (near Algiers), and Les Salines (near Bône). Two others, not as good, were at Blida and Sétif—with secondary fields at Tafaraoui, Constantine, and Tébessa. There were five good fields in Morocco—Cazes (near Casablanca), Port Lyautey and Rabat-Salé on the coast, and Meknès and Marrakech inland. These were all accessible by rail and road. In addition, there were five secondary fields. In Tunisia there were primary fields at Sidi Ahmed (near Bizerte) and El Aouïna (near Tunis). There were secondary fields at Gabès and Kairouan and many small fields capable of development on the coastal plain.

Gibraltar—sole Allied possession on the Western European Continent—was to play a key role in the invasion. The harbor, docks, dockyard facilities, and workshops were of prime importance, and the above-mentioned airfield was the only one available to furnish air support for the whole "Torch" operation. The Rock and its command facilities were placed at Eisenhower's disposal for the operation. It was true that, as Eisenhower wrote later, "Britain's Gibraltar made possible the invasion of northwest Africa," but there was one drawback: anything not actually buried deep in the Rock was open to observation by Axis and Spanish observers on nearby Spanish soil or from aircraft flying over Spanish air space. The airfield itself was separated from Spanish territory only by a barbed-wire fence. Despite this handicap, the exact time and direction of the Allied move remained a secret, and Axis surmise ran the gambit from a major operation to relieve Malta to the capture of Crete, the invasion of Sardinia or Sicily, landings at Dakar, in Algeria, or Tunisia. Malta and Dakar were the German favorites; the Italians, while warned about Sardinia and Sicily, were more inclined to see an invasion of North Africa as the main threat.

The delays in Allied strategic planning caused by the necessity of reconciling the divergent views as to the invasion's primary objectives threw the whole timetable off, and cut the operational period —before winter rains would hamper the movement of troops and vehicles—to a perilously small margin. Contributing to the delay was the reluctance of the Allied naval authorities, particularly those of the United States, to furnish the "Torch" planners with lists of vessels available. It was not until September 4 that the U. S. Navy reported the units it could commit. The final agreement on an overall strategic plan was not submitted to the Combined Chiefs of Staff until September 20.

The grand strategy finally disposed of—work on the tactical planning had now to be rushed to completion. The agreement reached on September 5 by Roosevelt and Churchill on the three main points of attack and the general makeup of the forces to be employed had allowed definitive planning on the tactical level to begin. But with D-Day set at November 8, and despite the fact that some lower-level planning had begun as soon as the first decisions as to an African invasion had been made in July, there was little time for the enormous amount of detailed work entailed in mounting so huge an undertaking.

The scope of Eisenhower's command over the British forces is shown in the directive from the British War Office to General Anderson and other British commanding officers.

"The First Army has been placed under the

Supreme Command of the Allied Commander-in-Chief, Lieutenant General Dwight D. Eisenhower, United States Army. In the exercise of his command, the national forces at his disposal will be used toward the benefit of the United Nations and in pursuit of the common object. You will carry out any orders issued by him.

"In the unlikely event of your receiving an order which, in your view, will give rise to a grave and exceptional situation, you have the right to appeal to the War Office, provided that by so doing an opportunity is not lost, nor any part of the Allied Force endangered. You will, however, first inform the Allied Commander-in-Chief that you intend so to appeal, and you will give him your reasons."

The invasion troops were divided into three task forces—the Western Task Force, under Patton; the Center Task Force (Fredendall) and the Eastern Task Force (Ryder). The Western Force was to land near Casablanca, Safi, and Port Lyautey; the Center close to Oran, and the Eastern at Algiers. The Western Force came from the United States, under U.S. naval command (Rear-Admiral Hewitt, U.S.N.); the Center and Eastern from Britain, under the Royal Navy (Commodore Troubridge, and Vice-Admiral Burrough, respectively).

The Western Force was an entirely American affair. The Center, transported mainly in British ships and supported by British naval units, was also American, with American backup troops. The Eastern Task Force, transported and supported in the same manner, was made up of both American and British troops. This force, to be built up with British reinforcements was, immediately after the landing, to become the British First Army.

The naval forces were organized basically in escort, covering, air, and fire-support groups, besides numerous special units and groups. Altogether, the maritime forces engaged in the initial operation numbered 323 ships. This included Force H (Vice-Admiral Syfret) and the fueling force. A breakdown is given with each Task Force operation.

There is not space to recount the preliminary, and in many cases hasty, training exercises on both sides of the Atlantic. Enough to say that when the first boats came ashore there were many lessons still to be learned—from major tactical and logistical planning to small-boat handling and operations at company level and below. But as Admiral Cunningham afterward wrote: "There are times in history when we cannot afford to wait for the final polish. . . . for 'Torch' particularly we could not afford to wait and . . . the risk of embarking on

these large-scale operations with inadequate training was deliberately accepted. . . ." In the postmortem summing up, few Allied leaders could deny that the success of the invasion was due in part to the feeble opposition put up by the French—although in places, as we shall see, this was stronger than expected. But before following the fortunes of each task force, there was one drama to be played out on shore, and that under the very noses of the pro-Vichy authorities.

In the middle of October Marshall informed Eisenhower that French General Mast, through Murphy, had requested a meeting with a senior American general at a rendezvous at Cherchel, 90 miles west of Algiers, on the night of October 21-22. General Mark Clark, with a small staff, therefore flew to Gibraltar (the two B-17s carrying the party were the first such aircraft to land at the Rock), and that night—October 19—embarked on the British submarine P-219. Due to the late start the submarine reached the Algerian coast too late for the original meeting, but Gibraltar relayed a message from Murphy setting a date for the night of October 22-23. At midnight a light from shore was seen, the submarine moved in to within two miles of the beach, and the party, with three British commandos, embarked in "folbots" for the trip ashore.

Emerging from the surf, the party carried their craft ashore, were met by Murphy, and conducted to a nearby villa. Mast arrived with his staff at about 0500, and talks went on all day. A telephone call warning that police were on the way brought the meeting to a hurried end, and Clark and his companions were bundled down into a wine cellar, while Murphy and two of his friends staged a "party" overhead. That night, through a rising surf—after several capsizes, and the loss of one boat, a money belt filled with gold coins, some valuable and secret papers, and the general's trousers—the party reached the submarine, which had been brought almost into the edge of the surf, and by daylight were on their way to Gibraltar.

From this meeting came the decision to call in Giraud—as mentioned earlier. As Mast was soon to be relieved of his command and Giraud's influence proved to be nonexistent, the expedition achieved little. But it was an exciting little affair, well handled and a credit to the participants.

On October 22 and 23—while P-219 lay submerged off the Algerian beach—the assault convoys were leaving the Clyde and Hampton Roads for their appointed positions off the North African coast. While the Moroccan landings were not strategically as important as those inside the Mediterranean, it may help the continuity of the invasion account if the operations of the Western Task Force are considered first.

The composition of the Western Naval Task Force is given below. It should be noted that once the landings began, the groupings became flexible —some vessels, for instance, assigned to screen or covering duties being used for fire support or miscellaneous tasks.

WESTERN NAVAL TASK FORCE
(TASK FORCE 34)
Rear-Admiral H. Kent Hewitt in *Augusta*
TG 34.1 Covering Group
Rear-Admiral Robert C. Giffen
BB *Massachusetts*
CAs *Wichita, Tuscaloosa*
          Screen: Captian D. P. Moon
DDs *Mayrant, Wainwright, Rhind, Jenkins*
AO *Chemung* (tanker)

SOUTHERN ATTACK GROUP (TG 34.10)
Rear-Admiral Lyal A. Davidson
Fire Support Group—BB *New York*, CL *Philadelphia*
Control and Fire Support DDs—Captain C. C. Hartman
DDs *Mervine, Knight, Beatty*
          Southern Attack Group Transports
          Captain Wallace B. Phillips
Embarking Force X, "Blackstone": 47th Regimental Combat Team (9th Division), 3rd, and parts 2nd/67th Armored Regiment (2nd Armored Division), and special units. Total all ranks, 6,423—54 light, 54 medium tanks. Major General E. N. Harmon commanding.
APs *Harris, Calvert, Dorothea L. Dix, Lyon, Lakehurst*
AK *Titania*
          Screen: Commander H. C. Robison
DDs *Cowie, Quick, Doran*
Assault DDs *Cole, Bernadou*
DMSs *Howard, Hamilton;* CM *Monadnock* (minecraft)
AOs *Housatonic, Merrimack* (tankers)
Beacon submarine *Barb*
          Air Group
CVE *Santee* 14 F4F-4s, 8 TBFs, 9 SBDs
          Air Group Screen
DDs *Rodman, Emmons*
AT *Cherokee* (ocean tug)

CENTER ATTACK GROUP (TG 34.9)
Captain Robert R. M. Emmett
Fire Support Group—CA *Augusta*, CL *Brooklyn*
Control and Fire Support DDs—Commander E. R. Durgin
DDs *Wilkes, Swanson, Ludlow, Murphy*
          Center Attack Group Transports
          Captain Emmett
Embarking Force Y "Brushwood": 1st/67th Armored Regiment (2nd Armored Division) and special units. Total all ranks, 19,870; 79 light tanks. Major General J. W. Anderson commanding.
APs *Leonard Wood, Thomas Jefferson, Charles Carroll, Joseph T. Dickman, William P. Biddle, Joseph Hewes,° Tasker H. Bliss,° Edward Rutledge,° Hugh L. Scott,° Ancon, Elizabeth C. Stanton, Thurston*
AKs *Procyon, Oberon, Arcturus*
          Screen: Captain John B. Heffernan
DDs *Bristol, Woolsey, Edison, Tillman, Boyle, Rowan*
          Minecraft—Commander A. G. Cook, Jr.
DMSs *Palmer, Hogan, Stansbury*
CMs *Miantonomah, Terror*
AM *Auk*
          AIR GROUP (TG 34.2)
          Rear-Admiral Ernest D. McWhorter
CV *Ranger*—1 TBF, 54 F4F-4s, 18 SBD-3s
CVE *Suwannee*—29 F4F-4s, 9 TBFs
          Air Group Screen
CL *Cleveland*
DDs *Ellyson, Forrest, Fitch, Corry, Hobson*
Beacon submarines *Gunnel, Herring*
AO *Winooski* (tanker)

NORTHERN ATTACK GROUP (TG 34.8)
Rear-Admiral Monroe Kelly
Fire Support Group—BB *Texas*, CL *Savannah*
          Northern Attack Group Transports
          Captain Augustine H. Gray
Embarking Force Z, "Goalpost": 60th Regimental Combat Team (9th Division), 1st/66th Armored Regiment (2nd Armored Division), 1st/540th Engineers, plus special units. Total all ranks, 9,099; 65 light tanks. Brigadier General Lucian K. Truscott, Jr., commanding.
APs *Henry T. Allen, John Penn, George Clymer, Susan B. Anthony, Florence Nightingale, Anne Arundel*
AKs *Electra, Algorab*
          Screen: Commander D. L. Madeira
DDs *Roe, Livermore, Kearny, Ericsson, Parker*
          Air Group
CVE *Sangamon*—9 TBF-1s, 9 SBD-3s, 12 F4F-4s

° Sunk in action.

CVE *Chenango*—76 Army P-40Fs (for basing at Port Lyautey and Casablanca)

Air Group Screen—Captain Charles Wellborn, Jr.
DDs *Hambleton, Macomb*

Special Units

DDs *Dallas, Eberle,* AO *Kennebec,* AMs *Raven* and *Osprey,* SS *Contessa,* AVP *Barnegat*
Beacon submarine *Shad*

For security reasons the 105 vessels were not concentrated before sailing. The Air Group with attendant units went early to Bermuda for brief training, from which place they joined the expedition in mid-Atlantic. The Covering Group left from Casco Bay, Maine. The Center Group left Hampton Roads, Virginia, ostensibly for Britain, on October 24, and the Northern and Southern Groups a day later—as if bound for Bermuda. The Groups and the Covering Force rendezvoused on October 26 and were joined by the Air Group on October 28. Five submarines (TG 34.11) took departure from Montauk Point on October 19 and 20; four to reconnoiter the landing beaches and help the transports locate them; *Blackfish* to operate off Dakar.

The united task force, including screen, covered an area of some 60 square miles. Ringed by more than 40 destroyers and preceded and flanked by battleships and cruisers, the transports, tankers, and cargo vessels steamed in nine columns. Some miles astern came the carriers and their screening vessels. Overhead patrols of cruiser-based and carrier-based aircraft kept anti-submarine watch. At a steady 14 knots, zigzagging by day and steaming a straight course at night, the armada forged ahead —changing course on October 28 to suggest to any watching U-boat that Dakar might be the objective. Fueling took place on October 30 and 31, and on November 2 the course was changed to the northeast, as though bound for the Straits. Up to now the weather had been favorable, but by November 5 a northwest wind had piled up such seas

that one battleship was in danger of losing her boats and her forecastle-mounted 20mms. On November 6 reports of 15-foot surf on the Moroccan beaches made chances of a landing look slim. Hewitt would have to decide whether to wait more favorable conditions or attempt to make the landings inside the Mediterranean on the Moroccan coast east of Spanish territory. Weather predictions for D-Day from Washington and London were gloomy, but the task force aerologist was of the opinion the storm would pass and that conditions would permit landings on November 8.

Admiral Hewitt decided to take the risk, and at dawn of November 7 the Southern Attack Group broke away for Safi. The Covering and Air Groups next departed for their respective stations, and at 1600 the Center and Northern Attack Groups parted. The Groups were to be on station at midnight, allowing four hours to get their landing craft launched, loaded, and under way by 0400. As Admiral Samuel Eliot Morison points out, after a voyage of some 4,500 miles, the time of arrival differed among the three forces by only 15 minutes.

The Southern Landings

Safi was chosen mainly because it offered the only harbor in the area where medium tanks could be landed (see map). A direct approach to the harbor of the heavily defended city of Casablanca was out of the question, and these mediums were needed for the landward assault on that port. But the ex-Port Everglades–Havana train ferry *Lakehurst,* of over 8,000 tons, carrying the mediums, could be berthed in the little harbor of Safi.

Counting on surprise, a direct assault had been decided upon, and while the transports moved into position and began the difficult task of loading their landing craft in pitch darkness and a considerable ocean swell, the old stripped-down four-stackers *Bernadou* and *Cole* steamed in toward the

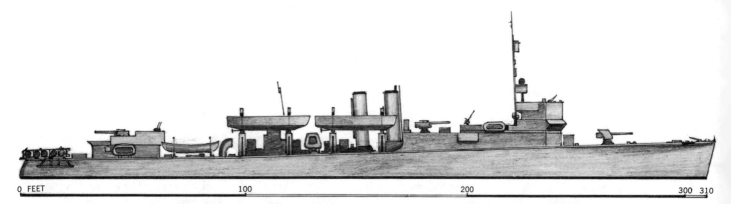

HIGH SPEED TRANSPORT (APD) CONVERTED "FLUSH DECK" DESTROYERS
Launched 1917–20. Converted 1942–43.
Displacement: 1,020 tons. LOA: 314½′. Beam: 31¾′. Draft: 8¾′. Twin Screw. 13,000 hp=
25 knots. Armament: three 3″, two 40 mm; anti-aircraft 20 mm. Complement: 200.

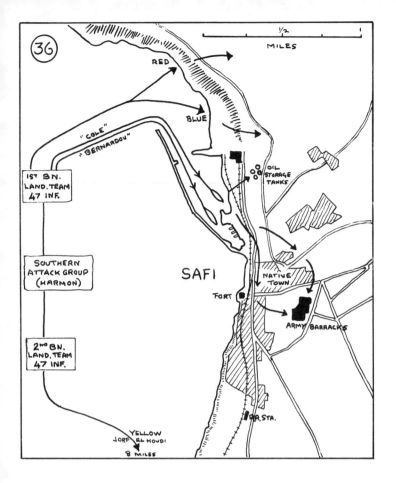

harbor mouth.

Each carrying nearly 200 raider-trained soldiers, they were to steer in behind the long breakwater and land their troops on the quay. As *Bernadou* approached the narrow harbor entrance she was challenged and almost immediately (0438) engaged at close range by 75mm guns and machine guns. As starshell lighted up the scene her own 3-inchers and automatic weapons opened up and silenced the French fire, and she moved on undamaged.

When the fireworks started, a coastal battery of four 130mm guns (Batterie Railleuse) opened up on DD *Mervine*. She signaled "Batter Up" (the agreed signal that the French had opened fire), and at 0439 the flagship replied "Play Ball" (the command to shoot back)—the first of the three Moroccan-bound forces to do so. *Bernadou*, unable to moor to the quay, grounded herself, and the assault troops clambered down a net over her bows. *Cole*, a trifle late, drew little fire as she entered at 0517. A string of landing boats followed her and landed at Beach Blue. This daring entry and debarkation cost only one man wounded. By 0530 light tanks were ashore at Beach Green, and the French Legionnaires and Moroccan infantry were being driven into the hills above town.

It was still dark and Batterie Railleuse ceased fire after a few rounds, as did *New York*, *Philadelphia*, and *Mervine*. At dawn the battery opened up again and straddled *New York* several times at 16,000 to 18,000 yards but scored no hits. *New York* replied with her 14-inchers, and after firing some 60 rounds, at about 0800 she scored a lucky hit on the observation slit of the battery's fire-control station, killing all inside and smashing the instruments. At 0850 the battery ceased fire and was occupied later in the morning.

Snipers were gradually driven from the town and vicinity, and tentative attempts at counter-attacks were brushed aside. The natives treated the invasion as a holiday occasion. Oblivious of naval shellfire and snipers' bullets they hung around the attackers. "Street intersections were crowded with natives turning their heads like a tennis gallery in trying to watch the exchange of fire." Later many drifted down to the beaches, where they helped unload the landing craft for small handouts—plus what they could steal (tons of rations and ammunition were later found on native fishing boats).

In the early afternoon *Lakehurst* entered, followed by AK *Titania*. By 1600 all objectives had been attained and a beachhead extending about 15,000 yards from the port had been secured. Fortunately, due to this success, few troops were landed at Beach Yellow, some nine miles to the south, which was being pounded by a heavy surf.

French air resistance was halfhearted—a good thing, as *Santee*'s air crews were as green as the ship herself. Flying fewer sorties than any of Task Force 34's carriers, she lost 21 out of 31 planes aboard, only one believed to be from enemy action. They did, however, destroy some parked planes on Marrakech airfield and bombed a couple of French road convoys headed for Safi. Admiral Davidson relied heavily on his scout aircraft catapulted from *New York* and *Philadelphia*, and it was some of these that silenced a mobile battery of 155mms that had survived a plastering by *Philadelphia*'s 6-inchers.

It had been believed by General Bèthouart that General Martin, commanding at Marrakech, would aid the American landing or at least not oppose it. But, like many French officers, Martin was torn between personal feelings and his sense of duty. Orders came to resist, and resist he did, but with a marked lack of enthusiasm, and it was not until 1350 on November 9 that troops were seen on the Marrakech–Safi road, just east of Bou Guedra. These and two other small columns were attacked and at least delayed by planes from *Santee*. First contact was made between these troops and U.S. infantry accompanied by light tanks and artillery at 1700, 1½ miles east of Bou Guedra. Night put an end to a brief skirmish, and in the morning there was an exchange of artillery fire. But Harmon's orders were to protect Safi and advance to Casablanca and not venture inland; and judging that his forces on the spot could contain the French, he went ahead with plans to move his mediums (Combat Command B, 2nd Armored Division) toward that city.

The last tank had hardly been swung ashore from *Lakehurst* (about 1400) before orders for a night march were issued, and at 1900 on November 10 the tanks moved out. *Cole* (later followed by *Bernadou*) conducted a small convoy of landing craft carrying drums of gasoline to provide the tanks with a refueling en route—a use that the old four-stackers' designers could scarcely have foreseen. Mazagan was reached early next morning and

the garrison surrendered about the same time as word of Darlan's cease-fire order ended the fighting at Casablanca.

All troops and tanks had been put ashore by 1800 on November 10, and all ships were completely discharged less than 6 days after arriving off the beaches. Much of the work of unloading had to be done by sailors; the Army's attitude, as Morison puts it, was, "Good-bye, Jack, thanks for the trip; rush that stuff ashore, I've got to go and fight." (Halfway around the world, the Navy had found that the Marines had much the same idea—see *The Campaign for Guadalcanal*, p. 34). Because of the decision to use the beaches inside the breakwater, only 1 landing craft was destroyed and 8 damaged (later salvaged) out of 121.

The Safi landing was a most successful operation, carried out with neatness and dispatch and a minimum loss (47th Infantry's casualties totaled 7 killed, 41 wounded, and 2 missing).

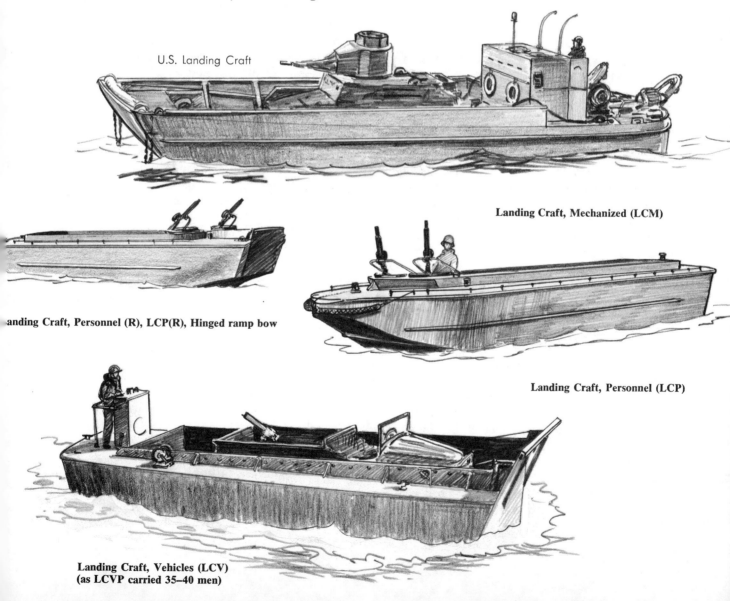

U.S. Landing Craft

Landing Craft, Mechanized (LCM)

Landing Craft, Personnel (R), LCP(R), Hinged ramp bow

Landing Craft, Personnel (LCP)

Landing Craft, Vehicles (LCV)
(as LCVP carried 35–40 men)

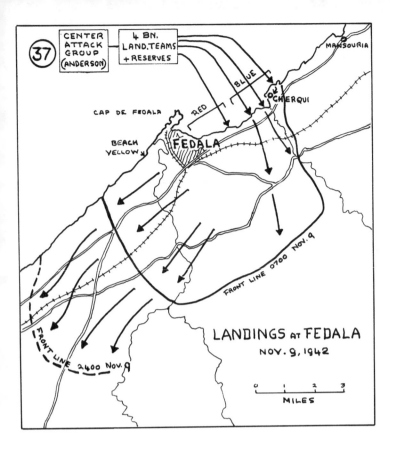

CENTER ATTACK GROUP (ANDERSON)

4 BN. LAND. TEAMS + RESERVES

MANSOURIA

BLUE

COL CHERQUI

RED

CAP DE FEDALA

FEDALA

BEACH YELLOW

FRONT LINE 0700 NOV. 9

FRONT LINE 2400 NOV. 9

LANDINGS at FEDALA

NOV. 9, 1942

0 1 2 3

MILES

THE LANDINGS AT FEDALA AND THE NAVAL ENGAGEMENTS AT CASABLANCA

The force to be put ashore at Fedala for the assault on Casablanca was the largest of the three, and its ultimate objective the most important. Much care had been taken in the planning, which had been worked out in great detail. But as is so often the case in ship-to-shore operations, the unpredictable ocean worked havoc with the most carefully laid plans. A strong and unexpected current set the convoy several miles off course, and in the ensuing maneuvers the transport formation straggled raggedly.

The plan called for scout boats, with infrared flashers, to reconnoiter and anchor (just beyond the line of surf) off each of the four selected beaches. The landing craft, once lowered and loaded, were to rendezvous with four control destroyers each 1,000 yards south of the four leading transports. Each destroyer would then conduct her waves of landing craft to a position 4,000 yards off shore. From this line of departure the landing craft would proceed to shore guided by the infrared flashing lights of the scout boats.

All very neat—on paper. But the front-line transports could not carry enough landing craft to disembark their own assault groups and had to rely on boats from other ships. These in some cases never

arrived at all—coxswains from ships whose relative positions could only be guessed at attempting to find other vessels in pitch darkness—and there was delay and confusion. Even when boats had assembled, disembarking took far longer than anticipated. Most troops, other than the first wave, carried some 60 pounds of equipment (too much, the Navy maintained) and were understandably cautious in clambering down the landing nets into the small landing craft heaving and surging alongside (one net on *Jefferson* carried away, spilling men into the sea). Some men were drowned in the surf while landing—knocked down by the waves and too overburdened and waterlogged to rise.

H-Hour (0400) was postponed, and it was 0500 before the first wave (or as much of it as had been collected) made for shore. Fortunately the surf was not too high, but a few boats went astray and were wrecked on rocks. *Jefferson's* scout boat went astray by two miles, and many of that vessel's craft were holed on a rocky shore. On Beach Blue—a narrow strip between two ledges—of 25 of *Carroll's* boats in the initial waves, 2 were wrecked by collision, 2 more by flooded engines, 3 holed on the rocks, and 10 broached—that is, were turned broadside in the surf and rolled over or swamped and driven up on the beach. Seven of the 25 retracted through the surf safely and returned for more men, but of these, 5 more were lost in the second landing.

Jefferson lost 16 boats out of 33; *Wood* lost 21 out of 32 in the original landing and 8 more during the day. *Carroll*, as noted above, lost 18 and 5 more later. *Dickman* came off best, losing only 2 out of 27.

Despite the delays, losses, and foulups, some 3,500 troops were put ashore between 0515 and just after 0600, when the guns opened up. While many units found themselves ashore on other than their assigned beaches, all shore objectives were attained and with enough manpower to hold them.

If there was some confusion among the invaders, there was considerably more in the ranks of the defenders. In the interests of security the exact date or locations of the landings had not been divulged to the few French leaders involved in the plot. This policy, while ensuring against leaks, also precluded any immediate co-operation with the French Army. So well was the secret kept that when the shooting began many Frenchmen did not know who their opponents were. On the other hand, the American commanders of the individual landing operations neither knew who the anti-

Vichy French leaders were nor what sort of reception to expect.

General Bèthouart's plan was to seize temporary control at Rabat by a *coup,* then issue orders to the garrisons to stay put in their barracks and let the invasion take place unopposed. He was not informed of the date of D-Day until the very last minute. He then hastened to Rabat, where he sent a message to Noguès, informing him that an invasion was imminent, that Giraud was taking control over North Africa, and that he, Bèthouart, was to take over command of all Army troops in Morocco and to aid the American landings. Orders for garrisons and airfields not to oppose the landings were being issued, and Noguès was asked either to confirm these orders or absent himself until the takeover was complete. Bèthouart, at headquarters, guarded by a battalion of French colonials whose loyalty to the Allied cause was assured, sent Lascroux, nominal commander of all troops in Morocco, to Meknès under open arrest and got an agreement from General Lahoulle, commanding officer of air forces, not to resist if the Army did not. Lahoulle later reversed his position after a talk with Michelier and was also arrested.

The stumbling block was the French Navy. The higher echelons, at least, were believed to be staunchly pro-Vichy, and when Admiral Michelier received a message similar to the one handed to Noguès he refused to believe it and advised Noguès by telephone to ignore it also. He assured Noguès there was no invasion force offshore, that any rumored landings would be mere commando raids, and he ordered the deputy commander of the Casablanca Division to cancel Bèthouart's orders and man the defenses.

Now the secrecy with which the invasion forces had proceeded worked to the Allies' disadvantage. Had a single French plane or ship reported the armada heading for the coast, Noguès might have been convinced. But the beaches at Rabat, where a landing might certainly be expected, were quiet and the sea empty. Telephone calls to the garrison commanders at Meknès and Marrakech revealed they would still obey his orders. A note from President Roosevelt arrived late and was set aside, and the President's proclamation, broadcast a half hour after the landings at Algiers (0100), does not appear to have been heard by anyone in authority— although it was picked up by the invasion fleet and caused some consternation, predating the Moroccan landings as it did by four hours. In fact, word of the Algerian landings did not reach Morocco

until 0300.

Noguès did not telephone a reply to Bèthouart until the Americans were ashore and fire had been exchanged. He then ordered Bèthouart to withdraw his colonials, which he did to avoid bloodshed, and the latter was arrested and sent to Meknès on a treason charge. But the admiral's coastal batteries had long since been in action, and by midmorning rolling clouds of smoke covered the port area as American shells fell in the harbor and the French batteries and naval vessels replied.

Although Michelier did not believe any invasion was likely, he did order an *alerte* at 0130 and followed with an *urgente* at 0227. The landing parties encountered no opposition, however, and the only excitement was when a French trawler escorting a small steamer blundered into the transport area. After a brief exchange of automatic weapons fire, a prize crew was put aboard the Frenchman. About 0520 a couple of searchlights ashore were shot out by assault craft, but about 0604, as dawn was breaking, machine guns and finally coastal batteries opened up, and Commander Durgin ordered "Batter Up" radioed to Hewitt (0607).

By the time "Play Ball" was signaled (0617), the support destroyers were already engaging the batteries at Cape Fedala and Pont Blondin (usually referred to as Sherki), and *Brooklyn* was coming in fast from patrol to her fire-support station. She fired her first main battery salvo at Sherki at 0622. The 4 138.6mm guns there had already put a shell in *Murphy's* engine room, but salvoes from *Brooklyn's* 15 6-inchers finally silenced the battery, which was occupied by American troops about 0750. The 2 75mms and the 3 100mm guns of the Batterie du Port on Cape Fedala were harder to subdue, being emplaced close to oil-storage tanks, which the invaders hoped to use later. Careful fire by destroyers and *Augusta* silenced the du Port guns more than once, but they continued to harass the troops on the beaches until the Army moved in around noon. The two 75mms were knocked out by *Palmer* about 1010, after they had hit her twice.

With the silencing of the shore batteries resistance ended, although the beaches were strafed by aircraft several times during the afternoon. The transports were brought closer inshore, and the work of debarkation and landing supplies went forward. As the sea was building up, the landing craft were directed to use the harbor. Losses in landing craft amounted to over 40 per cent. Of these 150-odd boats, only 2 or 3 were destroyed by enemy gunfire. Unskilled crews were probably the main reason for the heavy loss. Many that could have been saved were needlessly abandoned, to be battered to pieces by the surf as the tide turned and stranded boats floated free.

Even so, by 1700 on D-Day some 7,750 out of about 19,500 (reports differ) in the total force had been landed, along with some 275 vehicles. Losses had been comparatively light (20 killed and 128 wounded), indicative of the efficiency of the naval gunfire, the swiftness and surprise of the first assault waves, and the slight resistance put up by the French.

Resistance by the French Army may have been less than determined, but the French Navy and part, at least, of the Air Force made strenuous, if hopeless, efforts to drive off the invaders. As dawn broke, Admiral Giffen's Covering Group was steaming off Casablanca, roughly parallel to the shore and some 20,000 yards distant. Their mission was to guard against a possible attempt at interference by the powerful squadron at Dakar (the new battleship *Richelieu* and three cruisers), prevent the naval vessels in Casablanca from sortieing and silence the shore batteries, if they fired. At 0610 the Covering Group catapulted aircraft, and 9 planes winged shoreward on spotting and antisubmarine missions. Ten miles farther out, *Ranger* and *Suwannee* had launched aircraft, and by 0700 18 of *Ranger*'s SBDs were over Casablanca.

At 0650 one of *Massachusetts'* spotters reported two submarines leaving Casablanca Harbor, and a minute later, as anti-aircraft shells exploded close aboard, he signaled "Batter Up." French aircraft were also in evidence, and one was shot down by *Massachusetts* at 0701. Almost at the same moment tall pillars of water rose around the battleship as the 194mm guns at El Hank and *Jean Bart*'s 15-inchers opened fire. Giffen ordered "Play Ball," and at 0704

Massachusetts let go a 16-inch salvo at *Jean Bart* at a range of 24,000 yards. *Tuscaloosa* opened on the same target while *Wichita* fired at El Hank. At 0720 a shell from *Massachusetts* (her fifth hit) jammed *Jean Bart*'s forward turret in train (her No. 2 turret had never been installed). Firing was continued at the submarine berthing area and other shipping and the shore batteries.

These last were temporarily silenced, but single gun emplacements make poor targets at ranges of over 15 miles, and nothing but a direct hit could knock one out. By about 0747 3 merchant ships and 3 submarines had been sunk—most of them by dive bombers. Despite bombs and shells, 8 submarines sortied between 0710 and 0830.

At 0815 ships of the French 2nd Light Squadron, (5 destroyers and the 2 destroyer leaders, *Milan* and *Albatros*, followed at 0900 by the cruiser *Primauguet*,) steamed out of port to do battle (even the admiral in command, Lafond, was ignorant of the nationality of their opponents). Giffen's squadron was by now 25 miles away from the transports off Fedala and there were anxious moments as the fast French vessels, undeterred by strafing and bombing attacks, drew close. *Augusta*, *Brooklyn*, *Wilkes*, and *Swanson* were ordered to intercept. Under heavy fire the French destroyers temporarily withdrew, making skillful use of smoke screens. At about 1000, *Primauguet* joined the action, and shortly after, two destroyers closed to attack the Covering Group with torpedoes. One of these, *Fougueux*, was sunk; at the same time *Massachusetts*, *Tuscaloosa*, and *Brooklyn* were narrowly missed by torpedoes. In the somewhat confused action *Brooklyn* sank the *Boulonnais*, and *Primauguet*, badly battered, headed for the harbor, where she was joined by the heavily damaged *Milan* and *Brestois*. The retreating French ships were strafed

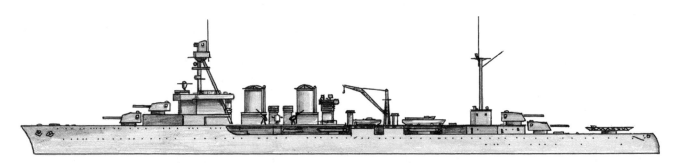

Primauguet (Fr.) *Duguay-Trouin* Class Light Cruiser (three ships)

Launched May 1924.
Displacement: 7,249 tons. LOA: 595'. Beam: 57½'. Draft: 17¼'.
Four screws. 100,000 hp=34 knots.
Armament: eight 6.1″ (4✕2), four 3″ (4✕1), twelve 21.7″ torpedo tubes (4✕3), automatics.
Aircraft: 2, one catapult.
Armor: armored deck, splinter shields.
Complement: 577.

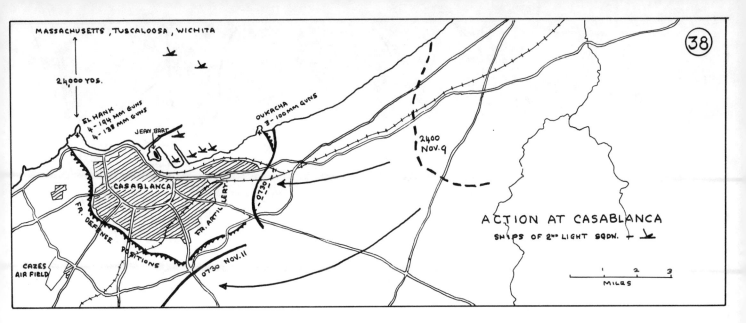

ACTION AT CASABLANCA
SHIPS OF 2ND LIGHT SQDN.

repeatedly by the carriers' Wildcats. One such attack on *Milan*'s bridge left 29 dead. A few minutes later, *Frondeur* was also damaged and returned to harbor, while bombs from *Ranger*'s SBDs left already damaged *Albatros* dead in the water. *Alcyon* alone retired undamaged. Hits from French destroyers had temporarily put *Ludlow* out of the fight; a shell had exploded in *Massachusetts,* injuring no one; another had slightly wounded 14 in *Wichita,* and *Brooklyn* had been hit by a dud. One casualty of the battle had been General Patton's landing craft, hanging ready to go overboard. The general had been about to disembark from *Augusta* when the naval action started and the blast from the flagship's after 8-inch turret, trained forward, blew the craft to pieces. The general, although anxious to get ashore, thus became an interested spectator of the morning's battle.

Primauguet was severely damaged by bombing in the afternoon and was beached, burning. After repeated but ineffectual attempts to silence the battery at El Hank, the action was finally broken off. The port had been hard hit. Ten cargo and passenger ships had been sunk, a destroyer leader and 2 destroyers undergoing repairs severely damaged, and 3 submarines sunk at anchor. Of the 2nd Light Squadron only *Alcyon* remained undamaged. Of the 8 submarines that left port just before or during the attack, only 3 survived.

Preparations were made on D plus one to secure positions from which the advance on Casablanca could be made on the following day. Patton himself spent the forenoon of November 9 on the beaches at Fedala—not liking what he saw. He found much confusion and slackness, lack of leadership and, during a French air attack at 0800, enough disruption of work due to "cold feet" to ex-

asperate the doughty general. The movement toward Casablanca that day met light resistance and occasional strafing but was badly hampered and finally halted by the slow rate of unloading. Guns, vehicles, and radios were either still aboard ship or lost or damaged along the beaches. By making full use of the meager port facilities of Fedala the situation improved during November 9, but it was not until midnight of November 9–10 that the advance was continued.

On November 10, against stiffening resistance, the American troops pushed forward into the outskirts of Casablanca. *Jean Bart,* her turret now repaired, again opened fire but was promptly hit by 2 1,000-pound bombs by *Ranger*'s dive bombers. The airfield at Port Lyautey was not yet in U.S. hands, nor had the medium tanks (Combat Command "B") arrived from Safi, but Patton decided to go ahead with an assault in co-ordination with naval support fire at 0730 on November 11. Word then came that *Chenango*'s P-40s were on the Lyautey airfield and that CC "B" was on its way.

Not counting the men manning the coast defense batteries, the French defending Casablanca numbered some 4,000, plus naval units from the damaged ships and about 90 guns. An encounter in which the city might have suffered severely, with heavy casualties on both sides, was averted when Darlan's orders to stop the senseless struggle were transmitted to Noguès at his headquarters in Fès. He in turn radioed Casablanca and Marrakech to suspend active hostilities until an armistice could be arranged next day. The French reply was received only minutes before the attack was to begin. Just before noon the defenders of Casablanca surrendered (Americans to take key positions, the French to remain in barracks but to retain their

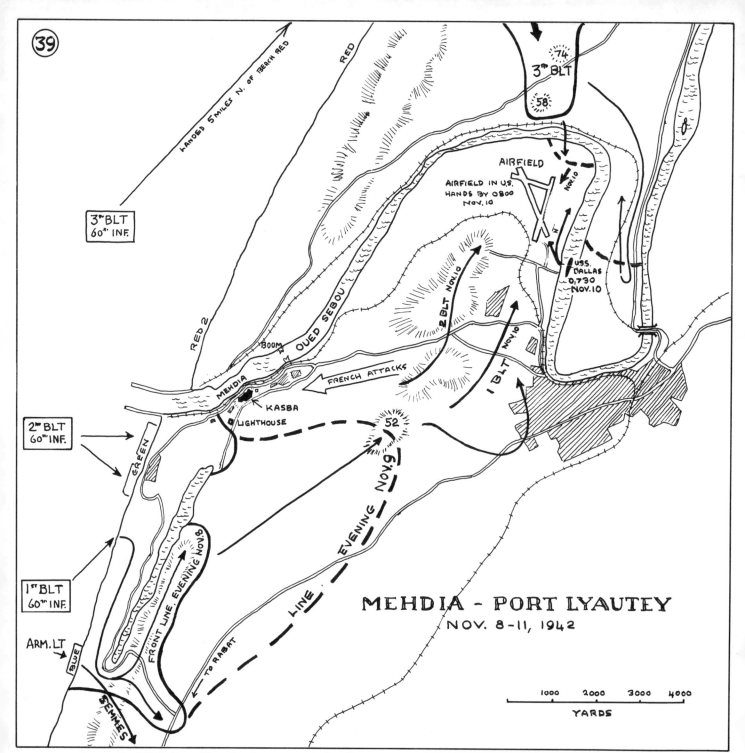

Map labels

(39)

LANDED 5 MILES N. OF BEACH RED

RED

3rd BLT
60th INF.

3rd BLT

74

58

AIRFIELD

AIRFIELD IN U.S.
HANDS BY 0800
NOV. 10

NOV. 10

2nd BLT NOV. 10

U.S.S. DALLAS
0,730
NOV. 10

1st BLT NOV. 10

RED 2

BOOM

OUED SEBOU

MEHDIA

FRENCH ATTACKS

KASBA

LIGHTHOUSE

2nd BLT
60th INF.

GREEN

52

FRONT LINE EVENING NOV. 9

1st BLT
60th INF.

FRONT LINE EVENING NOV. 8

TO RABAT

ARM. LT

BLUE

SEMMES

MEHDIA - PORT LYAUTEY
NOV. 8-11, 1942

1000   2000   3000   4000

YARDS

---

weapons). Michelier, Noguès, Lascroux, Lahoulle, Patton, Hewitt et al. met at Fedala about 1400 on November 11. The terms were generally the same as agreed on in Casablanca, a few hours earlier with the added proviso that no one was to be punished for aiding the Americans. Further terms were to be settled at Algiers.

The Northern Group

One of the prime objectives of the Moroccan invasions was the airfield at Port Lyautey, with the only all-weather concrete landing strip in north-western Africa. As the map shows, the airport lies in a loop of the winding Wadi Sebou—the town 1½ miles farther upstream. At the rivermouth is a small village, Mehdia. Above the village, on high ground, is an old Portuguese fort, the Kasba. A boom had been positioned across the river near this point. The ancient walled citadel had no military significance but close by were six coastal defense guns of 138.6mm caliber (2 of them modern pieces, armored and in sunken positions). All had a range of about 11 miles. Below were 2 75mms and assorted automatic weapons.

The troops of the Northern Attack Group were to land on 5 beaches (see map). The 4 beaches on the coast were good, but steep ridges paralleling the shore and, south of the river, a 4-mile-long lagoon narrowed the possible areas of penetration to the interior. It was estimated that the French garrison at Port Lyautey defending this area consisted of a single regiment of infantry (just over 3,000 men) with artillery. These could be reinforced within hours by 1,200 mechanized troops and 45 tanks from Rabat. Two infantry regiments could march in from Rabat and Meknès in 5 days. The fifth beach, Beach Brown, was on the river near Mehdia. Destroyer-transport *Dallas* was to proceed up the river with 75 men of a special raider force to Beach Brown 2—near the airport.

There was some trouble due to navigational errors and the usual delay and confusion in assembling the landing craft and debarking the assault waves, so it was about 0540 on November 8 before the first boats hit the beaches. What with the delay, the constant repetition of the President's message, and the blundering into the transport area of some French coasters, it was obvious that there was not much chance of surprise. At 0545 a searchlight illuminated one of the guide scout boats, a rocket went up, and shots were heard. A few minutes later the battery near the Kasba opened fire and was answered by *Eberle*. Shortly after 0600, machine guns drove off the assault boat with the party assigned to cut the boom. There was only scattered firing during darkness, but at first light the guns on both sides opened up in earnest. Around 0630 French aircraft began to strafe and bomb the landing boats, and at 0730 Admiral Kelly asked for air support. Aircraft from *Sangamon* and *Ranger* responded. They shot down some nine French aircraft and then beat up the fields at Port Lyautey and Rabat-Salé. No further French air attacks were reported.

Fire from the Kasba battery drove the transports 15 miles offshore—which greatly hampered unloading. The battery was engaged by the warships and silenced temporarily but continued to fire off and on during the day. Troops from Beach Green attempted to storm the Kasba but were held up by U.S. naval gunfire from ships trying to knock out the battery. Naval fire by general order was limited to counter-battery fire and requests for support from shore fire-control parties. Truscott's plan had been for surprise infantry attacks, delivered before dawn, and need for a naval bombardment had not been anticipated. By the time the troops

were ashore and engaged they were too close to their objectives for *Texas* to blast the Kasba area with her 14-inchers, and the old fortress held out until early morning of November 10.

The Northern Attack Force seemed doomed to trouble. An attempt to urge Colonel Charles Petit, the French commander at Port Lyautey, to cooperate met with failure. A Jeep, with white flags and a tricolor, was first passed through the French lines near the Kasba but was fired on near Port Lyautey. One of the emissaries, Colonel D. F. Craw, was killed. The other, Major P. M. Hamilton, was taken to French headquarters, where he found Petit sympathetic but bound by orders. There was nothing for it but to fight it out, and, to their surprise, the advancing Americans met stiff resistance—stiffer than at Safi or Fedala.

The 1st Battalion Landing Team (1st BLT) landed without opposition (though nearly two miles too far north). But, after setting up defensive positions to guard against French moves from the south, an attempt to move northward along the high ground met with fire from concealed machine guns and bogged down. Not until late evening did supporting artillery dislodge the defenders, and 1st BLT dug in for the night.

The 2nd BLT landed at Beach Green (where they were strafed by French fighters) and proceeded toward the Kasba area. Unfortunately the area, as noted above, was under counter-battery fire from warships offshore. As shells roared overhead and exploded a few hundred yards to their front, the infantry halted and the attack broke up in some confusion. The naval gunfire ceased and a second attack was organized. The area near the lighthouse was taken, but as the Kasba defenses were neared, a second naval bombardment again drove the attackers into a hasty retreat. The 2nd BLT's troubles were not over. A renewed attack was ordered, but the order was misunderstood and, leaving a company facing the Kasba, most of the battalion bypassed the fort to the east. Here, at a native village, they were counter-attacked by French from Rabat, including artillery, and, later in the afternoon, three tanks. The battalion had already been badly shaken by the events of the morning (it had been rumored that the French would greet them with open arms). Straggling back in small parties they dug in for the night around the lighthouse, losing a number of prisoners in the retreat.

Due to the confusion in the transport area, 3rd BLT did not approach the beach until daylight. The

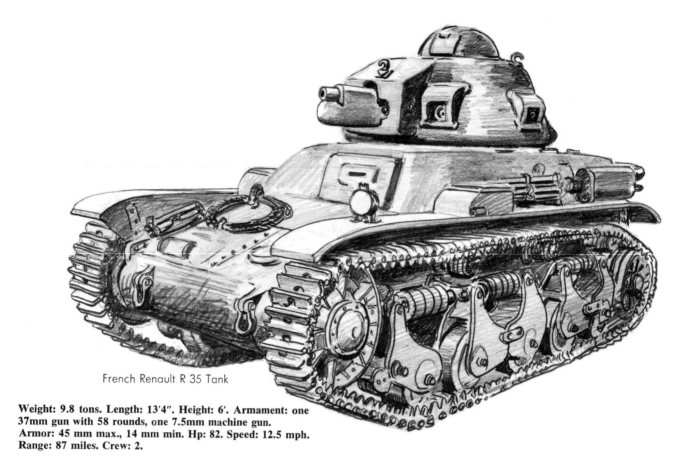

French Renault R 35 Tank

Weight: 9.8 tons. Length: 13′4″. Height: 6′. Armament: one 37mm gun with 58 rounds, one 7.5mm machine gun. Armor: 45 mm max., 14 mm min. Hp: 82. Speed: 12.5 mph. Range: 87 miles. Crew: 2.

decision was made to ignore Beach Red 2 and land both elements on Beach Red. Actually the landing was made five miles to the north of Beach Red. Two boats were lost to bombing and strafing (fortunately with no casualties), and machine guns hastily emplaced on the dunes downed two of the attackers. There was no opposition on land, and after a long hard hike across rough country the troops (without artillery) reached Hill 58—a position just across the river from the airfield. A fire-control post was set up on Hill 74, 1,000 yards to the north, and naval gunfire adjusted on a French battery of 155mms and an ammunition dump. During the night, artillery was dragged up from the beach and emplaced on Hill 74, and rubber boats were sent up in half-tracks, ready for an advance across the river next day.

The situation at nightfall looked none too good for the invaders. Mounting seas and the 30-mile round trip between ship and shore slowed landings to a trickle, and by nightfall no light tanks or heavy weapons could be handled at all. Seven light tanks (Stuarts) under Colonel H. H. Semmes were sent to block the Rabat–Port Lyautey highway. The long sea voyage had rendered their radios inoperative, and their guns were not sighted in. In the meantime, French reinforcements were on the way from Fès and Meknès, though with the coming of

daylight these were heavily strafed. Some reached the Kasba, where they added to 2nd BLT's worries, but the main threat was in the South. As Semmes' light tanks advanced toward the Rabat road at daylight they inflicted severe losses on a company of French infantry in the woods nearby. Then, about 0640, some 14 to 18 Renault tanks, with two battalions of infantry, could be seen coming down the road from Rabat. In the ensuing action four French tanks were destroyed and the infantry driven back with heavy casualties. Gunfire from *Savannah* and aerial bombing completed the discomfiture of the French. More tanks and some anti-tank guns had been landed by this time and joined Semmes in time to repulse a second French attack about 0900. The action in this sector quieted down, but firing continued throughout the day.

D plus one saw 1st BLT pushing northeastward, despite fire from the Kasba and lighthouse area in its flank and rear. Hill 52 was reached about 1500, but the battalion was stopped by heavy machine-gun and mortar fire. A French counter-attack was checked by tanks, artillery, naval gunfire, and bombing, and the advance was about to be resumed when unhappily a few bombs and shells fell into the American lines (not marked by identification panels). Thus disorganized, the advance was postponed until next morning.

The 2nd BLT, in some disarray after the first day's fighting, failed to get itself completely sorted out during the night. The French, reinforced, attacked again in the morning and drove the Americans from the lighthouse area and Mehdia itself. Despite a great advantage in army artillery, naval weapons, and aircraft, the 2nd BLT could not move forward, and the battle remained a stalemate.

The American 105s on Hill 78 dueled with French guns and dominated the airfield, while 3rd BLT prepared an attack for the night of November 9–10. One company was to cross the river onto the airfield, while two more were to capture the bridge at Port Lyautey. The river was crossed without trouble and a lodgment made on the south bank, but the attempt to seize the bridge failed. In a simultaneous attack from the southwest, elements of 1st BLT made disjointed but finally effective efforts to reach the high ground overlooking the airfield. French resistance now showed signs of slackening, at least in certain quarters. When Colonel Petit was captured early on November 10, he ordered the 1st Moroccan Tirailleurs to cease fire. He was paroled at his own headquarters in custody of his erstwhile captive, Major Hamilton. Later in the morning another regiment was ordered to cease fire.

The commander of 1st BLT, Major McCarley, and part of one of his companies, on the other hand, blundered into the edge of Port Lyautey in the dark and were taken prisoners by a battalion of the Foreign Legion, who showed no signs of giving up.

The boom across the river near the Kasba was finally cut and *Dallas*, with a local pilot aboard (a Gaullist previously sneaked out of Morocco by OSS for this purpose), entered the river. She rammed the boom, which had not fully opened, and started upstream, though peppered by automatic weapons and shelled by the Kasba battery and assorted 75-mms. She sliced through mud a couple of times, so shallow was the channel, but she was unhit, and

replied with good effect with her 3-inchers. At 0737 she grounded finally off the airport and her raiders took to their boats without a casualty.

While *Dallas* was churning upstream, elements of 2nd BLT, supported now by its artillery, attacked the Kasba. Held up by machine-gun and mortar fire, they called for air support. Dive bombers from *Sangamon* were soon overhead; clouds of dust and debris rose from the fort, the troops charged in, and the garrison came out—hands in air. In the meantime, the airfield had been secured, and at about 1030, P-40s from *Chenango* began landing.

Last shots were from *Texas*'s 14-inchers, which dispersed at a range of 17,000 yards a column of motorized infantry heading toward Port Lyautey. Admiral Kelly then broadcast an appeal to the French, ending: "Join with us. Stop this useless waste of lives and use them later in the fight against your real enemy—Germany."

With the fall of the Kasba the transports moved in and anchored from 1,500 to 3,000 yards of the rivermouth. Beach Brown soon became so crowded that craft went upriver to Port Lyautey. Darlan's order to General Mathenet, commanding French troops at Port Lyautey, to cease resistance was followed by a meeting between Mathenet and Truscott at 0800 on November 11. Fighting had already stopped, but the Frenchman agreed to put the airfield at Rabat-Salé under American control.

This concluded the operation and wound up the whole Moroccan venture, for they were talking now instead of fighting at Casablanca and in hours would agree to a cease-fire for the entire colony. There only remained the loose ends—landing the rest of the equipment and supplies, arranging harbor space for the follow-up convoy (now marking time out in the Atlantic), promoting co-operation between the French and their unwelcome guests, and not least, ensuring that the authorities took no steps to punish those who had openly sided with

Sangamon (U.S.) Class Escort Carrier (four ships)

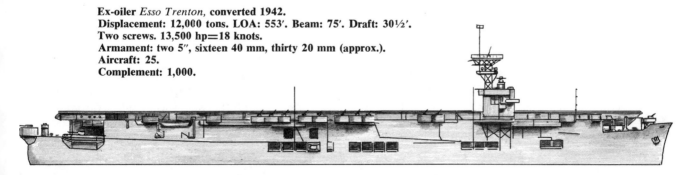

Ex-oiler *Esso Trenton,* **converted 1942.**
Displacement: 12,000 tons. LOA: 553'. Beam: 75'. Draft: 30½'.
Two screws. 13,500 hp=18 knots.
Armament: two 5", sixteen 40 mm, thirty 20 mm (approx.).
Aircraft: 25.
Complement: 1,000.

Launched February 1930.
Displacement: 9,050 tons. LOA: 600'. Beam: 66'. Draft: 16½'.
Four screws. 107,000 hp=32.7 knots.
Armament: nine 8" (3×3), eight 5" anti-aircraft, four 40mm quads plus 20 mm, two
triple 21" torpedo tubes.
Armor: vertical side 3", deck 1", gunhouses 1½".
Complement: 611.

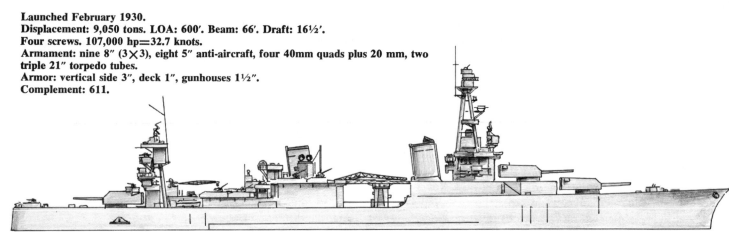

the invaders; for the French military, although now officially allied with their erstwhile enemies, were inclined to deal harshly with those who, in their eyes, were traitors to the armed services. Noguès, for instance, took steps to bring Bèthouart to trial, and it was not until November 17 that, on orders from Eisenhower, Bèthouart and the commander of the troops who supported him at Rabat on the night of the unsuccessful *coup* were released and flown to Algiers. Others were not so lucky. The policy of co-operation with Darlan and the so-recent followers of Vichy and Laval—necessary at the time to maintain the administration of the country —meant that these same authorities, military and civil, remained in control. Patton wrote Eisenhower, "The anti-Darlan-Noguès group does not have the personnel nor is it in a position to control Morocco if given that mission." He was probably right, but his support of the shifty Noguès and his commanders made life very difficult for the pro-Allies, Giraudists, De Gaullists, left-wingers, and the like.

And there was the butcher bill to tot up. Not too bad for a big operation, but French adherence to orders and the chain of command—the need to make at least a show of resistance to satisfy military honor and *la gloire*—had cost some 350 American dead, nearly 700 wounded, and well over 100 missing.

There would soon be more. The German U-boats had been caught off balance, but when the direction of the Allied thrust became apparent the undersea craft sped toward the beaches like sharks smelling blood.

Warnings that U-boats were concentrating were received on the afternoon of November 11, and ships were alerted to be especially vigilant. There were 15 transports and supply ships then anchored off Fedala. At Casablanca berths had been cleared to accommodate 12. Captain Emmett recom-

mended immediate transfer of as many ships as possible to the safety of the harbor. At a conference on the *Augusta* that evening Admiral Hewitt decided that these berths be kept open for the D plus 5 follow-up convoy. Within an hour a torpedo slammed into transport *Joseph Hewes*. Seven minutes later the nearby tanker *Winooski* and destroyer *Hambleton* were also hit.

Hewes went down in less than an hour, taking her captain and several seamen with her—and 90 per cent of her cargo. *Winooski,* hit by good luck in a sea-ballasted tank, was little damaged. *Hambleton* lost 20 men, but was towed into Casablanca. The submarine, *U-173,* was attacked but escaped, only to be sunk by depth charges on November 16.

Again Hewitt decided to risk the remaining transports. Despite reports of increased U-boat activity, unloading continued off Fedala during November 12. And while winches rattled and landing craft shuttled to the harbor, *U-130* was creeping along the shore—so close that she scraped bottom. At 1758 she fired 5 tubes. All torpedoes hit, and 3 transports—*Tasker H. Bliss, Edward Rutledge,* and *Hugh L. Scott*—burst into flames and began to list. All went down before morning. Casualties were well over 100 dead, and more injured. Emmett then ordered the remainder to get under way. *U-130* made good her escape.

The last victim was *Electra*, of the Northern Group, torpedoed as she headed for Casablanca. She was badly holed, but, assisted by two minesweepers and a tug, she was beached off Casablanca and later salvaged.

Hewitt's decision had been an unfortunate one, and the loss of 4 transports and the damaging of another, an oiler, and a destroyer, made an expensive ending to an otherwise successful naval enterprise. But Morocco was secure, no threat had developed from Spain, and the Allied efforts could be concentrated on the main target, Tunisia.

IV

"Torch":

THE CENTER AND EASTERN TASK FORCES

THE ALLIED LANDINGS AT ORAN AND ALGIERS

The Mediterranean landing operations actually began on October 2 when the first of the six advance convoys (tankers, colliers, ammunition ships, cased gasoline carriers, auxiliaries, etc.) left the United Kingdom for Gibraltar. These numbered altogether 84 ships, with 42 escorts, the last sailing from the Clyde on October 30. Of the Assault Convoys the 2 slow convoys, carrying tanks, vehicles, and stores, left the Clyde and Loch Ewe October 22, followed on October 26 by the 2 fast convoys with the troops. As these steamed south, well out in the Atlantic, several naval forces were also proceeding south. These included 4 battleships, 8 cruisers, 2 fleet and 2 escort carriers, 28 destroyers, and 4 smaller escorts.

It was too much to expect that some 240 merchant ships and transports and over 140 naval vessels, many steaming on widely separated courses, could escape the notice of German submarines and aircraft. Actually, sightings were reported by four U-boats and a Focke-Wulfe aircraft. These sightings were interpreted by the Germans as merely the preliminary to another large Malta convoy, and they persisted in this belief even when large concentrations of shipping were reported at Gibraltar. It was perhaps also too much to expect that none of these vessels would fall victim to submarine attacks en route. But none did—while two U-boats were sunk by patrolling aircraft. Luckily for the invaders, the U-boats of the only group in the ap-

BRITISH ADVANCE CONVOYS

CONVOY	COMPOSITION AND ESCORT	SPEED IN KNOTS	SAILING DATE	DEPARTURE PORT	DATE DUE AT GIBRALTAR
KX.1	5 ships 7 escorts	7½	10/2/42	Clyde	10/14/42
KX.2	18 ships 13 escorts	7	10/18/42	Clyde	10/31/42
KX.3	1 ship 2 escorts	13	10/19/42	Clyde	10/27/42
KX.4A	20 ships 8 escorts	7½	10/21/42	Clyde	11/4/42
KX.4B	8 ships 2 escorts	6½	10/25/42	Milford-Haven	11/3/42
KX.5	32 ships 10 escorts	7	10/30/42	Clyde	11/10/42

BRITISH ASSAULT CONVOYS

CONVOY	COMPOSITION AND ESCORT	SPEED IN KNOTS	SAILING DATE	DEPARTURE PORT	DATE DUE AT GIBRALTAR
KMS(A).1 (for Algiers) KMS(O).1 (for Oran)	47 ships 18 escorts	8	10/22/42	Loch Ewe and Clyde	11/5/42 11/6/42
KMS.2	52 ships 14 escorts	7	10/25/42	Loch Ewe and Clyde	11/10/42
KMF(A).1 (for Algiers) KMF(O).1 (for Oran)	39 ships 12 escorts	11½	10/26/42	Clyde	11/6/42
KMF.2	18 ships 8 escorts	13	11/1/42	Clyde	11/10/42

proaches to Gibraltar were busy with an unfortunate convoy (SL 125) returning from Freetown to the United Kingdom, sinking 12 ships.

The punctual arrival of these convoys, ships, or groups of ships at or off Gibraltar and their orderly passage through the Straits called for precise planning, navigation, and staff work, while at Gibraltar the fueling arrangements and dock facilities were taxed to the limit.

The first two convoy sections, those for Algiers, began to enter the Mediterranean at 1930 on November 5. The section for Oran passed the Rock during the afternoon of November 6. By daylight of November 7 the Eastern and Center Task Forces and Force "H" were well within the Mediterranean. The Axis powers had by now realized that something bigger than a large-scale operation for the relief of Malta was under way, but the direction of the thrust was still a mystery. As late as November 7 Hitler still believed Tripoli or Benghazi to be the target, with four or five divisions landing to cut off Rommel—even then retiring from his shattered El Alamein positions. The Duce thought French North Africa was the likely goal. Supermarina (Italian Naval High Command) was convinced early on November 7 that the area Algiers–Bougie–Tabarka was the target, but allowed itself to be overborne by its German counterpart. Toward evening the Italians changed their minds and ordered their submarines, most of which had been concentrated farther east, shifted westward. The Germans now admitted the possibility of landings in Algeria as well as in Libya. The nine U-boats available in the Mediterranean at the beginning of November were deployed east of a line Cartagena–Oran. Without air reconnaissance so far west the Oran convoys were not spotted at all. The Algiers convoys passed over the U-boat line, but the number of Allied escorts and patrolling aircraft prevented all but two U-boats from reaching firing positions, and these failed to score.

German aircraft had also been alerted, and at dawn of November 7 an air-dropped torpedo (there is a question about this and some maintain the attack was made by submarine) struck the transport *Thomas Stone*. The first casualty of Operation "Torch" occurred some 50 miles east of Cartagena. The hit was in the stern and there were only 9 killed or wounded, but the ship was stopped with a damaged rudder and propellers. The corvette H.M.S. *Spey* stood by but as the sea was calm it was decided that *Stone*'s most seaworthy landing craft, with some 800 men of 2nd BLT, 39th U. S. Infantry, should attempt the 150-mile voyage to the beach.

Two British destroyers and a tug from Gibraltar were on their way, and as night fell, *Spey* and the 24 assorted landing craft began their long journey.

not without difficulty, into Algiers on November 11.

On the afternoon of November 7, Force H, cruising south of the Balearics, was attacked by Ju 88s and a destroyer damaged, but the Algiers Fast Assault Section, then within sight, was not harmed. During daylight of November 7 the courses maintained by the various task forces were such as to give the impression of a Malta-bound operation. After sunset courses were changed, and the Center and Eastern Task Forces headed southward to their appointed positions off the beaches.

Before continuing with the account of the landing operations, it is necessary to describe briefly the situation in Algeria, where a small group of pro-Allies Frenchmen waited and prepared for the coming of the Americans.

The disastrous consequences of a leak in security —and there were no guarantees that there would

---

Naval Covering Force for Oran and Algiers Landings
FORCE "H"

Vice-Admiral Sir Neville Syfret

Battleships *Duke of York, Rodney*
Battle Cruiser *Renown*
Fleet Carriers *Victorious, Formidable, Furious*
Cruisers *Bermuda, Argonaut, Sirius*
17 Destroyers

Azores Covering Force

Cruisers *Norfolk, Cumberland*
3 Destroyers

Fueling Force

2 Tankers
1 Corvette
4 A/S Trawlers
Rodney, Furious, and three destroyers detached to support Center Naval Task Force
Bermuda detached to support Eastern Naval Task Force

Six knots were the best the landing craft could do, and as the sea kicked up, this was cut to 4. Breakdowns were so numerous that at dawn the wet, seasick troops were taken aboard *Spey*. There was an attempt to save some of the precious landing craft (others were scuttled), but this too had to be abandoned. *Spey* finally brought her passengers to a quay in Algiers Harbor on the morning of November 9—all resistance ashore having ceased by then. It was a minor incident in such a great undertaking, but the saga of *Stone*'s boats showed great spirit and determination. *Stone* herself was towed,

be none—precluded any but the most general plans being made known to the pro-Allies sympathizers. The disclosure by Murphy on November 4 that the landings were scheduled for November 8, therefore, came as an unwelcome surprise, and Mast's first reaction was to ask for a three-week delay. This, of course, was out of the question, and last-minute arrangements had to be rushed to completion.

The plans for Oran centered on Colonel Paul Tostain, Chief of Staff of the Oran Division. He was to be aided by a group of military and civilians. Units of the 2nd Zouaves Regiment were to gain control of the main military installations and furnish arms to civilian units, who would seize centers of communications and arrest key government officials—including the commander of the Oran Division, General Robert Boissau, if he refused to cooperate. But Tostain got cold feet—insubordination on this scale was too much for him. So Mr. Edgeway Knight, American vice-consul, radioed Gibraltar a warning that resistance at Oran might be expected.

At Algiers there were detailed plans for seizure of key points and officials, all under Mast's control. As we shall see, these plans were complicated by the unforeseen presence of the No. 2 man in the Vichy government, Admiral Darlan himself.

fast and slow convoys now united, turned back from its eastward course (one pointing toward Malta) and steamed south for the three landing beaches (X, Y, and Z). The columns for each sector had already been formed, and left the others in turn for their respective stations. Beacon submarines were in position off each beach, and these boats were located about 2130. British doctrine called for launches to be sent to each submarine to pick up piloting officers. Each of these launches would then join the landing craft and guide the leading waves in to the assigned beaches. The submarines, meanwhile, would proceed closer inshore and drop off teams in collapsible boats who would station themselves even closer to the beaches. Once the first waves hit the beach the transports, some 7

CENTER NAVAL TASK FORCE
Commodore Rear-Admiral T. H. Troubridge

Headquarters ship *Largs*	2 Cutters
Auxiliary carriers *Biter, Dasher*	1 Landing Ship Infantry (large)
Cruisers *Jamaica, Aurora*	2 Landing Ships Infantry (medium)
AA ships *Alynbank, Delhi*	3 Landing Ships Infantry (small)
13 Destroyers	3 Landing Ships Tank
2 Submarines	1 Landing Ship Gantry
2 Sloops	8 A/S Trawlers
8 Minesweepers	10 Motor Launches
6 Corvettes	

While the convoys were steaming toward their final positions, a minor crisis had arisen at Gibraltar. About 1500 on November 7, General Giraud arrived at Gibraltar. He had been picked up off Toulon as arranged, by the British submarine *P-219*, with an American naval officer in temporary command as a "front" to appease the Frenchman (he had wanted a U.S. submarine). Later he was transferred to a Navy PBY Catalina and flown to the Rock. Unfortunately the doughty general was under the impression that he was immediately to assume command of the whole operation. Eisenhower spent several uncomfortable hours trying to convince Giraud of the impossibility of such a step, but the general insisted that personal and national honor demanded that he be made Commander-in-Chief. The nonproductive argument went on past midnight, but a night's sleep brought a change of heart, and it was agreed that he would go to North Africa and assume command of all French forces there.

Oran—The Center Task Force Landings

At dusk on November 7 the Center Task Force,

miles offshore, would move in closer to the beaches through channels swept clear of possible mines.

ORAN WESTERN LANDING GROUP
(Partly formed from Center Naval Task Force)

1 Landing Ship Infantry (large)
2 Landing Ships Infantry (medium)
1 Landing Ship Tank
4 Mechanical Transport Ships
Cruiser *Aurora*
1 Destroyer
2 Corvettes
1 A/S Trawler
1 Motor Launch

The ships for "X" Sector's two beaches ("X" Green and "X" White), 7 transports, and a tank landing ship carried some 2,250 men of the armored task force (Task Force Green, Combat Command B., 1st Armored Division) under Colonel Paul M. Robinett. With them were a cruiser,

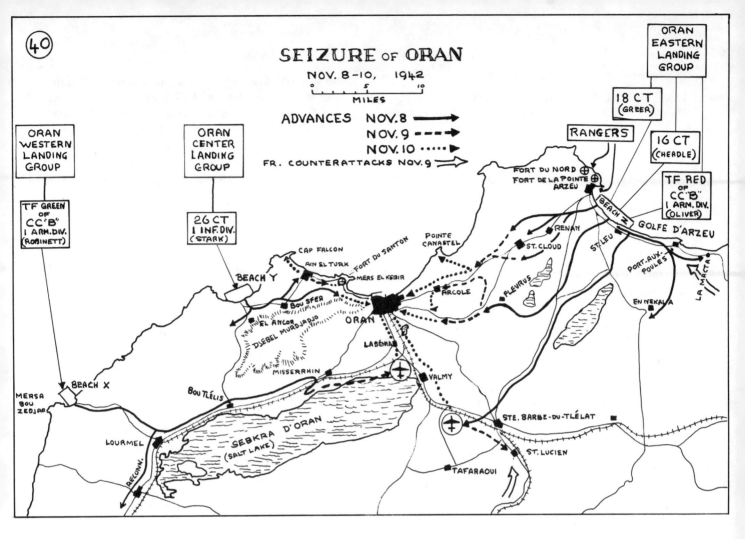

H.M.S. *Aurora,* a destroyer, two corvettes, an A/S trawler (equipped with anti-submarine gear), and an M.L. (motor launch). They had been forced to slow down to avoid a small French convoy that crossed their path. One of these vessels (there were 5 of them escorted by an armed trawler) was stopped and boarded. The other 4 steamed east until they sighted the "Y" Beach ships, reversed course, and finally beached themselves. The escort escaped. This delayed touchdown of the first wave of landing craft until 0130 (H-Hour was 0100) on November 8.

There was no opposition, and after the first assault teams ashore had secured the beachhead, landing craft with supporting troops and vehicles and the LST *Bachaquero* began to come in. The tank-carrying craft was, or had been, a shallow-draft oiler used on Lake Maracaibo, Venezuela. There were three of these odd-looking vessels altogether (two others were assigned to the Eastern Group). They averaged about 375 feet long by 60 feet and, trimmed down by the stern, they drew only 7 feet forward. Huge hinged doors and a bow

landing ramp had been built in, and they could carry some 22 light tanks or 40 5-ton vehicles. They were the forerunners of the standard LSTs then being built in the United States. They proved of great value in "Torch."

The waters of Mersa Bou Zedjar Bay are shallow, and *Bachaquero* grounded some 360 feet from shore. It was not until around 0700 that U. S. Army Engineers readied a pontoon bridge and the first of 20 light tanks rolled ashore. All were off by 0815, and by then many troops and vehicles were ashore. A line of steep dunes rose some 30 yards inland from the beach, and bulldozers went to work while engineers laid steel matting.

Reconnaissance units pushed inland down the blacktop highway to the village of Lourmel followed by a flying column (Task Force Green) under Lieutenant Colonel John Todd. The force proceeded east on the highway, breaking through a couple of French roadblocks, and bedded down for the night just west of Misserrhin.

Off the two "Y" beaches were the five transports carrying the 26th Combat Team of the 1st Infantry

ORAN CENTER LANDING GROUP
(Partly formed from Center Naval Task Force)
3 Landing Ships Infantry (large)
2 Mechanical Transport Ships
2 Destroyers
4 A/S Trawlers
5 Motor Launches

Division under Brigadier General Theodore Roosevelt and Colonel A. N. Stark, Jr.—some 5,400 men and almost 400 vehicles. Disembarking was slower than expected (the heavily laden soldiers having difficulty with the landing ladders on some vessels). Even so, some of the leading craft were at the beach at 0116. But a further delay was caused by an unexpected sandbar just offshore. As with many such bars, there was deeper water on the landward side, and the first three LCMs to ground there offloaded Jeeps and guns, which promptly disappeared. A way around was soon found, and by 0500 half the troops and 33 vehicles were ashore. Landings were speeded up as a result of the transports moving close (some 2,000 yards) inshore and anchoring. About dawn the French sloop La Surprise slipped out of Oran and attempted to attack the transports. She was engaged by destroyer H.M.S. Brilliant and sunk at 0715.

While part of the invaders set up defenses at the village of El Ancor (at about 0800 they destroyed 3 French armored cars coming up the road from Bou Tlélis), the major part of the force proceeded eastward (see map). Bou Sfer was occupied and the advance continued to within some 4 miles from Oran, where it was pinned down about 0740 by artillery, rifle, and machine-gun fire. At the same time troops moved from Bou Sfer to Aïn el Turk.

The city of Oran was protected by 13 batteries of coastal guns, and at daylight one of the most powerful of these, the 4 7.6-inch guns of Fort du Santon, began shelling the transports off "Y" Beach. One was damaged and moved west out of range, while from her position several miles offshore H.M.S. Rodney replied with her 16-inchers, temporarily silencing the battery. The battery fired intermittently during the day, hitting the Monarch of Bermuda once and driving it west. Fire from Rodney repeatedly silenced it but could not knock it out.

The main landings were in the Golfe D'Arzeu, either at the town itself or on the "Z" beaches to the east. Here 34 transports and over 20 escorting warships prepared to land the 16th and 18th Regimen-

tal Combat Teams (of 1st Infantry Division: Major General Terry Allen) and Task Force Red, of Combat Command B, 1st Armored Division, Brigadier General Oliver Lunsford. A Ranger force was to land north of the town and capture two coastal-defense batteries there while others took the town.

ORAN EASTERN LANDING GROUP
(Partly formed from Center Naval Task Force)
6 Landing Ships Infantry (large)
3 Landing Ships Infantry (small)
2 Landing Ships Tank
1 Landing Ship Gantry
1 Cable Ship
15 Mechanical Transport Ships
6 Merchant Vessels
Cruiser Jamaica
AA Ship Delhi
3 Destroyers
5 Corvettes
2 Cutters
1 Sloop
8 Minesweepers
3 A/S Trawlers
4 Motor Launches

At H-Hour four companies of Rangers swarmed ashore, scaled the cliffs of Cap Carbon, and took the battery at Fort du Nord from the rear after a brief skirmish. Two more companies in small boats entered the little harbor at Arzeu, surprised the garrison, and took the guns at Fort de la Pointe (aided by an American captain in the Foreign Legion stationed at the fort). As a green flare announced the success of this undertaking, a mixed U.S. and British naval party entered in a landing craft and seized 4 small vessels moored in the harbor. The port was put to immediate use, and although harassing fire opened up at daylight, it was quickly silenced.

The three beaches in "Z" Sector were good, though exposed, with easy approaches. The 18th Combat Team (7,092 men, Colonel F. U. Greer) began landing on "Z" Beach Green at 0120. The 1st Battalion went straight inland, destroying with bazookas 5 armored cars that attacked at Rénan, and penetrated as far as St. Cloud. Here it was checked by heavy fire from a colonial infantry regiment, a battalion of the Foreign Legion, and a battalion of artillery. Reinforced by self-propelled 105s and the 2nd Battalion, the Americans tried again at 1530,

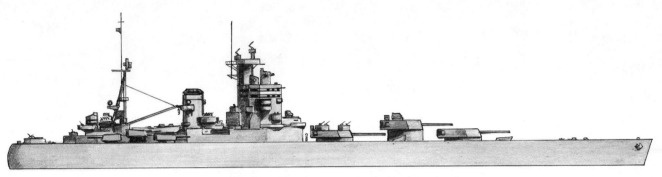

Rodney (Br.) Nelson Class Battleship (two ships)

Launched December 1925.
Displacement: 33,900 tons. LOA: 710′. Beam: 106′. Draft: 30′.
Two screws. 45,000 hp=23 knots.
Armament: nine 16″ (3✕3), twelve 6″ (6✕2), six 4.7 anti-aircraft, two 24.5″ torpedo tubes,
40 mm, 20 mm, and machine guns.
Armor: belt 14″, turret 6″, deck 6.2′.
Complement: 1,314.

but were beaten back once more. The 3rd Battalion, which had captured the barracks and the naval base at Arzeu (including 13 seaplanes, fueled and loaded with torpedoes), now arrived, and a concerted attack was ordered for 0700 the next morning, November 9.

The 16th Combat Team (5,608 men, Colonel H. B. Cheadle) hit the beaches "Z" White and "Z" Red, right on schedule at 0100. Third Battalion, 16th Infantry landed on "Z" White and proceeded inland south of St. Cloud to the village of Fleurus, about nine miles east of Oran, where a strong point was established. Landing on "Z" Red, 1st Battalion 16th Infantry took two small villages and secured the beachhead for the armored force. The battalion then moved east through Port-aux-Poules, sending a force southeast to En Nekala. Opposition was met at La Macta, held by elements of the 2nd Algerian Infantry Regiment. An attack, supported by artillery and the guns of destroyer H.M.S. *Farndale,* went in at 1230, and by 1400 the town was secured and a defense line set up to the east.

The armored task force (CC "B," 1st Armored Division, 4,772 men, Brigadier General L. E. Oliver) were brought to "Z" Beach on two transports and two of the Maracaibo tankers converted to LSTs. These latter beached about 0400 and began unloading two hours later. Despite harassing fire from a battery near St. Leu they were unloaded at 0759. A reconnaissance force, followed by a flying column, took the road southwest to the crossroads village of Ste. Barbe-du-Tlélat, and from there to the airfield at Tafaraoui. This was secured about noon, and at 1215 the welcome news went out that the airfield was in Allied hands. At 1630 two squadrons of Twelfth Air Force Spitfires landed from Gibraltar.

So important was the field at Tafaraoui that a parachute assault had been planned. The aircraft, C-47s, did not rendezvous off Cornwall until 2200 on November 7. Their route lay across Spain's northern mountains, and poor weather, faulty radio communications and running lights, and the climb through clouds to 10,000 feet completely dispersed the formation. To make matters worse, the beacon ship off Oran transmitted on a wrong frequency, and its signals were not received. One aircraft landed at Gibraltar, two in French Morocco, and three in Spanish Morocco, while a seventh dropped its troops over that territory. Of 32 transports that reached Algeria, 12 dropped their parachutists near Lourmel, at the wrong end of Sebkra d'Oran, while most either dropped or landed at the western end of the lake. After the ground forces captured Tafaraoui an attempt was made to fly the grounded planes from around Lourmel, but some were forced down by French aircraft from La Sénia and others were hit by flak. At the end of D-Day only 14 of the air transports were operational. Needless to say, the airborne attack accomplished nothing, and by November 15 only 300 of the 556 paratroopers could be assembled for the next operation.

Naval air support of the "Z" Beach landings began at first light. Eight Albacore dive bombers from H.M.S. *Furious,* each armed with 6 250-pound bombs and escorted by Hurricanes from the auxiliary carriers, flew over the La Sénia airfield and were met with heavy anti-aircraft fire and hostile fighters. Hangars were wrecked, grounded aircraft destroyed, and 5 French fighters were shot down in dogfights. A few minutes later Seafire fighters strafed the La Sénia and Tafaraoui airfields. Three British aircraft were lost and some others forced down from lack of fuel. Other aircraft

Walney (Br.) Ex-U.S.C.G. cutter *Sebago*

Launched 1930.
Displacement: 1,980 tons. LOA: 250'. Beam: 42'. Draft: 16'.
Two screws. 3,220 hp=16 knots.
Armament: one 5", three 3", automatics.

patrolled the beaches and the main roads, but the French pilots fought only in defense of their fields and there was almost no activity over the landing areas.

The bloodiest (and most unnecessary, as it turned out) actions of the day resulted from a frontal assault on Oran Harbor. This was carried out by two ex-U.S.C.G. cutters, renamed H.M.S. *Walney* and H.M.S. *Hartland*, carrying nearly 400 officers and men of the 6th Armored Infantry (1st Armored Division), 5 officers and 22 seamen of the U. S. Navy, 6 U. S. Marines, and 52 Royal Navy officers and ratings, as well as the ships' crews. The plan was to seize key port facilities and, by special boarding parties, attempt to prevent the scuttling of ships at the wharves or in the harbor entrance.

Had the operation ("Reservist") been planned for H-Hour or a few minutes before, it might just possibly have succeeded. Timed as it was for 0300, the mission was termed "suicidal" by Rear-Admiral Bennett, U.S.N., in a letter to Eisenhower on October 17. In Bennett's opinion the operation should not begin until the French were convinced that resistance was hopeless and that the time should be flexible, rather than fixed in an operational plan. He also protested to Admiral Cunningham, but the original plan was adhered to.

At 0300, *Walney*, flying large American flags as well as the White Ensign, neared the 200-yard-wide harbor entrance. This gap was covered by shore batteries, the guns of the warships in harbor,

dual-purpose anti-aircraft weapons, and machine guns. As the cutter, accompanied by two motor launches, steered for the entrance, she was lit up by searchlights and struck by cannon and automatic weapons fire. Partly shrouded in smoke released by the M.L.s, she broke the booms and steamed into the harbor. The sloop *La Surprise* was just sortieing on what was to be her last voyage, and the Frenchman raked the cutter in passing at pointblank range. Badly damaged and on fire, *Walney* staggered up the harbor, fired at by every warship whose guns would bear. Casualties were very heavy, her engines were wrecked, and at last the survivors were ordered to abandon ship. She finally capsized and sank about 0445.

Hartland, a few minutes behind, suffered a like fate. Her gun crews were cut down after they had fired only a few rounds, and as she steamed in she came under fire from the destroyer *Typhon* at a range of less than 50 yards. Burning and out of control, *Hartland* drifted on until the few survivors able to do so finally abandoned her about 0400. She finally blew up and sank about 1015. The butcher bill came high: 9 officers and 180 enlisted men of the 6th Armored Infantry dead, 5 officers and 150 enlisted men wounded. Three U.S. sailors and 2 Marines were killed, and 7 wounded. Royal Navy losses were 113 dead and 86 wounded. Admiral Bennett had been right.

Shortly after the unhappy attempt at a direct assault had come to grief, the three French destroyers then operational left port to attack the transports. They were promptly engaged by the cruiser H.M.S. *Aurora* and her attendant destroyers. Two Frenchmen were beached in sinking condition while one, damaged, returned to port. Three of the four French submarines also sortied. Two were sunk by H.M.S. *Wescott* and H.M.S. *Achates,* and another was harried into Spanish territorial waters. From there she proceeded to Toulon, where, on November 13, she was scuttled along with the rest of the Toulon squadron.

With the exception of the "Reservist" disaster and the air-drop fiasco, D-Day had been fairly successful. The beaches were secure; the little port of Arzeu had been taken in working order and was in full use. Attempts by the French Navy to interfere with the landing had been repulsed with loss, French air opposition had been negligible, and one of the major fields, Tafaraoui, was in Allied hands. Over 14,000 troops had been landed, although landings of vehicles had been slow (only 340), and a rising sea had caused much damage to landing craft and forced suspension of beach operation except in the small bay at Mersa Bou Zedjar.

It had been expected that French resistance might stiffen on D plus one. There were an estimated 10,000 troops in Boissau's Oran Division plus some 4,000 naval and anti-aircraft gunners. There were more troops inland, and it was thought that another 8,000 might join Boissau within 24 hours. The first threat came early on November 9 at La Macta. At the same time air reconnaissance showed motorized columns on the way from Sidi bel Abbès (main base of the French Foreign Legion) toward Tafaraoui.

Such infantry as could be spared, as well as armored reinforcements (including the only two medium tanks then ashore), were hurried toward La Macta, while Albacores of the Fleet Air Arm dive-bombed a suspected French battery position. The cruiser H.M.S. *Jamaica* joined *Farndale* to furnish gunnery support if needed. The French counterattack was checked without much trouble and without calling for naval bombardment. At the same time aircraft bombed and strafed columns advancing from Sidi bel Abbès. A minor threat to "Y" Beach was disposed of, while Combat Team 26 made slow progress, against stiff resistance and shelling, toward Mers-el-Kébir.

A French advance, with armor, hit elements of CC "B" near St. Lucien, seven miles east of Tafaraoui. American tanks and tank destroyers drove the French off, with the loss of 14 French E-35 tanks. In the meantime the interrupted advance to

La Sénia was continued and the airfield was reached shortly after sunup by advance units of Colonel Todd's Task Force Green. The field was secured by 1000 hours, but shelling by French batteries near Valmy proved a hazard until they were driven off with the loss of three of their guns by a detachment of Todd's force.

Following Todd's advance party was Colonel Robinett with the bulk of the Task Force. Their advance eastward was checked at Misserrhin, which strong point had been bypassed by Todd. The unsuccessful attacks on the place, hampered by lack of infantry, induced Robinett to bypass it also, and at dusk he followed in Todd's footsteps and joined up with him about 0100 on November 10.

St. Cloud was attacked at 0700 on D-Day, but the village was strongly held. The attack, after penetrating the village, was checked, and a massive artillery bombardment, followed by an advance from three sides by three battalions, was prepared. After a personal observation General Allen decided to bypass the place, contain it with a reinforced battalion, and press on westward to be ready for a final attack on Oran on November 10.

In the Cap Falcon–Mers-el-Kébir sector the 26th Combat Team made little headway. Like all the American units, the 26th was short of guns, vehicles, and ammunition. Landings at "Y" Beach had been stopped during the night due to the heavy surf, and lack of materiel was beginning to tell. The batteries at Cap Falcon were still active, and fire from French troops dug in above Mers-el-Kébir was heavy.

An attempt during the day by destroyer leader *Epervier* and *Typhon* to break out of port ended with *Epervier* beached and burning and *Typhon* driven back to harbor. That evening all remaining ships—4 submarines, 7 minesweepers and patrol craft, and 13 merchantmen—were sunk in the fairway or alongside the docks. *Typhon* was scuttled across the harbor entrance.

Despite slow progress on November 9 most troops were in position for the advance set for 0715 on November 10. The armored force at Tafaraoui moved to join Robinett's armor at La Sénia at dawn, and although shelled from Valmy and by coastal guns firing inland, by early morning CC "B" was ready for its advance into Oran. Counter-battery fire knocked out some of the Valmy guns and others were overrun by infantry, while naval gunfire soon silenced the shore batteries. On the east 3rd Battalion, 16th Infantry had actually reached the suburbs. Although many strong points were left intact, Oran was now threatened on three sides.

CC "B" advanced on Oran in two columns, on parallel roads about a mile apart. The affair at Valmy had delayed the start until after 0900, but by 1015, the leading elements had roared across the open ground (unharmed by sporadic fire from large-caliber guns), blasted away some roadblocks, and entered the city. The streets were deserted, and only sniper fire met the invaders. Colonel Todd's column made for General Boissau's headquarters, while others released the Allied prisoners (some 500), and moved into the areas about to be attacked by 1st Infantry Division. The infantry was able to march in unopposed, and at 1215 a cease-fire was ordered, pending the signing of a formal surrender. The terms were much the same as in Morocco—with Boissau retaining his command and policing the city while the American units took over all key positions. So sudden was the fall of the city that word of the cease-fire did not immediately get through to all units, French and American. An hour later there was still fighting around Mers-el-Kébir and it was not until 1330 that *Rodney* stopped firing on the Du Santon battery and it was occupied by troops of Combat Team 26. St. Cloud still held out, and attacks by 1st Battalion, 18th Infantry had all been beaten off, although negotiations for surrender were under way when news of the cease-fire finally arrived.

This was the last organized resistance, although there was some sniping in spots, and isolated units were still firing on Allied aircraft on November 11. Organization of the area proceeded rapidly. The inner port was blocked, but transports still loaded moved into the outer harbor, Mers-el-Kébir, and Arzeu. Salvage operations were got under way at once, and the French put pilots, tugs, lighters, and all available equipment at the disposal of Admiral Bennett, Commander U. S. Naval Operating Bases, Oran Area.

As in Morocco, the American hands-off policy to-ward the civil government worked great injustice and hardship on the pro-American Frenchmen who had risked life and liberty to prevent useless resistance. There were many Axis sympathizers and pro-fascist elements left in positions of authority and their activities caused deep resentment among the Frenchmen who had supported the Allied cause.

In spite of the heavy casualties incurred in the ill-advised frontal assault, over-all losses had not been too high. The 1st Infantry Division lost 85 killed, 221 wounded, and 7 missing. Apart from the losses in *Walney* and *Hartland,* listed above, 1st Armored Division's losses were negligible. One French report put their dead at 165.

The Occupation of Algiers

Casablanca and Oran were mere sideshows compared with the big prize, Algiers. Not only was it the capital of Algeria, but also the seat of government for all French North Africa. Moreover, its port and rail facilities and two airfields made it a key point from which to undertake the advance into Tunisia. As the hub of political activity it was also the center for the pro-Allies party, and the outcome of the inevitable conflict between these and the Vichyites would decide to a great degree the reception the landing forces might expect. The situation was made more complicated by the unlooked-for presence of the No. 2 man of the Vichy government, Admiral Jean François Darlan. If he could be talked over, the French might well give in without firing a shot. If he decided to fight to the last—and he was, obviously, a firm supporter of Pétain, as well as a rabid Anglophobe—then the success of the landings might be in doubt.

The huge convoy and its attendant warships steaming eastward off the Algerian coast had not gone unnoticed, and on the evening of November 7 the French naval commander in the Algiers region had pointed out to General Juin that the Allied force was in a position where it could easily turn south during the night and arrive off the Algiers

---

EASTERN NAVAL TASK FORCE
Vice-Admiral Sir H. M. Burrough

Headquarters Ship *Bulolo*	3 Sloops
Cruisers *Sheffield, Scylla, Charybdis*	7 Minesweepers
Carrier *Argus*	6 Corvettes
Auxiliary Carrier *Avenger*	2 Landing Ships Infantry (large)
AA Ships *Palomares, Pozarica, Tynwald*	2 Landing Ships Gantry
Monitor *Roberts*	8 A/S Trawlers
13 Destroyers	8 Motor Launches
3 Submarines	

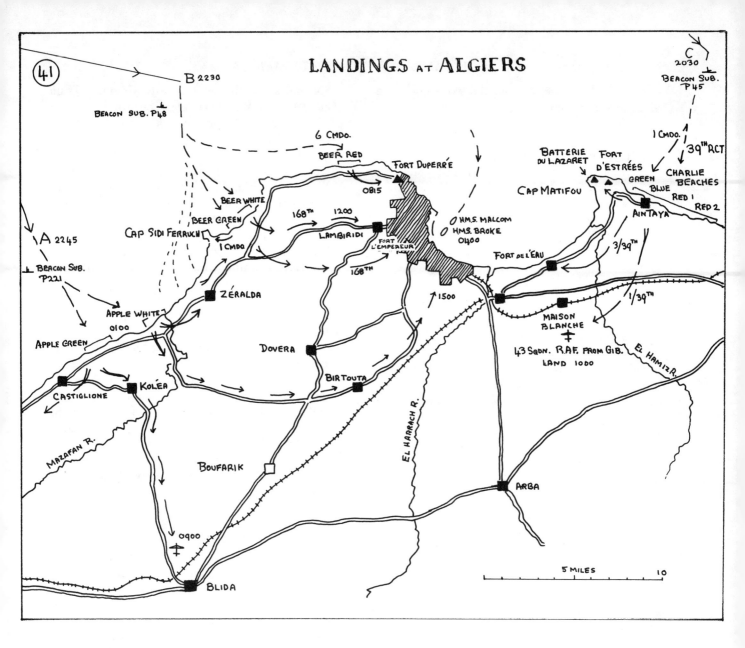

beaches before daylight. But no alert was sounded, and in places General Mast's co-conspirators had passed the word not to resist an Allied landing.

The Allied planners, while hoping for an unopposed landing, were well aware of the strength of the French forces near the capital. Some 7,000 were believed to be in or around the city itself, with 4,500 more to the west and 3,500 to the east, within 25 to 30 miles. There were about 90 operational aircraft at the two airports, while a dozen fortified batteries dominated the seaward approaches to the city. All-out resistance meant a hard fight, many casualties, and much time—and a great deal depended on Mr. Murphy and his friends.

So there was tension ashore and afloat as, one hour after sunset, the ships of the fast convoy turned south toward the coast. An hour later the transports for the eastern landing with their escorts headed for the beacon submarine northeast of Cap Matifou; the others formed a double column and steamed toward Cap Sidi Ferruch. About 2130, when some 30 miles northwest of the cape, the columns separated and steered for their rendezvous with the beacon submarines off their respective beaches. At the same time the slow convoy, which had steered a shorter course closer to the African coast, split into three sections, one for each landing sector. At about 2230 the assault convoys made contact with the beacon submarines and hove to. Conditions were ideal: There was little sea running, the night was clear, and the twinkling shore lights gave promise of a peaceful reception.

ALGIERS WESTERN LANDING GROUP
(Partly formed from Eastern Naval Task Force)

- 3 Landing Ships Infantry (large)
- 1 AA Ship
- 1 Landing Ship Gantry
- 4 Mechanical Transport Ships
- 2 Sloops
- 2 Corvettes
- 3 Trawlers
- 3 Motor Launches

The landings to the west, near Castiglione, were made by the 7,230 men of the British 11th Infantry Brigade Group. Their A beaches were designated Apple Green and Apple White. The brigade's mission was to establish itself on the road to Bir Touta as a flank guard for B (Beer) Sector to the east (where the major part of the French forces were stationed) and if necessary to be ready to support an attack on the airfield at Blida, some 15 miles southwest.

Despite a 5-knot current, which swept the ships out of position while unloading, the first waves picked up their pilots from the beacon submarine *P-221* and homed in on the signal flashing from the submarine's collapsible boat team only 400 yards off the beach. The first troops came ashore on the dot of H-Hour, and by 0230 the brigade's commander (Brigadier E. E. Cass) and staff were ashore and the leading elements of the force were on their way to their objectives. Castiglione, Koléa and Zéralda, were taken—the French troops encountered in the barracks at Koléa stating they had been ordered not to resist.

ALGIERS CENTER LANDING GROUP
(Partly formed from Eastern Naval Task Force)

- Headquarters Ship *Bulolo*
- 1 AA Ship
- 7 Landing Ships Infantry (large)
- 9 Mechanical Transport Ships
- 1 Landing Ship Gantry
- 4 Destroyers
- 1 Sloop
- 2 Corvettes
- 3 Minesweepers
- 3 A/S Trawlers
- 3 Motor Launches

Six miles to the east, 168th Combat Team (Colonel John W. O'Daniel), consisting of 4,355 Americans and 1,065 British (with part of 1st Commando and all 6th Commando, British and American, attached), landed at beaches Beer Green, White and Red. First Commando took Fort de Sidi Ferruch without any resistance on the part of its garrison; General Mast welcomed the invaders and formally surrendered the position and its batteries to Lieutenant Colonel Trevor, British commander of the detachment. The 6th Commando was delayed waiting for its boats (from other ships) to come alongside. Some units did not reach the beach, Beer Red, until 5 hours after H-Hour, and they did not reach and surround their objective, Fort Duperré, until 0815. There was some resistance, and not until a dive-bombing attack by Albacores during the afternoon, followed by an infantry attack, did the fort, with 3 7.5-inchers, surrender. The 168th's landing ran into trouble also. The motor launch could not find the beacon submarine to take off the pilot, and landing craft with elements of each battalion were soon scattered over 15 miles of beach—some landing in Apple Sector of 11th Infantry Brigade. The submarine duly moved inshore and sent her pilot in with a wave of landing craft, most of them successfully reaching Beer Green. Tank-landing craft were scarce, which delayed the landing of vehicles, heavy equipment, and weapons. There was a heavy swell at the beaches, and Beer White was soon closed while Beer Green was badly congested. To add to the difficulties, many radio sets had been damaged in the landings, and it was hard to make a co-ordinated advance. Despite this, elements made their way toward La Bouzaréa and Lambiridi against sporadic resistance.

By noon elements of all three battalions were on the outskirts of Lambiridi, but resistance was encountered as the leading company reached the center of the town, and fighting continued throughout the afternoon. The 1st Battalion's Colonel E. J. Doyle, with some 25 men, penetrated Algiers itself, captured the Palais d'Eté, and started to seize the police station when the colonel was killed by sniper fire. Other units bypassed Lambiridi and reached Fort l'Empereur. The attackers, about 100 men all told, felt it wiser to wait for reinforcements, and an assault was planned for the next morning. That the advances were contested at all was due to events in Algiers, of which more later.

The capture of Blida airfield had been assigned as only a secondary role to elements of 11th Infan-

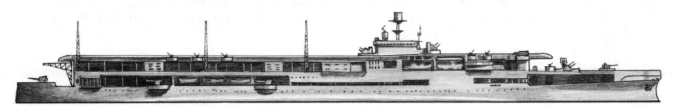

Furious (Br.) Aircraft Carrier. Designed as 18″ gun armored cruiser.

Launched 1916. Several extensive alterations 1917–18, 1921–25, 1939.
Displacement: 22,450 tons. LOA: 786′. Beam: 90′. Draft: 22′.
Four screws. 90,000 hp=31 knots.
Armament: Twelve 4.5″ dual purpose, eight multiple pom-poms, twenty-two small.
Aircraft: 33.
Armored decks and belt (up to 3″).
Complement: with air crews, c. 1,200.

try Brigade. The field was held by forces under command of pro-Allies Brigadier General de Monsabert, and the air commander there would obey his orders (at least early in the morning). But it was necessary to act quickly, in case the situation at headquarters in Algiers changed, and Mast was anxious to rush Allied troops to Blida as soon as possible. He persuaded Colonel Trevor to lead a detachment of 1st Commando there and even provided French military transport.

The French air commander had by now received orders not to surrender the field. Aircraft of the Fleet Air Arm had been patrolling the airfields since daybreak, and when about 0830 a flight of Martlets from H.M.S. *Victorious*, seeing white handkerchiefs fluttering on the field, landed, their leader (Lieutenant B. Nation) received a written agreement from the French Commanding Officer that Allied aircraft might land (but not take off). Thus when Colonel Trevor arrived at about 0900 the field was officially closed. Arrival during the morning of most of 2nd Battalion Lancashire Fusiliers ensured the continued neutralization of the field.

By afternoon elements of 11th Infantry Brigade were in the outskirts of Algiers and the forces landed west of the city had finally achieved their objectives, short of taking the city itself. Slowness in disembarking, confusion at the beaches, and shortage of landing craft (especially of those capable of handling tanks and vehicles) had set the operation far behind schedule, with grave consequences to the plans of the pro-Allies group in the city.

As at Oran an attempt was made to enter the harbor, seize ships and port facilities, and prevent sabotage. Operation "Terminal" called for the landing in the harbor of teams from two veteran British destroyers, H.M.S. *Malcolm* and H.M.S. *Broke*. The force included 662 Americans of 2nd Battalion, 135th Infantry Regiment, 74 Royal Navy personnel,

British Fairey Albacore, Fairey Aviation Co., Ltd. Torpedo-bomber. Updated version of the Swordfish.

Span: 50′. Length: 39′9½″. Hp: 1,065–1,130.
Speed: max. 160 mph at 4,500′. Range: 930 miles.
Armament: three .303 cal. machine guns, one 18″ (1,610 lbs.) torpedo or 2,000 lbs. of bombs. In operational service: 1940–44.

and three British Army officers, all under Lieutenant Colonel Edwin T. Swenson, U.S.A. The defenses were too strong for a surprise attack to succeed, and it was believed that by the time (about 0400) that the ships entered the harbor the coastal batteries might have fallen to commandos and the attention of the defenders might be diverted elsewhere. Hopefully, each vessel flew large American flags.

Any chance of an unopposed entry was dispelled as the ships neared the opening between the sea wall and the shore jetties. The city lights went out, the searchlights came on, and as they picked up the two vessels, shells fell close aboard. The dazzling glare of the lights and blinding gun flashes made navigation difficult, and both vessels missed the entrance. Circling, *Malcolm* was hit in the engine room, a fire was started on deck, and she was forced to sheer off, with 10 dead and 25 wounded. *Broke* finally smashed through the boom at top speed and moored alongside the mole. Her landing party had come through the ordeal without casualties and by about 0530 were ashore and taking possession of the power station, the oil tank farm, and the street paralleling the waterfront. Resistance was slight, and it was hoped that American forces would even then be entering the outskirts of the city. Two delegations of police and civilians requested that arrangements be made for the surrender of Algiers to the Americans but at the same time warned of the approach of hostile troops (some companies of Senegalese).

By now the pro-Vichy forces at headquarters had the upper hand, and resistance stiffened. Fire from the northernmost jetty forced *Broke* to change her moorings twice; finally a howitzer ranged in on her and she sustained a series of hits and near misses. It was time to go, and her siren sounded the recall. Some 60 men nearby responded but Swenson, believing he could hold out until the arrival of the 168th Combat Team and that his men were safer ashore than afloat, decided to stay. At 1030 *Broke* steamed slowly out, partially hidden by a smoke screen and covered by fire from the destroyer H.M.S. *Zetland*. *Zetland* afterward took aboard *Broke*'s passengers and took *Broke* in tow for Gibraltar, but she sank the next day in rough weather.

Swenson's remaining force held off the Senegalese while Albacores dive-bombed the batteries at the northern end of the harbor. But ammunition was running low; no American troops from outside had arrived; at about 1130 the appearance of sev-eral French light tanks and armored cars marked the beginning of the end, and at 1230 Swenson surrendered. For one reason or another the port's defenders made no attempt to sabotage the installations. Like "Reservists" at Oran, "Terminal" was a risky operation. Had the invaders been on time and able to advance rapidly from the beaches it might have succeeded. As it was, casualties were light; of the landing party, 15 were killed and 33 were wounded. *Broke* lost 9 dead and 18 wounded, and *Malcolm* 4 wounded.

ALGIERS EASTERN LANDING GROUP
(Partly formed from Eastern Naval Task Force)
4 Combat Loaders (U.S.)
1 Landing Ship Infantry
1 AA Ship
3 Mechanical Transport Ships
2 Destroyers
1 Sloop
2 Corvettes
4 Minesweepers
2 A/S Trawlers
2 Motor Launches

At the eastern beaches the American 39th Combat Team (5,688 men) and 312 men of 1st Commando (198 British, 114 American), Major K. R. S. Trevor (British), all under Colonel Benjamin F. Caffey, Jr., landed from four combat loaders: *Samuel Chase, Leedstown, Almaack,* and *Exceller.* The *Thomas Stone,* best trained in amphibious operations, was under tow (as noted above) and her troops were on their perilous voyage in their landing craft. Her boats and 1,400 assault troops were to be badly missed. The battery of 4 7.5-inch guns on Cap Matifou (Batterie du Lazaret) left the transports alone and concentrated instead on destroyers H.M.S. *Cowdray* and *Zetland*. These promptly replied and temporarily silenced the battery at about 0400. Later cruiser H.M.S. *Bermuda* effectively took both these guns and those at Fort d'Estrées under fire.

There were the usual delays and mishaps, but the first waves were on the "Charlie" beaches (not all, of course, on the right ones) shortly after H-Hour. The sea was calm at the outset, but inexperienced crews caused unnecessary loss of all-too-scarce landing craft; some were stranded, some sunk through premature opening of landing ramps or overloading, and, as the sea made up, others broached.

Trevor's commandos landed (two hours late) on the westernmost beach—Beach Green—and moved west toward Cap Matifou. The village of Jean Bart and the signal station and barracks near Fort d'Estrées were soon taken, but Batterie du Lazaret and the fort refused to surrender. The force was too small for an assault with available weaponry, and naval gunfire was requested. H.M.S. *Zetland* obliged at 1040, but her 6 4-inchers proved too light for the job, and around 1430 shells from *Bermuda* and bombs from Albacores off H.M.S. *Formidable* pounded the area. Shortly after 1600 the commandos, supported by a 105mm SP gun, attacked, and the battery surrendered at 1700. Half an hour later an assault was made on Fort d'Estrées but was repulsed, and the attack was broken off at 2000.

An advance along the coast road by 3rd Battalion, 39th Infantry was stopped at Fort de l'Eau by French infantry and three tanks. The important field at Maison Blanche was to be taken by 1st Battalion, 39th Infantry before daylight. The supporting 105mms and AT guns could not be maneuvered up the steep bluffs behind the beaches in time to support the advance, but the battalion proceeded without them. After a swift 10-mile march the field was reached at 0615. French tanks put up a token resistance then withdrew, and the field was officially surrendered at 0830. At Gibraltar Air Marshal Welsh, without waiting for news of the field's capture (which had been planned for 0730), took the risk of sending off the first R.A.F. fighters, although fuel did not permit a return if things went wrong. The Hurricanes of 43 Squadron took off at 0800 and landed at 1000. Spitfires of 81 Squadron followed two hours later, with two more squadrons of Spitfires following in the afternoon. Unfortunately the rapidly rising swells and surf at the beaches played havoc with the landing craft carrying R.A.F. ground crews and supply units and their vehicles, and in consequence the field could not be used at anything like expected efficiency. But despite lack of fuel and maintenance some aircraft managed to get aloft over Algiers and Cap Matifou by late afternoon. Lacking radio equipment, a Walrus amphibian of Fleet Air Arm was flown into the field and used to transmit messages to Gibraltar via the headquarters ship *Bulolo*.

In the city itself there was great confusion and uncertainty. At about 0030 the irregular forces of the French resistance began to occupy strategic centers. The police headquarters and other stations were soon under their control as were the telephone system and the Algiers radio station. The Algiers garrison was temporarily immobilized and guides went to the beaches to help hasten the arrival of American troops into the city. The city was virtually in pro-Allied hands until after 0700, long after the expected time of arrival of the invasion forces. General Giraud was expected (at the Blida airfield), but when he had not arrived by 0700 (he was still sulking at Gibraltar) an appeal was broadcast in his name. As time went by without the appearance of either Giraud or the Americans, control began to slip from the hands of the pro-Allied forces. Sniping began, and there were casualties in the ranks of the French resistance and their Army supporters.

As the first waves of landing craft were on their way to the beaches, Murphy called on Juin at his official residence in Lambiridi to inform him that the invasion was minutes away. Juin, who had warned Murphy that he was under orders to resist, now insisted that the American invitation to cooperate under the leadership of Giraud must be submitted to Darlan, as Commander-in-Chief of the Armed Forces. Darlan, who was in Algiers at the bedside of his son, stricken with polio, was brought at short notice to Juin's villa. His first reaction was surprise and anger that he had not been notified sooner. He then stated that he would agree to negotiate but only if Pétain assented and no "rebel Frenchmen" (in which he included Giraud) should interpose between him and the Americans. A radio message to Vichy was drafted but while he, Juin, and Murphy were awaiting the reply, Gardes Mobiles drove off the pro-Allied guards surrounding the villa. The tables were now turned. Murphy was put under house arrest and Darlan and Juin drove to Fort l'Empereur, where Juin set about regaining control. General Koeltz, commanding the region, who had been arrested, was released and relieved Mast of command of the Algiers Division. He was replaced by General Toubertie, with orders to maintain "elastic but nonaggressive" contact with the American troops.

Marshal Pétain was handed President Roosevelt's message (stating that "Germany and Italy intend to invade and occupy French North Africa," consequently "the intervention of American armed forces had been decided upon") by the American Chargé d'Affaires at Vichy, Mr. S. Pinkney Tuck, just after 0900 on November 8. The reply, already prepared, was signed by the Marshal and given to Tuck. As was to be expected, this attack on the French Em-

"TORCH" LANDING OPERATIONS

	SAFI	FEDALA	PORT LYAUTEY
November 8	0438—French batteries at Safi open fire 0445—First U.S. troops ashore in Morocco land in Safi Harbor 0530—French driven from dock area at Safi 0850—Batterie Railleuse silenced at Safi 1600—Beachhead secured at Safi	0500—First waves ashore at Fedala 0604—French batteries open fire at Fedala 0700—*Massachusetts* and *Jean Bart* exchange fire at Casablanca 0750—Troops occupy Sherki battery at Fedala 1000—Naval battle begins off Casablanca; *Fougueux, Boulonnais* sunk 1200—Batterie Du Port captured at Fedala	0540—First landings at Mehdia
November 9	1700—French from Marrakech clash with U.S. troops east of Bou Guedra		0640—Tank battle south of Mehdia
November 9–10			U.S. night attacks around Port Lyautey airfield; French resistance slackens
November 10	c. 1900—CC "B" starts from Safi toward Casablanca. c. 1900—Darlan's orders for cease-fire received in Morocco	c. 1900—Darlan's orders for cease-fire received in Morocco	0730—*Dallas* steams up Sebou, reaches Port Lyautey airfield 1030—Kasba surrenders; U.S. aircraft land on airfield c. 1900—Darlan's orders for cease-fire received in Morocco
November 11	0600—Mazagan entered	0730—Cease-fire agreement; final attack on Casablanca averted 1400—U.S.-French leaders negotiate an armistice at Casablanca	0400—Fighting ends at Port Lyautey

pire was to be resisted, and later in the day diplomatic relations with the United States were broken off.

The Marshal's reply to Darlan's report was an authorization to act on his behalf and expressing complete confidence. This left the admiral with several options. He chose to be realistic, and allowed Juin to persuade him to negotiate a cease-fire for Algiers and vicinity. As bugles repeated the command from post to post the sporadic firing died away, giving way to an uneasy truce. It was not until around 1600 that one of Murphy's staff lo-

cated General Ryder, commander of the Eastern Assault Force, with news that Juin was ready to negotiate. Passed through the French lines, Ryder met with Juin at Fort l'Empereur and agreed to a cease-fire at 1840 on November 8—control of the city to pass to American hands at 2000. A formal armistice was to be discussed next morning. At a later meeting that night Darlan gave permission for the Eastern Task Force to begin using Algiers Harbor at dawn of November 9.

Ryder reported the arrangements to Gibraltar and asked Eisenhower for permission to conclude

	ORAN	ALGIERS	MISC.
November 8	0100—H-Hour for Center Forces 0300—*Walney* and *Hartland* approach entrance to Oran Harbor 0715—*La Surprise* sunk off Oran 0740—Advance on Oran halted by artillery and small arms fire 1200—Tafaraoui Airfield secured 1400—La Macta secured 1530—U.S. attacks held at St. Cloud 1630—Two squadrons of Spitfires from Gibraltar land at Tafaraoui	0100—H-Hour for Eastern Task Forces 0300—French Resistance takes control of strategic points in Algiers 0400—*Broke* and *Malcolm* approach entrance to Algiers Harbor 0530—Troops go ashore from *Broke* in Algiers Harbor 0830—F.A.A. Martlets land at Blida 0830—Maison Blanche officially surrendered 1000—First Spitfires land on Maison Blanche from Gibraltar 1030—*Broke* leaves Algiers Harbor 1230—Colonel Swenson surrenders troops in Algiers Harbor 1430—Fort Duperré taken. c. 1500—U.S. troops in outskirts of Algiers 1600—Ryder informed that Juin seeks truce 1700—Batterie du Lazaret taken 1735—Attack on Fort d'Estrées beaten off 1840—Ryder and Juin meet—agree to truce 2000—Control of Algiers passes to Americans	
November 9	0600—French counter-attack at La Macta 1000—La Sénia Airfield secured	0700—Allied ships begin to enter Algiers Harbor 1630—First German air raid—30 Ju 88s and He 111s attack shipping; 4 shot down	

an armistice on mild terms (as previously planned in case of a token resistance). No reply had been received when he met the French in the afternoon of November 9 (Eisenhower complained, "Our radios constantly functioned poorly, sometimes not at all."), so he offered the armistice terms on his own responsibility. The conditions were the same as in Morocco and at Oran—with the same unfortunate results for the pro-Allies.

However, with the principal French leaders now at the conference table and the seat of government for all French North Africa in Allied control, it was obviously essential to see that the cease-fire arrangements at Algiers were now extended to the rest of Algeria and Morocco—where fighting was still going on—and to ensure active French cooperation in an advance into Tunisia. The narrative of events so far related has embraced such large and widely scattered areas that a short chronology may be in order.

Early on November 9 General Giraud arrived by air from Gibraltar. His reception was chilly. Darlan refused to see him. Giraud's name obviously had no magic in it for the vast majority of Frenchmen. His radio broadcast, announcing his assumption of leadership of French North Africa and ordering a universal cease-fire, fell on deaf ears. It was, in Eisenhower's words, "a terrific blow to our expectations." But if Giraud's name meant nothing, Darlan's meant everything. Darlan was obviously the man to deal with—although this inevitably meant a storm of criticism from well-meaning people in England and America to whom the idea of doing business with a Vichyite—and the second most powerful man in the government at that—was abhorrent. Clark had arrived with Giraud (who now vanished temporarily from the scene), and Eisenhower was soon informed that nothing could be accomplished without Darlan's co-operation. Pétain was the avowed leader of the French, and the French authorities, civil and military, would do nothing toward ordering a general cease-fire or aiding in expelling the Axis troops even then arriving in Tunisia without a legal order—that is, either from Pétain or his deputy in North Africa.

On the evening of November 9 Clark and Murphy met with Juin and Darlan. A note was handed Darlan outlining armistice conditions. He agreed to meet them again next morning. Clark was understandably impatient—delay meant continued fighting at Oran and in Morocco—while the Axis was getting ready for full-scale intervention in Tunisia. That night Juin saw Giraud, and both agreed that only through Darlan could anything be accomplished. The meeting began at 0900 on November 10. It was a stormy one, with Darlan evasive—saying he agreed personally with the armistice terms but must have Pétain's approval, and Clark angry at the delay and refusing to deal with Vichy—which had just broken off diplomatic relations with his government. Clark, tired of the shilly-shallying, tried the direct approach. If Darlan refused to sign, then he would be held in custody and the Americans would treat with Giraud. In the heated arguments Juin played a conciliatory role—knowing that his control over his forces must ultimately depend on the authority from his commander-in-chief, while at the same time trying to make the impatient American general see the necessity for the legal chain of command so dear to the French military. Darlan at last agreed, and drafted an order in Pétain's name to all forces in French North Africa to cease opposition to the Americans.

This ended the fighting but left the question of French co-operation against the Axis up in the air. Nor did the events of the next few days clarify the issue. Pétain, it seems, approved of the agreement, but under pressure from Pierre Laval—who was about to meet with Hitler and Ciano—the aged Marshal disavowed Darlan's actions. Darlan then informed Clark that he was powerless to treat with him further and he considered himself Clark's prisoner. There seems no doubt that the old warrior in Vichy retracted his disavowal of Darlan a few hours later and so notified Darlan in a message in a cypher known only to Darlan and Admiral Auphan, Minister of Marine.

Hitler was also tired of French lack of co-operation. After informing the Germans that airfields in Tunisia were open to them, the French then qualified this by insisting that no Italians be allowed in Tunisia. Hitler demanded full collaboration in Tunisia with both Axis partners, and when the shifty Laval temporized, saying only Pétain could make such a decision, orders went out for the occupation of Vichy France, and at midnight November 10–11 some 10 German divisions roared across the demarcation line, while 6 Italian divisions moved into eastern France.

Darlan now commanded Juin to order resistance to Axis landings in Tunisia by ground and air forces. But Pétain, presumably at Laval's insistence, now made public his earlier disavowal of Darlan and transferred authority to Noguès. In Tunisia the conflicting orders—from Juin and Vichy—caused great confusion. It was believed there that Darlan and Juin were American prisoners, and the orders to resist the Axis were questioned and in cases disobeyed. To Clark this seemed like double-dealing on the part of Darlan and Juin—and Clark's anger with the delays and procrastination was in no way abated by Darlan's and Giraud's (when the two finally met) opinion that nothing could be done until Noguès arrived from Morocco. Precious time was wasting—and the French commanders still demanded the legal chain-of-command approach. The Marshal—and it must have seemed to the angry and impatient Americans and British that in French eyes the ancient hero of Verdun outranked God himself—had vested his mantle on Noguès, and there it rested.

Noguès did not arrive in Algiers until November 12, and it was not until the next day that Clark, after meeting with Eisenhower (who arrived on November 13 with Cunningham for a few hours to get a firsthand account of affairs), managed to wangle an agreement; Darlan was to be High Commissioner and naval Commander-in-Chief, while Giraud would be Commander-in-Chief of ground and air forces. Juin was to command in the East (Algeria and Tunisia), while Noguès retained his role (and an effective one) as Resident General of Morocco and Commander in the West. All French resources would be directed to aiding the Allies in clearing the Axis out of Tunisia, and ultimately out of Metropolitan France.

As had been anticipated, the necessary (from the military point of view) expedient of incorporating Darlan into a working agreement with the French and Allied officials for prosecuting the war against the Axis met with general disapproval in America and England and bitter reaction from the Fighting French. Eisenhower, with his customary straightforward approach to things political, refused to be swayed by adverse criticism and held to his pragmatic opinion, believing (quite rightly, under the circumstances) that the end justified the means. The end in this case meant French co-operation against the Axis, the closing of Tunisian ports and airfields to German and Italian aircraft, and hopefully the acquisition of the powerful French naval forces based at Toulon. It was a high stake to gamble for, and had it succeeded, would have paid off handsomely in lives, ships, and equipment of all kinds. But too much time had already been wasted. Conflicting orders from Vichy and Algiers; the reluctance of many professional soldiers to take any initiative that might adversely affect their careers ("blotting their copybooks," as the British say); conservatism (often to the point of pro-fascism) on the part of some officers, who blamed the defeats of 1940 on the liberals and left-wingers; fear of Axis reprisals against the helpless French at home; and above all the swiftness with which the Germans presented the confused French military leaders in Tunisia with a *fait accompli* resulted in an almost unopposed Axis takeover in Tunisia—its ports, facilities, and airfields.

Anglo-American leaders might bitterly question the Gallic logic that prompted the French to oppose with arms landings by Americans (whom presumably, they liked) while allowing an uncontested occupation by Germans and Italians (whom, presumably, they detested). But allow it they did—with dire results.

The announcement by Vichy on November 9 that airfields in Tunisia and the Department of Constantine (eastern Algeria) would be made available to the Luftwaffe permitted the arrival of German liaison officers, and by afternoon of November 9, fighters, bombers, and transports began landing at El Aouïna, near Tunis. German paratroopers and Kesselring's headquarters guard were among those landed. They were confined to the field by French troops, but the Commanding Officer of Fliegerkorps II (General der Flieger Bruno Loerzer) was passed through the French cordon to obtain from Admiral Estéva guarantees of passive reception of German forces in any part of Tunisia. The admiral still held to Vichy's "no Italians" demands; nevertheless, on the morning of November 10 a flight of 28 Italian fighters arrived.

Along with the Axis move into Vichy France in the early hours of November 11 came a directive for the occupation of Tunisia. This was to be a strong force, ostensibly to "protect" the French from the Anglo-American invaders and to transport and supply it, all available sea and air transport was temporarily to be diverted from supplying the Afrika Korps. The Tunisian Division was to be disarmed in the event it proved to have pro-Allies leanings. The French fleet was to remain at Toulon.

The occupation of Vichy France and Corsica (by the Italians) failed to rouse any opposition in the French Tunisian command. The Axis airlift continued and on November 12 the first Axis ships arrived, 2 transports and 5 destroyers with 1,000 Italian troops and 1,800 tons of supplies. By the end of November the airlift alone brought in a total of 15,273 men and 581 tons of supplies. By the same date 28 shiploads had brought in 1,867 men, 159 tanks (a few of them the 88mm "Tigers"), and armored cars, 127 guns, 1,097 vehicles, and 12,549 tons of supplies. The immediate occupation of all Tunisia was not contemplated. The front, at least at first, was to be kept short, on defensible terrain and a reasonable distance from the principal supply ports. The air strength was to be built up rapidly to gain local air superiority. The reinforcement of Fliegerkorps II in Sicily had in fact begun in October—partly because of the British preparations for their offensive at El Alamein and also as reports came in of increased shipping and air activity at Gibraltar. By November 10, operational strength in Sicily was 455 aircraft—from 283 the previous month—while air transports rose from 205 to 673. On November 15 an estimated 81 fighters and 28 dive bombers were in Tunisia. Some of the fighters were the formidable FW 190s—generally superior to any Allied fighter aircraft.

Neither Admirals Estéva nor Derrien (the naval commander) did anything to oppose the Axis invaders. General Barré, on the other hand, while obeying Vichy's orders not to oppose the invaders, withdrew the bulk of his forces (over 9,000 men, but with little artillery) westward, while still maintaining a show of correct relations with the Axis commanders.

With the Allies ashore in strength in Morocco and Algeria, and the Axis establishing a firm bridgehead in Tunisia, the chapters on the "Torch" landings end. The results had in some respects been spectacular. The two westernmost of the French North African possessions had fallen, at a cost of some 2,000 dead (about evenly divided between British and Americans) and a slightly larger number of wounded. In other ways it was a disappointment. Tunisia had not been taken, and the campaigns for that colony were to take another six months, with a price tag of over 80,000 American, French, and British dead, wounded, and missing. With a little more daring—and several of the Allied leaders were in favor of landing at Bizerte, Admiral Cunningham among them—it is possible that the campaign in Tunisia would have been unnecessary. Or if the French in Tunisia had resisted the Axis with the same determination they displayed at Casablanca against the Americans. More "ifs," which make for interesting speculation—but not history.

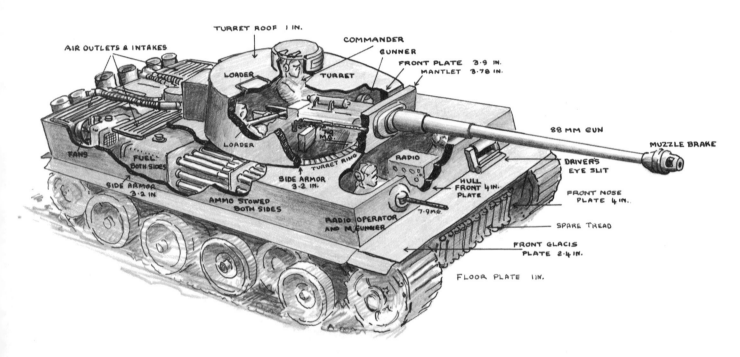

Pz Kw VI Tiger I (E)

Weight: 55 tons. Length: 20.35'. Width: 12.24'. Height: 9.38'.
Armament: one 8.8 cm. KWK 36 L/56 gun, two 7.9 machine guns. Armor: as shown.
Hp: 700. Speed: road 23 mph. Crew: 5.
   First German combat tank with overlapping wheel suspension. Eight independently sprung torsion bar axles per side. Combat track was 28" wide. A narrower 20–25" track was used for travel, with the outer wheels removed. The first 495 produced had Snorkel attachments allowing river crossing to a depth of 15'. Subsequent numbers could wade to a depth of 4'.

V

Too Little and Too Late

With Algeria under nominal Anglo-American control, the pressing need was to push eastward as rapidly as possible with the hope of seizing the ports of Bizerte and Tunis before the Axis forces made their bridgehead secure. The original plan, based on total French co-operation, was for parachute troops and commandos to seize the airfields at Bône, Bizerte, and Tunis on November 11, 12, and 13, respectively. The attitude of the French precluded such an operation, and at 1600 on November 10, a convoy of 5 cargo ships and 10 warships left Algiers for Bougie. A fast convoy of 4 R.N. Landing Ships, Infantry: *Karanja, Awatae, Marnix,* and *Cathay*—and six warships followed at 1830, carrying the 36th Infantry Brigade Group (British). The troop convoy, overtaking the slow

convoy en route, arrived off Cap Carbon at 0430 on November 11. The landings near Bougie were unopposed, but heavy surf frustrated a landing near Djidjelli (to seize the airfield there), and these troops were disembarked in the sheltered bay at Bougie. At the same time a small mobile column ("Hart Force") set out by road from Algiers with Bône as its destination. The failure to take the field at Djidjelli left the shipping at Bougie without cover except for aircraft operating from Maison Blanche, more than 100 miles to the westward. The carrier H.M.S. *Argus* had flown air support for the landings but it was not considered wise to risk her so far east, and she was ordered back to Algiers.

German air raids in the afternoon of the eleventh did no damage, but a heavy attack at dusk sank

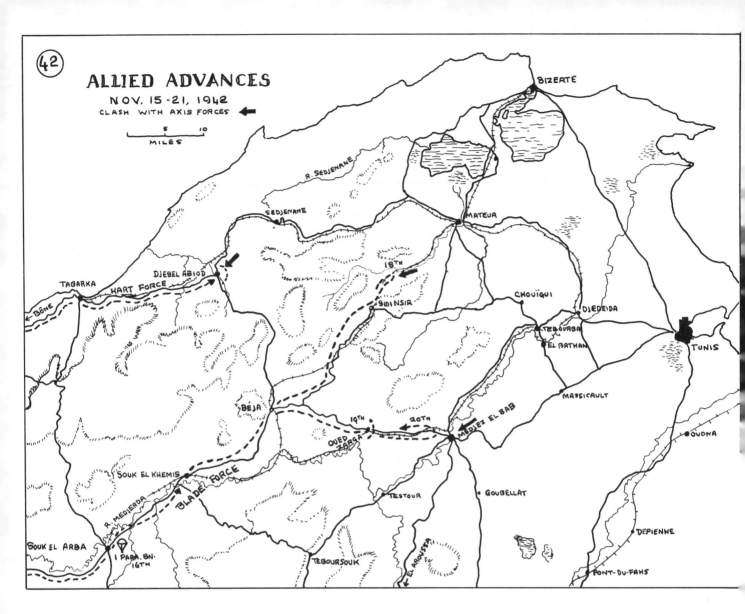

ALLIED ADVANCES

NOV. 15-21, 1942
CLASH WITH AXIS FORCES ←

5   10
MILES

(Map labels: BIZERTE, R. SEDJENANE, SEDJENANE, MATEUR, CHOUIGUI, DJEDEIDA, TABARKA, DJEBEL ABIOD, HART FORCE, SIDI NSIR, 18TH, TEBOURBA, EL BATHAN, TUNIS, BÔNE, BEJA, MASSICAULT, OUDNA, 19TH, 20TH, OUED ZARGA, MEDJEZ EL BAB, SOUK EL KHEMIS, BLADE FORCE, R. MEDJERDA, TESTOUR, GOUBELLAT, DEPIENNE, SOUK EL ARBA, 1 PARA. BN. 16TH, TEBOURSOUK, EL AROUSSA, PONT-DU-FAHS)

Awatae and *Cathay* and damaged the monitor
H.M.S. *Roberts.* Just before dawn the AA ship
H.M.S. *Tynwald* was sunk, and shortly afterward
Karanja was set on fire and sunk. In the meantime
the field at Djidjelli had been occupied, but lack
of fuel grounded the Spitfires there, and it was not
until November 13 that there was active air opposition to Axis attacks.

An air assault on November 12 by two companies (312 men) of British 3rd Parachute Battalion and simultaneous landings by part of 6th Commando from two destroyers secured the airfield
and port of Bône, 125 miles to the east of Bougie.
AA equipment, maintenance crews, fuel, etc., were
flown in, and by November 14 two squadrons of
Spitfires were operating from the field. Also, on
November 12, a reinforced battalion of the Argyll
and Sutherland Highlanders occupied the town and
airfield at Sétif. Bône was an important objective,
with accommodations for docking some two dozen

ships and railroad connection to the main Algiers–
Tunis line. Bône also became an important target
for Axis bombers.

The British First Army (it was one in name
only; an incomplete division [the 78th] part of an
armored division, some parachutists, commandos,
and an AA brigade) commenced a forward movement on November 14 (the day the first follow-up
troops finished disembarking at Algiers). It was
Anderson's hope that by forcing the pace he might
yet forestall a sizable Axis buildup and reach
Bizerte and Tunis before it was too late. "Blade
Force," an armored regimental group of 6th Armored Division, with advance elements of 11th Infantry Brigade Group, was ordered to advance
through Souk Ahras to Souk el Arba. The 1st (British) Parachute Battalion, in U.S. transports and escorted by U.S. fighters, dropped on the airfield at
Souk el Arba on November 16. French troops were
both friendly and helpful. The previous day 2nd

Battalion, 509th U. S. Parachute Regiment (Colonel E. D. Raff), escorted by R.A.F. Spitfires, dropped unopposed at Youks-les-Bains. Part of the force then proceeded to Tébessa.

In the North "Hart Force" reached Tabarka on November 15, followed a day later by part of 36th Infantry Brigade. "Hart Force" pushed on to Djebel Abiod on the night of November 15–16 and a liaison officer from 36th Infantry Brigade made contact with General Barré at Béja. His force of some 10,000 men and half-dozen guns were in several groups—with orders from Giraud to cover the British concentrations from Teboursouk north. General Koeltz, with the XIX Corps—(the Constantine Division and the Algerian Division [not yet arrived])—was to do the same from Souk el Arba south. As the British units moved eastward from Bougie, Sétif, and Djidjelli, they were replaced by elements of the 34th Infantry Division from Algiers.

The Axis forces necessarily arrived in Tunisia in bits and pieces—at first by air alone. The arrival of the first vessels at Bizerte on November 12, with 17 tanks, 4 guns, trucks, fuel, and ammunition, provided a little weight while troops continued to be airlifted in at the rate of some 750 per day. The command of the rapidly increasing German force went to General Nehring, recovered from his wounds received in the Western Desert at Alam el Halfa. His headquarters (designated XC Corps) began modestly, with a complement of 2—the general, one staff officer, and a French taxicab for transport. A state of complete confusion was recorded, with "no means of communication other than the French postal network." Teutonic efficiency soon asserted itself, and two bridgeheads, one at Bizerte and one at Tunis, were firmly established, and one of the familiar, and effective, battle groups was scraped together and assembled at Mateur. True to his Afrika Korps training, Nehring believed the best defense to be attack, and on November 17 he ordered Battle Group Witzig westward from Mateur toward Tabarka.

At the same time, Italian troops, mainly the Superga Division under General Lorenzelli, were coming in as fast as transport became available, and later Lorenzelli took over much of the southern front. Sousse, Sfax, and Gabès were occupied, securing a line that ultimately became Rommel's supply route.

The advance of Battle Group Witzig produced the first action on the ground, near Djebel Abiod. A patrol of "Hart Force" reported tanks and mechanized infantry approaching from the direction of Mateur. These were engaged by leading elements of 36th Infantry Brigade at 1430 on November 17. The Axis column retired as darkness fell, having lost 8 tanks. British casualties were considerable, with several guns and vehicles destroyed or damaged. Sporadic fighting went on for the next two days—with little advantage to either side.

A German reconnaissance force of light and heavy armored cars sent from Mateur toward Béja was ambushed and wiped out near Sidi Nsir by a patrol of the British 1st Parachute Battalion on November 18. Advance elements of "Blade Force" had passed through Oued Zarga on November 18—and a few units of "Blade Force," including the 175th American Field Artillery Battalion, had reached Medjez el Bab on the night of November 18–19. Some of Barré's French were holding that important road junction. An order by General Nehring to allow passage to an Axis force from Tunis was ignored, and at 0900 on November 19 the Germans broke off their attempts to negotiate and ordered an advance. Despite heavy Axis air attacks two light German assaults were repulsed, but as no reinforcements were available and ammunition was running low, the town was abandoned during the night and a new defense line set up some three miles east of Oued Zarga. The Germans had won an easy victory, but more important than the temporary loss to the Allies of the town and the bridge over the Medjerda was the fact that French troops were at last actively opposing the Axis.

On November 21 an Italian patrol moving toward Béja by way of Sidi Nsir was driven off by the French with the loss of 4 tanks, while on November 23 a German probe toward El Aroussa was thrown back by Allied infantry and some British tanks.

Far to the south, Colonel E. D. Raff's 2nd Battalion, U. S. 509th Parachute Infantry, with attached units (named the Tunisian Task Force) co-operating with the French, had the task of watching the passes and roads in the area Tébessa–Kasserine–Sbeitla–Gafsa.

On November 20 a mixed French and American garrison (a French command and a small detachment of Colonel Raff's 2nd Battalion, 509th Parachute Regiment) at Gafsa retired before the advance of an Italian motorized column from Gabès. Two days later the Allied force, slightly reinforced, returned, and, driving out a few German airborne troops, met the advancing Italians near El Guettar. The Italians were sent hurrying back toward Gabès, but at Sbeitla a German armored column drove out the French garrison on November 22. When the German column started back to Tunis they left an Italian force in Sbeitla. These were attacked by a detachment of Colonel Raff's parachutists and some French and in turn the Italians were driven out. A strong French force now garrisoned Sbeitla, which was held against an Axis attempt to recapture the place on November 24.

While this skirmishing was taking place in central Tunisia, Anderson was gathering his forces for his attack on Bizerte and Tunis. Major General Vyvyan Evelegh's British 78th Division began to concentrate, in spite of difficulties due to shortage of motor transport and the inadequacy of the French railway system. Occasional ships went directly from the United Kingdom to Bône, but usually men and supplies were transshipped at Algiers into smaller vessels or landing craft. From Bône cargoes went by landing craft to La Calle or Tabarka. These coastal convoys were frequently attacked by air, as the Allied air forces were stretched too thin to provide adequate cover, but losses were small. Air attacks on the ports were numerous, Bône being a favorite target.

To support the still incomplete 78th Division various mobile U.S. units were sent eastward from Oran and Algiers. These included light and medium tanks, tank destroyers, armored infantry, and artillery. The largest formation was CC "B," U.S.

1st Armored Division (Brigadier General L. E. Oliver).

The railhead for the main offensive was at Souk el Arba. The journey by rail from Algiers took four to six days, with a maximum at that time of nine trains a day. Of these, two hauled coal for the locomotives and generating plants, and one necessities for the civilian population. Another railhead was at Tébessa (for the Tunisian Task Force). As noted above, motor transport for the Allied units were far below the normal strength, and even by pressing into service all French transport that could be made to run there was still a serious shortage. Labor at the forward ports and at railheads was also insufficient, with the result that materiel began to pile up.

The shortage of transport also hindered the Allied air effort. Fuel and materiel had to be delivered to the fields, and difficulties in supply adversely affected the number of aircraft operational at any given time. This and the small number of fields available in forward areas told heavily against the Allies at a time when Axis aircraft were operating from airfields often only a few miles from the combat zone. The fields at Souk el Arba were 80 miles from Tunis, at Bône 135 miles, and at Youks-les-Bains 155 miles. The field at Maison Blanche was used by bombers, such as the B-17s of U. S. 97th Bombardment Group, which on November 16

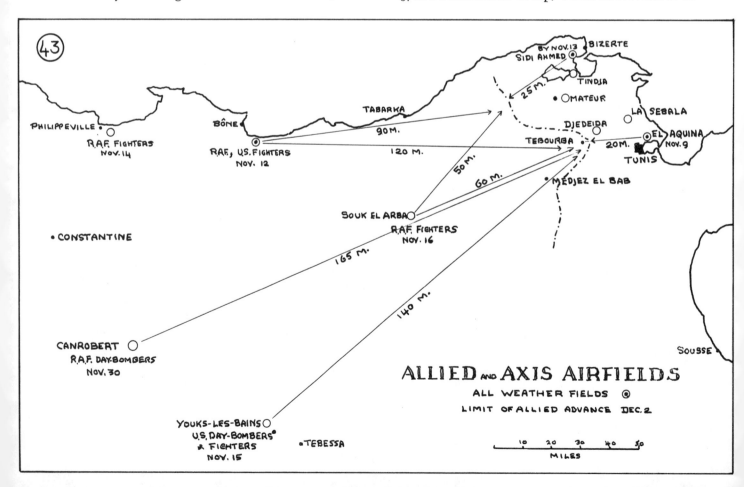

ALLIED and AXIS AIRFIELDS

ALL WEATHER FIELDS ⊚

LIMIT OF ALLIED ADVANCE DEC. 2

Curtis P-40 (R.A.F. Kittyhawk)
Single-seater Fighter

**Span: 37′4″. Length: 33′4″. Engine: 1,325 hp
Merlin Rolls-Royce in line. Speed: max. 373
mph. Armament: six .50 cal. machine guns.
A 170-gallon drop tank was carried for
extended range.**

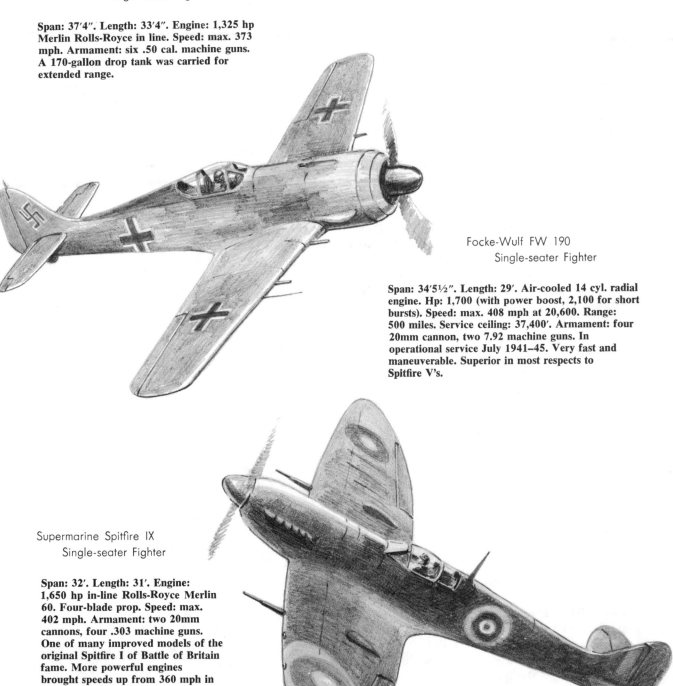

Focke-Wulf FW 190
Single-seater Fighter

**Span: 34′5½″. Length: 29′. Air-cooled 14 cyl. radial
engine. Hp: 1,700 (with power boost, 2,100 for short
bursts). Speed: max. 408 mph at 20,600. Range:
500 miles. Service ceiling: 37,400′. Armament: four
20mm cannon, two 7.92 machine guns. In
operational service July 1941–45. Very fast and
maneuverable. Superior in most respects to
Spitfire V's.**

Supermarine Spitfire IX
Single-seater Fighter

**Span: 32′. Length: 31′. Engine:
1,650 hp in-line Rolls-Royce Merlin
60. Four-blade prop. Speed: max.
402 mph. Armament: two 20mm
cannons, four .303 machine guns.
One of many improved models of the
original Spitfire I of Battle of Britain
fame. More powerful engines
brought speeds up from 360 mph in
MK I to 448 in MK XIV. Armament
varied greatly.**

began raids on the Axis fields at Sidi Ahmed (Bizerte), El Aouïna (Tunis), and the fields near Cagliari (Sardinia). These fields also were targets of Wellingtons from Malta. Blida was used by Bisleys (Bristol Blenheim Mark Vs), and Spitfires were based at Djidjelli. Of the forward fields only Bône was an "all-weather" installation, and as the rainy season approached it was found that the grass or earth runways severely restricted operations. The 2,000-odd tons of steel mat needed to surface one runway would at this time have utilized the entire capacity of the railways for two days.

Demands on the fighter and fighter-bomber squadrons were already heavy. The ports and airfields underwent frequent heavy attacks by the Axis (mostly by the Luftwaffe), and defensive patrols alone engaged much of the Allied strength. It was not surprising that in the coming offensive the Axis fighters and dive bombers, operating from their nearby all-weather fields, often achieved local superiority and gave the unfortunate Allied infantry the impression that the skies belonged almost exclusively to the Luftwaffe. The inefficiency of the old practice, in which large numbers of Allied fighters were tied down in flying patrols over the British ground forces, had led to the abandonment of the "air umbrella" tactic. As laid down by Churchill in his instructions prior to "Crusader," "Nevermore must the troops expect, as a matter of course, to be protected against the air by aircraft." This sound argument had been reinforced by the arrival in the desert of 250 light AA guns.

But the exigencies of the invasion had cut equipment, including light AA weapons, to the minimum. Also, and just as important, the troops were inexperienced, and attack from the air was in many cases demoralizing. Despite the shortage of the larger automatic weapons, many vehicles, particularly U.S. ones, were equipped with a 50-caliber machine gun. A convoy, attacked from the air, could theoretically put up a respectable amount of ground fire. But at first, in too many cases, Allied troops took to the nearest ditch, and the ground strafers and dive bombers had it all their own way. In time good march discipline and battle experience changed this, and Luftwaffe pilots learned that such targets could not be attacked with impunity. The same battle experience held true of the infantry, and later on low-flying Axis aircraft (and often, unfortunately, Allied aircraft too) were liberally sprayed with fire from all available weapons. Until the green troops became seasoned,

however (and also began to receive an adequate number of AA weapons of 20 or 40 mm), Axis air attacks did much damage, inflicted many casualties—and caused disruption often out of proportion to the weight of the attack.

The Allied fighters, as they became available, took the war to the enemy—striking at their airfields, transport, and concentrations. The intensity of their assault in the months to come finally broke the power of the Axis air forces, but in the opening weeks of the battle for Tunis the support given the German ground troops by the Luftwaffe did much to check the Allied advance.

Axis forces at this time amounted to some 15,575 German and 9,000 Italian troops. As noted, the main Italian strength was in the South, so that most of the fighting fell to the Germans. Of combat troops, there were 9 battalions of infantry, an anti-tank battalion, a tank battalion and part of another, a field artillery battalion, about 2½ anti-aircraft battalions (including 20 new dual-purpose 88mms), 2 reconnaissance companies (one with armored cars with 75mm guns), a motorcycle company, and a motorized anti-tank company. In support the Axis Air Commands could muster 4 German fighter groups and an Italian fighter group (Gruppe, equivalent to R.A.F. Wing, of about 30–36 aircraft), a group of dive bombers, and a squadron of short-range reconnaissance aircraft. These were stationed in Tunisia and were backed up by bombers based on Sicily and Sardinia.

The Allied Advance—Medjez el Bab

In spite of the shortages Anderson, who had moved his headquarters from Algiers to near Philippeville on November 19, believed the 78th Division strong enough to advance, and on November 24 he ordered it to seize the line Tebourba–Mateur and from there northwest to the coast. After that Evelegh was to drive for Tunis and Bizerte. The 11th Infantry Brigade was to take Medjez el Bab on November 25, "Blade Force" on their left was to move on the Sidi Nsir–Chouïgui road and take El Bathan and Djedeida, while farther north the 36th Infantry Brigade was to pass through Sedjenane and on to Mateur. The three columns were reinforced with American armored and artillery units.

The initial attack on Medjez el Bab, a three-pronged affair, failed. The reinforced battalion that was to cross the Medjerda River north of the town on the night of November 24–25 was pinned down by heavy mortar and machine-gun fire, and finally dispersed with many casualties by a counter-attack by tanks and infantry. The southern attack seized the heights of Djebel Bou Mouss (Grenadier Hill) but lost it to an armored counter-attack. But the pressure on the Axis troops was strong, and rather than commit more troops, Nehring ordered the town abandoned on the night of November 25–26 (Kesselring later disapproved of this move).

In the North the 36th Infantry Brigade attacked a day late and found no opposition. Advancing cautiously, the brigade made contact west of Djefna on November 28. "Blade Force," with over 100 tanks, advanced at 0700 on November 25 and seized the road junction (see map) south of Mateur shortly after noon. Part of the force (1st British Parachute Battalion) moved north toward Mateur while the rest pushed east, across the Tine River toward the Chouïgui Pass. Here, about two miles northwest of the entrance to the pass, the 1st Battalion, U. S. 1st Armored Regiment (Lieutenant Colonel J. K. Waters), made contact with German parachute engineers and some Italian anti-tank guns. The Axis force retired to a walled French farm ("Coxen's Farm") a couple of miles inside the pass and could not be dislodged. The enemy retired to Mateur during the night. A reconnaissance by Company "C" (Major R. Barlow) advanced down the Tebourba Road, bypassed that place (overrunning Axis patrols), and reached the vicinity of the newly activated airfield at Djedeida unobserved at about sunset. In a rare clash between tanks and aircraft, the 17 tanks of Company "C" roared onto the field, destroyed 20 or more parked aircraft, and shot up the defenders, buildings and supply dumps before retiring westward. This exploit led to false reports to Axis headquarters that Allied forces were within 9 miles of Tunis and did nothing for Nehring's peace of mind. Although Colonel Waters' battalion was withdrawn from Chouïgui Pass before dawn, the alarmed Nehring ordered the retirement of the Axis troops from Djedeida, El Bathan, and St. Cyprien, with the intention of concentrating more of his troops for close-in defense of the Tunis bridgehead. Kesselring advised him to adopt a bolder policy, however, and early on November 26 a small German force of tanks and infantry moved from Mateur toward Tebourba. This force was engaged by Colonel Waters' battalion in the first clash of the war between U.S. and German armor.

When the German force, including 6 Mark IVs with 75mm guns, attacked part of the U.S. M3s (Stuarts) to their front, other Stuarts, concealed in defilade, knocked the 6 Mark IVs and a Mark III

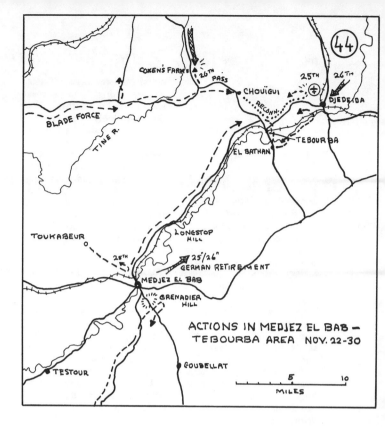

ACTIONS IN MEDJEZ EL BAB – TEBOURBA AREA NOV. 22-30

out at close range from flank and rear. Motorized German infantry arriving at the farm position were destroyed or driven off, while British guns and tanks accounted for at least another Mark III. U.S. losses included 6 M3s. "Coxen's Farm" was then occupied by a company of the 1st British Parachute Battalion.

German forces reoccupied Djedeida on November 26, and the Luftwaffe struck hard at Allied forces—making movement on open ground dangerous. At noon of the same day American tanks and British infantry entered Medjez el Bab; opposition was almost nonexistent, but one span of the important bridge had been destroyed by the retreating Germans. The gap was repaired by a Bailey bridge span during the night, and shortly after midnight of November 26–27 the 1st Battalion, East Surrey Regiment and some artillery took Tebourba. An Axis counter-attack in the morning by battle Group Lüder (which included 2 Tiger tanks) resulted in an all-day battle in the outskirts of the town. At dusk the enemy retired toward Djedeida. Eight of his tanks were destroyed and 4 damaged. The Surreys lost heavily, and all 8 guns of a supporting battery were knocked out. The 5th Battalion, Northamptonshire Regiment, and most of the 2nd Battalion, U. S. 13th Armored Regiment were ordered up from Medjez el Bab. French infantry and American artillery units took over the defenses there.

Guns vs. Armor

The vital importance of armored warfare, as shown by the 1940 *Blitzkreig* in France and Belgium, revived the old "gun versus armor" race that had occupied the minds of naval tacticians and designers from the late nineteenth century to World War II. Improvements in armor were met with guns (usually larger in caliber) throwing shells of better design. In naval vessels this race resulted inevitably in larger vessels, able to carry the huge weapons capable of penetrating the thickest armor, and protected in turn by massive plates of steel. This was true to a degree in tank design, but moving a

metal monster across water is one thing, and across country quite another. The huge, unwieldy vehicles that appeared toward the end of the war in Europe were not universally successful. Besides difficulty of production, shipping and transportation had to be taken into account, and such things as width of railroad tunnels and roads, and capacity of bridges. There were limitations on power, too, and speed and maneuverability over open country had to be taken into account. With the exception of the 55-ton Pz Kw VI "Tiger I," used in limited numbers in Tunisia, the tanks that fought in the desert and in French North Africa were mediums or lights.

Despite the disadvantages, tanks tended to get larger and more powerful as the war went on, but by then the fast plane, armed with cannon, rocket, or bomb, had to be reckoned with.

Even more dangerous was the development of the shaped-charge projectiles, both for artillery and for the new hand-held launchers: the American "Bazooka," the British "PIAT," and the German Panzerfaust. Armed with one of these, a lowly infantryman might (although at fairly close range and at great risk to himself) pierce the armor of the mightiest tank.

Shot or shell? Armor piercing, or AP projectiles (wholly or in part of hardened steel), were of two types. Solid shot relied on the lethal effects of the projectile itself, plus fragments of plate driven through on penetration. Armor piercing shell (AP) contained a small charge of high explosive (HE) and a fuse in the base, which exploded the charge a fraction of a second after entry. This sounds more deadly, but in practice, in the confines of a tank the

shower of white-hot fragments driven in by solid shot was usually sufficient. Whatever advantage the shell had was offset by the weakness of the hollow projectile, the small bursting charge, and the vagaries of the delicate fuse. The British held to this view, and did not bother with shell in small calibers. But small-caliber tank guns firing solid or AP were of little use against infantry or dug-in positions. For such targets a gun capable of firing an HE shell fused to burst on impact or in the air over the target was necessary. Some tanks, designated "infantry" or close-support tanks, were armed with howitzer-type weapons; the short 75mm Pz Kw IV is an example. The 75 mm of the Grant and Sherman could fire both HE or AP (the AP of the former with only moderate effect, owing to the comparatively low velocity). The long 75 of the German

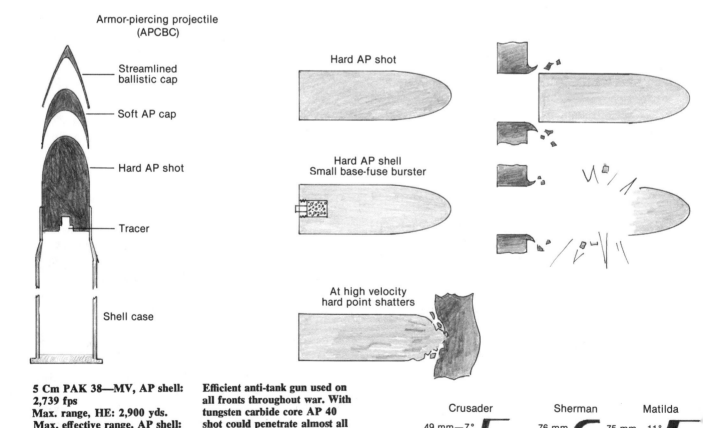

Armor-piercing projectile (APCBC)
- Streamlined ballistic cap
- Soft AP cap
- Hard AP shot
- Tracer
- Shell case

Hard AP shot

Hard AP shell
Small base-fuse burster

At high velocity hard point shatters

5 Cm PAK 38—MV, AP shell: 2,739 fps
Max. range, HE: 2,900 yds.
Max. effective range, AP shell: 1,640 yds.

Efficient anti-tank gun used on all fronts throughout war. With tungsten carbide core AP 40 shot could penetrate almost all types of heavy Allied tanks.

61 mm—30° 50 mm—30°
500 m 1,000 m

Crusader
49 mm—7°
40 mm—0°
20 mm—60°
33 mm—29°
50 mm—53°
50 mm

Sherman
76 mm
50 mm—43°
50 mm

Matilda
75 mm—11°
78 mm—0°
47 mm—67°
78 mm

Mark IV and the 88 of the Tiger could use both most effectively.

Increased thickness of armor called for heavier projectiles and higher velocities. Due to wartime production problems it was usually more efficient to upgrade a weapon than design a new one. One way of increasing velocity was with a larger charge using a longer barrel. For instance, the KwK 7.5 cm L/24 (24 calibers in length) firing an HE shell had a muzzle velocity of 1,263 feet per second (fps), while the 7.5 cm L/43 was rated at 2,427 fps.

Higher velocities produced another problem: The tip of the projectile shattered instead of penetrating. Solution: protect the tip with a cap of softer metal, which spread the impact over the shoulder of the projectile (APC capped). And, because the most efficient cap was blunt, cover it with a streamlined wind shield or ballistic cap (APCBC). While the Germans furnished different types of ammunition for almost all their guns, APCBC shot was not available for the British 2-pounder and 6-pounder nor at first for the Grant's 75 mm. A grave disadvantage, as by now some German plates were face-hardened. Also, a Mark III Special captured in July 1942 showed a 20mm plate bolted to the main armor but separated from it by a 4-inch airspace. Purpose: to destroy the AP cap and reduce the chances of penetration of the plate behind.

As armor protection became more effective, the gunners tried a new approach—make the projectile harder than any steel it might attack. Tungsten carbide was a natural but it was much heavier than steel. A 6-pounder shot might weigh 10 pounds, and fired with a full charge it would probably have wrecked the gun. So a tungsten core, surrounded with a light composite shell, was developed. On impact the outer shell disintegrated and the heavier but smaller core punched through the plate. With the lighter projectile a larger propelling charge could be used, boosting muzzle velocity. The German Pzgr (Panzergrenate or AP) 40 was very successful and in the 5 cm KWK 39 L/60 reached 3,930 ft/sec, with a penetration at 250 yards of 109 mm of armor at 30° from the vertical. However, due to the light weight in relation to the cross section, velocity fell off with range and at 750 yards had no more penetration (46 mm) than the British 2-pounder. The German PzB 41 "Squeeze Gun" had a 28mm bore tapered to 20 mm at the muzzle.

On firing, the light alloy covering was swaged down around the tungsten core emerging at 4,600 ft/sec. Penetration at 250 yards was estimated at 50 mm, very good for a projectile weighing only .28 of a pound.

Finally, the assessment of gun vs. tank performance. Here theoretical figures mean little. Velocities of projectiles and penetration of x number of inches of armor under ideal conditions may be known or demonstrated, but battlefield conditions are seldom ideal. A moving tank, partly shrouded by dust and smoke, is no easy target. The angle at which a projectile meets a plate, the "angle of attack," varied constantly, and shot that might be expected to penetrate might glance harmlessly off. "Maximum thickness" means just that. No tank was equally heavily armored all round, and a slow vehicle impregnably armored at bow and turret might fall victim to more agile opponents striking at its comparatively vulnerable sides or rear.

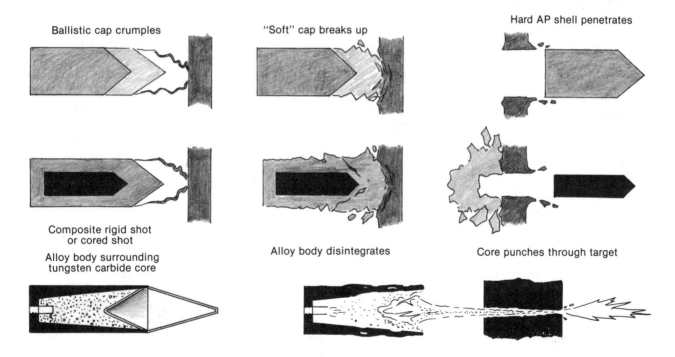

Ballistic cap crumples

"Soft" cap breaks up

Hard AP shell penetrates

Composite rigid shot or cored shot

Alloy body surrounding tungsten carbide core

Alloy body disintegrates

Core punches through target

Hollow-charge shell, with base fuse, ballistic cap, and copper lining.

Detonation of the charge converts the liner to a jet of metal particles and hot gas. This jet is propelled at very high velocity, over 20,000 feet per second. In a microsecond it literally burns its way through the opposing plate, emerging in a spurt of searing flame and molten metal, setting fire to anything inside the tank. Velocity of the projectile mattered little. The German hand-held Panzerfaust 60 propelled its 6½ lb. hollow-charge bomb at a muzzle velocity of only 148 fps, yet it could penetrate 200 mm (nearly 8 inches) of armor at 30°.

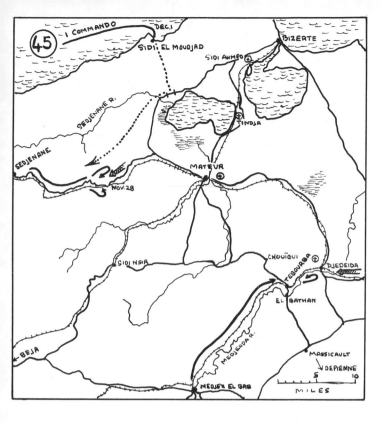

The 78th Division now planned to attack toward both Mateur and Tunis—the advance on the former serving to cover the northern flank of the latter movement. To aid these attacks the British 1st Commando (including some U.S. troops) was to land west of Bizerte at Sidi el Moudjad and cut the Bizerte–Mateur road, while the 2nd British Parachute Battalion was to be dropped at Depienne, wreck the airfield at Oudna, and guard the southern flank of the advance.

The attack on Djedeida failed. The attack began at 1300, November 28, and was met with heavy fire from concealed artillery. The 2nd Battalion of the 13th lost several tanks and withdrew, nor could the Northamptons make headway. The advance guard of the 36th Infantry Brigade from Sedjenane along the coast road ran into an ambush between Djebel Adjred and Djebel Azag—its leading carriers hosed with 20mm automatic fire. An attack on the night of November 29–30 failed to drive the enemy off positions on Green Hill, north of the road, and the force finally retired toward Sedjenane. A second attack at Djedeida on November 29 by the Northamptons and some tanks of the 2nd Battalion of the 13th also failed to make any gains, while the incessant enemy strafing and dive-bombing attacks were very effective. On November 30 the attack on Djedeida was called off until the Allied air effort could be increased.

The Commandos landed in the early morning of December 1. They reached the coast road and held a sector of it for three days but with supplies and ammunition running low, no sign of 36th Infantry Brigade, and being unable to make contact with it by radio, the Commandos made for Sedjenane, which was reached on December 5. Casualties amounted to 134. The parachutists, some 500 men, dropped near Depienne, but found the airfield not in use. News of the postponement of the attack on Tunis came via radio, and the force made the best of its way back to Medjez el Bab. Between attacks by Axis air and ground forces and forced marches at night the force became badly scattered and suffered heavily—19 killed, 4 wounded, and 266 missing.

Eisenhower had moved his headquarters from Gibraltar to Algiers on November 23. His first task was to clarify the situation in French North Africa (as relating to Darlan in particular and the French in general) to the leaders of the British and American governments. As noted above, there was great criticism of any dealings with pro-Vichy French officials, but the Commander-in-Chief's message did much to clear up the popular misconception that the inhabitants of French North Africa were only waiting a leader to throw off the Nazi-controlled Vichy yoke. There were patriots, but they were proportionally few, while there was much resentment (especially when bombs began to fall on Algiers and other centers). An excerpt from one of Anderson's dispatches is revealing: ". . . I can safely generalize by saying that at first, in the Army, the senior officers were hesitant and afraid to commit themselves, the junior officers were mainly in favor of aiding the Allies, the men would obey orders; amongst the people, the Arabs were indifferent or inclined to be hostile, the French were in our favour but apathetic, the civil authorities were antagonistic as a whole. The resulting impression on my mind was not one of much confidence as to the safety of my small isolated force should I suffer a severe setback." Due to Darlan's influence one advantage had been won by the Allies during this period: General Pierre Boisson, Governor of French West Africa, had agreed on November 22 to accept Darlan's authority. In subsequent meetings with Eisenhower, Boisson was persuaded to sign an agreement offering full cooperation with the Allies and incidentally opening up the harbor at Dakar. This important acquisition—which obviously could not have been gained without Darlan's co-operation—somewhat appeased those who were crying for the admiral's scalp.

Three days after moving into his new headquarters, the Commander-in-Chief, accompanied by Clark, set off for the front—a journey on which Eisenhower experienced firsthand the perils of travel under enemy-dominated skies. The weather was deteriorating, and mud—of a particularly viscous kind—confined traffic to the rapidly disintegrating roads and gave the Allied commander a forewarning of troubles to come. He found Anderson and his men in good heart, but even with slowly increasing U.S. support the task of the understrength elements of First Army was becoming increasingly difficult. On the Axis side, German troops and materiel were reaching the front in growing numbers, although badly hampered by Allied bombing of ports and airfields.

Tebourba—The Germans Counterattack

On his return to Algiers on November 30 Eisenhower reported, "My immediate aim is to keep pushing hard, with a first intention of pinning the enemy back in the Fortress of Bizerte and confining him so closely that the danger of a breakout of a heavy counteroffensive will be minimized." But Nehring had already, under Kesselring's prodding (he visited Tunis on November 28 and condemned Nehring as being too cautious and defensive-minded) begun plans to mount a counter-attack in the Tebourba sector, and ordered it to begin no later than December 1. Commanding the attacking forces was General Wolfgang Fischer, Commanding Officer 10th Panzer Division, elements of which had already arrived at the front. He organized his scanty forces in four groups. Groups Lüder and Hudel were to attack "Blade Force" (including supply and service units, screened by 1st Battalion, U. S. 1st Armored Regiment, and a squadron of 1st Derbyshire Yeomanry) at Chouïgui, then move on Tebourba from the west. Group Koch was to attack at El Bathan, while Group Djedeida was in reserve, ready to exploit any successes.

Allied forces were widely scattered—with an advance force (2nd Battalion Hampshire Regiment) on a ridge near Djedeida; a company of 1st Battalion, East Surrey Regiment on a hill, Djebel Maïana, to the west; while Tebourba was held by units including 2nd Battalion, U. S. 13th Armored Regiment, U. S. 5th Field Artillery Battalion, and 5th Battalion, Northamptons. El Bathan was held by two companies of the East Surreys.

Striking "Blade Force" from two sides on the morning of December 1, Groups Lüder and Hudel dispersed the Allied force and drove it down the road to Tebourba. An attempt to relieve the situation by 17th/21st Lancers failed, with the loss of 5 Crusaders, and the regiment pulled back west of Tebourba in support of the 11th Brigade Group. Surviving units from "Blade Force" were attached to the Lancers as they came in from Chouïgui. German pursuit toward Tebourba was cautious and further slowed by British armored cars acting as rear guard. Tebourba Gap is a narrow passage between Djebel Lanserine (569 meters) to the north and the lower Djebel el Guessa, almost due east, through which runs the road, the railway, and the Medjerda River. One object of the German northern drive was to cut the road between the town and the Gap. Allied artillery on high ground near the Gap prevented this, although enemy fire temporarily denied the road to the Allies.

While Groups Lüder and Hudel were held just north of the road, Group Djedeida attacked the Allied troops holding the ridge to the west of the village. Although led by Fischer in person and supported by two Tiger tanks, they could not force the 2nd Hampshires off the objective. To the south Group Koch moved up east and south of El Bathan. As darkness fell, the Allied hold on Tebourba was precarious, with the route to the west only a narrow strip close to the river. The scanty forces to the east were extended in a 4-mile line from the town to the ridge. Scattered units of "Blade Force" continued to arrive—rallying to the north of Tebourba Gap alongside the 5th Northamptons. Reinforcements were on the way in the shape of elements of CC "B," U. S. 1st Armored Division (light and medium tanks, armored infantry, and artillery). A German attempt in the night to halt this move by blocking the Gap with an armored detachment failed, and the unit was driven toward Chouïgui.

Fischer's efforts on December 2 were hampered by the poor quality of some of his infantry—replacement battalions, with untrained troops badly officered. Even so, Allied losses in the day's fighting were heavy. The Hampshires held Group Djedeida all day at the ridge, but with such casualties that at midnight they were withdrawn to Djebel Maïana. Pressure from Group Koch—elements of which infiltrated the flank of their position—finally forced the withdrawal across the river of the company of Surreys at El Bathan. To the north Allied superiority in numbers (not quality) of tanks was reduced by rash use of American armor. Over 30 Stuarts of the 13th Armored Regiment, without artillery support, attacked a forma-

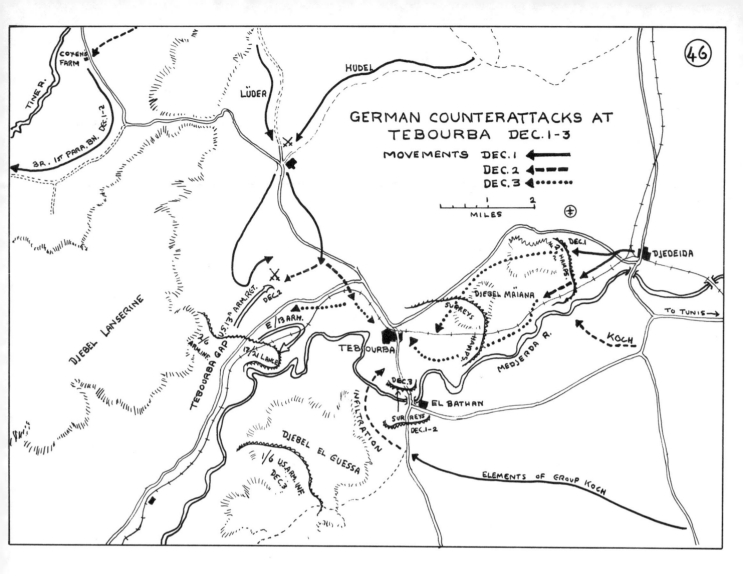

GERMAN COUNTERATTACKS AT
TEBOURBA DEC. 1-3
MOVEMENTS   DEC.1
              DEC.2
              DEC.3
MILES

tion of Mark IVs and were repulsed with heavy loss. Shermans of the regiment's Company "E," sent to reinforce the remainder of 2nd Battalion, U. S. 13th Armored Regiment, exposed themselves to heavy anti-tank fire, losing 8 tanks to no purpose. Well-placed Allied artillery prevented Groups Lüder and Hudel from cutting off the town and caused them considerable loss.

It was fairly obvious by now that, even if the Germans should be forced to withdraw from the area, the Allies would be in poor shape to continue a drive on Tunis. They were not to be given the chance. Reinforced by Panzer Grenadiers flown from Italy, Group Djedeida took Djebel Maïana on December 3 and held it despite valiant counter-attacks by 2nd Hampshires and 1st Surreys. Axis air assaults had become more frequent and Tebourba was under heavy dive-bombing attack when, at 1800, it was decided to evacuate the village. The main road to the Gap was dominated by enemy fire, and a track along the riverbank was the only route out. As the long column of vehicles ground its

way west under artillery and machine-gun fire, vehicles in front were hit and set on fire. The column came to a halt, part of the track gave way, and the retreat bogged down. The troops moved on foot cross country to the Gap. Transport, guns, tractors, and supplies, unable to move, had to be abandoned. Fortunately elements of Group Koch, which had infiltrated the high ground west of El Bathan, had been driven out by U.S. infantry and artillery so that the road from the Gap west was free from harassing fire.

The Allied advance had been checked and turned back with considerable loss. Fischer estimated that the 4-day action had cost the Allies 55 tanks, 4 armored cars, 4 anti-tank guns, 6 100mm guns, 6 120mm guns, 13 smaller guns, many machine guns and mortars, 300 vehicles, and over 1,000 prisoners. German losses are not known but were necessarily less, especially in materiel.

The action at Tebourba was a severe setback to Eisenhower's plan to take Tunis before the rainy season. It also demonstrated not only the Germans' determination to take the offensive, but also the rapidity of their buildup and the effectiveness of their co-ordinated air effort. The substantial aid afforded the Axis by this arm is reflected in Eisenhower's report of December 3 to the Combined Chiefs of Staff, the first two items of which dealt solely with the air: "1. We have gone beyond the sustainable limit of air capabilities in supporting ground forces in a pell-mell race for Tunisia. Consequently, although our air forces have been working at maximum pace without even minimum repair, supply, and maintenance facilities, the scale of possible support is insufficient to keep down the hostile strafing and dive-bombing which is so largely responsible for breaking up all attempted advances by ground forces. 2. The Air Commanders report that from 2 days to 1 week more of present-scale air operation, under existing conditions, will leave them near or at complete breakdown, yet this scale of air support is not sufficient."

To implement the Axis decision to make a major effort in French North Africa, the status of the German forces there was raised to that of an army—the Fifth Panzer Army (PzAOK5)—and its new commander, General Oberst Juergen von Arnim, took over from Nehring on December 9.

The Action at Djebel el Guessa—December 6

The failure of the first offensive toward Tunis was regarded by Eisenhower as only a temporary reverse, and preparations were made for a continuance of the assault. The line as now held ran from Chouïgui Pass south through Tebourba Gap to Djebel el Guessa.

Reinforcements had arrived on both sides. As troops and materiel arrived from Italy, units moved to the front, while on the Allied side the bulk of CC "B," now united and anxious to avenge its recent reverses, was deployed southeast of the Medjerda near Djebel el Guessa. Elements of the British 6th Armored Division (Major General Sir Charles Keightley) was assembling in the area east of Souk el Arba, and 1st Guards Brigade (Brigadier F. Copland-Griffith) arrived at Béja on December 6. The remains of "Blade Force" rejoined the British 6th Armored. French troops held a line east of Medjez el Bab and the sector north of Béja, while others held the slopes of Djebel el Ang north of Medjez el Bab. In central Tunisia French units took Faïd Pass on December 3, Fondouk el Aoureb on December 8, and Pichon on December 19. Anglo-American headquarters would have preferred to use more of the poorly equipped French

as line-of-communication troops, releasing British and American units for front-line duty, but French feelings had to be deferred to. It was only after November 24, for instance, that Giraud allowed French troops to serve under British commanders. The system of command on land was to be a continued problem for Eisenhower and Anderson and one that necessitated a mixture of firmness and tact.

The Allied plan for regrouping followed by a renewed advance, was forestalled by Fischer on December 6, striking first at Djebel el Guessa from El Bathan and from near Massicault. The American defenders (1st Battalion, U. S. 6th Armored Infantry), their line of retreat threatened, made a hasty and costly withdrawal. A counter-attack with other elements of CC "B," under Lieutenant Colonel H. Bruss, northeast of Djebel Bou Aoukaz, was stopped with the loss of several tanks. The Germans did not push the attack and later retired. The American tactics—tank vs. tank, without mutual support of guns and infantry—came to grief, just as had similar British tactics in the Western Desert. Nor had the Americans yet learned that tanks were usually at the mercy of powerful, concealed anti-tank guns.

The reverse at Djebel el Guessa caused General Evelegh to order CC "B" back to Djebel Bou Aoukaz and 11th Infantry Brigade to Longstop Hill. The V Corps (Lieutenant General C. W. Allfrey) now took over command from headquarters, 78th Division, with headquarters at Souk el Khemis. The principal formations were: 6th Armored Division (British)—one armored and one infantry brigade—concentrating near Teboursouk; 78th Division—3 infantry brigades (elements of all 3 had suffered considerable losses); CC "B"—also a bit battered; 1st British Parachute Brigade—3 battalions (these had been in action since the beginning of the offensive in mid-November); and 1st and 6th Commandos (which had also lost heavily). Even with Corps troops, numerous attached units, and the French, it was not an imposing force with which to hold a front of some 75 miles and to battle its way through a mountainous region against strong opposition.

The chances of an immediate renewal of the Tunis offensive now looked dim. General Allfrey, V Corps commander, suggested a shortening of the Allied line, behind which fresh preparations for the advance could be made. There was a hassle over Medjez el Bab: Allfrey wanted to abandon it, the French protested, and finally it was decided at the highest level to continue to hold it. Some shuffling of forces was ordered, but before they could be carried out, the Germans struck again. The 86th Panzer Grenadiers advanced on both sides of the Medjerda, spearheaded by tanks, while the 7th Panzer Regiment (—) moved from Massicault toward Medjez el Bab via Sidi Mediene ("Peter's Corner") supported by elements of the 501st Panzer Battalion, with "Tiger" tanks, anti-tank guns, and artillery.

The northern prong, on the left bank, was held by U.S. tanks and artillery at the railway station of Bordj Toum while the advance on the south side of the river ran into stiff defense by the U. S. 6th Armored Infantry at Djebel Bou Aoukaz and Djebel el Asoud. The 7th Panzer's attack, after scattering some elements of the 1st Battalion, 1st Armored Regiment, was held up at a roadblock by French infantry and artillery and lost 4 tanks. The German column then pulled back to meet a flanking attack

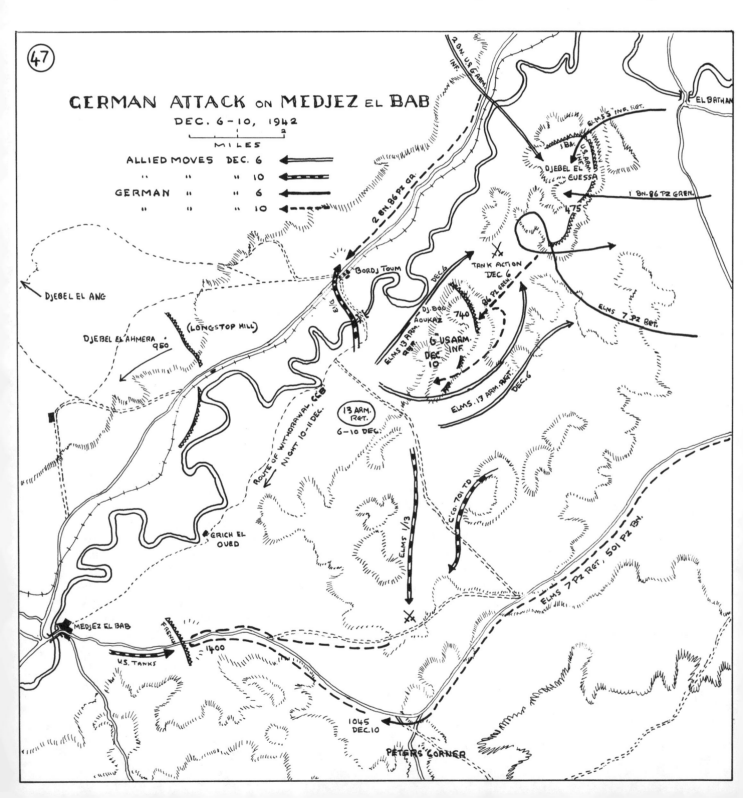

from the north by elements of 1st Battalion U. S. 13th Armored Regiment and some tank destroyers. Nineteen of the light American tanks were lost and most of the tank destroyers, although the latter claimed 10 German mediums. The enemy then retired to Massicault.

At an evening conference near Medjez el Bab attended by Allfrey, Evelegh, Oliver, and Robinett, CC "B's" retirement through Medjez el Bab was arranged, with British units covering the route. The command began its withdrawal from Djebels Bou Aoukaz and el Asoud that night—lining up in a crowded column on a track, flanked by mud, leading to the Bordj Toum bridge. The advance guard crossed the bridge, but did not find the covering force. A skirmish with a small German force near the railway station started a rumor that the Germans were attacking the bridgehead. The noise and misleading reports caused the officer in command, Lieutenant Colonel J. R. McGinness, to divert the leading vehicles from the bridge route to a dirt track that ran close to the east bank of the river. The leading vehicles got through, but those following became hopelessly mired and were ordered abandoned while the crews continued to Medjez el Bab on foot. A few vehicles were extricated before the Germans could advance, but CC "B" was temporarily useless as a fighting unit. Eighteen tanks, 41 guns, and some 140 half-tracks and other vehicles were lost, not including the casualties of December 10, and a frantic scramble began in the rear areas to strip units of their equipment to replace CC "B's" losses. Twenty-six mediums, for example, were sent from Morocco by rail from 2nd Armored Division.

The steady flow of Axis troops and materiel into Tunisia allowed von Arnim to merge the two defense perimeters around Bizerte and Tunis and establish a "front" of a more or less interlocking series of defensive positions (although by no means the continuous system associated with World War I). This ran from the coast some 25 miles west of Bizerte, south to Djefna, southeast to Djebel Lanserine, and across the Medjerda near Bordj Toum. It then passed east of Ksar Tyr, by way of Zarhouan to near Enfidaville. Von Arnim now decided to move southward, to occupy Pont-du-Fahs and the defiles through the mountains from that place south to Maknassy (taking Faïd Pass and other key points defended by the French), then southwest to the area of El Guettar. This move on December 16 established Axis forces along the edge of the central Tunisian highlands, in a position to guard against any sudden moves toward the coastal road. Rommel had already retired from El Agheila into Tripolitania on the first leg of the long two-month retreat to Mareth. The fall of Tripoli (the cost of sailing supplies into that port was already prohibitive) was obviously not far off, and it was essential that the lifeline to the east be kept open.

Plans for what the Allied command hoped would be the final attack went forward, while desperate efforts were made to prepare forward airfields for the fighters and fighter-bombers. Intermediate fields at Télergma and Canrobert were put in operation. A "dry" field at Biskra, southwest of Constantine, on the edge of the desert, was used by heavy bombers, as was the all-weather field at Maison Blanche. Youks-les-Bains was used by light and medium bombers (because of the distance, fighters based there were usually for area defense only). The effective Allied combat forces were estimated by Allied Force Headquarters at 20,000 British, 11,800 Americans, and 7,000 French (there were some 40,000 French in all, but most were poorly armored and badly equipped). Axis strength was set at some 25,000 combat and 10,000 service troops. There were believed to be some 80 German tanks, some few of them the massive "Tigers." Allied tanks were more numerous but in general inferior to the German Mark IIIs and Mark IVs. The Allies had the edge in heavy artillery while the Axis could, temporarily, put up more planes—at least in the combat areas.

Much of the Allied chance of success hinged on the weather, which was deteriorating rapidly. The main offensive was scheduled to begin on the night of December 24–25, but to win the approaches to the Tebourba area a reinforced company of 3rd Grenadier Guards was to take Grich el Oued, northeast of Medjez el Bab on December 22–23, while 2nd Battalion, Coldstream Guards, followed by 1st Battalion, U. S. 18th Infantry Regiment, took Longstop Hill. The 5th Northamptons were then to move through the mountains from Toukabeur and retake Tebourba Gap, Bordj Toum, and Djebel el Guessa. While the 78th Division was thus securing the northern flank, the main drive was to be by the 6th Armored Division through Massicault.

Longstop Hill, nearly seven miles northeast of Medjez el Bab, has two main heights (although this was not realized at the time) separated by a ravine. The high point, 290 (meters) was taken, and handed over, amid some confusion in darkness and heavy rain, to the relieving 18th Infantry. The fact that the lower (243) was still occupied by the

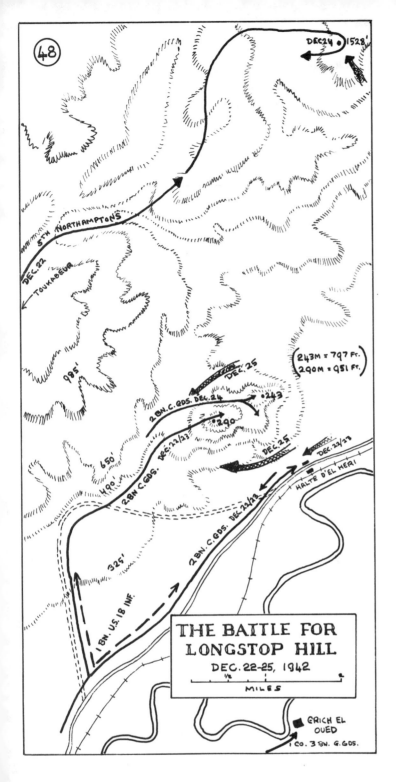

THE BATTLE FOR LONGSTOP HILL
DEC. 22-25, 1942

position. The attack went in at 1700, behind a rolling barrage, and again the Germans were driven off the crest. The lower peak was then "discovered" across the ravine, and although strongly held, was also taken, only to be lost again in the darkness. Next morning, December 25, a heavy two-pronged German attack with armor support dispersed some French troops to the north, took the 18th Infantry in the rear to the south, and isolated the Coldstreams on 290. Their position was soon untenable, and with their withdrawal the battle of Longstop (or Christmas Hill, as the Germans named it) came to an end.

The Northamptons, with an improvised mule train, had meanwhile started on their mission. Then, on December 24, Eisenhower and Anderson, visiting the front, decided to call off the attack on Tunis. Rain was now coming down in buckets and could be expected to continue for a couple of months. Roads were almost impassable, and any vehicle venturing off the highway was instantly mired. Eisenhower recounted afterward, "We went out personally to inspect the countryside over which the troops would have to advance, and while doing so I observed an incident which, as much as anything else, I think, convinced me of the hopelessness of an attack. About thirty feet off the road, in a field which appeared to be covered with winter wheat, a motorcycle had become stuck in the mud. Four soldiers were struggling to extricate it but in spite of their most strenuous efforts succeeded only in getting themselves mired into the sticky clay. They finally had to give up the attempt and left the motorcycle more deeply bogged down than when they had started.

"We went back to headquarters and I directed that the attack be indefinitely postponed. . . ."

The Northamptons, moving only at night, succeeded in taking a German post a few miles north of Longstop and stood off several counter-attacks. Division and Corps had been trying vainly to contact them (even to sending out search aircraft), but only after their Commanding Officer guessed that the main attack had been called off did the battalion return to Toukabeur. The Grenadier company that had taken and held Grich el Oued was also recalled, and the Allied attempt to take Tunis and Bizerte before the rains set in came to an end. As Eisenhower wrote, "It was a bitter decision."

Action on the Naval, Air, and Political Fronts

The following chapter tells of the efforts to carry on the fight in central Tunisia, but before outlining

Germans went unnoticed until dawn, when a strong counter-attack drove the Americans off 290. A counter-attack by 18th Infantry failed, and the Coldstreams, who had just reached Medjez el Bab, were ordered back again. The downpour had turned the roads into mudholes, vehicles could not operate, there were no mules, and ammunition and supplies had to be carried by hand. It was not until 0600 on December 23–24 that the battalion was in

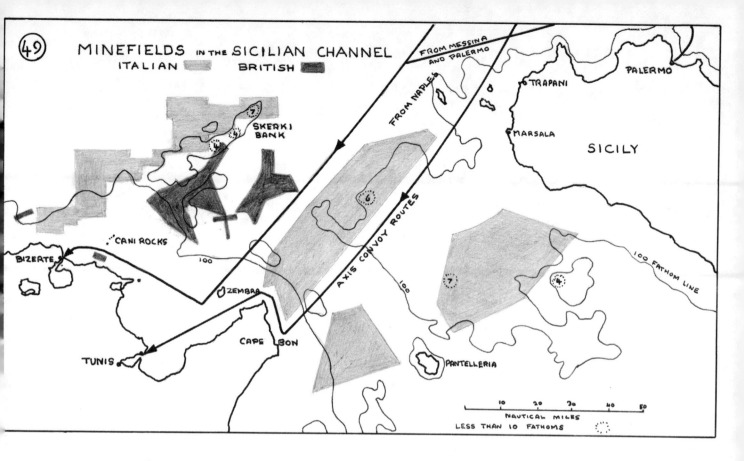

MINEFIELDS ɪɴ ᴛʜᴇ SICILIAN CHANNEL
ITALIAN ▨   BRITISH ▦

FROM MESSINA AND PALERMO

FROM NAPLES

PALERMO

TRAPANI

MARSALA

SICILY

SKERKI BANK

AXIS CONVOY ROUTES

CANI ROCKS

BIZERTE

ZEMBRA

CAPE BON

TUNIS

PANTELLERIA

100 FATHOM LINE

```
10    20    30    40    50
   NAUTICAL MILES
LESS THAN 10 FATHOMS
```

the campaign it is necessary to recount briefly events naval and political that occurred while the actions noted above were taking place.

On the naval front the relative quiet with which the landings took place was broken when the Axis undersea forces, recovering from their initial confusion, rallied and began (aided by the Luftwaffe) to take their toll of Allied shipping.

On November 10, *U-431* sank the destroyer H.M.S. *Martin* northeast of Algiers. On November 11, *U-407* sank the 19,600-ton *Viceroy of India* north of Oran and the 11,600-ton *Nieuw Zeeland* southeast of Gibraltar. Both fast troopships were returning empty. On November 13 the Dutch destroyer *Isaac Sweers* fell to *U-431*, and another sank the 6,500-ton motor vessel *Maron* north of Oran. Aircraft also scored and torpedoed destroyer H.M.S. *Ibis* on November 10. The 16,600-ton liner *Narkunda* was sunk on November 14.

Allied anti-submarine warfare was stepped up as the cease-fire arrangements released more warships and aircraft for this duty, and in the Western Basin between November 9 and November 17, 5 German and 2 Italian submarines were sunk—3 by aircraft, 3 by escort vessels, and 1 by submarine. Two German submarines were sunk west of Gibraltar—1 by destroyer, another by aircraft. These heavy losses, coupled with damage to other boats, caused a temporary lull in the U-boat campaign.

A glance at the map explains the initial failure of Allied submarines and surface forces to do more to halt the Axis buildup in Tunisia. (See also the chapter on Malta.) It was due to a number of factors, the main one being the shortness of the passage (from Trapani to Tunis is only 130 miles). A fast (15-knot) ship could make this in 8½ hours, and a warship in half that time. This allowed the runs to be made under cover of darkness. The waters were heavily mined (see map), with numerous shallow banks—poor submarine "country" —while the area was within easy reach of Axis airfields. Also, much of the British naval and air action in November and December was devoted to cutting Rommel's supply route to Libya, while Malta was only just getting back on its feet after the heavy assaults of the autumn and was still desperately short of supplies. Thus it was that in November over 30,000 tons of materiel and more than 13,000 military personnel were convoyed to Tunisia by sea without loss.

The run of luck for the Axis, however, ended with the reconstituting of Force "K" at Malta on November 27 (usually 3 cruisers and 4 destroyers) and the stationing of a comparable force "Q," (3 cruisers, 2 destroyers) at Bône. On the night of December 1–2 the latter intercepted and wiped out a convoy (shadowed and illuminated by Malta-based aircraft). Sunk were 3 Italian supply ships, a

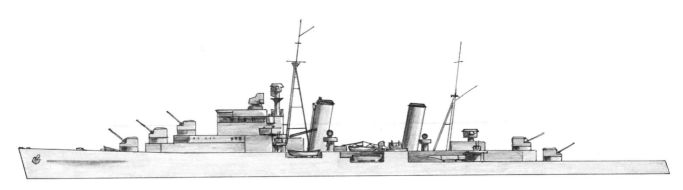

Dido (Br.) Class Light Cruiser (nine ships)

Launched July 1939.
Displacement: 5,450 tons. LOA: 512′. Beam: 50½′. Draft: 14′.
Four screws. 62,000 hp=22 knots.
Armament: ten 5.25″ DP (5×2), 16 smaller, six 21″ torpedo tubes (2×3).
One aircraft.
Armor: turrets 1″, sides 2″.

German transport, and one of the escorting destroyers. Destroyer *Quentin* of Force "Q" was sunk by a torpedo-bomber on the return to Bône. (After this massacre nearly all the troops entering Tunisia by sea were carried over by destroyers. All told, these Italian destroyers made 155 trips to Tunisia, landing some 52,000 men.) On the following night destroyers of Force "K" finished off the remains of a convoy already shattered by air and submarine attack. Altogether 4 merchantmen and the veteran destroyer *Lupo* were sunk. This began a month in which the air and sea pressure on the Axis was intensified (although not without loss on the Allied side) and, while tonnage landed in December increased to nearly 59,000 tons, losses amounted to 23 per cent.

The weight of Allied air assaults forced the withdrawal of Italian naval units to northern bases (a raid on Naples on December 4 sank a cruiser and badly damaged 2 more cruisers and 4 destroyers), and by the end of November points of departure in Sicily had to be abandoned also, and the convoys then generally used Naples or Leghorn. The importance of the Allied air effort is shown by the following figures: Of 46 Italian ships sunk from all causes in November (just over 52,000 tons), 21 (41,000 tons) or 79 per cent, were sunk by air (this included those sunk in port). Bad flying weather reduced this figure in December—but the increased activity of the British submarines (33,400 tons sunk in December) raised the total for the month to over 76,000 tons. Losses of German-operated vessels for the period August to December were 44,430 tons from all causes, of which 22 per cent were sunk by air.

There were other events of major importance during the period November–December 1942. On November 27 the Germans completed the seizure of unoccupied France by attempting to take possession of the French fleet at Toulon. Darlan had appealed (not ordered, be it noted) in vain to Admiral Jean de Laborde to sail for North Africa and join the Allies—although it is fairly certain that Darlan did not believe that his "invitation" to Laborde would be taken seriously. Laborde, under the eye of the Vichy government (and a pronounced Anglophobe), had no intention of sailing for Dakar, as Darlan had suggested. On the other hand, Laborde had no intention of handing his ships over to the Axis, and as German tanks broke through the gates to the Navy yard he ordered the fleet scuttled. A total of 3 battleships, 7 cruisers, 32 destroyers, 16 submarines, a seaplane tender, and 18 sloops or smaller craft—77 vessels in all—went to the bottom, tragically vindicating the French Navy's promise in 1940 that they would never permit their ships to fall into German hands.

On December 8 Rear-Admiral Edmond Derrien, naval commander at Bizerte, was ordered by the Germans to comply with Pétain's order of December 5, acceding to Axis demands that all French forces be demobilized. On receipt of an ultimatum threatening death and destruction if he did not comply, Derrien surrendered the small naval squadron, forts, and all other installations. Some 6,000 sailors and 3,500 soldiers were demobilized as well as 7,000 Senagalese (battalions of Barré's that should have accompanied him in his withdrawal).

On December 24, while Allies and Germans were battling for Longstop Hill, Darlan was assassinated by a young Frenchman, Fernand Bonnier de la Chappelle. While possessing the obedience and respect of most French naval and military officers Darlan had made many bitter enemies, from both the far left (who hated him as a Vichyite and collaborator) to the far right (who damned him for co-operating with the Allies). What the young man's motives were, or which faction, if any, was implicated were never revealed, as he was tried on Giraud's orders on Christmas Day and executed (with what some have considered suspicious haste) early the next morning.

Admiral Darlan's place in history is hard to assess. He was aware of the dislike of many of the Allied leaders and that Roosevelt had felt it necessary to justify any dealings with him as a "temporary expedient." In a letter to Clark, Darlan wrote, "I am, perhaps, only a lemon which the Americans intend to throw away after squeezing it." Yet, in Eisenhower's words, "His reputation was that of a notorious collaborator with Hitler, but during the time he served as administrator of French North Africa he never once, to our knowledge, violated any commitment or promise." There is no doubt that without him the winning of French acceptance of the "Torch" landings, grudging as it was, would have proved far more difficult, if not impossible.

Giraud was named temporary administrator by the local French officials, a task for which he was not suited and one that he did not desire. He professed to have no interest in politics—no recommendation for such a position in French North Africa, where factionalism was rampant. Eisenhower himself, in fact, had to tread a difficult path, which he managed to do with his customary skill in reconciling, at least temporarily, individuals and groups of widely divergent views. On one hand were the old Vichy appointees—some of whom, like the wily Noguès, he would have liked to be rid of but for the undoubted value they had in dealing with the Arabs. Then there were the pro-fascist veterans, the pro-communists (some of them deputies deported from France in 1939), those who wanted no part of the war, and others who demanded full co-operation with the Allies and the ouster of all former Vichyites. There were those few in the Army who had helped the Allies and were now all but ostracized by their brother officers, and there were the Jews, outnumbered 40 to 1 by the Arabs and victims of repression by Arabs and Vichyites alike. Not least was the large Arab population, potentially explosive unless handled by experts (who, in turn, were mostly ex-Vichyites themselves).

To add another ingredient to the seething mixture, it was obvious that sooner or later De Gaulle and his Free French, hated by most of the French Army and government officials, must have a share in the running of affairs. His increasing popularity with the French civilians guaranteed that; but it was not until May 30, 1943, that "Le Grand Charles" arrived in Algiers. De Gaulle's rise to power is no part of this story, but as might be expected, when the Committee of National Liberation was formed 4 days after his arrival, with Giraud as co-chairman, the hatred of the Free French for those who had obeyed Vichy soon began to make itself felt. Among others, Governor General Boisson was dismissed and arrested, while Noguès fled to Portugal to escape a similar fate.

Estéva, the Governor General of Tunisia, was removed from office by the Germans prior to the recapture of Tunis and sent back to France. He was arrested after the liberation of France in 1944, and was later tried and imprisoned. He was freed in 1950, a dying man, and passed away shortly after his release. A like fate awaited Admiral Derrien, who was sentenced to life imprisonment, served 2 years, and was released, to die 12 days later.

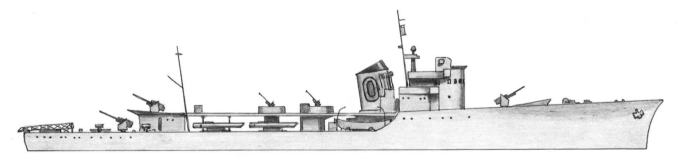

Lupo (It.) *"Partenope"* Class Torpedo Boat (sixteen ships)

Launched November 1937.
Displacement: 679 tons. LOA: 267'. Beam: 26'. Draft: 7¾'.
Two screws. 19,000 hp=34 knots.
Armament: three 3.9", six 37 mm (2✕3), four 18" torpedo tubes.
Complement: 94.

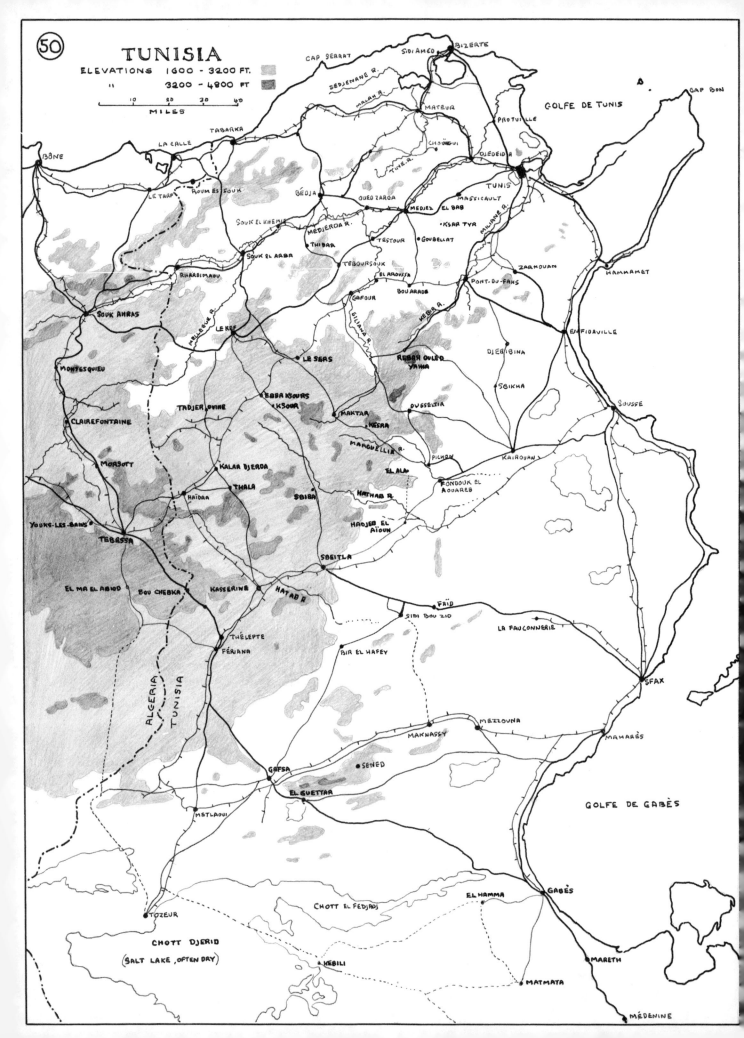

50

TUNISIA

ELEVATIONS 1600 - 3200 FT.
" 3200 - 4800 FT

10   20   30   40
MILES

CAP SERRAT
SIDI AMED
BIZERTE

SEDJENANE R.
MALAH R.
MATEUR
PROTUILLE
GOLFE DE TUNIS
CAP BON

TABARKA
LA CALLE
BÔNE
LE TARF
ROUM ES SOUK
BÉDJA
OUED ZARGA
CHOÜIGUI
DJEDEIDA
TUNIS

TINE R.
MASSICAULT
MEDJEZ
EL BAB
KSAR TYR
MILIANE R.

SOUK EL KHEMIS
MEDJERDA R.
THIBAR
TESTOUR
GOUBELLAT
SOUK EL ARBA
TEBOURSOUK
RHARDIMAOU
EL AROUSSA
ZARMOUAN
HAMMAMET
GAFOUR
BOU ARADA
PONT-DU-FAHS
SOUK AHRAS
LE KEF
SILIANA R.
KEBIR R.
EMFIDAVILLE
MONTESQUIEU
LE SERS
REBAA OULED YAHIA
DJEBIBINA
TADJEROUINE
EBBA KSOURS
KSOUR
SBIKHA
CLAIREFONTAINE
MAKTAR
KESRA
OUSSELTIA
SOUSSE
MORSOTT
KALAA DJERDA
MARGUELLIR R.
PICHON
KAIROUAN
THALA
HAÏDRA
SBIBA
EL ALA
HATHAB R.
FONDOUK EL AOUAREB
YOUKS-LES-BAINS
HADJEB EL AÏOUN
TEBESSA
SBEITLA
EL MA EL ABIOD
BOU CHEBKA
KASSERINE
HATAB R.
FAÏD
SIDI BOU ZID
LA FAUCONNERIE
THÉLEPTE
FÉRIANA
BIR EL HAFEY
ALGERIA
TUNISIA
SFAX
MEZZOUNA
MAKNASSY
MAHARÈS
GAFSA
SENED
EL GUETTAR
GOLFE DE GABÈS
METLAOUI
EL HAMMA
GABÈS
CHOTT EL FEDJADJ
TOZEUR
CHOTT DJERID
(SALT LAKE, OFTEN DRY)
KEBILI
MARETH
MATMATA
MÉDENINE

VI

"Head 'Em off at the Pass"

THE CAMPAIGN IN CENTRAL TUNISIA

The topographical map of Tunisia is not easy to read and at first appears a bewildering jumble of mountains, plains, and valleys. To clarify matters somewhat, the accompanying maps are over-simplified but give the general features of the terrain, without which the maneuvers and battles of central Tunisia are meaningless.

Beginning at Cape Bon Peninsula, 3 connected mountain ranges form an inverted Y, the stem at the peninsula, the fork south of Pont-du-Fahs near Djebel Fkirine (988 meters). One prong (the Eastern Dorsal) runs south for some 125 miles to Maknassy. The other (the Western Dorsal) projects southwest past Fériana. Across the wide part of the Y is an east–west chain on a line Maknassy–El Guettar–Gafsa. The enclosed triangular plateau is itself subdivided by numerous disconnected ridges running roughly parallel to the Western (or Grand) Dorsal and crossed by several streams and watercourses (sometimes dry in summer) draining from the higher ground in the west

to the eastern coastal plain. The average annual precipitation of 16 inches falls mostly in the winter, but, rather surprisingly, there is enough at many spots for orchards, grainfields, and forage. In the winter rains, the streambeds fill and dry soil gives way to a thick, slick slush. In other places the plateaus and valleys, seamed by erosion, are covered with bunch grass, cactus, and scrub.

Between the Eastern Dorsal and the sea the coastal plain stretches from Enfidaville in the North to the narrow Gabès Gap in the South.

Access from the plain to the triangular plateau and from the plateau westward is through breaks in the mountain chains. The main passes through the Eastern Dorsal are at the Karachoum Gap at the fork of the Y, the Kairouan Pass at Pichon, Fondouk el Aoureb, Faïd, Maknassy, a defile east of El Guettar, and a gap at Gafsa. Through the Western Dorsal the main passes are at Maktar, Sbiba, Kasserine, and Fériana.

The link between the Axis forces in the North

and those facing the Eighth Army lay along the coastal plain. Naturally this was a sensitive area, and any threat, real or fancied, caused grave concern at Commando Supremo and OKW. As the campaign for Tunisia opened, the Axis partners took the precautions of ensuring their coastal positions by occupying (November 17–18) Sousse, Sfax, and Gabès. To hinder any Allied push southeastward, Gafsa was seized by a German airborne demolition team (November 20–21). The weak French garrison, reinforced by a small detachment of U.S. paratroopers, retired unmolested to Fériana. On November 22, slightly strengthened, the Allies returned, drove out the Germans, and headed for Gabès, where they encountered an Italian motorized column en route to Gafsa. The Italians hastily retired. At the same time another small Allied detachment headed for Sbeitla which was threatened by another Axis force.

This force, headed by a German armored column, passed through Kairouan, drove out the small French garrison (November 21), then turned back for Tunis leaving the Italians in possession. The dust of the departing German vehicles had hardly settled before the French came back and ejected the Italians in their turn. On November 24 an unsuccessful Axis attempt was made to retake the place; then a temporary quiet settled over the central front.

Any Allied planning now had to take into consideration the likelihood of future co-operation between two Axis armies. Rommel was being pressed farther northwest along the coast by the Eighth Army and in the foreseeable future would be forced out of Tripolitania and into Tunisia. Thus while the Allies gained the invaluable port of Tripoli (entered by the Eighth Army, on January 23, 1943), the retreat hastened the junction of the Axis forces (which Rommel had advocated) and shortened the southern army's supply line.

With the rainy season now putting an end to major operations in the North, the planners at Allied Force Headquarters began eying the drier central and southern front. A thrust toward the coast to cut the German-Italian Panzer Army's supply route from the north seemed to offer possibilities, and an outline of an attack toward Sfax (Operation "Satin") was approved on December 28. To aid in such an attack by pinning down enemy forces, Anderson agreed to make subsidiary attacks in the North.

The difficulty of building up supplies was enormous. The great distances from viable ports, short-age of transport, and inadequate rail and road facilities made any offensive dependent on the amount of ammunition, fuel, and food that the hard-working G-4s estimated could be stockpiled in support. Coupled with the supply problem was the unwieldy arrangement under which the Allied commands functioned. Giraud, who on December 17 proposed that he be appointed Eisenhower's tactical commander over all operations in Tunisia (a plan that was quietly shelved), would not put French forces under British command. Likewise, although U. S. II Corps was concentrating on the British First Army's southern flank, it was not under Anderson's command.

On January 21, Eisenhower decided that while Anderson could "co-ordinate" British and American forces he could not move the latter about, and Anderson could only "request" Juin's co-operation. Finally, on January 26, a new directive gave Anderson control of all troops, including, besides First Army, U. S. II Corps, and a Composite Corps, to consist of 34th Division (less detachments) and French troops under a French Corps commander.

In limited offensives the French had gained important positions from the Italian defenders around the Karachoum Gap and Kairouan Pass. To offset this, on January 3 a force of German armor and infantry, its way prepared by artillery and air strikes, had struck at Fondouk el Aoureb, driving the French defenders west with the loss of over 300 men and several guns.

A counter-attack was planned with American assistance, and on January 8 Combat Command B (CC "B") of U. S. 1st Armored Division—Brigadier General Paul Robinett—moved to Sbeitla to take part. II Corps established a depot at Tébessa, and supplies were accumulated at other points as far east as Kasserine. By this time "Satin" had been scrubbed—mainly because Eighth Army was not yet in a position to make a forward move in support.

The French were not long left in possession of their gains at Karachoum and Kairouan. Von Arnim launched a powerful thrust ("Eilbote I") with the object of taking Djebel Mansour and the great reservoir and dam on the Kebir River (some 12 miles southwest of Pont-du-Fahs), then striking due south and taking the positions at Karachoum and Kairouan from the rear. While the main force (Kampfgruppe Weber) was engaged in this operation, 10th Panzer Division and other elements were to strike the southern end of the British V Corps line toward Bou Arada in a diversionary move.

"Eilbote I" got under way early on January 18. The Bou Arada thrust was met by V Corps. Little ground changed hands, but casualties on both sides were heavy in a week's intermittent fighting. Around Kebir and to the south, the French were unable to hold against the German onslaught, spearheaded by the new Mark VI "Tiger" tanks, and the attacking force, in three sections, took the reservoir area and Djebel Mansour. By evening of January 19 the road near Sidi Saïd was blocked and the attackers had reached Hir Moussa. The French were now calling for assistance, and both British and American forces were put in motion—the British toward Rebaa Oulad Yahia and CC "B" from Kesra toward Ousseltia.

By 0930 of January 21, CC "B" was assembled some 5 miles southwest of Ousseltia, while elements of British 36th Brigade reached Rebaa before daylight. Robinett, under orders from French XIX Corps' Koeltz, counter-attacked eastward along the Ousseltia–Kairouan road after readying artillery and air support. CC "B" made progress, and at nightfall the German Armored Group Lüder (one of Weber's three sections) fell back into defensive positions, enabling French troops cut off in the hills near the pass to escape.

Next morning Robinett was ordered to suspend his eastward attack and drive up the Ousseltia Valley toward Hir Moussa. This movement was checked by stiff German resistance. Robinett estimated he would need two battalions of infantry, tank destroyers, and artillery to clear the path for his advance, and Fredendall at II Corps told him to hold on where he was (French orders to advance notwithstanding).

Reinforcements for Robinett in the shape of elements of the U. S. 1st Infantry Division now began to arrive, and on January 25 an advance was begun toward Kairouan. By this time Weber's Germans had begun their withdrawal, leaving the defense of the area to the Italians. The 1st Division men (3rd Battalion, 26th Infantry Combat Team) pushed the Italians back toward the western end of the pass, where any further advance was checked by stiff German resistance.

The Germans could be well satisfied with "Eilbote." Their new line ran west of the northern passes, and Allied losses (mainly French) had amounted to more than 4,000 POWs. German claims included 24 tanks, 52 guns, 27 anti-tank guns, and over 200 vehicles. On the Allied side of the score the Germans had also suffered some losses, and the inner-Allied command problems

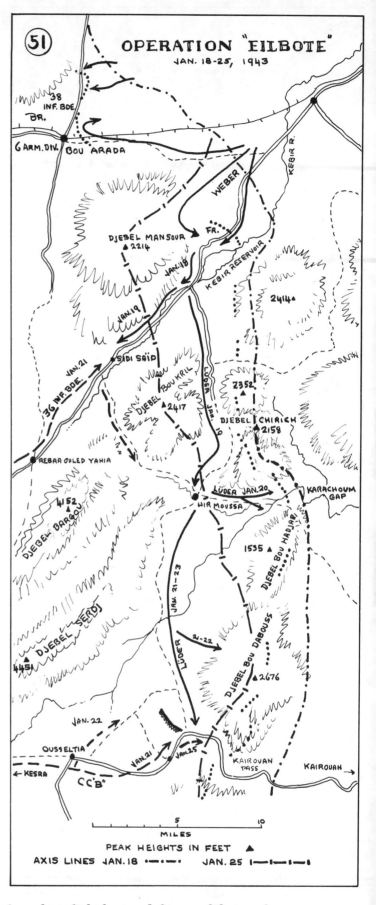

brought to light hastened the consolidation of command (January 26) noted above.

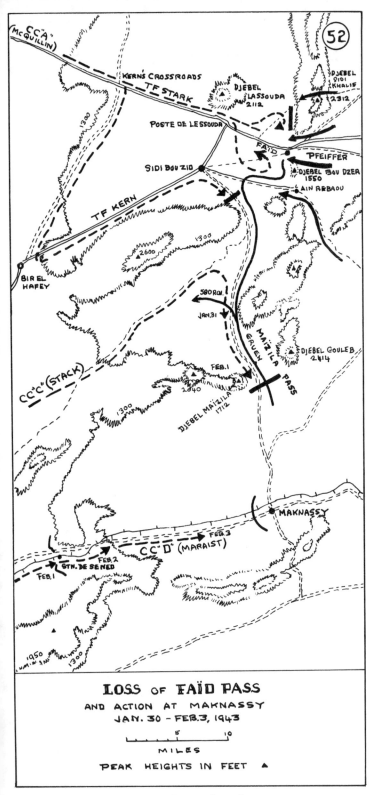

LOSS of FAÏD PASS
AND ACTION AT MAKNASSY
JAN. 30 - FEB. 3, 1943

0   5   10
MILES

PEAK HEIGHTS IN FEET ▲

Loss of Faïd Pass

U. S. II Corps was now attached to First Army, and Fredendall was ordered to assume command of the American, British, and French forces south of a line running roughly from Morsott–Thala–Sbiba–Fondouk el Aoureb and north of a line from Gabès to the salt marshes (below that was, or soon would be, Eighth Army hunting grounds). In effect II Corps was to hold the Army's right flank. At the

same time, many French units were to be withdrawn for re-equipment and retraining. Under the circumstances, it was difficult to heed Eisenhower's admonition to Anderson to keep the U. S. 1st Armored Division concentrated. Axis forces now held the eastern passes north of Fondouk el Aoureb, and an attack, and it was likely there would be one, might come at any one of several points. The French thought that Faïd Pass and Gafsa Oasis should be strongly held; at the same time it was desirable to concentrate a sufficient force to take the offensive if at all possible. "Eilbote" had in fact disrupted an ambitious plan of Fredendall's for four simultaneous assaults on Fondouk el Aoureb, Maknassy, El Guettar, and Bir Mrabott (these last in the Gafsa area). CC "B" was engaged at Ousseltia, and the attacks on El Guettar and Bir Mrabott were dropped, but CC "C," U. S. 1st Armored Division, was assigned the Maknassy operation.

Against the advice of Generals Ward (commanding U. S. 1st Armored Division) and Welvert (commanding the French Constantine Division), who feared it might tip the Germans off to the prospective attack, Fredendall ordered a raid against Sened (January 24–25). It was probably good for CC "C's" morale and netted some 96 prisoners for no American losses. As it turned out, the Maknassy plan came to nothing, and 1st Armored soon had its hands full. Early on the morning of January 30 the veteran 21st Panzer Division, aided by Italian units, attacked Faïd Pass.

The pass through the Eastern Dorsal at Faïd is a broad one, through which runs the main road from Sfax to Sbeitla. There were two other gaps, crossed by trails at Sidi Khalif and Aïn Rebaou, a few miles north and south of Faïd Pass, respectively. The 21st Panzer Division was organized for this operation in two groups—Kampfgruppe Pfeiffer—subdivided into three small task forces, and Kampfgruppe Gruen. The three columns of the former attacked the passes at Faïd, while the latter attacked through Maïzila Pass, farther to the south, in an encircling move that would enable it to attack Faïd village from the rear (see map).

The French defenders, about 1,000 men, were finally forced back from the flanking passes into Sidi Bou Zid, and by midafternoon Faïd village was taken. CC "A" at Sbeitla had received orders to counter-attack—but without weakening the Sbeitla defenses! After some delay a reconnaissance company went east followed by a company of tanks, one of armored infantry, and a battery of field artillery. At 1400 the reconnaissance company reported the area from Faïd village to Rebaou Pass held by enemy infantry and tanks. Reinforcements following from Sbeitla were attacked by enemy aircraft, and Brigadier General R. McQuillin, Commanding Officer of CC "A," decided not to attack until next morning. In the meantime the defenders of Faïd Pass itself, cut off in the west, still stubbornly held the eastern end of the pass.

By morning the German forces had dug in their weapons and placed their tanks in defilade. An attack by U.S. medium tanks ran into anti-tank fire from concealed weapons and lost several vehicles. The infantry could make no progress, and the artillery was brought under long-range counter-battery fire. Enemy air intervention was effective, while weak Allied air efforts failed to prevent the movement of enemy reinforcements.

With no American aid forthcoming, Faïd Pass was taken by midafternoon (bringing a strong protest from French headquarters regarding the tardy U.S. response).

Colonel R. Stack's CC "C" had meanwhile been ordered (1300, January 30) to start northeastward from Gafsa toward Sidi Bou Zid and bivouacked some 30 miles southwest of that place. Next morning as CC "C" was nearing the Faïd battle area, Stack received radioed orders to turn south to co-operate with CC "D" (Colonel R. Maraist) in an attack through Maïzila Pass on Maknassy. This was the result of overoptimism at II Corps' headquarters as to what was happening around Faïd—American troops believed advancing had already been beaten back. Also, Stack was not in direct communication with McQuillin so could not get the true picture from him. General Welvert, who seems to have had a better grasp of the situation than II Corps, saw Stack personally and got him to question the order with the U. S. 1st Armored Division commander. Ward confirmed Fredendall's order, so CC "C" went on toward Maïzila while CC "A" and the remaining French tried once more to regain Faïd Pass.

Despite heavy artillery preparation, McQuillin's infantry were soon pinned down by machine guns, mortar, and artillery, while a flank attack by Panzers from Faïd threw the northern flank into confusion. A battalion (3rd, 1st Armored Regiment) of tanks was met by heavy fire from well-concealed weapons. A second German onslaught by some nine Mark IVs, although ultimately driven back by tanks, self-propelled guns, tank destroyers, and artillery, further discomfited the infantry, and

the American attack petered out. The Allies remained in Sidi Bou Zid, while the Axis forces, supported by heavy long-range artillery (some of 210mm), held all the approaches to the western end of Faïd Pass.

Stack's attack on Maïzila Pass on February 1 encountered an enemy strongly reinforced during the night. An Axis counter-attack was repulsed, but orders from Division held up the advance until about 1700. As darkness fell, part of the western end of the pass was in American hands, but next morning orders came canceling the operation and recalling CC "C" north to Hadjeb el Aïoun.

Maraist's CC "D" attack through Sened to Maknassy was equally unsuccessful. The assault on Sened began late on January 31 and was repeatedly harassed by German aircraft. Stukas "stunned the infantry and caused substantial casualties" (Official History of the U. S. Army in World War II) and forced the delay of the attack until the next morning. Reinforcements sent up during the night were mistakenly guided into the enemy's rear area and many were captured. Sened was finally entered about 1640 and held during the night. Maraist was not only harassed by enemy aircraft, but also by conflicting orders from Corps and Division (both in conflict with Eisenhower's directive that the U. S. 1st Armored Division be concentrated for defense of the central front, even if it meant giving up the Eastern Dorsals, evacuating Gafsa and the important forward airfield at Thélepte).

Undeterred, Maraist pushed his attack toward Maknassy next morning. His tanks were heavily dive-bombed, but by noon his force held the ridge east of Sened. Here, at 1600, an enemy counter-attack nearly brought about a disaster. The infantry were badly shaken by Stuka attacks and the appearance of 16 enemy tanks on the left flank caused a panic. Troops retired on the run and the road west was jammed with fleeing vehicles. It was not until 1900 that the rout was checked and the position restored.

The attack was renewed next morning—tanks, tank destroyers, and self-propelled guns out in front of the infantry to guard against more tank attacks—and by noon reconnaissance units were within six miles of Maknassy. At this point, II Corps ordered CC "D" back to Gafsa.

The entire operation was disappointing, marked by conflicting orders and little singleness of purpose at II Corps' headquarters, and showing the difficulty of operating with green troops during a period of enemy superiority in the air.

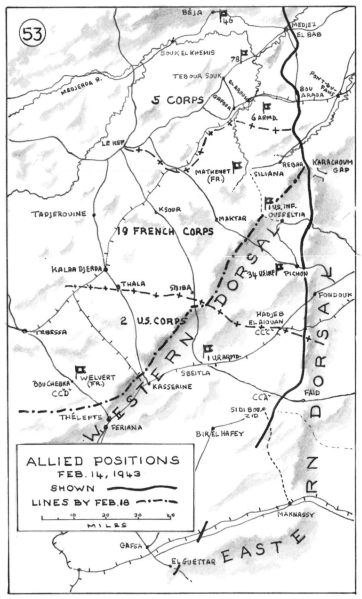

At the same time as the Faïd operations, von Arnim ordered an attack made against Hir Moussa and the heights northeast of Rebaa Oulad Yahia. An armored column was beaten back just short of the latter place by the British 36th Brigade on January 31. Between February 3 and 5, troops of the 1st Guards Brigade and 1st Parachute Brigade tried unsuccessfully to drive the Germans from Djebel Mansour and the area around the Kebir reservoir lost in the "Eilbote" operation on January 18.

The Axis Attacks II Corps

It was anticipated at Allied headquarters that von Arnim would attack again at some point or points in central Tunisia. Movements of his armored units were carefully watched, and Allied forces were located at strategic points. Meanwhile, First Army was beginning the often-deferred formation of a substantial reserve—necessary for the

all-out offensives planned for early spring. The British 6th Armored Division was to be relieved and refitted with Sherman tanks, while the British 46th Division and the 133rd and 135th Combat Teams of U. S. 34th Infantry Division moved up. There was considerable shifting of other troops with the object of reuniting and consolidating units, notably the U. S. 1st Infantry Division, some of whom had been separated for many weeks. The map shows roughly the areas where the various units were concentrated on the eve of the German offensive.

Eisenhower and Anderson met at Fredendall's headquarters near Tébessa on February 13. After reviewing the situation the Commander-in-Chief concluded arrangements were "as good as could be made pending the development of an actual attack. . . ." That evening he went as far forward as Sidi Bou Zid, returning to Tébessa late that night. Late that same day word had been sent from First Army headquarters that the enemy would attack the next day.

The Axis attack was a co-ordinated affair planned by Rommel and von Arnim. The two commands were not yet united, but Rommel believed the moment ripe for a successful drive, providing it was done speedily, before the Eighth Army was in a position to interfere and while American strength in the area was still building up. There was considerable chaffering as to who was to control which divisions, and Commando Supremo's original plan to attack Gafsa with all available mobile forces was revised. The final plan was for an initial operation against Sidi Bou Zid by the 10th and 21st Panzer Divisions and Superga Division ("Operation Fruehlingswind") under General Heinz Ziegler while a later attack would be made by Rommel in the Gafsa area when elements of 21st Panzer could be released to him. Available for the attack on Sidi Bou Zid were more than 200 Mark III and IVs plus 11 or 12 Mark VI "Tigers." The force to attack Gafsa was a Kampfgruppe from D.A.K. with some 53 German and 17 Italian tanks.

For the actual attack 10th Panzer organized three assault groups—Gerhardt, Reimann, and a reserve—while 21st Panzer split into two groups—Schuette and Stenkhoff. On February 13, Rommel, von Arnim, and the Luftwaffe commander met Ziegler just east of Faïd Pass. Plans were reviewed and finalized and at 1630 the next morning German tanks and armored infantry rolled out from the western mouth of the pass where Combat Command "A" was waiting.

The Battle of Sidi Bou Zid

Rising out of the plain north of the little village of Sidi Bou Zid is Djebel Lassouda (644 meters high). Stationed there was Lassouda Force (Lieutenant Colonel J. Waters), comprised of tanks, tank destroyers, artillery, and infantry. These occupied positions on the flat during the day and retired to the hill defenses at night. Southeast of Sidi Bou Zid was Djebel Ksaira (550) where a force of infantry and artillery was posted under Colonel Drake. Observation posts on both hills were in communication with the command post of CC "A" in Sidi Bou Zid. Near the village was a mobile reserve of some 40 tanks under Lieutenant Colonel L. Hightower.

Patrolling tanks of Lassouda Force were the first to engage the enemy. One of the first tanks knocked out was the company commander's, and radio communication with Colonel Waters was lost. The prepared artillery barrage on the pass was therefore not requested. CC "A" then sent tanks and tank destroyers out from Sidi Bou Zid. These ran into 88s and "Tigers" and were outranged and checked. Strong enemy tank forces were now moving past Lessouda (see map) from north and south. Hightower attempted to check these movements but was forced to retire with heavy loss.

The southern flanking movement through Maïzila Pass (Kampfgruppe Schuette) was engaged by Colonel Drake, fighting continuing all afternoon. The Stenkhoff group, after an unopposed left hook to Bir el Hafey, turned northeast toward Sidi Bou Zid. General Ward believed at first the situation was under control, but reports of heavy losses and the presence of strong enemy forces made it plain that the troops at Sidi Bou Zid would have to be pulled back. Djebel Lassouda was surrounded and Drake's forces were cut off on Djebel Ksaira. McQuillin was authorized to retreat, and by 1405, CC "A's" headquarters was some seven miles southwest of Sidi Bou Zid. The remnants of Hightower's tanks were fighting a rear-guard action, covering CC "A's" withdrawal.

A protective line was established by infantry and light tanks from Sbeitla under Colonel Kern at a crossroads (Kern's Crossroads) 11 miles northwest of Sidi Bou Zid. Here badly battered CC "A," harried in their retirement by tank and artillery fire, rallied for the defense of Sbeitla. Hightower personally led his few remaining tanks in foiling enemy attempts to disrupt the retreat. At the end of the day his tank was destroyed but he and his crew escaped.

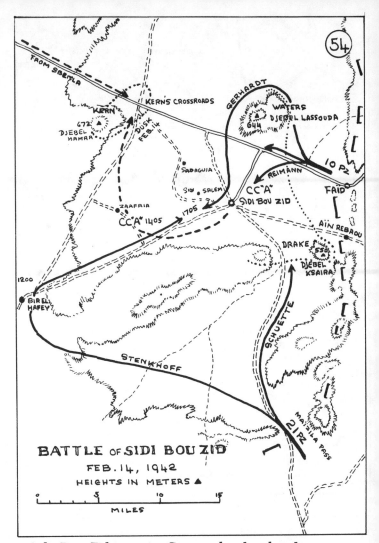

BATTLE OF SIDI BOU ZID
FEB. 14, 1942
HEIGHTS IN METERS ▲

Sidi Bou Zid was in German hands, the defenders of Djebel Lessouda and Djebel Ksaira were isolated, and the line of retreat was marked by burning or abandoned U.S. vehicles. Losses included 44 tanks, 15 self-propelled guns, 9 105mm pieces, and all the 155s of 2nd Battalion, 17th Field Artillery.

A counter-attack was at once ordered to restore the situation and bring out the Americans under Drake cut off on Djebel Ksaira and a smaller group on Djebel Garet Hadid. Water's force holding Djebel Lassouda would be relieved in a subsequent operation. For the counter-attack Stack's CC "C" was ordered south from Hadjeb el Aïoun, and II Corps pried loose 2nd Battalion, 1st Armored Regiment (Lieutenant Colonel J. Alger) from CC "B" near Maktar. The strength of the German attack had been underestimated, and although Welvert appealed to First Army through II Corps to release all of CC "B," Army headquarters refused. As no units from 10th Panzer had been identified so far in the Sidi Bou Zid operation it was, therefore, believed to be still facing (and threatening) the French XIX Corps, so CC "B's" presence at Maktar

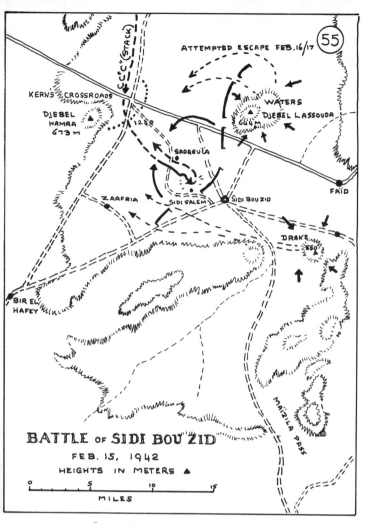

BATTLE of SIDI BOU ZID
FEB. 15, 1942
HEIGHTS IN METERS ▲

0   5   10   15
MILES

was deemed necessary. At the same time it was felt that the defense of Gafsa stretched Allied resources too far and it was ordered evacuated. This was done the night of February 14–15, the troops pulling back to Fériana.

Colonel Stack's force assembled near Djebel Hamra, some 13 miles from Sidi Bou Zid. At 1240 the attack began, tanks and self-propelled guns in the lead, followed by artillery and infantry in half-tracks, with tank destroyers on the flanks. Luftwaffe bombers and fighters strafed the column, then the German artillery opened fire. Radio reports from Waters and Drake described enemy movements, unfolding on the plain at their feet. As CC "C" rumbled forward, resistance increased, and the U.S. artillery went into position and began counter-battery fire. The little village of Sidi Salem was reached, but attempts to pass it were beaten back. Alger's tank was one of those knocked out, and he was among the prisoners. Strong enemy forces were now moving in on either flank, and a retreat began. The armored infantry escaped the envelopment, but the battered armored force had to fight its way back through fierce anti-tank fire from both flanks. Only four tanks returned that

evening. German claims listed 39 tanks, 17 half-tracks, and 3 self-propelled guns, as well as artillery pieces and some 100 vehicles taken or destroyed. The Americans claimed 13 Mark IVs as well as 88s and artillery pieces damaged or destroyed (German reports also mention that all their tanks were salvaged). Personnel losses were heavy. On the night of February 16–17 the forces left in the hills tried to break out on foot after destroying their equipment and heavy weapons. They were surrounded at daylight of February 17, cut down by machine-gun fire, and all but a few survivors were captured. Colonels Waters and Drake were among the nearly 1,500 taken. Two of 1st Armored's Combat Commands had been shattered with little but bitter experiences to show for it.

Axis troops occupied Gafsa on February 15 while Ziegler ordered 10th Panzer Division to push toward Sbeitla early on February 16 and to be prepared to attack the town later in the day. During this period, elements of the 10th and 21st Panzer were mopping up Waters' and Drake's strongly defended positions in the hills. It was not the Allies' intention to retain Sbeitla permanently; at the same time, it was vital to hold it long enough to win time to organize the defense of Sbiba Gap. On February 15, Anderson, realizing that the plan to hold forward positions had been too ambitious, wrote Eisenhower that a withdrawal to the Western Dorsal should be considered and pointing out that losses incurred in trying to hold positions to the east might endanger the whole southern flank. "I think," Anderson wrote, "it is essential that we hold the Grand [Western] Dorsal itself, and I am prepared to fight all out to insure this."

Loss of Sbeitla

The eastern approaches to Sbeitla were screened by forward positions near Kern's Crossroads and Djebel Hamra. General Ward's main line of resistance was at the edge of olive groves some 3 miles east of the town. The southern sector was to be held by CC "B" (finally released by First Army) and the northern by the battered CC "A," now reinforced and with CC "C" attached. As the German advance force (Group Gerhardt) made contact—about 1700 on February 16—the screening forces withdrew fighting while CC "A" completed its move from Djebel Hamra into its defensive positions. A second German group (Pfeiffer's) was to pass through Group Gerhardt and make the actual attack.

It was dark by the time Pfeiffer's advance units opened fire on the dimly seen tanks of the American rear guard. "Overs" fell into the olive groves, where there were parked vehicles and fuel and supply dumps. The troops were tired and dispirited after the actions of the past 3 days. Few had undergone a night attack. As random shells burst among the olive trees and engineers began demolitions in the town, some vehicles pulled out and started to move west. Others followed and the roads through Sbeitla became jammed with vehicles of all descriptions. Fortunately other units of CC "A" kept their positions, and the Germans, unaware of the panic, decided to wait for daylight to resume their advance.

Ward's report of the situation reached Anderson who, at 0130 on February 17 authorized Fredendall to withdraw Ward from Sbeitla and a force under Stark (previously at Gafsa) from Fériana. Anderson also ordered a mixed Anglo-American force under Brigadier C. Dunphie to the defense of the Sbiba Gap. All aircraft from Thélepte were to be flown off at dawn and demolitions carried out (a setback for the badly needed tactical air support, as operations at that sandy field were never interrupted by rain). Thirty-four aircraft unable to fly

were destroyed. Fériana and the airfield were occupied by D.A.K. later in the day. Ward's force retired into the defenses of the Kasserine Pass during the night of February 17–18.

The delaying action at Sbeitla now fell to Robinett's CC "B." The German attack was delayed until noon. The first onslaught, in great strength, struck a tank-destroyer battalion (601st). These, no match for the German Panzers, were soon in hasty retreat. Some were rallied near CC "B's" command post. Most were swept along in the stream of vehicles heading for Kasserine. A frontal attack on the tanks of the 2nd Battalion 13th Armored Regiment (Lieutenant Colonel H. Gardiner) was beaten off. The U.S. tankers waited hull down until the enemy was at close range, then let fly a salvo that knocked out at least 5 enemy tanks and sent the others to the right about. An hour later the attack was renewed on the southern flank. Robinett had by now received an order to begin a gradual withdrawal toward Kasserine Pass. The disengaging movement began around 1430 and was completed, not without loss, after dark.

Combat Command A, what was left of it, headed

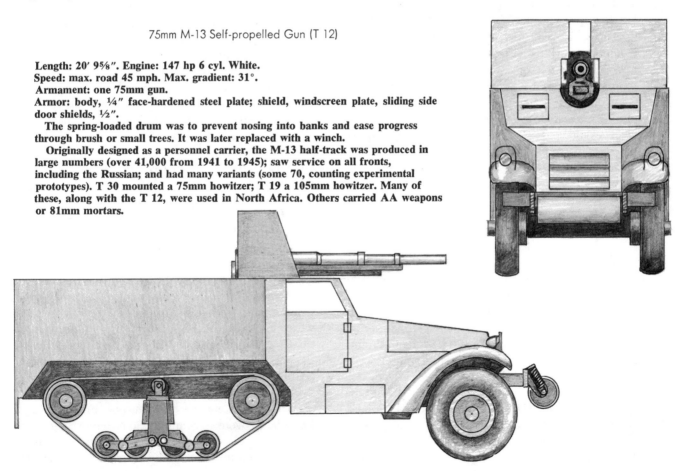

75mm M-13 Self-propelled Gun (T 12)

**Length: 20' 9⅝". Engine: 147 hp 6 cyl. White.
Speed: max. road 45 mph. Max. gradient: 31°.
Armament: one 75mm gun.
Armor: body, ¼" face-hardened steel plate; shield, windscreen plate, sliding side door shields, ½".**
  The spring-loaded drum was to prevent nosing into banks and ease progress through brush or small trees. It was later replaced with a winch.
  Originally designed as a personnel carrier, the M-13 half-track was produced in large numbers (over 41,000 from 1941 to 1945); saw service on all fronts, including the Russian; and had many variants (some 70, counting experimental prototypes). T 30 mounted a 75mm howitzer; T 19 a 105mm howitzer. Many of these, along with the T 12, were used in North Africa. Others carried AA weapons or 81mm mortars.

for Tébessa, via the Sbiba position, while CC "C," after covering McQuillin's retirement, broke off contact with the Germans and retreated in good order to Kasserine. The enemy entered Sbeitla about 1700. Bridges and the aqueduct supplying Sfax had been blown up and most supplies destroyed or removed. By February 18, the U. S. 1st Armored Division, more or less in one piece, took up positions near Tébessa. In the meantime Group Gerhardt of 10th Panzer was moving north (slowed by mines) to take Pichon and trap the Allied troops in the upper leg of the Eastern Dorsal. These, however, got away in good time, and 10th Panzer's thrust missed its mark—at a time when it could have been better employed elsewhere.

Rommel's Offensive—Kasserine Pass

The offensive, as originally conceived, had fulfilled its purpose, and the Allies, after suffering considerable loss, had been driven back to the Western Dorsals. But to Rommel it seemed that there was now an opportunity for a far more sweeping advance—the sort of operation he had envisaged when arguing for early withdrawal of his army from Libya to Tunisia. He proposed nothing less than a powerful drive through Tébessa, which, if successful, might reach Bône itself, which in turn would mean Allied withdrawal from Tunisia.

Von Arnim felt this was too risky. Tébessa was some 50 miles past Kasserine; Tébessa's approaches were dominated by high ground, and it was supplied by two roads and two railroads. An advance on it would call for a smoothly operating supply system with ample transport, which was not available (Rommel had a reputation for brushing aside such details).

To carry out his plan Rommel wanted the 10th and 21st Panzer Divisions, and also a holding attack in the north by the Fifth Panzer Army. Von Arnim had no intention of releasing any more units to Rommel than he could help and ordered a halt to operations westward of the crest of the Eastern Dorsals. Rommel appealed to Commando Supremo and to Kesselring, who gave his full approval. On the night of February 18, Commando Supremo directed Rommel, with 10th and 21st Panzers and any available units of his German-Italian Panzer Army, to attack toward Le Kef. The Fifth Panzer Army was to launch a holding attack and even, in co-operation with Naval Command, Africa, to land troops at Tabarka. The Second Air Force was to drop a parachute mission to destroy the bridges at Le Kef.

Rommel got his armor (though von Arnim still retained part of 10th Panzer, including its heavy Panzer battalion—for which Kesselring upbraided him later) but was unhappy that Le Kef instead of Tébessa (as he and Kesselring had planned) was named as the primary objective. Le Kef, he felt, was in the very center of the Allied reserves, whereas Tébessa was a vital base and starting point for II Corps' drive to Gabès. But time was precious and rather then get into a lengthy hassle with Commando Supremo, he gave orders for the advance to begin at dawn on February 19. D.A.K. (Angriffsgruppe Nord) was to attack into Kasserine Pass, while 21st Panzer tried the gap at Sbiba. The 10th was ordered back from the Pichon area to Sbeitla, to be ready to move to whichever pass proved the easier. Mobile units of Centauro Division were ordered to advance on Tébessa from the southeast.

Allied defense of the western passes called for some rapid shuffling of available units, and by February 19 there were considerable forces at or in support of Sbiba and Kasserine. Nine miles north of Sbiba at Rohia was headquarters of the British 6th Armored Division. Elements of that division, under Brigadier C. Dunphie, moved to Thala. In the vicinity of Sbiba were British 1st Guards Brigade; 18th U. S. Combat Team (1st Infantry Division); three battalions of the U. S. 34th Infantry Division; 16th/5th Lancers (6th Armored Division); 2nd Hampshires; 3 U. S. Field Artillery battalions; parts of two R.A. anti-tank regiments, and some French detachments. The U. S. 1st Armored Division was reorganizing at Tébessa. Combat teams and task forces of II Corps were scattered along the front. At Kasserine, Colonel Stark commanded a miscellaneous group including 1st Battalion, 26th Infantry; 33rd Field Artillery Battalion; 805th Tank Destroyer Battalion; elements of the U. S. 19th Combat Engineers, and a battery of French 75mms (Stark Force). At the pass at El Ma el Abiod was 3rd Battalion, 26th Combat Team (Bowen Force). A Franco-American force under Welvert was strung along the high ground in between. The weary and battered 1st Armored was to be responsible for the defense of Tébessa, lay mines, cover the passes with artillery fire, and be ready to mount counter-attacks if necessary.

Plans for the defense of Kasserine Pass were only partially complete by morning of February 19. Mine fields were incomplete. Some mines, for lack of proper tools, were strewed unburied. Stark had hardly set up his command post when 88mm shells began bursting nearby. At midmorning enemy troops were seen unloading southeast of the pass and scaling the heights on either side.

The initial attack was made by two battalions of the veteran Panzer Grenadier Regiment Afrika. After heavy fighting these were checked by intense fire, and a battalion of Panzers moved up in support. Five tanks were crippled in a mine field, and the attack made slow progress against heavy American anti-tank and machine-gun fire. By dark the Grenadiers had succeeded in taking a high hill on the north side of the pass and captured some 100 prisoners, but the pass was not yet won.

Both Stark and the German commander, General Buelowius, had received some reinforcements during the action. Dunphie drove in from Thala in the afternoon, thinking his command might be committed. He felt Stark's situation was deteriorating and asked First Army for permission to commit his (Dunphie's) armor. This was refused by Brigadier McNabb, First Army Chief of Staff. Only a detachment of 11 tanks, a battery, some anti-tank guns, and a company of infantry, under Lieutenant Colonel A. Gore, were sent, arriving at the northwestern end of the pass about 0400 on February 20.

Rommel had originally planned to send 10th Panzer through Sbiba while merely sealing Kasserine Pass. But 21st Panzer's attack through the Sbiba Gap ran into mine fields covered by accurate artillery fire. Finding the pass well defended, Rommel then decided to route 10th Panzer through Kasserine, where the attack was progressing more favorably.

At the latter pass, German troops had gained ground during the night, especially in the northern sector—the U.S. 26th Infantry being hard hit. On the morning of the 20th Gore's detachment advanced to support the main line of resistance in the pass, while Stark sent other troops to try to restore the situation on the northern flank. Buelowius' infantry continued their attack supported by all his artillery, including 88s and a battery of the new rocket projectors (150mm "Nebelwerfer"). The attack did not progress fast enough for Rommel, who ordered in two battalions and then a third. At 1630 he directed an all-out assault with tanks and infantry and a very heavy concentration of artillery. By this time the command post of the 19th Combat Engineers had been overrun and the regiment was falling back. As the German tanks began to break out of the mine fields, the U.S. artillery was pulled back, while the French ran out of ammunition for their 75mms and disabled and abandoned them.

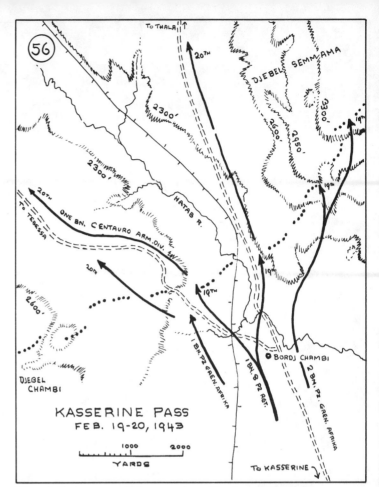

KASSERINE PASS
FEB. 19-20, 1943

The defense was disintegrating. Tanks of D.A.K. and 10th Panzer, plus 5 German and one Italian infantry battalions, supported by 5 battalions of artillery, advanced up the pass. Gore's British detachment fought ("a valiant stand") until their tanks were all destroyed, then made a fighting retreat toward Thala. Many U.S. units were cut off on Djebel Semmama and much equipment lost.

Kesselring himself was at the pass on February 20. On his way back to Rome he saw von Arnim, who asked for 10th Panzer to be returned to his control. Far from complying, Kesselring ordered the Fifth Panzer Army to make diversionary attacks at once and recommended to Commando Supremo that Rommel assume command of such elements of the Fifth Panzer Army as were, or would be, participating in the offensive. He also ordered the parts of the 10th Panzer Division withheld by von Arnim sent to Rommel immediately. It was too late for these units to arrive in time for the big push on February 21 but, having left von Arnim with "a flea in his ear," so to speak, Kesselring headed for Rome while Rommel organized his drive with the forces at hand.

In the meantime, Allied units were being moved into the battle area—part of the U. S. 1st Infantry Division to Bou Chebka and CC "B" toward Thala. Brigadier Dunphie's 26th Armored Brigade (less

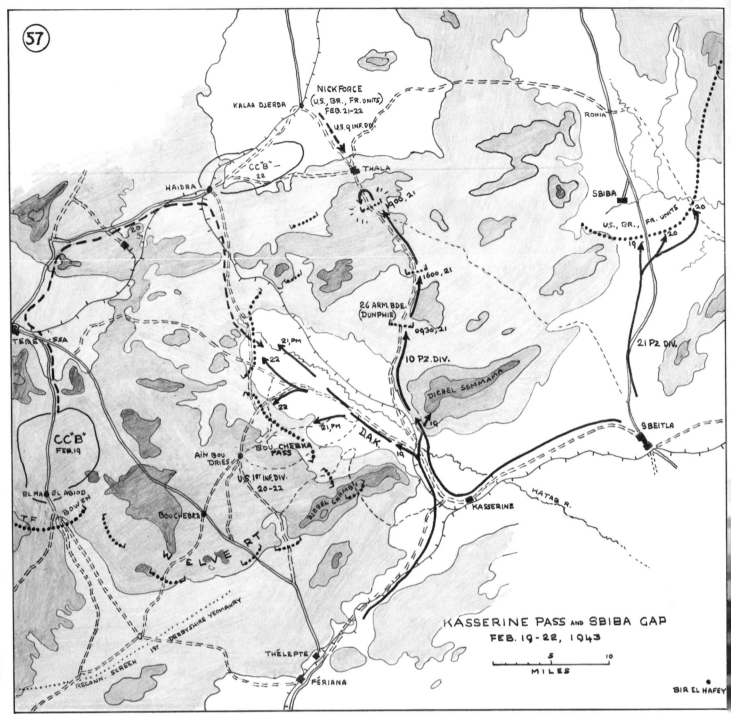

KASSERINE PASS AND SBIBA GAP
FEB. 19-22, 1943

5   10
MILES

16th/5th Lancers at Sbiba) established a line 9 miles north of the pass on the road to Thala. Fredendall now being convinced that the main threat was to Tébessa, he ordered Robinett to stop this advance while Dunphie was to guard Thala. For this operation Dunphie was put in sole command—an impossible task considering the distance between the various commands and the poor communications. First Army further complicated things by ordering Brigadier C. Nicholson (second in command, British 6th Armored Division) in control of all troops south of Thala. "Nickforce," containing British, American, and French units, made ready to

meet Rommel's next move.

On February 20, 21st Panzer had made another effort to break the Allied defenses at Sbiba. Poor weather hampered the Luftwaffe but not the Allied artillery, whose accurate fire stopped what was felt to be an irresolute attack. Rommel therefore ordered the division to make an active defense, and withdrew a reconnaissance battalion to help at Kasserine.

Sbiba was now held by 11 infantry battalions, 3 artillery battalions, and other troops, including a British unit with 25 of the new Churchill tanks.

Rommel had now come to a fork in the road,

both literally as well as figuratively. He did not have sufficient strength to attack strongly along both the road through Thala to Le Kef and the one toward Tébessa. Uncharacteristically he hesitated, prepared for an Allied counter-attack, and sent reconnaissance forces along each road. Dunphie was astride the road to Thala and CC "C" was organizing a defense along the Djebel Hamra ridge (1112). Among the defenders there were stragglers from Kasserine Pass and even from Drake's ill-fated command at Djebel Ksaira. South around Bou Chebka, 2nd Battalion, U. S. 16th Infantry Regiment, and some French Senegalese units were watching the steep, rough passes there.

Rommel's reconnaissance forces ran into opposition on both roads and withdrew. He now decided to throw part of 10th Panzer against the Allies south of Thala while Kampfgruppe D.A.K. secured his western flank by taking the passes at Djebel Hamra. Accurate tank and artillery fire checked D.A.K.'s first attack. The ground was open and dominated by Allied artillery. A night flanking march was decided on but missed in the dark and rain, and the attack was delivered some seven miles southeast, near Bou Chebka. Eight American guns and some 30 vehicles were captured, but the line was pulled back more or less intact. An attack in the right direction toward Djebel Hamra ran into the same deadly artillery concentrations as before. It was obvious there was no chance of forcing a way through the Djebel Hamra passes, and a retirement after dark into Kasserine Pass was planned. By this time a counter-attack organized by 1st Division's General Terry Allen had retaken the ground lost in the morning plus the guns and vehicles. As a bonus a few of CC "B" tanks overtook a retreating Italian battalion, scattered it, and captured vehicles and supplies.

On the Thala road Brigadier Dunphie, with part of his 26th Armored Brigade, fought a delaying action on February 21 against some 50 tanks and self-propelled guns, of 10th Panzer, supported by infantry in half-track carriers. Fifteen of Dunphie's outgunned Crusaders (about to be replaced with Shermans) had been lost by 1600 hours, but it was dark before 10th Panzer, under Rommel's personal command, forced the British tankers to retreat to the last ridge before Thala, where an infantry battalion (2nd Battalion, 5th Leicestershires) with artillery, anti-tank guns, and 4.2-inch mortars held the last defense line. In the dark the German armor followed the last of the British (Dunphie's command vehicle) through a gap in the defenses, not

opening fire until they were well inside the lines. A firefight at point-blank range followed, lit by burning vehicles, flares, and flash of artillery and tank fire. The German troop carriers were on the heels of their tanks and churned after them into the British positions. Nicholson issued "no withdrawal" orders, scraped together the "odds and sods"—every man capable of firing a rifle, and after three hours' pandemonium the enemy withdrew with nearly 600 prisoners. It was a close shave; the defense line was wrecked and the Leicestershires lost heavily, but during the night the U. S. 9th Infantry Division's artillery arrived, after an uninterrupted 4-day march of over 800 miles, and went into position at once.

An abortive dawn counter-attack cost Nicholson 7 more tanks but had the effect of making the German commander (General von Broich) believe that a heavy attack would follow (the arrival of Allied reinforcements must have been audible, if not visible). The morning passed in artillery exchanges, and later in the day Rommel gave orders to go on the defensive. The chance for a drive on Le Kef thus passed, and every hour the Allied positions grew stronger. On the Axis side, fuel and ammunition were running short, and on the afternoon of February 22, Rommel told Kesselring that the offensive now had no chance of success. No help was forthcoming from von Arnim, and Rommel was anxious to return to Mareth. That evening Commando Supremo halted the offensive and ordered a retirement.

The Allied follow-up was hesitant. Not realizing that Rommel had shot his bolt, a day was wasted preparing for an attack that did not come, although Eisenhower had urged Fredendall to counter-attack at once.

It was not until February 25 that the Allies moved cautiously to the attack of the eastern end of the pass. Their advance was unhindered except for mines, demolitions, and booby traps. The enemy had gone.

A shuffle in command within II Corps also had much to do with the delay. Fredendall proposed to Eisenhower that Ward be replaced by Major General E. Harmon, Commanding Officer of 2nd Armored Division (under Patton in Morocco). This was not done, although Harmon was brought in as deputy corps commander. As it turned out, it was Fredendall who went. He had lost the confidence of his divisional commanders and Alexander's opinion of him was unfavorable, as was that of Eisenhower's Chief of Staff, Brigadier General Walter

Bedell Smith, and Major General Omar Bradley, who visited the front as the Commander-in-Chief's personal representative. On March 7, the shrieking sirens of a column of scout cars and half-tracks announced the arrival at II Corps headquarters of the new Commanding Officer, Major General George S. Patton.

Besides a slight dislocation of the Allied timetable, the German offensive had little effect on the outcome of the campaign. Allied losses in men and materiel had been heavy but could be made up. Units in the West had, in many cases, been stripped of their equipment to bring the depleted regiments up to strength.

For the period February 16 to 24, the Germans took just over 4,000 prisoners, nearly two thirds American. They also claimed to have destroyed or taken 235 tanks, 110 self-propelled guns and reconnaissance vehicles, 67 anti-tank guns, 95 personnel carriers and 13 pieces of artillery, besides many trucks, etc. Killed or wounded probably totaled 4,000 more. German losses were almost 1,000, with 20 tanks (which they could ill afford) and other equipment in proportion. To these must be added those of the Italians—although their losses were lighter, as they were not heavily engaged.

Kasserine had an ugly name for a while, but despite some hasty (and unauthorized) withdrawals by some units, the bulk of the green American troops had fought well. They were often up against veterans of the desert fighting, and while usually numerically superior their Stuarts, Grants, and even Shermans were no match for the Panzer Mark IVs and "Tigers." The Americans were also under the disadvantage of operating at a time when enemy air strength was comparatively great. Frequent and often unopposed air attacks can be unsettling even to veterans; to raw troops they can be shattering. By and large, while experiencing the defects of training and leadership to be expected of newly raised armies, the troops of II Corps had little to be ashamed of.

During the whole operation the aircraft of both sides had been engaged as often as the bad weather permitted. Close support by Allied aircraft had been limited by the loss of the comparatively rain-free field at Thélepte, while on February 21 the field at Tébessa had been evacuated because of mud, and the American squadrons there were moved to the overcrowded field at Youks-les-Bains (where one steel-mat strip had been laid). The strips at Gafsa and Sbeitla had been evacuated on February 14 and 15. U.S. aircraft had flown an average of only a little more than 200 sorties a day. Stuka attacks and ground strafings were frequent and often unopposed, and the Allied ground forces, at times, felt that their airmen had let them down.

On the other side of the coin, identification and fire discipline of ground units were often poor, resulting in the destruction or damaging of friendly planes. In the excitement of an air attack a Spitfire might possibly be mistaken for an Me 109, but there was little excuse for shooting up 5 P-38s—an unmistakable plane. But errors were not all with the ground forces. A B-17 raid on Kasserine missed the target in cloudy weather, and the formation bombed Souk el Arba, an important town 100 miles behind Allied lines!

Actually there were numerous attacks on enemy supply columns and airfields, while the bomber squadrons continued their attacks on Axis ports and points of concentration. As more fields were put in operation and more U.S.A.A.F. and R.A.F. fighter squadrons came into action, the enemy air attacks were frequently met and broken up, while damage to enemy ground forces increased.

During February and March the balance of air power tipped gradually in favor of the Allies—and not only because U.S. and British squadrons increased in number, while Axis strength dwindled. The creation of the Mediterranean Air Command, Air Chief Marshal Sir Arthur Tedder as Air Officer Commanding in Chief for all the "Torch" air forces, provided the unified air command so badly needed since the invasion began. Air Marshal Sir Arthur Coningham, on taking over as Commanding Officer, Northwest African Tactical Air Force, found that in many cases little of the knowledge gained in the Western Desert had been applied in Tunisia. Air/ground co-operation was not as advanced as in the Western Desert, nor was the organization for the quick and efficient servicing of aircraft in the forward areas. Fighters, he felt, had been used too defensively to attempt to create "umbrellas" over the ground forces. Instead, he believed an air force always on the offensive gave the troops better protection by carrying the fight to the enemy, denying him use of his fields, and ultimately driving him out of the air. Under Coningham's central control there were rapid improvements not only in maintenance, repair, salvage, and supply but also in ground–air control, communications, and training. Coningham called for a continuous offensive against the Luftwaffe in the air and on his airfields. At the same time, attacks on enemy concentrations and supply truck convoys were stepped up while the raids on ports, freight yards, and depots were not only maintained but even increased as more bomber squadrons became available.

A good part of the increase in Allied front-line strength, both air and ground, can be attributed to the improved supply situation. The invasion force had been short of vehicles from the beginning. Losses through enemy action, improvised maintenance, and general wear and tear over bad roads had made matters worse. By swift co-operation between the War and Navy departments the first of a special shipment of 5,400 trucks began to arrive in Africa less than 3 weeks after Eisenhower requested them. At the same time, U.S. railway engineers managed to more than triple the daily tonnage of 900 tons delivered by the shaky French lines to the front. When diesel engines and rolling stock began to arrive from the States, this tonnage was further increased.

There were command changes on both sides in February. On February 19 General Sir Harold Alexander took command of the newly formed 18th Army Group, succeeding Mark Clark as Deputy Commander-in-Chief, Allied Forces. On February 23, Rommel was (reluctantly) made commander of Army Group Africa (a little too late for the success of his offensive)—and with the understanding that when he was ready to leave he would turn the command over to von Arnim. The German-Italian Panzer Army was, as of February 20, renamed the First Italian Army (AOK1).

Even as Rommel's troops were retiring from their positions west of Kasserine, plans for future operations were being made at both Allied and Axis headquarters.

The next major move on the Allied side was to be made by Eighth Army, driving northward through the Mareth defenses. Simultaneously First Army was to regroup for its main offensive, meanwhile engaging in small holding attacks to draw as much enemy strength away from Montgomery's front as possible. Meantime, new airfields close to the front were to be constructed to accommodate the growing number of Allied squadrons. On the southern front, II Corps would make limited attacks to improve training and morale (in both of which, in Alexander's judgment, II Corps was sorely lacking).

On the Axis side, it was agreed that pressure should be put on in the North while Rommel was withdrawing and regrouping for a blow at Eighth Army. Also, an attack in the North would hopefully

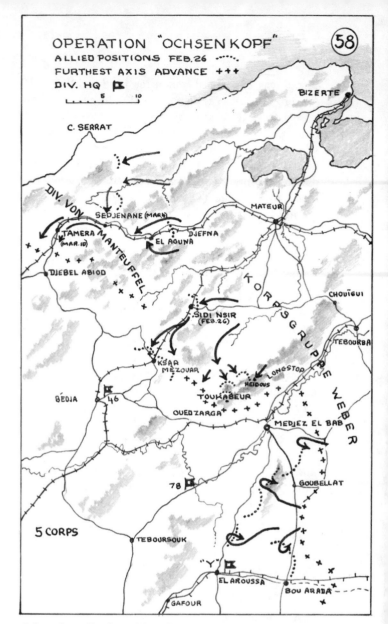

delay the Allied buildup for the offensive expected in the spring. Originally, von Arnim planned a spoiling attack in the Medjez el Bab sector on February 26. But on February 24, the German commander flew to meet Kesselring in Rome (without Rommel's knowledge), and from this conference came a plan for a major offensive along the northern front. Rommel, who was requested to keep 10th and 21st Panzer Divisions in a position to threaten Le Kef, later called it "completely unrealistic."

Operation "Ochsenkopf"

Operation "Ochsenkopf," a drive toward Bou Arada, Medjez el Bab, Teboursouk, and Béja by Korpsgruppe Weber, and a weaker thrust near the coast by von Manteuffel at Djebel Abiod, began on February 26. Von Manteuffel's attack succeeded in driving into the British positions, held in part by two French battalions. The radar station at Cape

Serrat was evacuated and after hard fighting the Axis forces took Sedjenane (March 4). Tamera was defended stoutly but fell on March 10. By March 19, Manteuffel was within 2½ miles of Djebel Abiod. That was as far as he could get. His weary troops had fought a stubborn battle in difficult country, and they were too weakened by losses to continue. They had gained considerable ground and taken 1,600 Allied prisoners and taken or destroyed 16 tanks, 17 artillery pieces, 13 anti-tank guns, and 70 vehicles.

One part of Weber's attack, spearheaded with 77 tanks, including 14 "Tigers," first struck at Sidi Nsir. This was taken by evening of February 26 after a day of sharp fighting. The delay gave time for Allied reinforcements to converge on the danger spot, and when the attack resumed next day—the tanks moving up the valley in fours, interspersed with motorized infantry and armored cars—they came under fire from 5 batteries of artillery and a battery of anti-tank guns. Tanks began to "brew up" and the armored column halted in confusion, the leading section unable to back up or leave the road. At least 11 tanks were destroyed and some 30 more damaged, and the attack fizzled out. By March 1, the commander of this column, Colonel Lang, had only some 5 runners left and he was being nicknamed "Tank Killer." After 4 more days' fighting the front stabilized near Ksar Mezouar. The attack toward Medjez el Bab was also held, after 2 battalions of French Algerian infantry suffered heavy casualties. Fighting continued in this sector until March 2.

A little farther south, Weber's troops, including a mountain regiment, gained ground on February 26, were held the next day, and were driven back on the 28th after losing heavily. Total results claimed by von Arnim for "Ochsenkopf" were 2,500 prisoners and the capture or destruction of 16 tanks, 20 guns, 17 anti-tank guns, and other materiel. His own losses included over 1,000 casualties, 22 tanks destroyed, and nearly 50 damaged. His tank losses, in fact, ran close to 90 per cent—a totally unacceptable figure. The operation had been hastily prepared, poorly planned (with armor used in mountainous terrain), and too late to coincide with Rommel's attempt on Thala. On the positive side, the Axis had won themselves some strong and commanding positions, from which they would later have to be driven before the Allied advance on Tunis began.

By now, despite the bad weather, Allied air power was beginning to assert itself. Enemy records indicate that by March 1, movement of transport by day was almost impossible, while raids on Axis airfields were causing serious damage. Ports, freight yards, and facilities of all kinds came under heavier attack, and cumulative damage made even temporary repairs a lengthy affair. Meanwhile, Allied aircraft from North Africa and Malta sank over 43,000 tons of shipping bound for Tunisia during February, submarines contributing another 18,000 tons.

The Battle of Medenine—March 6, 1943

The Eighth Army's methodical advance from Tripoli, slowed by the need for a massive buildup of fuel and supplies, had been too late to take any pressure off Anderson's forces during the Kasserine crisis. But by February 25, some units were west of Medenine, while the rest of XXX Corps and the New Zealanders were moving up.

Montgomery expected (and welcomed—"exactly what we would like . . .") an enemy spoiling attack, and at 0600 on March 6 it came. The point of assault was at Medenine, an important road and track junction. Rommel had submitted his proposal that his forces, too weak to hold a long front, should retreat, link up with von Arnim's, and hold a line from the northern Tunisian coast through the area around Djebel Mansour (southeast of Pont-du-Fahs) to Enfidaville. This was logical, but it meant that the First and Eighth Armies would unite and also meant giving up many important Axis airfields. On March 8, Kesselring told Rommel that his proposal had been turned down by Hitler and Commando Supremo. In the meantime, Rommel, Messe, Ziegler (acting Commanding Officer of D.A.K.), and the commanders of the German armored divisions discussed plans for the attack. Rommel was not well and no doubt discouraged and bitter about the lost opportunities and the repeated flouting of his advice. Unlike the dynamic commander of old, he did not press his own views of the coming battle and allowed Ziegler and Messe to make the final plans.

The attack was to be made by D.A.K. (10th, 15th, and 21st Panzer Divisions, 2 battalions of infantry and artillery) advancing toward Medenine and the high ground to the northwest while Column Bari (4 battalions of German and 4 of Italian infantry, with artillery and "Nebelwerfers") attacked southeast astride the Mareth–Medenine road. Exact Italian strength is not known but Axis records (incomplete) suggest that the German units had some 124 field guns, 33 88s, and 58 anti-tank guns. As of March 4, D.A.K. could put 144 "runners" into action, mostly Mark IIIs and IVs. Axis aircraft were estimated at about 160.

Montgomery had reinforced XXX Corps (Lieutenant General Oliver Leese) with the New Zealand Division and 8th Armored and 201st Guards Brigade. The combined forces held a front of some 24 miles. In round numbers, Leese had 3 veteran divisions, the equivalent of a fourth, 300 tanks, 350 guns, and 460 anti-tank guns, with 3 fighter wings (about 300 aircraft) based on forward fields.

Men and guns were well dug in. Anti-tank guns were well sited and used for once in their primary role of killing tanks, not protecting the infantry or artillery. The artillery was zeroed in on prearranged squares. The tanks were dispersed in the rear of the infantry, ready to counter-attack when necessary.

A frontal attack on such a position was doomed from the start. The anti-tank gunners had a field day, while massive artillery concentrations pinned down the advancing infantry and wrecked tanks and vehicles (XXX Corps Artillery fired some 30,000 rounds). German sources mention the deadly effect of shell bursts on stony ground, showering infantry and gunners with fragments; also that the artillery regiments suffered severely from attacks by low-flying aircraft. Three batteries of "Nebelwerfers" were destroyed by fighter-bombers.

At the few points where penetrations of the British lines were made, counter-attacks soon restored the situation. Beaten back in their first attempt, the Panzers and Panzer Grenadiers tried again at 1430. Once again a rain of shells on the concentration areas drove the infantry to seek cover and brought the Panzers to a halt. As darkness fell, the D.A.K. disengaged, losing several more tanks in the process. Any hope of renewing the attack next day was abandoned, and Rommel's last battle in Africa was

over. Ironically, it was a repeat of some of his early victories—tanks advancing against murderous gunfire from well-concealed positions. There were even some anti-aircraft guns used in anti-tank roles. Only this time the anti-tank guns were British and the blazing wrecks were Panzers—52 of them. British casualties were negligible.

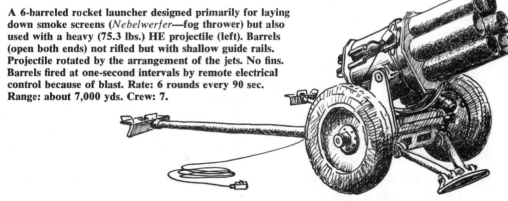

German 15cm Nebelwerfer (Werfer) 41

A 6-barreled rocket launcher designed primarily for laying down smoke screens (*Nebelwerfer*—fog thrower) but also used with a heavy (75.3 lbs.) HE projectile (left). Barrels (open both ends) not rifled but with shallow guide rails. Projectile rotated by the arrangement of the jets. No fins. Barrels fired at one-second intervals by remote electrical control because of blast. Rate: 6 rounds every 90 sec. Range: about 7,000 yds. Crew: 7.

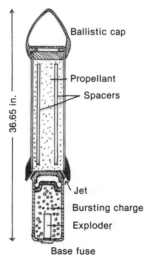

- Ballistic cap
- Propellant
- Spacers
- 36.65 in.
- Jet
- Bursting charge
- Exploder
- Base fuse

BATTLE OF MEDENINE
MAR. 6, 1943
MILES
1   2   3

59

90 LT DIV
7 BN. ARGYLL & SUTH.
7 B WATCH
1 BW
154 BDE.
SPEZIA
1/5 QUEENS ROYAL RGT.
131 BDE.
617 FT
1/7 QUEENS
1/6 QUEENS
2 SGDS.
22 ARM. BDE.
8 ARM. BDE.
3 MILES →
6 GREN. GDS.
201 GDS. BDE.
15 PZ DIV.
886 FT
KSAR REBOUNTEN
3 COLDM GDS.
6 N.Z. BDE.
21 PZ DIV.
7 ARM. HQ
METAMEUR
MEDENINE
10 PZ DIV.
28 N.Z.
5 N.Z. BDE.
21 N.Z.
23 N.Z.
WADI ZESSAR
To MARETH

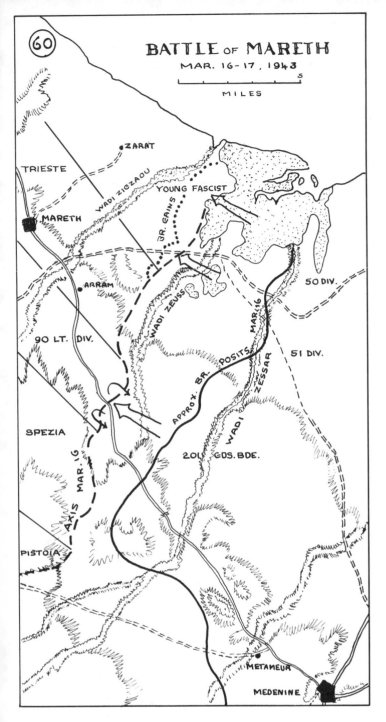

60

BATTLE OF MARETH
MAR. 16-17, 1943

MILES

ZARAT

TRIESTE

WADI ZIGZAOU

YOUNG FASCIST

BR. GAINS

MARETH

ARRAM

WADI ZEUSS

50 DIV

APPROX. BR. POSITS. MAR.16

90 LT. DIV.

WADI ZESSAR

51 DIV.

SPEZIA

AXIS MAR. 16

20L. GDS. BDE.

PISTOIA

METAMEUR

MEDENINE

The Mareth Position

The battle over, Montgomery resumed his task of building up supplies and reserves for his assault on the very strong Mareth positions. These consisted in part of the old French defense system —built before the war to thwart a possible Italian invasion. They ran from the Matmata hills some 22 miles to the coast. This part of the country is cut by many wadis or watercourses—the most important being the Wadi Zigzaou and the Wadi Zeuss. The main defenses ran along the former, whose steep banks had been scarped into an anti-tank ditch. The wadi itself averaged some 60 feet wide. It was defended by nests of pillboxes—some large enough to hold half a battalion—connected by deep trenches. In addition there were miles of wire and some 100,000 anti-tank and 70,000 anti-personnel mines.

The Axis outposts lay just north of the Wadi Zeuss, and between the two wadis were strong fieldworks. Farther south, in the higher ground, the line was not as strongly held, but to guard against a possible flank attack, Axis forces held positions (thinly, because of the length of the line) to the northwest. In the area of the valley between the northwestern end of the Matmata hills and Djebel Tebaga (the Tebaga Gap) the defenses were stronger—wire, an anti-tank ditch, and some 18,000 more mines. To defend the Mareth positions (see map) the Axis had, beginning at the coast: Young Fascist Division; Trieste; 90th Light; Spezia; Pistoia; and on the flank near Ksar el Hallouf, 164th Light.

The armored divisions (10th, 15th, and 21st) were well in the rear and widely separated. Among them they could muster some 142 "runners." Opposed to this, Eighth Army had some 743. In artillery Montgomery could dispose of some 692 field and medium pieces and 1,033 anti-tank guns as against about 445 and 728, respectively. Infantry battalions were equal in number (43 on each side), but the Axis formations were inferior in men and equipment.

Rommel had left Africa on March 9. There were several explanations for his departure. Ill health had certainly something to do with it—but Eisenhower's statement that he "escaped—desiring to save his own skin" can be dismissed. Sick and disgusted he might have been and certain by then that disaster for the Axis forces was inevitable, but to desert his troops would, to a man like Rommel, have been unthinkable. His own explanation, given to his family, was that he flew out to try once more to convince Hitler that the end was in sight and that at least the German troops should be withdrawn while there was still time. Hitler refused and accused him of defeatism. When Rommel then proposed to return and fight with his troops to the bitter end, permission was denied.

Von Arnim now took command of the Army Group. At a conference of Army leaders, Kesselring said the line must be held, from Cape Serrat in the north to Mareth. Von Arnim's objection that the front was too long and too lightly held was overruled, and next day he ordered the vital forward defenses held to the last man. At the same time, the shorter line of Wadi Akarit—40 miles to the northwest of Mareth—was to be strengthened as quickly as possible. Messe was told that in the event of a British breakthrough at the Mareth position and/or the secondary Matmata–Tebaga line, AOK1 was to withdraw to the Wadi Akarit—but not without von Arnim's orders. While Messe was nominally Commanding Officer of AOK1, in fact the German units in his command took their orders from Bayerlein, the Chief of Staff, who had no high opinion of Messe and often acted on his own.

Montgomery's plan of attack was basically a simple one—a frontal attack by XXX Corps (50th Division, 51st Division, 4th Indian Division, 201st Guards Brigade) while Freyberg's New Zealand Corps (New Zealand Division, 8th Armored Brigade, Leclerc's "L" Force) was to pass around the enemy's right flank by Ksar Rhilane, break through the secondary defense line, and try to cut the Axis retreat route by reaching the Gabès–Matmata road. ("L" Force was a mixed force of French and French colonial troops assembled by General Leclerc, Commanding Officer of French troops in Chad. He cleaned the Italians out of the Fezzan region, then marched across Libya and Tripolitania to Tripoli, reaching it on January 26, 1943.) The X Corps (1st and 7th Armored Divisions, the Fighting French Flying Column [a small mixed force of tanks, armored cars, anti-tank and anti-aircraft guns and motorized infantry]) were to be in reserve, ready to exploit XXX Corps' breakthrough. This Corps arrived (March 14) from around Benghazi—for some units a move of 1,300 miles (on the march close to 1.2 million gallons of fuel had to be deposited at strategic dumps along the route).

To aid the Eighth Army, Alexander directed U. S. II Corps to capture Gafsa, threaten Maknassy, and attempt to take El Guettar.

The attack on the Axis outpost positions began on the night of March 16–17. The 50th Division, with heavy artillery support, pushed across the Wadi Zeuss, while on its left, the 51st Division also took its objectives without too much opposition. Farther south, a diversionary attack by the 201st Guards Brigade suffered heavy casualties in an anti-personnel mine field and met strong opposition from 2 battalions of 90th Light. Most objectives were reached, but because of heavy shelling and mortar fire, the Guards could not bring up supporting weapons. They were withdrawn early on March 17. The 50th Division made further gains during the day, and tracks and a crossing were

made over the Wadi Zeuss. Before and during the assault, heavy attacks were made by Allied aircraft of all types. Bombs were dropped on the Mareth strong points, guns and troops positions, and enemy airfields. Strength of the Western Desert Air Force in the Mareth operations was 22 squadrons of fighters and fighter-bombers (a total of 535 aircraft); 7 squadrons of bombers (140 aircraft), and almost 3 full reconnaissance squadrons.

II Corps Advances on Gafsa, El Guettar; Action at Maknassy

At the same time as the British began their attacks on the Mareth outpost line, II Corps, now commanded by Patton, began a well-prepared and limited assault toward Gafsa and El Guettar on the one hand and Maknassy on the other. On March 15, II Corps consisted of 1st, 9th, and 34th Infantry Divisions, 1st Armored Division, 13th Field Artillery Brigade, and the 7 battalions of 1st Tank Destroyer Group. These added up to some 88,000 men.

Spring rains, which had been falling for several days, confined heavy vehicles to the roads, filled the watercourses, and covered the rest of the countryside with mud. The approach marches to the assembly points were uncontested, although slowed somewhat by mines and the weather. The 1st Armored Division, from Kasserine via a newly bulldozed road from Thélepte to the Gafsa–Sidi Bou Zid road, was at a point some 12 miles northwest of Station de Sened by March 17. The 1st Infantry Division, meanwhile, had passed through Fériana and was in position just north of Gafsa. Units of the latter division entered Gafsa around noon—after artillery and air bombardment—only to find the enemy gone. The 1st Ranger Battalion occupied El Guettar on March 18, while the 1st Infantry Division organized the defense of Gafsa.

A three-pronged attack on Station de Sened by Combat Commands A and C, with Combat Team 60 (9th Infantry Division) was held up by heavy rains (which also hampered enemy air activity) until March 20. The Italian defenders were driven out by shellfire and the place was occupied on March 21. The original plan called only for a demonstration toward Maknassy, but Alexander now ordered II Corps to seize the high ground east of the town and to send a light armored raiding party to destroy installations at the airfields around Mezzouna.

Maknassy was brought under artillery fire around midnight on March 21–22 and was evac-

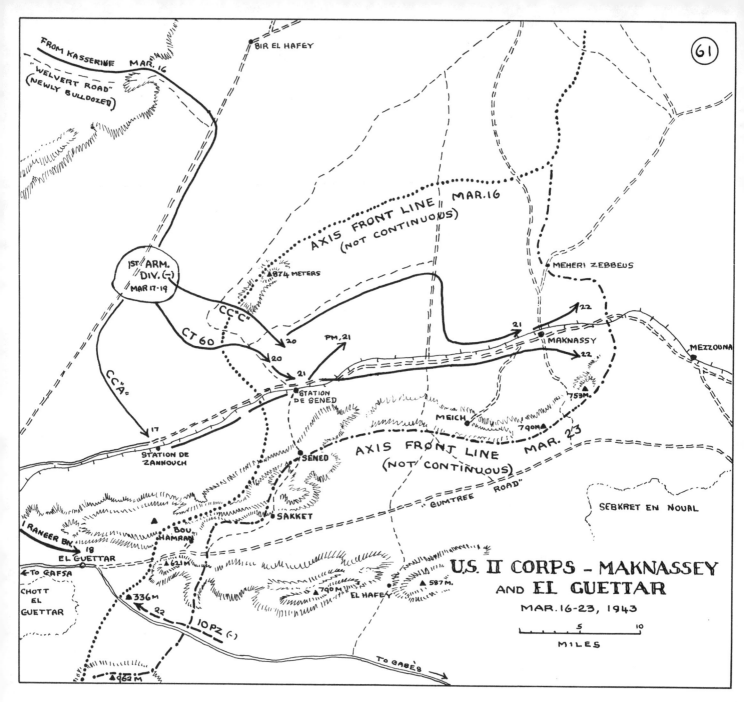

61

FROM KASSERINE MAR. 16
"WELVERT ROAD"
(NEWLY BULLDOZED)

BIR EL HAFEY

AXIS FRONT LINE MAR.16
(NOT CONTINUOUS)

MEHERI ZEBBEUS

1st ARM. DIV. (-) MAR 17-19

▲874 METERS

"CC 'C'"

CT 60

20

20

PM, 21

21

STATION DE SENED

21

MAKNASSY

22

22

MEZZOUNA

CC "A"

▲753M

17

MEICH

STATION DE ZANNOUCH

790M

SENED

AXIS FRONT LINE MAR. 23
(NOT CONTINUOUS)

SAKKET

BOU HAMRAN

"GUMTREE ROAD"

SEBKRET EN NOUAL

I RANGER BN

18

EL GUETTAR

▲631M

U.S. II CORPS — MAKNASSEY AND EL GUETTAR

TO GAFSA

CHOTT EL GUETTAR

▲336M

22

▲790M

EL HAFEY

▲587M

MAR. 16-23, 1943

5   10
MILES

10 PZ (-)

▲462 M

TO GABES

uated as the U.S. forces approached next morning, the enemy retreating to the hills 5 miles to the east. General Ward had the choice of trying to take the hills at once in daylight, or waiting until dark, when his own forces (and also the enemy's) were better prepared. He chose the latter, a decision that Patton later regretted. Patton then directed that the attack be made that night.

The assault was only partially successful. One of the key positions, Hill 322, dominating the gap beyond Maknassy through which passed the road and railway, was strongly held. The 3rd Battalion, 60th Infantry, assigned to the task, was pinned down and forced to dig in. The next morning they resumed their attack, supported by 1st Battalion, 6th

Armored Infantry. It looked as if the new assault would succeed, but Hill 322 was held by a unit composed of Rommel's former bodyguard. These had been reduced to 80 infantrymen when reinforcements arrived. Covered by fire from a few tanks, the newcomers partially restored the situation, and Hill 322 was held despite several more American attacks, supported by as many as 4 artillery battalions.

The next morning, March 24, 3 battalions of infantry and 2 companies of tanks and some tank destroyers assaulted the hill from 3 sides, heavily supported by artillery. Though only 350 in number, the enemy was well dug in and succeeded in throwing back the attackers. The failure to take

Hill 322 was jeopardizing the plan—one that appealed to Patton—of raiding around Mezzouna and possibly even farther. He therefore ordered Ward to personally lead a do-or-die attack the next morning. Ward did so and the 3 battalions gained some ground, but could not hold it under heavy fire. By noon, Ward, who had been slightly wounded, suspended operations while his troops recovered and reorganized.

South of El Guettar the 1st Infantry Division moved into the higher ground against Italians of the Centauro Division. Striking along both the road to Maharès and the road to Gabès, the division took several hundred prisoners and advanced some 8 miles under frequent air attacks, which knocked out guns and vehicles and caused over 50 casualties.

As the II Corps' attacks had been timed to coincide with Montgomery's assault on the Mareth positions, the Axis command could only spare part of 10th Panzer to check an American drive toward Gabès. While Allied headquarters was aware that a counter-attack by this division was imminent, the exact direction was unknown. This became apparent at 0300 on March 23, when 10th Panzer attacked along the Gabès–Gafsa road. Advancing slowly in a great hollow square formation, tanks, self-propelled guns, and troop carriers rolled up the wide gap between the hills on either side. Behind them, trucks carried more infantry. German tanks and infantry overran some American positions in hand-to-hand fighting—taking guns and prisoners and causing heavy casualties—but the heaviest attack, south of the road, ran into concentrated fire from artillery and 2 tank-destroyer battalions. Nearly 30 tanks were destroyed or damaged by the guns, and 8 more came to grief in a mine field running from Chott el Guettar across the road to Hill 336 (see map).

The 10th Panzer now pulled back, towed their disabled armor to a prepared maintenance point some 4 miles in the rear, and prepared for a second assault. Both air forces were active, and strafing and bombing attacks were carried out during the action. At 1645 the enemy attacked again, preceded by an assault by dive bombers. American reinforcements were now in the line and artillery airbursts ". . . crucified them with high-explosive shells and they were falling like flies . . ." as 18th Combat Team reported. Patton, who was watching, commented, "They're murdering good infantry. . . ." Several more tanks were damaged and the attackers withdrew.

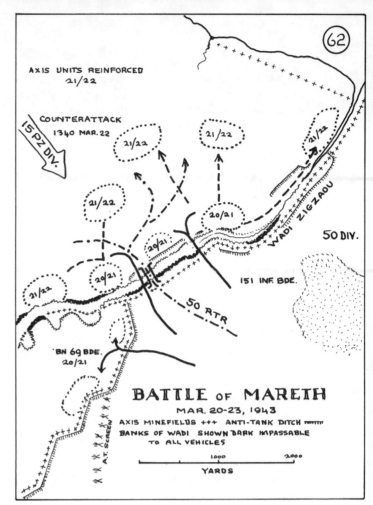

BATTLE OF MARETH
MAR. 20-23, 1943
AXIS MINEFIELDS +++ ANTI-TANK DITCH
BANKS OF WADI SHOWN DARK IMPASSABLE TO ALL VEHICLES

YARDS

The attacks had cost the Germans heavily in tanks and infantry, but they still held a good defensive position and even improved it in a series of small attacks on March 24 and 25. On March 26 the front was temporarily stabilized while II Corps gathered itself for another advance.

The Attack on the Mareth Positions

The Eighth Army, in the meantime, had begun its long-awaited assault on the Mareth positions. New Zealand Corps had already started its wide flanking movement, and when the main attack went in on the night of March 20–21, it was some 20 miles north of Bir Soltane.

The 50th Division's attack began with counter-battery fire followed by a barrage by 16 regiments of artillery. Headed by Scorpions to clear anti-personnel mines, the infantry—some carrying scaling ladders to climb the anti-tank ditches—forced their way through heavy fire to take their first objectives. The Valentines of 50th Battalion, Royal Tank Regiment, many with huge fascines, 10 feet long by 8 feet in diameter, to drop in the wadi, headed for the spot chosen for the crossing. Many of the fascines caught fire from the hot exhausts, and the leading tank stuck in 3 feet of mud and water, blocking the crossing. Under a deadly fire, the

Sappers cleared mines and blew in part of the anti-tank ditch while others managed to pass 4 tanks across. Heavy casualties among the Sappers delayed the making of two other crossings, and it was not considered feasible to continue the work in daylight. No anti-tank guns had been able to get across, a failure that was to have serious results on March 22.

The next day the Young Fascist Division was reinforced by German infantry, artillery and anti-tank guns, while the 15th Panzer was readied for a counter-attack. The 50th Division was ordered to complete a crossing that night (March 21–22), and while the reinforced infantry fought to enlarge their bridgehead, 42 Valentines of 50th R.T.R. managed to cross, hampered by heavy rain. In so doing, they damaged the crossing so that again no vehicles or guns could follow. The bridgehead had still not been consolidated when at 1340 hours 15th Panzer counter-attacked. Only a few of the Valentines had 6-pounders, the rest the inadequate 2-pounder gun; and there were no anti-tank guns. Some 30 Valentines were knocked out by the Mark IIIs and IVs, and the troops on the bridgehead were driven back to the edge of the wadi. At the time when it was most needed, air support was lacking, owing to the foul weather.

Preparations were made to build more crossings that night and re-establish the bridgehead. A fresh brigade was ordered up, and Grant and Sherman tanks of 5th R.T.R. were ordered to cross. Sappers of the 4th Indian Division readied 2 crossings during the night, under a hail of artillery and machine-gun fire. Then, about 0200 hours on the night of March 22–23, the counter-attack was canceled. By now Montgomery had realized that the main attack (by XXX Corps) had failed to produce a quick breakthrough. As he had done at El Alamein, he swiftly changed his plans and switched the main thrust around the flank, where Freyberg's New Zealanders were already fighting in the Tebaga Gap.

The New Zealand Corps—totaling some 25,600 men, with 151 tanks of 8th Armored Brigade (76 Shermans, 13 Grants, 62 Crusaders, plus some Stuarts of the New Zealand Division Cavalry Regiment and some tanks of "L" Force), 112 field guns, and 172 anti-tank guns—had made a swift approach march of some 48 hours, and by the afternoon of March 21 was probing the enemy positions defending the Tebaga Gap. Pausing briefly to reconnoiter and deploy, the veteran New Zealand infantry prepared to attack that night. This they did,

and captured Hill 201—a mesa rising in the middle of the gap and dominating the surrounding terrain, plus 850 Italians. Freyberg, however, vetoed a suggestion that 8th Armored Brigade attack through the gap the same night instead of at daylight—a move that might have succeeded had it been attempted.

Freyberg's flanking movement had not gone unnoticed by Axis air reconnaissance, and to meet the obvious threat, 21st Panzer had moved west followed by 164th Light Afrika Division. By morning any chance of a swift breakthrough by New Zealand Corps was gone as the Axis reinforcements dug in, and the next two days were spent by both sides in minor skirmishes, artillery duels, and mine lifting (by the New Zealanders) and mine laying (by the Axis forces). A counter-attack on Hill 201 by 21st Panzer was called off before it had well begun because of stiff opposition and poor going.

At 1630 on March 23, Montgomery informed Freyberg that Horrocks, his headquarters, and the 1st Armored Division of his X Corps (7th Armored was at the Mareth line) were on their way to reinforce his thrust. Jealous of possible interference with his New Zealand Division, Freyberg was not overjoyed. The situation was awkward with two generals sharing command, but the duo cooperated in implementing a plan by Montgomery for thrusting the armor through the gap under cover of a concentrated air bombardment and artillery fire. It was agreed that the earliest possible date was March 26.

Montgomery's name for the operation was "Supercharge," and it called for intensive low-level pattern bombing just prior to the infantry advance; then, as the infantry advanced, fighter-bomber runs in relays every 15 minutes. The infantry were to go into position the night before and stay concealed until jump-off time. The 8th Armored Brigade was to lead, covering the whole front of the attack, with the infantry close behind. The attack was scheduled for 1600, when the sun would be in the enemy's eyes. At 1810 hours 1st Armored was to pass through the New Zealanders and, when the moon was bright enough, drive for El Hamma. Heavy bombers were to attack targets in the battle area on the nights of March 24–25 and 25–26, destroying vehicles and disrupting communications—and sleep (400 tons of bombs were dropped in all on those nights). The best techniques learned in the desert were to be utilized—including direct radio links with R.A.F. ground observers, and colored smoke markers for objectives and to mark

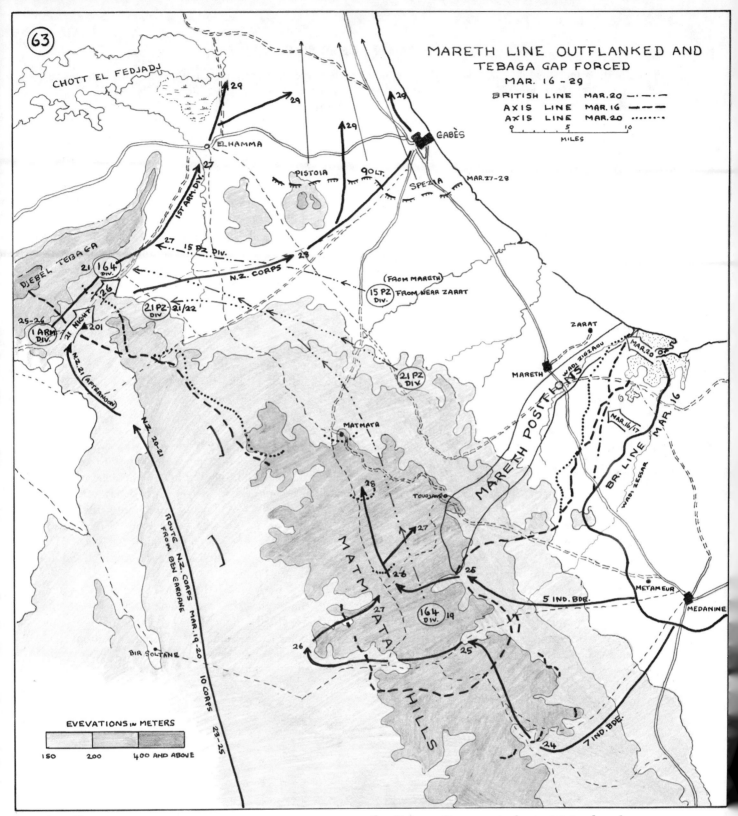

MARETH LINE OUTFLANKED AND
TEBAGA GAP FORCED
MAR. 16-29

BRITISH LINE MAR. 20 —·—·—
AXIS LINE MAR. 16 ————
AXIS LINE MAR. 20 ·········

friendly troops.

The ominous buildup of forces in the Tebaga Gap and the U. S. II Corps' threat to Gabès and Maharès had warned von Arnim that another retreat was inevitable. He therefore ordered Messe to disengage AOK1 from the Mareth front and withdraw to the Wadi Akarit positions. The defense of the Tebaga Gap was to be maintained as long as possible, and von Liebenstein (Commanding Officer of 164th Light Afrika Division and sector commander) was to cover AOK1's retreat.

Allied air activity had been growing in intensity and had caused considerable physical as well as mental damage. Axis records complain particularly of the night attacks—while even the armor was not safe by day. Hurricane II D tank destroyers claimed 11 tanks on March 25 though at a cost of 6 aircraft out of 10. Sandstorms on the airfields delayed the start of the supporting attacks on March 26, but by 1530 the pattern bombing began, followed by the fighter-bombers—relays of 30 aircraft every 15 minutes. German reports told of heavy damage to guns, equipment, serious interruption of communications, and complete stoppage of traffic to and from the front line.

At 1600 the artillery barrage began, and the tanks of the 8th Armored Brigade moved forward, followed by the motorized infantry. As was hoped, the enemy, used to night attacks by the Eighth Army, seemed taken by surprise, and the sun's rays and the clouds of dust and smoke blowing toward the Axis troops added to the confusion. Tanks and infantry swept forward beyond their final objectives, despite losses in men and armor. The 5th Panzer Regiment (21st Panzer Division) had been broken through, a battalion of Panzer Grenadiers dispersed, and many strong points taken when the 1st Armored Division went roaring into action. ". . . Straight through, no halting" was the order, and the forward objective was reached by 1930. At midnight the advance to El Hamma began—an advance that soon found the victorious British armored units mixed with elements of von Liebenstein's troops retreating to a point southwest of that place.

The German general managed to scrape together a few 88s and other artillery pieces and with these and elements of 21st Panzer, he checked the British armor about 3 miles from El Hamma. At the same time an attack on 1st Armored's rear by 15th Panzer was beaten back with the aid of some of the powerful 17-pounder anti-tank guns just then coming into service. A temporary lull followed in the forward area, although units were still battling for some of the bypassed high points in the flanking hills.

Leaving Horrocks and Freyberg poised at the gates of El Hamma, a quick résumé of the action at Mareth and the hills to the south and west is necessary to maintain continuity.

The 4th Indian Division had been stationed on XXX Corps' left flank. Under Montgomery's new plan following the failure of the frontal breakthrough, the division was sent to clear the enemy forces out of the hills to the south, follow up 164th Light Afrika Division's withdrawal, and eventually thrust in AOK1's rear in the direction of Matmata. At the same time, fresh preparations for another assault on the Mareth lines were being made on the 50th and 51st Divisions' front. But the success of the British at Tebaga Gap speeded AOK1's planned withdrawal, and on the night of March 26–27 the last units withdrew up the coast to the Wadi Akarit position.

The armored forces facing Horrocks and Freyberg were still in position on March 27, but a move by New Zealand Corps toward Gabès flanking the German positions on Djebel Halouga, just south of El Hamma, on March 28 forced von Liebenstein to pull his forces back—first north of El Hamma and Gabès, and the following night into the Wadi Akarit lines. Gabès was entered by the New Zealanders early on March 29, and the same day XXX Corps' 51st Division passed through on its way from Mareth.

The Mareth victory had been a considerable one, but there was the same lack of "push" at the last—as at El Alamein and Agheila. The enemy had been driven out of his strong positions and beaten, but once more had made a fighting withdrawal.

VII

Tightening the Noose

THE ALLIES CLEAR SOUTHEASTERN TUNISIA

Early on March 30, Horrocks reported to Montgomery that his (Horrocks') probing attacks on the Wadi Akarit defenses indicated that "If army commander prepared for heavy casualties might be possible to carry out blitz attack right through." Not wishing to cripple his mobile forces, which would be needed in the open country to the north once the Wadi Akarit position had been forced, Montgomery decided that the XXX Corps should make a set-piece attack and that the X Corps should be ready to exploit. He informed Alexander that he would attack on the night of April 4–5 (later changed to April 5–6). He wanted U. S. II Corps to advance on its front, "even a few miles; it would make my task very simple."

Alexander's overall plan was for the Eighth Army to force the Wadi Akarit position and move north into the coastal plain—aided by pressure on the enemy's flank by II Corps. The II Corps was then to switch north to the coast on the northern flank of First Army. It had been originally planned to send a good part of the Corps back to Constantine for additional training, but Eisenhower insisted that the II Corps be committed as an entity and given its share of the final drive from Tunis and Bizerte. For the moment the Corps was ordered to renew its drive eastward—to draw pressure off Eighth Army and, hopefully, to reach and harass the Axis line of communications—though without engaging in a major battle with the German armor.

For these more extended operations the U. S. 9th

Division (Major General M. Eddy) and 34th Division (Major General C. Ryder) were released to II Corps. The 9th Division (less 60th Combat Team) and U. S. 1st Infantry Division were to attack simultaneously from El Guettar. The 34th Division (less 133rd Combat Team) was to attack through the gap at Fondouk el Aoureb.

The attempt at Maknassy was to be given up. The 1st U. S. Armored Division (the designations 1st U. S. Armored Division, 1st British Armored Division, 1st U. S. Infantry Division, etc., were ordered on April 4 by Eighteenth Army Group to avoid confusion) was to leave a tank battalion, 2 artillery battalions, plus the 60th Combat Team on the defensive in the area, while 3 other tank battalions were to be readied in concealment for a thrust eastward from El Guettar.

El Guettar

The attack at El Guettar was begun on the night of March 28–29. To cover the Axis retreat from Mareth to the Wadi Akarit positions then in progress, D.A.K. had a strong defense along this front. Main elements were 10th Panzer, interspersed with units of Centauro Division. A night attack is a tricky business, even for veteran troops; 9th Division's operation went awry almost at the start. The objective of 47th Infantry Regiment was Hill 369 to the south of the Gabès road. Mistaking the silhouette of a nearby hill, 290, for the objective, 1st Battalion/47th and 3rd Battalion/47th assaulted it, took the ridge, but not the peak. To make matters worse, 2nd Battalion/47th lost direction altogether, wandered into a rugged jumble of enemy-held hills and ravines, and 232 enlisted men and 10 officers, including the battalion commander, were taken prisoner; 2nd Battalion was out of touch with Regiment for 36 hours. The reserve battalion also lost its way and was out of touch for 24 hours. A second attempt, the following night, also failed. The truck column carrying a battalion down the Gabès road for another try at Hill 369 came too close to the enemy positions, was hard hit, and most vehicles pulled back in near panic to the starting point. The troops who stayed were pinned down and, when daylight came, were unable to move.

The 1st U. S. Infantry Division was having more success north of the road, taking part of the high ground but not the important Hill 482 on Djebel Mcheltat overlooking the Gabès road. The failure of the two divisions to clear the shoulders of the pass now induced Eighteenth Army Group to order Patton to push armor through the gap and down

the Gabès road ahead of the infantry. Putting an aggressive officer, Colonel Benson, at the head of 1st U. S. Armored Division's task force, Patton ordered a renewed infantry assault, preceded by a heavy artillery bombardment. This attack went in at 0600 on March 30. The 9th Infantry Division got nowhere again. The 1st U. S. Infantry Division did better, gaining most of Hill 482 after two attacks. At noon, Task Force Benson moved into the gap. It did not move very far. A mine field between Djebel Mcheltat and Hill 369 stopped it, and before it could pull back, artillery and anti-tank guns knocked out 5 tanks and 2 tank destroyers.

That night a path through the field was cleared and another infantry attack at 0600 on March 31 finally forced the Germans to give up Hill 290 and fall back about a mile. Just after noon, Benson made a tank-infantry attack, and 2nd Battalion of 1st Armored Regiment passed through the mine field. The battalion succeeded in gaining ground north of the road after a sharp fight in which it claimed 6 tanks, several 88s, and other anti-tank guns at the cost of 8 tanks. The battalion was relieved the next day by 3rd Battalion of 13th Armored Regiment.

A diversionary attack by elements of the 1st U. S. Armored Division was made near Maknassy, but the troops had been engaged almost constantly since March 27 with Kampfgruppe Lang, and a rather weak assault was quickly beaten down by concentrated fire from heavy machine guns and artillery.

Task Force Benson had failed to punch through, and Alexander now ordered a return to the plan of using the infantry to clear the ground and adjacent hills for the armor. So the battered infantry again began the task of prying the enemy loose from his positions on the high ground on either side of the Gabès road. Losses were heavy and engineers had to be put into the line. The 1st Division managed to get as far as Sakket but no substantial gains were made elsewhere, and Hills 369 and 772 still were in enemy hands.

By this time (April 5–6) the battle for the Wadi Akarit position had begun, and D.A.K.'s armor had been ordered back from the El Guettar area. By the night of April 6–7 the Axis forces began to withdraw from their positions facing II Corps. The Axis forces successfully disengaged during the night and an all-out attack ordered by Patton at Eighteenth Army Group's urging met no resistance. Task Force Benson, prodded continually by Patton (who personally led the way through one mine

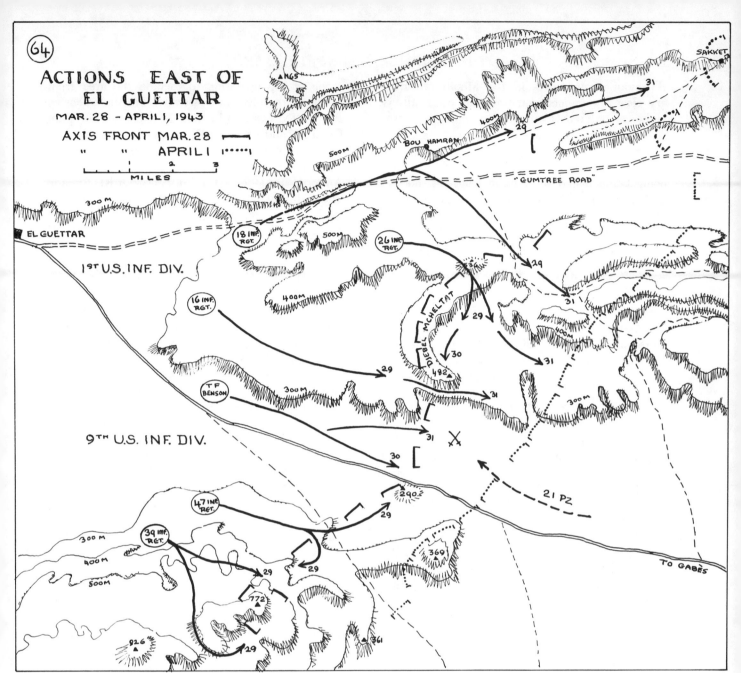

64

ACTIONS EAST OF
EL GUETTAR
MAR. 28 - APRIL 1, 1943

AXIS FRONT MAR. 28 ━━━
 "   "   APRIL 1 ·········

MILES

field in a Jeep) and under orders to keep rolling toward the coast "for a fight or a bath," as the II Corps' Commanding Officer put it, finally made contact with an Eighth Army reconnaissance patrol of the 12th Lancers—the first meeting between the two armies who had fought their way across North Africa. The enemy was gone, and Task Force Benson turned north on its secondary mission of cleaning out any remaining Axis forces in the vicinity of Mezzouna. The retreating enemy had been harried down the Gumtree Road by artillery and aircraft, while eastward of Maknassy Lang's Group evacuated their positions, leaving the long-contested pass open at last. The fighting had been costly. The 9th Division reported 120 killed, 827 wounded, and 316 missing. The 1st Division lost 126 killed, 1,016

wounded, and 159 missing. The 1st Armored's losses, including those of the 60th Combat Team, were 304 killed, 1,265 wounded, and 116 missing.

Numerous air attacks caused Patton to report to Eighteenth Army Group that enemy aviation was operating almost at will because of "total lack of air cover. . . ." Coningham took exception to this (actually during the first week of April despite poor weather, U. S. XII Air Support Command and North African Tactical Bomber Force had flown an average of 300 sorties a day, lost 23 planes, and downed 18 of the enemy) and fired back a tart rejoinder, upholding his airmen's efforts and suggesting, ". . . II Corps personnel concerned are not battleworthy. . . ." This enraged Patton, especially as copies of Coningham's reply were sent to all senior commanders in the Mediterranean. A first-class row seemed in the making, but finally Eisenhower ordered Coningham to apologize personally to Patton. It was another example of the "Where the hell are the goddamned fly-boys?" attitude of the exasperated infantryman who is sick of being bombed and strafed and longs for the sight of friendly aircraft. In actual fact, the Allied air effort, which may not have been very apparent to the men of II Corps, was rapidly whittling away the Axis air forces in Tunisia. Intensive bombings were causing more airfields to be evacuated, and the number of Axis planes destroyed on the ground, as well as in combat, was mounting. Whatever the losses and annoyance suffered by II Corps, the Axis ground forces were subjected daily to far worse treatment. In addition "Operation Flax," intended to smash the considerable enemy air supply route from Italy, was put into effect on April 5.

Fondouk el Aoureb

The actions at El Guettar were one of three operations occurring simultaneously. For the second —also involving American troops—we must turn to Fondouk, where the U. S. 34th Infantry Division was to gain the pass and demonstrate in the direction of Kairouan. The pass lies between Djebel ech Cherichera (462) to the north and a series of steep ridges leading to a higher hill formation known as the Djebel el Aoureb. At the village of Fondouk el Aoureb the pass is only some 1,000 yards wide and through it winds the shallow Marguellil river. On the northern side of the river is a steep-sided ridge, the Djebel Aïn el Rhorab (290). The area was thinly held by German units, with a battalion of Italians and some Arab troops.

The two regiments of the 34th Division—168th and 135th—began their attack on the northern end of the Djebel el Aoureb (Hill 306) at 0600 on March 27. The first phase line was reached by 1000 hours with no opposition, but the regiments soon came under increasing artillery, mortar, and machine-gun fire, and by 1400 the 135th Infantry was stopped and went to ground. The 168th had little better luck, and a night attack by the 135th gained some ground only to lose it again. A second attempt next day, after a heavy artillery shoot, got as far as the bottom of the main ridge. After 3 days of small infantry attacks the operation was called off and the troops withdrawn out of range (March 31–April 1 and April 1–2).

Realizing that the force originally committed was too small, General Alexander enlarged the scope of the operation to include the area from Fondouk 15 miles northeastward. For this offensive British IX Corps (Lieutenant General Sir John Crocker) and French XIX Corps (General Koeltz) were to be used. Main formations of Crocker's force were: British 6th Armored Division; (26th Armored Brigade; 1st Infantry [Guards] Brigade with artillery and anti-tank and AA Batteries); 1st Derbyshire Yeomanry; 51st Royal Tank Regiment less one squadron (Churchills); 128th Infantry Brigade; 34th U. S. Infantry Division (133rd, 135th, and 168th Infantry Regiments, 3 artillery battalions, 75th tank battalion; and part of 2 tank-destroyer battalions). Axis forces were not strong, although the 961st Infantry Regiment (of men released from prison, who had been graded "poor" by Allied Intelligence) fought surprisingly well.

British and U.S. infantry were to open the pass, then the British Armor (6th Armored Division) was to drive through to Kairouan. French and other British forces were to clear the hills north of Fondouk. Ryder's 34th Division was to attack south of the River Marguellil, while British 128th Infantry Brigade drove the enemy from Djebel Aïn el Rhorab (Hill 290).

Ryder did not like the plan of attack, as it called for the British first to attack the high ground east of Pichon and then move south. This meant that flanking fire from the north might be expected as his regiments attacked Djebel el Aoureb. Crocker and his Chief of Staff did not believe Hill 290 to be strongly held, and the plan was not altered.

The 128th Infantry Brigade crossed the river near Pichon on the night of April 7–8 and began its main attack at 0530. With a squadron of 51st Royal Tank Regiment it had reached its objective by noon and a regiment of infantry and the tanks began to move on Djebel Aïn el Rhorab at about 1500. By this time German reinforcements were coming up and helped the enemy hold his line about 2 miles from Hill 290.

In the meantime the 34th Division's attack was not going well. To minimize casualties, Ryder had planned his attack at 0300, but the troops were 2½ hours late in starting and consequently lost the cover of darkness and also of their supporting barrage. An attempt to rectify this by pulling the troops back and calling in an air strike failed when the aircraft did not arrive. The advance was not resumed until after 0930 and soon increased enemy fire drove the infantry to seek cover, nor could they be induced to go forward again. It was not until 1600 that the advance, supported by American

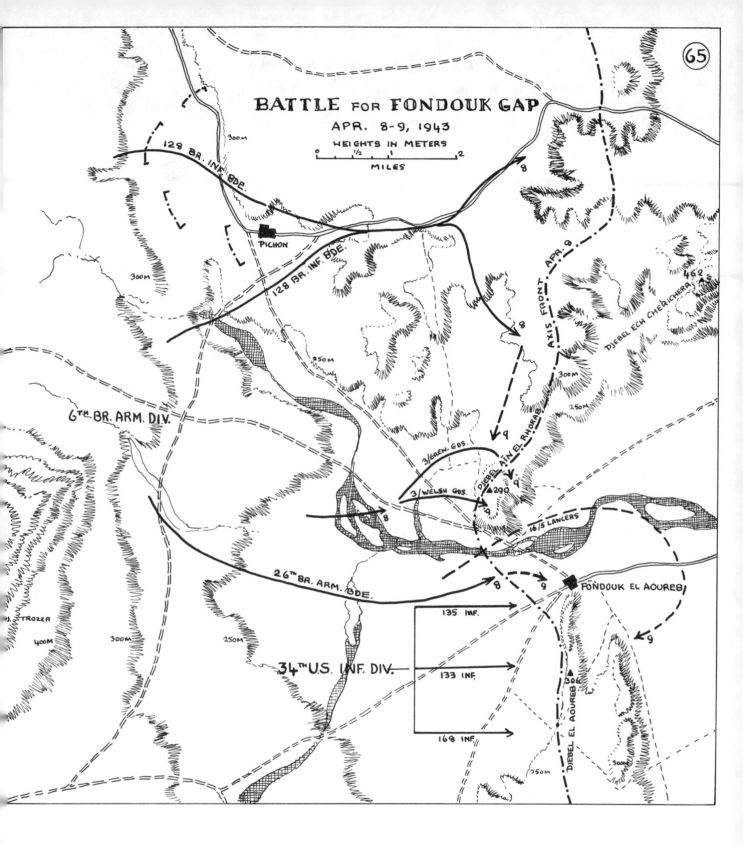

65

BATTLE FOR FONDOUK GAP

APR. 8-9, 1943

HEIGHTS IN METERS

0   ½   1   2
MILES

128 BR. INF. BDE.

300M

PICHON

128 BR. INF. BDE.

300M

250M

6TH BR. ARM. DIV.

AXIS FRONT APR. 9

462

DJEBEL ECH CHERICHERA

300M

250M

3/GREN. GDS.

DJEBEL AÏN EL RHORAB

3/WELSH GDS.

▲290

16/5 LANCERS

26TH BR. ARM. BDE.

FONDOUK EL AOUREB

135 INF.

34TH U.S. INF. DIV.

133 INF.

DJEBEL EL AOUREB

J. TROZZA

400M

300M

250M

168 INF.

250M

300M

tanks, was renewed. At about that time a Regimental Group of the 26th Armored Brigade, sent forward to probe the defenses, passed through the 34th Division, drawing fire and causing confusion. Some of the infantry reached enemy positions at the foot of the hills but could not hold them. British infantry were ordered to clear Djebel Aïn el Rhorab at daylight on April 9.

If Crocker was to intercept the Axis forces retreating from Wadi Akarit the British Armor must be on the plain south of Kairouan by April 10. Every hour counted. Alexander therefore ordered

Crocker to launch his armored division through the pass, regardless of 34th Division's failure. A path had to be found or cleared through the deep but irregular mine field (defended by at least 15 anti-tank guns) and Djebel Aïn el Rhorab taken. This last was not accomplished until the afternoon of April 9.

An attack by 31 of Ryder's tanks at about 0900 went unsupported by his infantry, who were again pinned down by fire. Five tanks were lost for no gain. A combined attack later was beaten down, mainly by fire from the northern flank. There would obviously be no clearing of the hills on the south side of the pass by 34th Division, but during the morning and early afternoon of April 9, British tankers and Royal Engineers found a lane through the mines that let a few tanks through. These were stopped by fire from Fondouk village, 400 yards beyond, but while others, aided by some American troops, tried to clear a second lane, the 16th/5th Lancers found a narrow way through. This crossed the river to the north bank, then about a mile farther crossed to the south again, behind Fondouk village. This operation cost a considerable number of tanks, but Allied artillery fire in return knocked out several anti-tank guns. The Coldstream Guards cleared the heights on the south side (in the U. S. 34th Division's zone), and by late afternoon the leading units of British armor were east of Fondouk village. Mines and anti-tank fire had taken a toll of 34 British tanks (many of which were only damaged).

By this time the enemy, their task accomplished, began to slip away, and an attack by 1st Battalion, 133rd Infantry on Hill 309 that night (April 9–10) found few defenders left. On the morning of April 10 the British armor was on its way toward Kairouan, but the Axis retreat from Wadi Akarit had by then been successfully carried out. The Italian elements of AOK1 had passed across the Kairouan plain on the night of April 8–9, and the remnants of the Panzers and the rest of D.A.K. on the night of April 9–10. Except for a couple of small clashes with the rear guard, which netted some 650 prisoners, 14 tanks, and 15 guns, Crocker's armor was too late to engage. Crocker blamed the 34th Division for this, and suggested it be sent to the rear to be retrained under British guidance. Ryder maintained that part of his division's failure was due to Crocker's dispositions whereby the 34th Division was exposed to fire from its flank. Recriminations were promptly squelched by Eisenhower and Alexander, and the division,

after intensive night training and some shake-up in command, was soon considered battleworthy. It must be admitted, however, that at this time the effectiveness of American troops was, rightly or wrongly, not rated very high by either their Allies or their opponents.

April 10 saw Patton lead CC "A," 1st U. S. Armored Division, through the Aïn Rabaou pass south of Faïd. By evening one of its reconnaissance units linked up with elements of the 168th Infantry east of Fondouk village. By the same evening French forces of XIX Corps had pushed through to the coastal plain in the area between Ousseltia and Kairouan. They took over 1,000 prisoners but lost General Welvert, killed by a mine.

Wadi Akarit

The third of the operations mentioned above, and by far the largest and most important, was the forcing of the Wadi Akarit positions by the Eighth Army. This natural barrier was the last remaining between the Eighth Army and the Tunisian coastal plain. It ran for some 18 miles from the sea to Djebel Haidoudi on the west. The wadi, broad and deep, formed a formidable obstacle for some 4 miles inland. Five miles from the coast and roughly parallel to it is the steep 500-foot-high Djebel Roumana. A mile-wide gap separates Roumana from ground that rises steeply to the 900-foot Djebel Tebaga Fatnassa, to quote the *Official British History*, ". . . a towering horrible-looking labyrinth of pinnacles, chimneys, gullies and escarpments." To the southwest there ran a line of hills some 500 feet high terminating in Djebel Haidoudi, overlooking the Gafsa-Gabès road. From there the flank was guarded by the great salt marshes of the Chott el Fedjadj.

It was a strong natural position, and one that Rommel had favored over the far longer Mareth line. But the latter had received the priority and little had been done to the Wadi Akarit defenses. Some anti-tank ditches and mine fields had been laid, but the position had no great depth, and von Arnim, pessimistic and harassed, classed them as "nothing special." In fact, by this time there was considerable doubt in von Arnim's mind that the Axis position in Tunisia itself, let alone that at Wadi Akarit, could long be held. He later said, "Even without the Allied offensive I should have had to capitulate by the first of June at the latest, because we had no more to eat." Evacuation of Tunis and Bizerte was considered politically impossible (Hitler was, of course, insisting that the Wadi

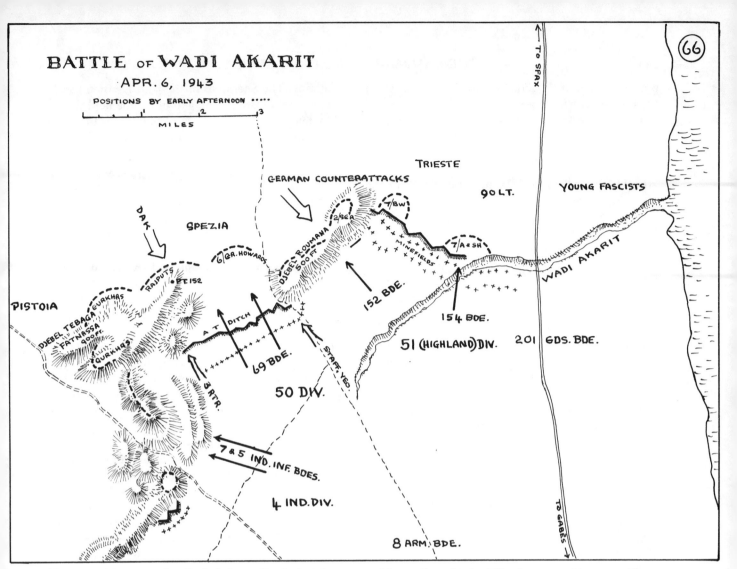

66

BATTLE of WADI AKARIT
APR. 6, 1943

POSITIONS BY EARLY AFTERNOON •••••

MILES

TO SFAX

TRIESTE

GERMAN COUNTERATTACKS

90 LT.

YOUNG FASCISTS

DAK

SPEZIA

7/BW

2/SCR

DJEBEL ROUMANA 500 FT

7/A & SH

MINEFIELDS

WADI AKARIT

6 GR. HOWARDS

PT. 152

RAJPUTS

GURKHAS

152 BDE.

PISTOIA

DJEBEL TEBAGA FATNASSA 900 FT.

GURKHAS

A T DITCH

69 BDE.

154 BDE.

51 (HIGHLAND) DIV.

201 GDS. BDE.

3 RTR.

50 DIV.

STAFF YEO.

7 & 5 IND. INF. BDES.

4 IND. DIV.

8 ARM. BDE.

TO GABES

Akarit position was the final defense line), but in-essential personnel were to be returned to Italy when transport was available.

Commando Supremo wanted the southern front held, but at the same time realized that the threat from U. S. II Corps to its flank and rear might force a retirement. The ever-optimistic Kesselring thought preparations for such a retreat might make von Arnim "retreat minded," and Major General Westphal, Kesselring's assistant Chief of Staff, accused Army Group of "peering over its shoulder." Von Arnim retorted that he was "peering for ships," and finished by saying, "We are without bread and ammunition, as was Rommel's Army before. The consequences are inevitable." He demanded 10,000 tons of ammunition and 8,000 tons of fuel by April 6—exclusive of Italian needs. As the entire tonnage of military cargo and fuel disembarked in April was to amount to less than 30,000 tons (over 12,000 tons went to the bottom), his request was little more than wishful thinking. A letter to Jodl at OKW asking what was to be done when all fuel and ammunition were expended went unanswered.

Messe thought it difficult to combine an all-out stand at Wadi Akarit with preparations for a retire-ment, and German records show that it was com-mon knowledge that a retreat was contemplated—not the best frame of mind for troops making a last-ditch stand.

About 12 German and 26 Italian infantry battal-ions garrisoned the line, with perhaps 200 pieces of field and medium artillery. Anti-tank guns were numerous and included 19th Flak Division's 63 dual-purpose 88s. The 15th Panzer was down to 26 serviceable tanks (21st Panzer had been sent to II Corps front to bolster 10th Panzer and Centauro Division). Transport was scarce. Shipments of ve-hicles from Italy had fallen short of losses, and the 200-odd types of vehicles in use in Africa made re-placement of spare parts and tires very difficult. On April 2, units not in the front line and all head-quarters had to turn over a quarter of their vehicles to the fighting units.

The Eighth Army's two Corps totaled 33 infan-try, 6 motorized, and 5 machine-gun battalions, some 400 artillery pieces, and 462 tanks. Ammunition was plentiful, and the artillery fired some 82,000 shells during the action.

The XXX Corps was to smash through the line, with the X Corps ready to pour through the breach. The original plan of attack was modified at the insistence of General Tuker, commanding the 4th Indian Division. He concluded that the Fatnassa Massif was the key to the position and, while outwardly formidable, needed a great number of troops to hold it properly (troops that the enemy did not have). Also, an attack there was hardly to be expected. Feeling that his mountain-wise Indians could do the seemingly impossible, he declared he could take the position in a night attack.

Montgomery did not wait for a full moon, and the speed of his preparations caught the enemy by surprise. Tuker's brigades attacked on the night of April 5–6, the 1st Battalion, 2nd Gurkhas leading. The Italians holding the mountain were no match for the kukri-swinging hillmen, and by daylight much of the Fatnassa Massif was in British hands and engineers were already preparing a way over the anti-tank ditch at the position's foot.

The 51st (Highland) Division, after moving into position in the dark, attacked Djebel Roumana after a bombardment that Messe described as "an apocalyptic hurricane of steel and fire," and by 0600 had seized the crest and were working along the ridge. An hour later the whole ridge was in British hands and Valentines of the 50th Royal Tank Regiment (RTR)—some of them towing anti-tank guns while their crews rode the tanks (a lesson learned from the Wadi Zigzaou)—were passing through the enemy position.

The 50th Division's attack met very heavy fire at the anti-tank ditch and two brigades were pinned down. Tanks and infantry were sent via the Highlanders' position to get at the enemy's rear.

In the meantime, Panzer Grenadiers and tanks of 15th Panzer counter-attacked Roumana and pushed the Highlanders off the crest of the ridge. 40th RTR came up but its Valentines were knocked out one by one. It was all the Highlanders could do to hang on, but hang on they did, in a day's hard fighting. The Shermans of the 50th Division had by now passed through the gap in a mine field west of Roumana, followed by the infantry (6th Green Howards), and by noon the division's objectives were nearly all taken.

Montgomery optimistically reported to Alexander that X Corps was "now in movement to pass through hole blown by XXX Corps." Unfortunately the hole was not very big, and X Corps' attempt to exploit it not very vigorous. The first regiments through were checked by concealed 88s, and the advance petered out. Some of D.A.K.'s tanks were on their way back from the El Guettar area and there were attacks by Panzer Grenadiers attempting unsuccessfully to retake ground from the Indians. Forty of D.A.K.'s tanks made a halfhearted assault near Pt. 152 but were repeatedly attacked by fighter-bombers and tank-busting Hurricanes.

While the British were apparently being held along much of the line, the Axis leaders had already decided the pressure was too great and the position must be abandoned. Army Group ordered a limited retirement at nightfall, but Messe sent the majority of his troops and all his artillery directly to Enfidaville. The Germans and the remaining Italians retired during the night of April 6–7.

The renewed British attack slated for the morning of April 7 proved unnecessary, and there was little to do but gather in the spoils and prepare to follow up the enemy once more. Enemy casualties had been heavy, and 125 Germans and 5,211 Italians were in the cages by nightfall of April 6, with more taken the next day (the disparity between the number of POWs of the two nations points up the bitter accusations of the Germans that their Axis partners were not pulling their weight). The Eighth Army lost some 1,290 men and 32 tanks.

There was some argument as to whether XXX Corps had made a sufficient opening for X Corps to charge through—or if X Corps had exploited the opening made to the utmost of its ability. In any event, the Axis were now driven into a comparatively small area in the northeast, had suffered further losses in men and equipment, and, perhaps more important, the loss of many vital airfields, 22 in all.

VIII

Operation "Vulcan"

Two divisions joined First Army during March and early April. The 1st British Infantry Division (Major General W. Clutterbuck) arrived in the forward area March 5–9, and the 4th Infantry Division (Major General J. Hawkesworth) reached the forward area April 3–6. Among other reinforcements were 56th and 54th Heavy Regiments, R.A., each with 16 7.2 howitzers. Some infantry also received the new Projector Infantry Anti-tank (PIAT), the British equivalent of the U.S. bazooka.

The arrival of reinforcements was due to the greatly improved supply situation. The problem at the beginning had been neither lack of men nor materiel but the sheer impossibility of maintaining more than a given number of units over a line of communication of over 500 miles. Among the tasks was the clearing and improving of port facilities, repair and building of railways, bridges, and roads, and the formation of repair depots for thousands of overworked vehicles racking themselves to pieces on rough mountain roads. Huge fuel dumps had to be stocked and replenished—in February, First Army alone used over 1,000 tons of fuel a day. The demands of the ever-growing air forces also had to be met, while the lavish use of artillery and mortar ammunition posed a problem of its own. A very large and efficient supply organization, plus the efforts of engineers, railwaymen, road builders, seamen, stevedores, port and transportation officers, and many thousands of truck drivers made the buildup for the final drive possible.

Paralleling the improvement in the Allied supply organization was the rapid deterioration of that of the Axis forces. The major factor in a situation which was rapidly becoming disastrous was the continual offensive waged by the Allied air forces, both tactical and strategic. The effects of the tactical air squadrons on and directly in the rear of the combat areas has been noted. Unseen by the troops, but of vital importance to the battles raging below, the blows dealt by the big bomber squadrons were crippling the Axis air forces as well as smashing the ports of embarkation and sinking ships at sea.

More squadrons had been added, and finally Northwest African Strategic Air Force's (Major General James H. Doolittle) American units included 16 squadrons of Fortresses, 8 of Mitchells, and 8 Marauders, plus 2 of R.A.F. Wellingtons. In Middle East Command's R.A.F. Mideast were 4 squadrons of Wellingtons and 1 of Halifaxes, plus Albacores of the Fleet Air Arm. Brereton's Ninth Air Force had 8 U.S. squadrons and 1 R.A.F. squadron of Liberators. The effect of this buildup on the Axis air forces is shown by the following figures. From March 31 to April 20 inclusive, raids on fields in Sardinia, Sicily, the mainland, and North Africa destroyed 45 German aircraft and damaged 48 more, while incomplete Italian records show 42 aircraft lost and over 100 damaged. This in addition to damages to repair shops and other installations. In fact, after April 15 all damaged German planes that could get off the ground were flown to Sicily for repairs. Surplus ground crews were formed into Luftwaffe field companies and used as infantry (the above figures do not include damage by the light bombers and fighter-bombers of North African Tactical Air Force or losses in combat).

Besides attacks on airfields the big bombers also plastered ports, railroad facilities, and concentrations of troops and transport. Even more devastating were the attacks on convoys and the Italian ports of embarkation. Northwest African Coastal Air Force (Air Vice-Marshal Hugh P. Lloyd) was responsible for sea reconnaissance, convoy escort, anti-sub operations, anti-shipping sweeps, and fighter defense of ports and convoys. Acting in close co-operation with N.A.S.A.F., the two commands inflicted severe damage on enemy shipping. For instance, on March 7, 6 U. S. Mitchells, escorted by 14 Lightnings, sank a convoy of 3 merchant ships totaling over 10,000 tons and damaged several of the escort. At the same time the Malta forces were operating around the clock, and on

March 12–13 Beauforts and Albacores sank a large tanker with 4,000 tons of fuel. On March 22, 13 American Marauders attacked a convoy northeast of Cape Bon, sank one ship, and set another on fire. She limped into Bizerte where she blew up. On the same day B-17s, escorted by Lightnings, hit an ammunition ship in Palermo. She exploded with such violence that the port became almost unusable for several weeks. The blast also helped sink 7 other vessels in port. And so it went on. Of 111,480 tons of Axis shipping sunk in the Mediterranean in March, aircraft accounted for 62,450.

The Axis High Command held another of their conferences in April, near Salzburg, partly to give Hitler a chance to bolster the Duce's flagging spirits. Both agreed Tunisia must be held (one reason being that the German High Command felt that collapse in Tunisia might have serious effects in Italy), but Mussolini's requests for more aid fell on deaf ears. In any case, even had the usual reassurances that reinforcements would be sent been more than wishful thinking, there was now no way to increase the trickle of men and materiel reaching North Africa. It was all very well for the Axis leaders to talk of counter-attacks on land and sweeps by the Italian Navy. No one knew better than Supermarina that its fuel-starved squadrons could do little but play the annoying but passive role of a fleet in being, while any move to relax the virtual blockade of North Africa by a naval action would be welcomed by the Royal Navy. And as the commanders on the spot in Tunisia realized all too well, any counter-attacks of theirs would of necessity be both local and severely limited.

In preparation for what all knew must be the final struggle, there was some shuffling in the Axis commands. D.A.K. (10th and 21st Panzer), which was to form an assault reserve, took command of the Italian Superga Division and remaining units of the Italian XXX Corps. Division Centauro would absorb all remaining Italian tanks and be attached to a German armored division. AOK1, which included 15th Panzer, 90th and 164th Light Divisions, and Trieste, Pistoia, Spezia, and Young Fascist Divisions, were to hold the left (southeastern) area, while PzAOK5 (including von Manteuffel, 334th, 999th, and Hermann Göring Divisions) would operate on the right.

There was even more rearranging on the Allied side. The final line-up of troops (see map 67) called for the transfer of the U. S. II Corps to the northern flank—no mean feat in itself—while units from Eighth Army were transferred to IX Corps. These

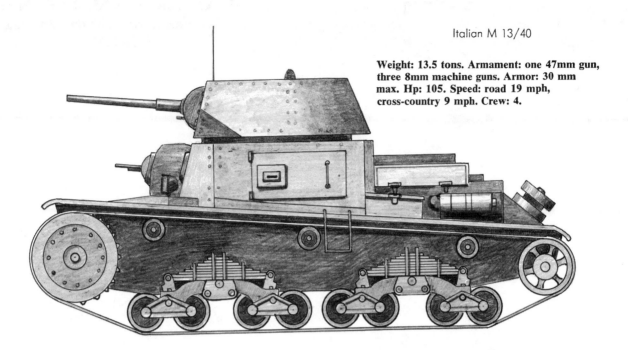

Italian M 13/40

Weight: 13.5 tons. Armament: one 47mm gun, three 8mm machine guns. Armor: 30 mm max. Hp: 105. Speed: road 19 mph, cross-country 9 mph. Crew: 4.

were only the major moves, and for weeks the rear areas were alive with convoys carrying men and mountains of shells, rations, fuel, and all the materiel needed to feed the fires of modern battle.

The II Corps' shift north, cutting across First Army's rear, meant moving 90,000 men and thousands of vehicles along inadequate roads, many of which were in use to supply First Army's forward areas. This called for timetables worked out with the British Movement Controls Branch and close schedules—with groups moving certain numbers of vehicles (some 2,400 a day) along stretches of road at specified times. All went well, with little inter-

ference from the battered Luftwaffe. At the same time, the 1st British Armored Division was moving up from the Eighth Army front. (Montgomery had asked Alexander for the 6th Armored Division to be sent to join him. In reply Alexander informed him that the main effort was to be by First Army and required him to send an Armored Division and an Armored Car Regiment to join IX Corps.)

The order of battle for the big offensive was—starting at the coast: U. S. II Corps (1st U. S. Armored Division [—]; 1st U. S. Infantry Division; 9th U. S. Infantry Division; 34th U. S. Infantry Division; 3 battalions, Corps Franc d'Afrique). British

Lockheed P-38F (Lightning)   Single-seater Long-range Fighter

Span: 52'. Length: 37'0". Height: 9'10". Weight empty: 12,264 lbs. Speed: max. 395 mph at 25,000 ft., 347 mph at 5,000 ft. Range: 400 miles at 330 mph at 25,000', 900 miles at 219 mph at 10,000' (drop tanks increased this to 1,750 miles at 213 mph at 10,000').
Power: two 1,225 hp Allison 12 cyl. Vee engines.
Armament: one 20mm cannon and four 0.5 machine guns, all nose-mounted, plus two 1,000 lb. bombs or two 21" torpedoes.

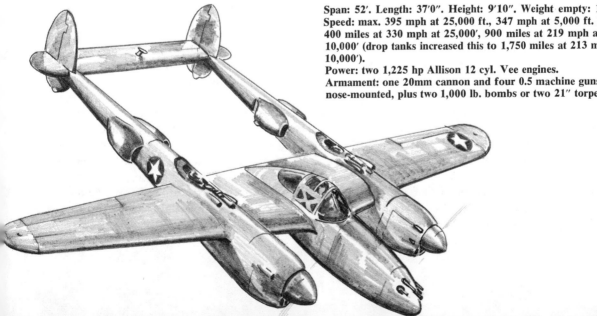

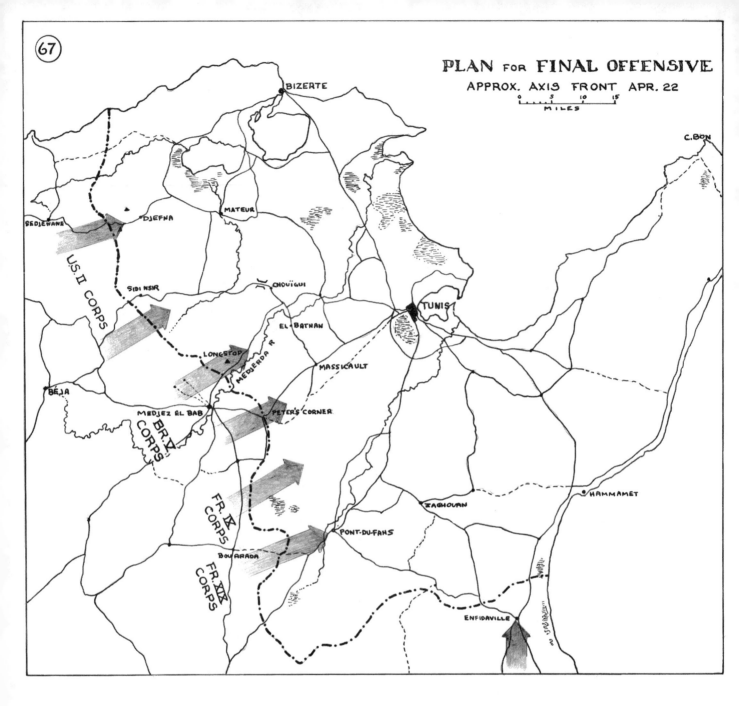

67

PLAN FOR **FINAL OFFENSIVE**
APPROX. AXIS FRONT APR. 22

0   5   10   15
MILES

V Corps (1st British Infantry Division; 4th British Infantry Division; 78th British Infantry Division; 25th Tank Brigade [—51st R.T.R.]). British IX Corps (1st British Armored Division; 6th British Armored Division; 46th British Infantry Division; 51st R.T.R.). French XIX Corps (Moroccan Division; Algiers Division; Oran Division; Armored Group; 1st King's Dragoon Guards).

Alexander's overall plan was for Eighth Army to attack the Enfidaville positions on the night of April 19–20, to draw Axis reserves to that part of the front and hold them by increased pressure. French XIX Corps was to advance on the right of First Army's line toward Pont-du-Fahs and Zaghouan. The IX Corps was to advance on April 22 to the left of XIX Corps, take the high ground northwest of Pont-du-Fahs, and threaten the Pont-du-Fahs–Tunis highway and aid V Corps as needed. The V Corps was to make the main attack (also on April 22) to retake Longstop Hill and "Peter's Corner" and capture the high ground between Massicault and El Bathan. U. S. II Corps' main objective was Bizerte. Part of II Corps was to advance from Béja toward Sidi Nsir and Chouïgui. Nearer the coast, the enemy was to be driven out of the Djefna positions due west of Mateur.

The idea of making the main attack along the Medjez el Bab–Tunis line (certainly the easiest in the matter of terrain) was to split the Axis armies rather than compress them—which having Eighth Army make the major thrust would tend to do—then turn south and drive the enemy against Montgomery's forces. At the same time this would, hopefully, give the enemy no opportunity for positioning himself for a last-ditch stand on the Cape Bon peninsula where he might hold out for weeks, thereby upsetting the timetable for the Sicilian invasion.

As a preface to the initial assaults of Operation "Vulcan" the British 46th Division had opened an attack (March 27) on the hills southwest of Sedjenane. Despite wet weather and difficult country the town was entered on March 30. By April 14, when the U. S. 9th Infantry Division took over the sector, most of the ground lost to the Axis since February 26 had been retaken.

The V Corps began the first phase of its central attack with an advance by 78th Division in the direction of Toukabeur and Chaouach. The former was taken April 8 and Chaouach a day later. As well as gaining ground, the attack had cost the enemy's 334th Division heavily and drawn in some of von Arnim's precious reserves.

In line with the policy of applying constant pressure, 4th Division advanced on Sidi Nsir while the 78th continued its attacks. The 4th Division ran into steadily increasing resistance before Sidi Nsir and was held up until April 16. On April 14, 78th Division moved on the heavily defended positions on Djebel Ang Ridge and Djebel Tanngoucha. In 3 days and nights of very sharp fighting the former was taken, lost, and retaken, while the latter was captured, but had to be abandoned when heavy firing caused the Arab muleteers of the supply train to bolt with their animals. Even so, good gains had been made, and German losses were heavy. Kesselring himself criticized the loss of 300 prisoners from a crack mountain regiment. The XIX Corps had pushed ahead from around Fondouk, and on April 13, near Djebel Sefsouf, it made contact with the left of Montgomery's X Corps.

The preliminary attacks on the ground had their counterpart in the air. Although the Me 109Gs and the FW 190s still outclassed all but a few of the Allied fighters (it was not until the end of January that a squadron of Spitfire IXs [maximum speed, 402 miles per hour] arrived in North Africa, and there were only a few of the new fast Mustang IIs [P-51A]), the Allies had overwhelming superiority in numbers. Not only that, but the efficiency of their servicing and repair facilities brought the proportion of serviceable aircraft even higher. From March 29 to April 21, North African Tactical Air Force and Middle East Air Command flew a daily average of over 1,100 sorties, excluding antishipping operations. Losses for the period were 203; at the same time, 270 German and 46 Italian planes were lost, plus nearly all the remaining Italian air transports.

In the southeast, Montgomery's X Corps took over the Kairouan area (April 12) from IX Corps and the 1st British Armored Division painted its light sandy desert camouflage dark green and got ready to join First Army. On Eighth Army's front the leading brigades were in contact with the Enfidaville positions. This was a mountainous area, overlooking the one good coastal road to Bou Ficha. Near the crossroads at Enfidaville (there was little else) was the steep hill of Takrouna. Some 4 miles to the west, Djebel Garci rose to 1,000 feet—a rugged complex of naked rock peaks and gullies. The country behind was even more forbidding, posing a special problem to Eighth Army's highly mechanized units.

Counting perhaps on the knowledge that the enemy had been beaten out of one position after another and that his morale might be somewhat shaken, it was decided that the 4th Indians and the New Zealanders would take Djebel Garci and Takrouna, respectively, pushing on ahead as opportunity offered. The attacks went in on the night of April 19 and developed, in many cases, into bloody hand-to-hand fighting. Casualties were heavy, one company being reduced to 17 effectives and another to 20. Counter-attacks were made and beaten off by bomb, rifle, kukri, or deadly artillery concentrations from 11 regiments of supporting artillery. But Takrouna and part of Djebel Garci were hardly worth the butcher bill, and on April 21 it was decided to attack astride the coastal road. Small attacks had been made on April 23 and 24 and some ground gained, but an attack on the night of April 28–29 by the newly arrived and inexperienced 56th Division failed. Montgomery asked Alexander to look over the ground, and the latter then decided that a large-scale offensive would be too costly. Small local attacks were to be continued, to pin down Messe's battered remnants (on April 14, redoubtable 15th Panzer was down to 4 "runners" and 21 tanks in the repair shops). The 7th Armored Division, 4th Indian Division, and 201st Guards Brigade were to join First Army. So

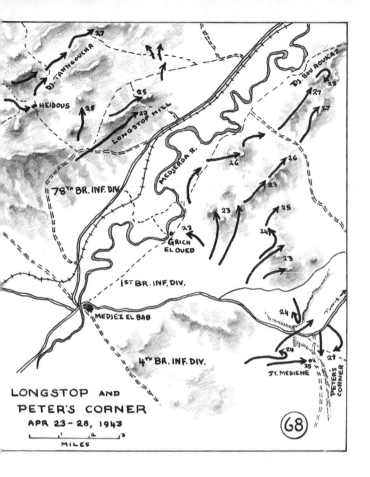

LONGSTOP AND
PETER'S CORNER
APR 23-28, 1943

68

MILES

ended Eighth Army's long march—back and forth across the desert, and from El Alamein to within 50 miles of Tunis. It was only fitting that some of its veteran units should be given the chance to be in at the kill.

The enemy was well aware that a major offensive was near, and the acting commander of Hermann Göring Division suggested a spoiling attack. Von Arnim agreed, and a powerful Kampfgruppe was collected, including a Panzer regiment and a detachment with 13 "Tiger" tanks. The attack went in in the early hours of April 21, and despite a warning by British Intelligence, there was heavy fighting before it was beaten back. The initial penetration was about 5 miles deep on a 12-mile front and caused some loss and confusion until at daybreak it ran up against the British main line of resistance where tanks and artillery drove the Germans back to their original lines. Despite the loss of some forward guns and about 300 prisoners it did not succeed in delaying "Vulcan," and IX Corps began the operation at 0340 on April 22. The other three corps of First Army followed at short intervals.

The British Attack

The 46th Division's initial attack in the el Kourzia area, while penetrating deeply into Hermann Göring Division's positions, was only partially successful, and 6th Armored Division, following it up, did not get as far as hoped. During the next 4 days more ground was gained by both 6th and 1st British Armored Divisions against determined defense by Hermann Göring and 10th Panzer Divisions. On April 26 Anderson, deciding that 6th Armored might do better exploiting V Corps' success, withdrew the division into reserve, leaving Crocker to keep up the pressure on the badly battered enemy divisions with 46th and 1st British Armored Divisions. The 10th Panzer Division at one time was reduced to about 35 "runners" (25 German and 10 Italian). British losses were also high, the Germans claiming 162 British tanks and 24 guns destroyed or damaged from April 20–26.

The V Corps' 78th Division attacked Longstop and Tanngoucha Ridge on the night of April 22–23. Longstop was taken after fierce fighting, 30 survivors of the assault companies finally winning the summit. Tanngoucha, swept by fire from well-fortified Heïdous Hill, was taken and lost again, and on April 24, 78th Division had to stop and reorganize. South of the Medjerda River, 1st British Infantry Division's 2nd Brigade gained some ground, lost part of it in a fierce counter-attack, retook it, and lost it again. Casualties were heavy, and 142nd Royal Armored Corps had 16 "runners" left out of 45. The next day 1st Division's 3rd Infantry Brigade recaptured the ground lost on April 23 while 4th Division fought its way toward "Peter's Corner."

The fighting continued during the next few days, with small gains and considerable losses. The 1st Division reached and captured Djebel Bou Aoukaz. Von Arnim grouped most of his remaining armor (less than 70 tanks) of the 10th, 15th, and 21st Panzer Divisions, and 501st Heavy Panzer Battalion ("Tigers") along with a grenadier regiment and artillery units under Colonel Irkens, Commanding Officer of the 8th Panzer Regiment. This composite force managed to recapture Djebel Bou Aoukaz and checked V Corps' advance.

U. S. II Corps Attacks

U. S. II Corps' task was primarily to take pressure off the Allied center, where the main thrust was expected to be delivered. It was also to protect the left flank of this thrust—for which purpose it was agreed that, though directly under the control of Alexander's Eighteenth Army Group, orders should come through Anderson. Alexander did, however, offer Bradley direct access to his head-

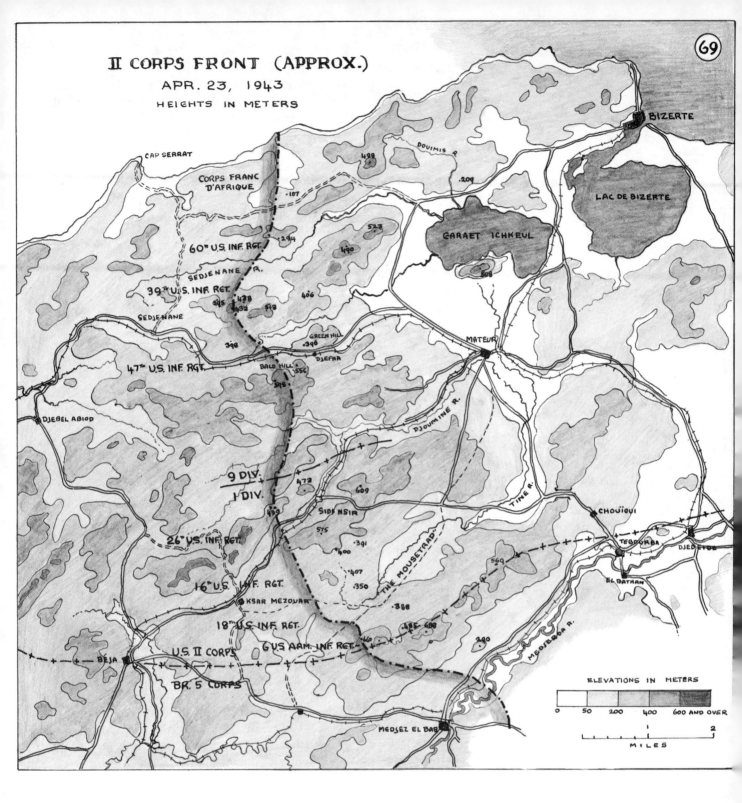

II CORPS FRONT (APPROX.)
APR. 23, 1943
HEIGHTS IN METERS

ELEVATIONS IN METERS

0   50   200   400   600 AND OVER

MILES

quarters at any time.

There were two principal roads from the American sector to Mateur. One led from Sedjenane through Djefna. The other, the longer one, led from Béja through Sidi Nsir, skirting the Tine River. The former, just west of Djefna, ran through a narrow neck between Green and Bald Hills—far too strong to be forced frontally. The lat-

ter ran up a relatively flat valley, suited to armor, but dominated on both sides by fortified djebels. The most prominent of these, 4 miles east of Sidi Nsir, was Hill 609. The valley between these enemy-held hills was, appropriately enough, nicknamed "The Mousetrap." A little to the north another opening followed the Djoumine River, but it too was dominated by high hills on either side and

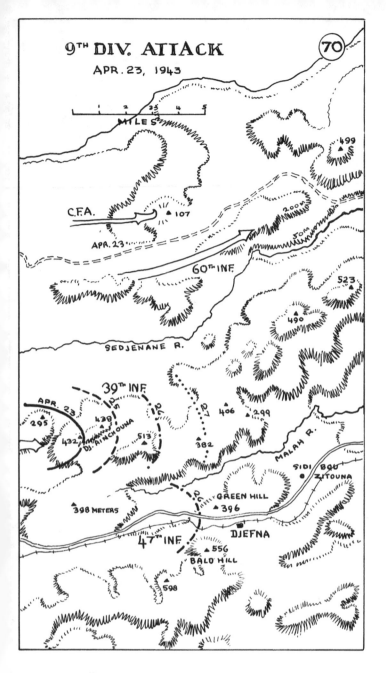

and beyond. The two operations were simultaneous but, separated by miles of rugged country, all but unconnected.

To take 9th Division's attack first, Eddy's troops and Corps Franc d'Afrique (C.F.A.) began their advance early on April 23, aided by a heavy artillery concentration. C.F.A. at the northern end of the line soon ran into strong opposition at Hill 107, but the 60th Infantry, to the north of the Sedjenane River, reached its objectives and pushed on beyond. South of the river, the 39th Infantry moved into a jumble of hills—295, 432, 438 (Djebel Aïnchouna), and 513. They took 295 and 432 and attempted to take 438 but were thrown into some confusion by a surprise counter-attack on 295 that overran the regimental observation post, captured the Commanding Officer, his executive officer, the Commanding Officer of the 2nd Battalion, and a small force with them before they themselves were driven off with loss. The fight was renewed the next day, but resistance was stiff and it was not until the afternoon of April 25 that Hill 438 was taken. Hill 513 was taken on April 26, and on April 27 a position was reached some 4 miles east of Djebel Aïnchouna. Here increased enemy fire from field artillery, 88s, mortars, and heavy machine guns brought the 39th's operation to a 4-day halt.

Farther south, 47th Infantry's task was to demonstrate aggressively in front of the Djefna position. This was done, and on April 26, patrols reached the foot of Green Hill. In the meantime, 60th Infantry had not only pressed forward on its own front but also had moved northeast to the aid of C.F.A., its objective to outflank Hill 499.

The 1st Division's attack began after very heavy artillery preparation, and early on April 23 the Division's three combat teams (16th, 18th, and 26th) moved out toward the ridges and valleys of the hilly region ahead. The hills were well defended with fire support from each adjacent crest. Good observation from the high knobs gave the enemy opportunity to direct artillery and mortar fire over wide areas. Progress was slow and casualties heavy (2nd Battalion, 18th Infantry alone had 224 casualties that first day). Counter-attacks were met and ground was lost and regained as the regiments scrambled on and up. Each crest gained brought fire from supporting positions on adjoining hills. It soon became clear that to take the hills directly north of the river it would be necessary to drive the enemy from the higher ground to the north of the Sidi Nsir–Mateur road. Allen's 1st Division had

furthermore was roadless. Nearer the coast the Sedjenane River Valley was covered with thick brush, in places almost impenetrable.

Bradley chose to make a two-pronged attack— the 9th Division to hack its way through the brush along the Sedjenane and in on the flank of the Djefna positions, cut the supply road to the rear and, if possible, to drive toward Bizerte, although it was expected at Eighteenth Army Group headquarters that Tunis would fall first and British forces would then move up to help take the city from the southeast. The 1st U. S. Infantry Division was to clear the hills overlooking the Tine River route, and when that was open, the 1st U. S. Armored Division would drive through to Mateur

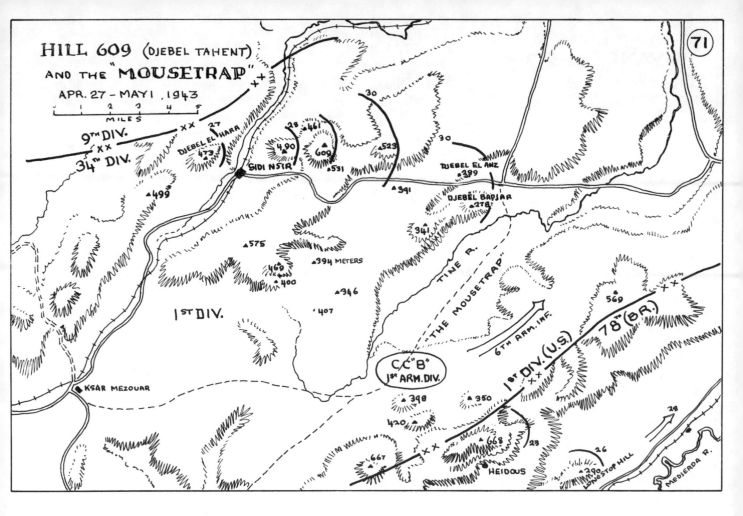

HILL 609 (DJEBEL TAHENT)
AND THE "MOUSETRAP"
APR. 27 - MAY 1, 1943

taken many casualties and was fully committed, but 34th Division had just completed its move from Fondouk, and Bradley decided to give Ryder and his men a chance to prove themselves and incidentally dispel any doubts Alexander might have about their fighting ability.

And prove themselves they did. The complex of hills—Djebel Grembil, Djebel el Hara, Hill 490—was dominated by the raw face of Hill 609. This peak was in a sense the key to the whole position north of the Tine, affording splendid observation for pinpointing artillery concentrations on the struggling 1st Division to the south. Ryder soon found that any direct assault on 609 was impossible without first clearing the nearby heights, and this he proceeded to do. An attempt to take Djebel el Hara on the night of April 26–27 failed (according to Bradley, at daybreak the assaulting battalion found itself trying to capture the hill from which it had started that night). In preparation for an afternoon attempt a massive artillery concentration was laid on, but called off in the nick of time when word came that Djebel el Hara had been taken. Hill 490 proved a tougher nut to crack, and it was not until April 28 that it was won and held in

spite of numerous counter-attacks.

The ground was ideally suited for defense. Attackers moving up the sheltered side of a hill would be pinned down on the bare, rocky tops by air bursts and heavy machine-gun fire from neighboring hills and from fire from troops dug in on the reverse slopes. Ravines up which troops might be expected to move were registered for mortar fire and often mined. Counter-attacks could be counted on before a defense could be organized. Understandably, progress was slow and costly. On April 27 Anderson urged II Corps to push the advance, bypassing 609 and its surrounding hills. Bradley met Anderson at Allen's command post and outlined his plans for the breakthrough—emphasizing the necessity for taking the high ground overlooking "The Mousetrap." Anderson evidently "got the message," as Bradley heard no more about bypassing 609.

The capture of 490 doomed Hill 609, and the strategic mount was finally taken on April 30 after a flank and rear attack using Sherman tanks as mobile artillery, with the assault troops right behind. The capture of this dominating feature did much to ease the pressure on Terry Allen's men as they

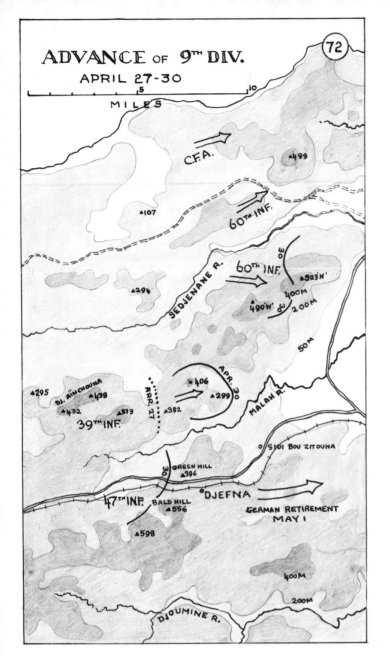

Hills 531, 523, and 461. Hill 523 in particular proved an expensive piece of real estate. It was taken with relative ease in a night attack on April 29–30 by 1st Battalion, 16th Infantry but it was anticipated that holding it would be another matter. Stone parapets were erected (it was impossible to dig foxholes on these bare, rocky summits, Axis positions had in many cases been drilled or blasted out of the rock), and preparations were made for the expected counter-attack. First came several hours of artillery and mortar fire, which wrecked the radios and cut all telephone wires. Then about noon an attack from two sides first encircled, then overran the men on the hill. Some 150 were taken prisoner, the rest killed. An attempt to relieve the battalion with tanks and infantry failed, and it was not until adjacent hills were taken that the position was secured.

Possession and retention of Hill 609 despite determined efforts to recapture it gave the American artillery observers the chance they had been waiting for. Overwhelming gunfire could now be brought on enemy concentrations, and attempts to regain the lost heights were broken up before they got under way.

While the fighting was going on around Hill 609, the heights overlooking the narrow mouth of "The Mousetrap" were also taken. Djebel el Anz (289) was taken and held against repeated German attempts to retake it. On April 30 five separate counter-attacks were beaten off. Possession of this hill enabled the attackers to take Djebel Badjar, a mile opposite on the south side of the Nsir–Chou-ïgui road. In the meantime, armored infantry of the 1st U. S. Armored Division were fighting along the high ground to the south of the Tine Valley, while engineers lifted mines and prepared roadbeds and crossings for the armored columns' advance.

The II Corps operations, physically separated by some 10 miles of rugged country, now interlocked strategically—with a sudden impact on the enemy defenses. The trigger was 9th Division's steady advance south of the Sedjenane River. Hills 382, 406, and 299 were taken on April 30. Possession of these afforded direct observation of enemy supply lines and a base from which an attack could be launched to cut the Sedjenane–Mateur highway. Meanwhile, to the northeast, the 60th Infantry had hacked its way to Hills 523 "N" and 490 "N" ("N" to avoid confusion with the hills around Hill 609 to the south).

The Djefna position was now threatened with isolation from Bizerte and Mateur, and the enemy

fought valiantly for the hills close to the Tine River. Casualties had been heavy. The attack in the south had cost II Corps (to April 30) 183 dead, 1,594 wounded, and 676 prisoners or missing. German losses had run high too, and although Bradley's push in the south had only netted some 400 prisoners, the constant attacks and heavy shelling had weakened the enemy (Luftwaffe Regiment Barenthin and part of 334th Infantry Division). Reinforcements and supplies had to be brought in under American fire, while the rear elements were subjected to the customary bombing and strafing by Allied aircraft.

The successful attack of April 30 took the Americans to the tops of several other nearby points—

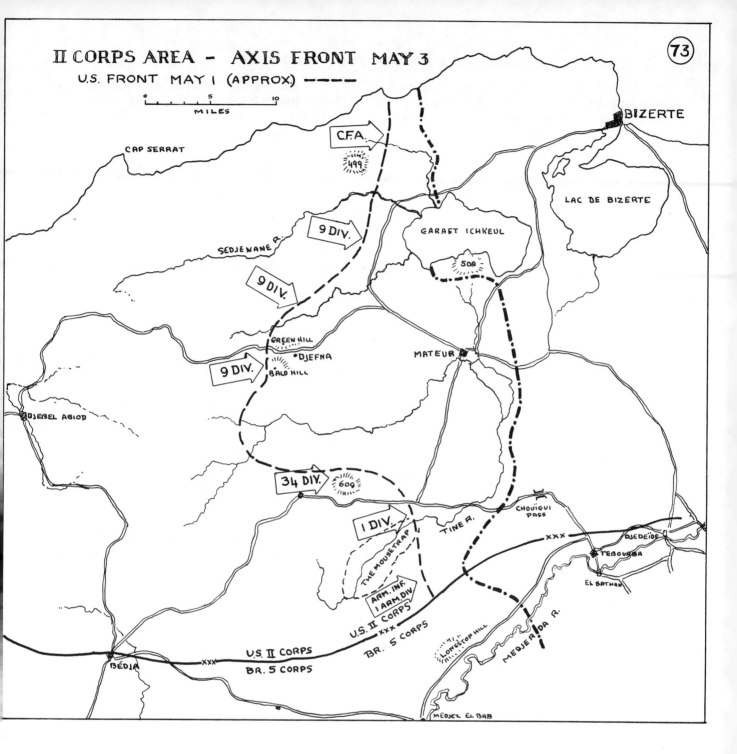

73

II CORPS AREA – AXIS FRONT MAY 3
U.S. FRONT MAY 1 (APPROX.) ――――

MILES

CAP SERRAT

C.F.A.
499

BIZERTE

LAC DE BIZERTE

9 DIV.

SEDJENANE R.

GARAET ICHKEUL

508

9 DIV.

GREEN HILL
•DJEFNA
BALD HILL

MATEUR

9 DIV.

•DJEBEL ABIOD

34 DIV.
609

I DIV.

THE MOUSETRAP

TINE R.

CHOUÏGUI PASS

xxx

DJEDEÏDE
•TEBOURBA

EL BATHAN

ARM. INF.
I ARM. DIV.
U.S. II CORPS

LONGSTOP HILL

MEDJERDA R.

U.S. II CORPS
xxx
BR. 5 CORPS

U.S. II CORPS
xxx
BR. 5 CORPS

BÉDJA

MEDJEZ EL BAB

at once began preparations for withdrawal. A retirement here obviously meant that the positions farther south around Hill 609 must also be evacuated or face encirclement. This was done stealthily without interference from the American forces on the nights of May 1–2 and 2–3—but by May 2 the glare of fires and heavy explosions showed unmistakable signs that the enemy was in general retreat. It was time to unleash Harmon's armored columns, and by the afternoon of May 3, 1st Armored was on the outskirts of Mateur. The bridge

over the Djoumine was blown almost in their faces but, despite enemy shelling, engineers of the bridging train had the first of five crossings ready by 2130. Elements of CC "B" had already forded the river to the east of the town and begun mopping up while others reconnoitered to the northeast and northwest.

By May 3 the enemy line (see map) ran east of Mateur almost due south from the Garaet Ichkeul to the Chouïgui Pass, and American units had pushed forward into contact.

Operation "Strike" and the End in Africa

While II Corps had been battling past Djefna and "The Mousetrap," Anderson's forces had been reorganizing for another, and final thrust for Tunis (Operation "Strike"). In the center of the line, 4th Indian Division and 4th British Division were to attack on May 6 on a narrow front and clear the enemy defenses, preceded by intensive artillery preparations, after which 6th and 7th Armored Divisions would push through to Tunis. The V Corps was to take Djebel Bou Aoukaz on May 5 to secure IX Corps' left flank. In a vain hope of deluding the enemy that the attack might come farther south (the "colossal traffic movement" around Medjez el Bab reminded Anderson of Derby Day), 70 dummy tanks were placed near Bou Arada (1st British Armored Division was also in the neighborhood). U. S. II Corps was to take the pass at Chouïgui, the river crossings at Tebourba and Djedeida, and push on to Bizerte. The XIX Corps was to take Zaghouan. The artillery preparation was to be on a lavish scale, and the greatest air-support program of the campaign was arranged.

The air war had been mounting in intensity, with dire results to the Luftwaffe and Regia Aeronautica. Their squadrons in North Africa were being shattered, while raids on the Italian fields were equally destructive. A raid on Bari on April 26 by Liberators of U. S. 9th Bomber Command destroyed 107 German aircraft on the ground and damaged 45 more (including 40 Me 109s and 41 FW 190s); 5 Italian planes were also destroyed. Other losses brought the total of German planes destroyed to 124—a black day for the Luftwaffe.

Knowing that the final offensive was coming, even though uncertain about the exact time and date, there was little von Arnim and his commanders could do. One thing was sure: It was not coming from the Eighth Army's front. The Germans were aware that powerful elements of that Army had been sent to Anderson, and von Arnim now followed suit by transferring all AOK1's tanks, most of the 88s, much artillery, and the remains of 15th Panzer to PzAOK5. These transfers were made extremely difficult, and in cases impossible, for want of transport and fuel. Besides an almost total lack of the latter there was a desperate shortage of ammunition, which had already seriously weakened the efforts of the German artillerists to check the American advance on II Corps' front.

The final blow, when it fell, was therefore something of an anticlimax, although there was to be hard fighting before everything was over and North Africa secured. The initial attack was made by 1st British Infantry Division's 3rd Brigade. Supported by the fire of over 600 guns, the brigade took Djebel Bou Aoukaz on the evening of May 5. At 0300 on May 6, an overwhelming rain of shells heralded the assault on a 3,000-yard front by the 4th Indian and 4th British Divisions. In 2 hours, 16,632 shells crashed down on the enemy in front of 4th British Division alone. Tactical air support was concentrated in an area 4 miles deep by 3½ miles across. This massive effort (in the 24 hours from the evening of May 5 to May 6, sorties in support of the ground action totaled 1,958), combined with the fire of over 650 guns, ensured the rapid success of the infantry. The armored divisions began to move after daybreak and by noon were near Massicault. Despite Horrock's and Alexander's emphasis on speed, the armored division commanders preferred to consolidate and bring up their mechanized infantry supports before advancing farther, and at nightfall on May 6, both divisions were not far beyond Massicault.

In the event the delay did not matter. The German defenses had been shattered. The veteran 15th Panzer had been all but destroyed, the Hermann Göring and 334th Divisions were worn out, and the Germans admitted that nothing could stop the British from reaching Tunis the next day. Sure enough, on resuming the advance next morning, the British armor met only scattered resistance, and patrols of the 1st Derbyshire Yeomanry and the 11th Hussars reached the center of the city in the afternoon. It was fitting that the unit that had led the Desert Army since Wavell's first offensive—the red jerboa insignia of the 7th Armored Division, the "Desert Rats," on their sand-colored vehicles—should tie for first place in the race for the enemy's key city with the outfit that had scouted ahead of the First Army's advance across Tunisia.

The city was a bedlam—cheering, yelling civilians mixed with dazed Germans and Italians. Many of these base troops had been sitting quietly drinking in outdoor cafes when the first armored cars roared in. Thousands of them surrendered as the British moved in. Others chose to fight, and in places the joyful crowds scampered for shelter as sudden shots rang out. So amid cheers, songs, the crackle of gunfire, the explosions of grenades, flags, flowers, and the smoke of burning vehicles and buildings, the British entered Tunis. The 6th Armored was ordered southeast and reached La Mohammedia by dark, while elements of the 7th Armored mopped up the city during the night.

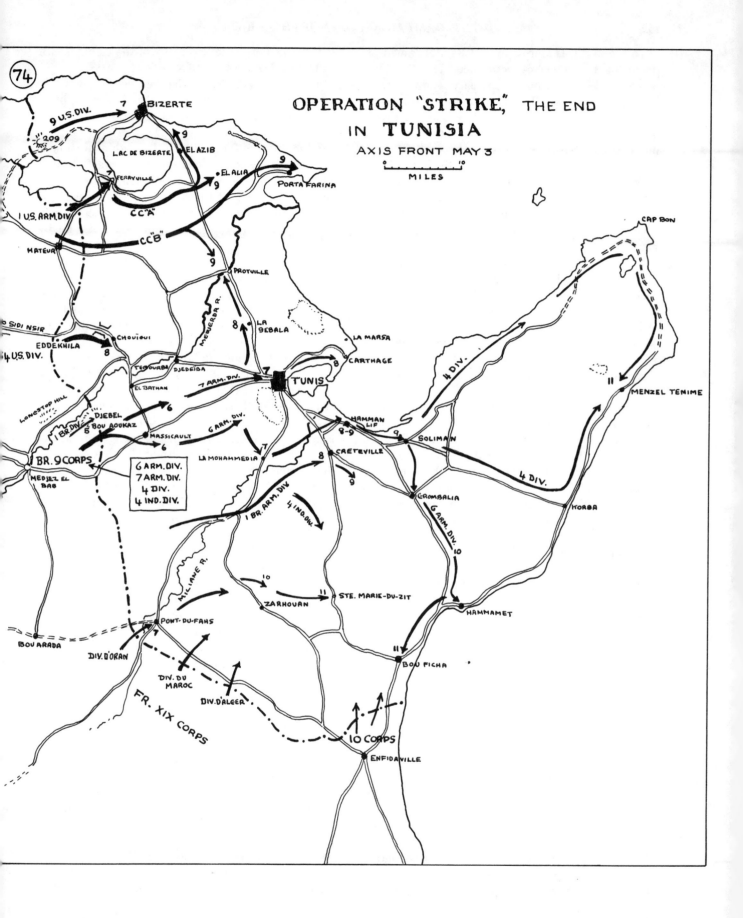

74

OPERATION "STRIKE," THE END
IN TUNISIA
AXIS FRONT MAY 3

MILES

9 U.S. DIV.   7   BIZERTE
"209"
LAC DE BIZERTE   EL AZIB
I U.S. ARM. DIV.   FERRYVILLE   9   EL ALIA   9
MATEUR   CC"A"   PORTA FARINA
CC"B"   9
PROTVILLE
SIDI NSIR   CHOUIGUI   8   LA SEBALA
EDDEKHILA   8   LA MARSA
4 U.S. DIV.   TEBOURBA   DJEDEIDA   8   CARTHAGE
LONGSTOP HILL   EL BATHAN   7 ARM. DIV.   7   TUNIS
DJEBEL   6   CAP BON
1 BR. DIV.   BOU AOUKAZ   6 ARM. DIV.   HAMMAN   4 DIV.
BR. 9 CORPS   MASSICAULT   6   LIF   8-9   11
MEDJEZ EL   LA MOHAMMEDIA   7   SOLIMAN   MENZEL TÉNIME
BAB   8   CREETEVILLE   4 DIV.
6 ARM. DIV.   9   GROMBALIA   KORBA
7 ARM. DIV.   1 BR. ARM. DIV.   4 IND. DIV.
4 DIV.   6 ARM. DIV. 10   HAMMAMET
4 IND. DIV.
MILIANE R.   10   ZARHOUAN   11   STE. MARIE-DU-ZIT   11   BOU FICHA
BOU ARADA   PONT-DU-FAHS
DIV. D'ORAN
DIV. DU
MAROC
DIV. D'ALGER   10 CORPS
FR. XIX CORPS   ENFIDAVILLE

MEDJERDA R.

To the north, II Corps pressed its attack against points of strong enemy resistance. The 60th Infantry took over from the weary Corps Franc d'Afrique and took Djebel Cheniti (209) north of the Garaet Ichkeul, crossed the Douimis River, and by noon were on their way to Bizerte, some 15 miles east of the river. Resistance was slight (the Germans had already abandoned the city), and mines and booby traps were the chief obstacles. Reconnaissance units of 894th Tank Destroyer Battalion entered the city at 1615 on May 7. Enemy demolitions and intensive Allied bombings had caused much damage and, despite scattered sniping, engineers cleared wreckage, mines, and booby traps during the night. Official entry was made May 8 by elements of the Corps Franc d'Afrique.

Enemy guns from positions southwest of the city kept up a sporadic fire. In the morning artillery observers on the roof of the Hôtel de la Marine directed counter-battery fire that knocked most of these out.

Although 34th Division was on 1st Division's left, Bradley decided that in view of 1st Division's heavy casualties, Ryder's men should take Chouïgui Pass, while Terry Allen held the high ground between the pass and Mateur. This involved not only crossing one division's route over another, but also both across the track of 1st U. S. Armored Division. The resulting traffic problem was successfully overcome and the crossovers made without incident, due in no small part to Allied superiority in the air.

The 34th Infantry Division ran into stiff opposition west of Eddekhila, and on May 7 had still not reached the pass. It was not taken until the next day, the defenders having withdrawn during the night of May 7–8.

On May 6, 1st U. S. Armored Division joined the general offensive by attacking northeast of Mateur. CC "A" moved toward Ferryville, took some of the high ground southwest of that town, lost it to counter-attacks, retook the ground that night, and reached Ferryville on the afternoon of May 7. CC "B" moved due east toward a road junction some 6 miles east of Mateur. Enemy anti-tank guns knocked out 7 tanks, and the attack was halted until artillery preparation could be laid on. Under cover of a barrage from 54 guns, some firing smoke shells to mask the enemy artillery, the tanks and tank destroyers pressed forward about 2 miles before dark. CC "B" lost 12 tanks destroyed and 15 damaged on May 6. At dawn the command pushed past the junction, taking prisoners and guns and

cutting off Ferryville and many of the enemy south of Lac de Bizerte.

The aggressive Terry Allen, not content with the assigned task of holding ground and exerting pressure, attacked eastward into the hills some 7 miles southwest of Mateur. His 1st Division soon ran into trouble in the form of the Barenthin Regiment (mainly Luftwaffe volunteers from parachute and glider schools and with a reputation for *esprit* and tenacity). Only 4 of the supporting tanks managed to cross the Tine River before the bridge collapsed, and heavy fire and fierce counter-attacks finally forced a withdrawal across to the west bank of the river. It was an unfortunate affair, with many casualties, and as Bradley wrote, even if the foothills had been carried, there were other higher hills behind, and the line of attack led nowhere anyhow.

The Axis forces in Tunisia were now on the brink of disaster. The capture of Tunis had cut these forces in two, and in accordance with plans for such an eventuality, those north of the Allied corridor remained under control of PzAOK5's von Vaerst, while those to the south were under Messe. By this time the shortage of fuel had immobilized some units, while most were suffering from lack of ammunition. With Allied armored columns breaking through the tenuous lines right and left, the number of German prisoners began suddenly to swell, and it was obvious the end was not far off. Only in the southeast opposite X Corps (Eighth Army) was the line still intact.

The Fifth Panzer Army (AOK5) had been broken into three pieces, with portions in the hills around the Lac de Bizerte, east of the Tine, and to the northwest of Tunis in the area of La Sebala and Protville. The next move on II Corps' part was to drive wedges into these sizable chunks and split them into smaller fragments. CC "A," 1st U. S. Armored Division, moving out from Ferryville on May 8, swung around the southern end of Lac de Bizerte, then west via El Azib despite the fire of numerous guns, including a battery of radar-directed dual-purpose AA 105s. The coast on the north near Bizerte was reached on May 9. At the same time, CC "B" was pressing forward toward Porto Farina, while another element of the command moved on Protville, which units of the British 7th Armored Division had reached on May 8. The 34th Infantry Division had taken the southern part of the Chouïgui Pass and were about to attack the northern side on May 7–8. But Tebourba and Djedeida were evacuated on May 7, and the pass was found to be undefended except for a few riflemen. Chouïgui village was reached by 0800 on May 8, and at noon a British patrol from Tebourba arrived.

"Unconditional Surrender"

Von Vaerst, with remnants of 10th and 15th Panzer and Manteuffel Divisions, cut off from von Arnim's command, made a last stand in the hills northeast of El Alia. At 1000 on May 9, emissaries requested Harmon for an armistice while details for surrender of all troops north of Tunis were worked out. When informed of this, Bradley's headquarters instructed, "unconditional surrender," and this was accepted by noon. Generals von Vaerst, Krause, Buelowius, and Borowietz of the Army and Bassenge and Neuffer of the Luftwaffe were among the almost 40,000 prisoners taken.

The bulk of the Axis forces lay to the south, facing the British V and IX Corps, French XIX Corps, and British X Corps (Eighth Army). The ground was in places, especially the Cape Bon Peninsula, well suited to defense, and the efforts of the Allied Corps were directed at heading off the enemy from these potential defense areas and, by keeping up constant pressure, preventing the dazed and disorganized enemy from rallying. The 6th Armored Division, therefore, was directed to take Soliman and Grombalia at the base of the peninsula, while the 1st British Armored Division advanced to Creteville.

There was a holdup at Hamman Lif. Here cliffs came down to within 300 yards of the surf, and for a day and a half the defenders held this Thermopylae against 6th Armored with the remains of D.A.K. and Hermann Göring Division and most of AOK1's heavy anti-tank guns. Finally, by attacking along the beach and in the edge of the surf, the passage was forced at the cost of 22 Shermans, and the armor poured through in the direction of Hammamet, which was reached on May 10. Von Arnim was now cut off from Messe, who was still resisting X Corps in the hills north of Enfidaville. On May 11, the 6th Armored swept south to Bou Ficha, where one element made wireless contact with X Corps and later in the day spotted bursts for X Corps' artillery. It was not often that observers in an army fighting its way south corrected fire for an army battling northward.

The peninsula was now isolated, and the 4th Division began the task of clearing it—10th Infantry Brigade moving clockwise while the 12th Brigade cut across to Korba, then north to Menzel Temime. To the southwest, XIX Corps was north and west of

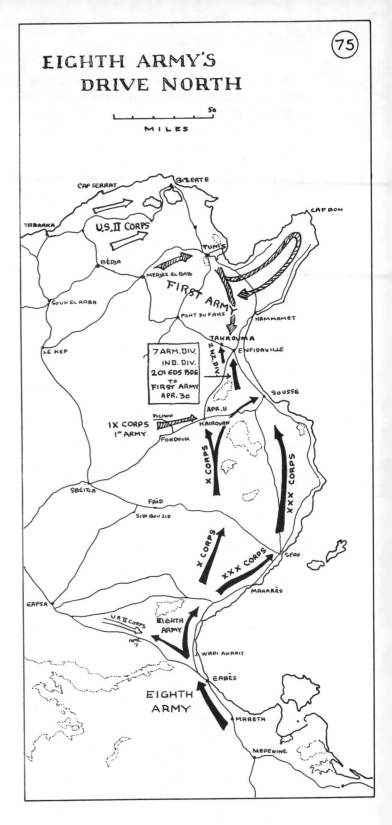

Zaghouan. On the left of the French, 4th Indian Division had swung east, linked up with Boissau's Oran Division, and by May 11 was at Sainte Marie du Zit. The 7th Armored turned north, taking prisoners and guns, to Carthage, La Marsa, and Protville.

Enemy resistance was unpredictable. In places it was fierce, and the Allies had to fight for every inch of ground. In other places, troops surrendered in droves. Allied air attacks did much to hasten the disintegration of the Axis forces. On May 9, the Luftwaffe flew off its remaining planes to Pantellaria or Sicily. The former island was used as a staging area for planes and small vessels on the Sicily–Tunis run, and was heavily raided on May 8, 9, and 10.

By May 12 the remnants of the Italian air force —57 planes—were flown off. On May 9, Allied air forces flew 1,657 sorties. Total (excluding shipping strikes) for May 7–11 was 6,363 sorties.

By the night of May 12, the Axis forces were near complete collapse. On the night of May 12–13, Cramer sent a final message from H.Q. Afrika Korps to OKH, ". . . ammunition shot off, arms and equipment destroyed. In accordance with orders received D.A.K. has fought itself to the condition where it can fight no more. The German Afrika Korps must rise again." The 10th Panzer, out of fuel, had dug in its remaining 7 tanks. When the last shells were gone the tanks were blown up.

Having done their best—and a splendid "best" it had been—the German troops in North Africa now began, in orderly fashion, to prepare for surrender. Von Arnim had by now joined his headquarters with D.A.K.'s in the hills north of Sainte Marie du Zit. After ordering his headquarters radios destroyed (presumably so that he would not have to order the surrender of his forces), von Arnim on May 13 sent staff officers to the nearest British command post. In the meantime an officer and rifleman of the 1st Battalion, 2nd Ghurkas saw a

white flag flying over the two headquarters and "captured" the waiting generals. By this time surrenders were taking place everywhere regardless of von Arnim. A whole army was laying down its arms. Observers were amazed at the number of prisoners—many marching in orderly ranks to the POW cages. Anderson had on May 12 issued orders for unconditional surrender, a cessation to the destruction of weapons and equipment, and the handing over of maps of all mine fields. It now remained for Messe to surrender his AOK1, which he did just after noon on May 13 (having received Mussolini's permission and a field marshal's baton) to Eighth Army's General Freyberg.

At 1415 on May 13 Alexander (later Earl Alexander of Tunis, and a field marshal) sent a report to Churchill: "Sir, it is my duty to report that the Tunisian campaign is over. All enemy resistance has ceased. We are masters of the North African shores."

So ended the campaign in North Africa. There was no attempt at a "Dunkirk." On May 8, Admiral Cunningham had issued his famous "Sink, burn, and destroy—let nothing pass" order, but for the Royal Navy too the end came as an anticlimax. Destroyers cruised watchfully off the Cape Bon Peninsula, while at night coastal craft patrolled close inshore. Less than 700 men are said to have escaped in small craft. Others, carrying some 800 Germans and Italians, were intercepted and taken. The rest of the Axis forces made their voyage from Africa in Allied ships.

In terms of men and equipment taken, the victory was as impressive as any in the whole war. Roughly a quarter of a million men laid down their

U.S. 105-MM. GUN HOWITZER

Range: 12, 330 yds.
Rate of fire: short burst 4 rounds per min. sustained fire 2 rounds per min.

Length of gun: 8'5"
Weight of gun: 1080 lbs.
Weight of shell: 33 lb.
Crew: 9

Spade

Spades are dug in when gun is put in firing position

7

G: Gunner lays for direction
1: Set elevation and fires
2: Loads
3 & 4: Operate fuse setter
5: Prepares charges
6 & 7: Ammunition handlers
C: Chief of Section

Right: Charge in case can be varied. For instance, for lobbing a shell in a high arc for a short distance the shell is removed from case and some of the small powder bags (increments) are removed.

The 105 was the workhorse of the artillery. Its range of elevation, −10° to +65° enabled it to be used as a gun (with a reasonably flat trajectory) or, as a howitzer, lob shells in a high arc into hidden enemy positions. It is usually towed by a 2½-ton 6-wheel truck.

arms (the Axis records are incomplete). Of these well over 100,000 were German (von Arnim's estimate: 100,000 German, 200,000 Italian; Rommel's: 130,000 German; Eighteenth Army Group's: March 20–May 13, 157,000 German, 86,700 Italian).

The Tunisian campaign had been costly to the Allies. Statistics vary, but the *Official British History* lists casualties as follows:

	KILLED	WOUNDED	MISSING	TOTAL
British First Army	4,094	12,566	9,082	25,742
U.S. forces	2,715	8,978	6,528	18,221
French	2,156	10,276	7,007	19,439
British Eighth Army	2,139	8,962	1,517	12,618

From February 3, 1943, total Allied casualties for the Tunisian campaign: 76,020.

It is difficult to write the epilogue to a campaign that was in itself a series of campaigns. The whole affair was on such a vast scale, involving large numbers of men, mountains of materiel, and fleets of ships. Statistics mean little in terms of death and suffering, but a few figures may indicate the scope of the conflict from military and economic points of view.

The big losers were, of course, the Italians. They lost their African Empire, along with over 17,000 dead, many wounded, and tens of thousands of prisoners in Tunisia and Libya alone. The Italian Navy lost over 20,000 dead and more than 300 warships, while some 2 million tons of Italian merchant shipping went to the bottom. Not only was the Italian merchant marine crippled, but also Italian ports and installations had suffered severe damage.

British losses were heavy—total casualties, including prisoners, from June 1940 to May 1943 were 10,763 officers and 163,282 men. These figures do not include the R.A.F. or the Royal Navy, which lost in the Mediterranean area (including Greece and Crete) a battleship, 2 carriers, 14 cruisers, 2 cruiser-minelayers, a monitor, over 40 destroyers, some 40 submarines, and over 100 escort vessels, minor auxiliary units, and MTBs.

German sources give their dead, wounded, and missing at 127,321 (this does not include all prisoners, the Luftwaffe, or naval units).

The problems in logistics were immense, yet despite the distances involved, men, materiel, and supplies were transported in great numbers and in tremendous tonnages. Almost 150,000 Italians and over 112,000 Germans were ferried to Africa by sea alone, while U.S. forces in Africa in May 1943 totaled over 395,000. The size of the British effort may be judged from the fact that in one period

alone (January through September 1942), Army and R.A.F. units and reinforcements arriving in Egypt from the United Kingdom (via the Cape) numbered more than 182,000—with 32,000 more from India. During the same 9-month period there arrived in Egypt 2,789 guns, 2,453 tanks (almost half from the United States), over 62,000 vehicles, and close to 570,000 tons of munitions and war materiel.

The complete victory in North Africa changed the course of the war. Besides ending the mighty effort to supply men and materiel to Egypt (thus releasing large numbers of merchant ships and escort vessels for duty elsewhere), it opened the way for the invasion of southern Europe, with the consequent drain on German forces necessarily committed to its defense; allowed increased aid to the Yugoslav partisans; and removed (in conjunction with the Soviet halting of the German drive in the Caucasus) any threat to the vital oil fields and the Suez Canal.

Under De Gaulle, who soon took full advantage of "Torch," the French gradually prepared to take their share in the recovery of their homeland, while the shattered Italians were by now in no mood to defend their country yard by yard, or, indeed, defend it at all. Sicily was invaded on July 10, 1943, and Messina fell on August 17. Mussolini resigned on July 25 and Marshal Badoglio, his successor, contacted Eisenhower on August 19 to arrange an armistice. It was signed in secret on September 3, as British and Canadian troops crossed the narrow Straits of Messina to the mainland, and announced on September 8. And so the first Axis partner was officially out of the war—although bitter fighting in Italy against the occupying German forces would continue until the collapse of Germany in May 1945.

Perhaps more important, the lessons learned (and they were many) helped perfect the techniques that, just over a year after the end in Africa, enabled the Allied forces to storm across the Channel and smash their way into Fortress Europe. Certainly, without that knowledge, the winning of the Normandy beaches would have been as bloody, and possibly as futile, as that of the shores of Gallipoli almost 30 years before.

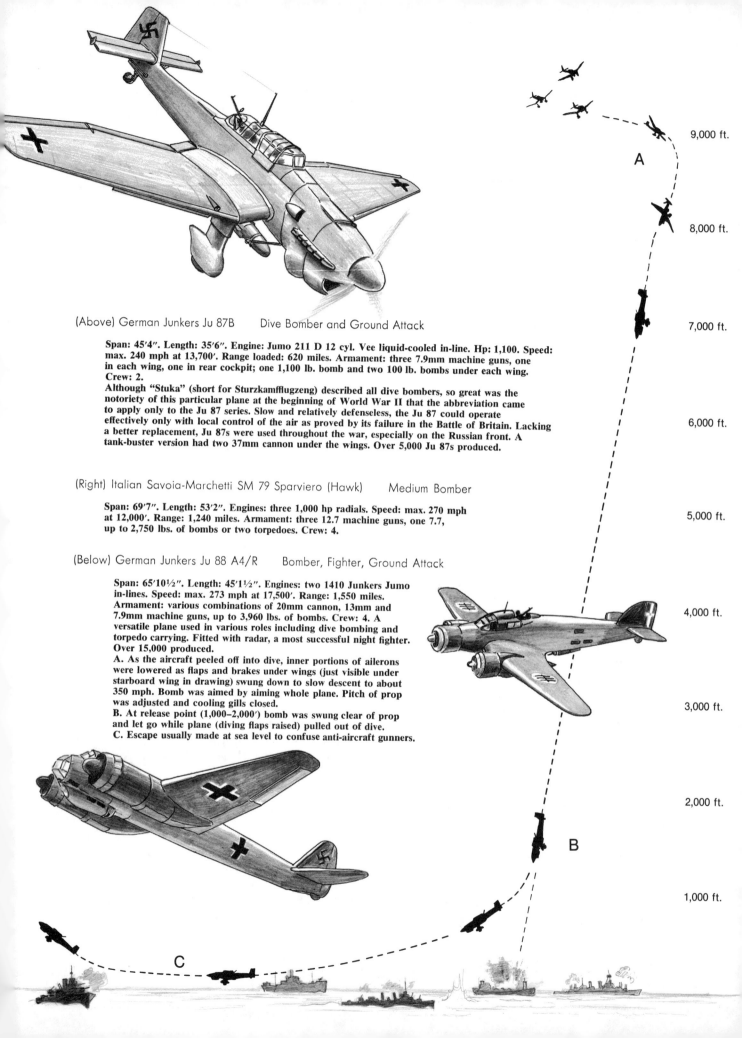

(Above) German Junkers Ju 87B   Dive Bomber and Ground Attack

Span: 45'4". Length: 35'6". Engine: Jumo 211 D 12 cyl. Vee liquid-cooled in-line. Hp: 1,100. Speed: max. 240 mph at 13,700'. Range loaded: 620 miles. Armament: three 7.9mm machine guns, one in each wing, one in rear cockpit; one 1,100 lb. bomb and two 100 lb. bombs under each wing. Crew: 2.
Although "Stuka" (short for Sturzkamfflugzeng) described all dive bombers, so great was the notoriety of this particular plane at the beginning of World War II that the abbreviation came to apply only to the Ju 87 series. Slow and relatively defenseless, the Ju 87 could operate effectively only with local control of the air as proved by its failure in the Battle of Britain. Lacking a better replacement, Ju 87s were used throughout the war, especially on the Russian front. A tank-buster version had two 37mm cannon under the wings. Over 5,000 Ju 87s produced.

(Right) Italian Savoia-Marchetti SM 79 Sparviero (Hawk)   Medium Bomber

Span: 69'7". Length: 53'2". Engines: three 1,000 hp radials. Speed: max. 270 mph at 12,000'. Range: 1,240 miles. Armament: three 12.7 machine guns, one 7.7, up to 2,750 lbs. of bombs or two torpedoes. Crew: 4.

(Below) German Junkers Ju 88 A4/R   Bomber, Fighter, Ground Attack

Span: 65'10½". Length: 45'1½". Engines: two 1410 Junkers Jumo in-lines. Speed: max. 273 mph at 17,500'. Range: 1,550 miles. Armament: various combinations of 20mm cannon, 13mm and 7.9mm machine guns, up to 3,960 lbs. of bombs. Crew: 4. A versatile plane used in various roles including dive bombing and torpedo carrying. Fitted with radar, a most successful night fighter. Over 15,000 produced.
A. As the aircraft peeled off into dive, inner portions of ailerons were lowered as flaps and brakes under wings (just visible under starboard wing in drawing) swung down to slow descent to about 350 mph. Bomb was aimed by aiming whole plane. Pitch of prop was adjusted and cooling gills closed.
B. At release point (1,000–2,000') bomb was swung clear of prop and let go while plane (diving flaps raised) pulled out of dive.
C. Escape usually made at sea level to confuse anti-aircraft gunners.

9,000 ft.

8,000 ft.

7,000 ft.

6,000 ft.

5,000 ft.

4,000 ft.

3,000 ft.

2,000 ft.

1,000 ft.

A

B

C

IX

Malta

THE UNSINKABLE CARRIER

The island of Malta has played a part in the history of the Mediterranean basin for more than 2,500 years. Carthaginians succeeded Phoenicians, followed by Romans, Arabs, Normans, Sicilians, French, Spaniards, the Knights of St. John, Bonapartist French, and finally the British. After the latter captured the island (with the support of the Maltese) from the French in September 1800 it became a useful naval base. With the introduction of steam into the Navy and later with the opening of the Suez Canal, Malta's importance increased, and by World War I it figured largely in British naval strategy.

The development of the bombing plane between the wars and the proximity of now hostile Italian airfields raised serious doubts about the value of Malta as a naval base, and consequently when war broke out the major units of the Mediterranean Fleet were based on Alexandria. However, due to the steady buildup at Malta of light attack forces, both sea and air, the tiny but strategically located island influenced the North African campaign to an extent out of all proportion to its size.

Situated athwart the enemy supply lines, the damage the Malta strike forces caused—by air, on the sea, and

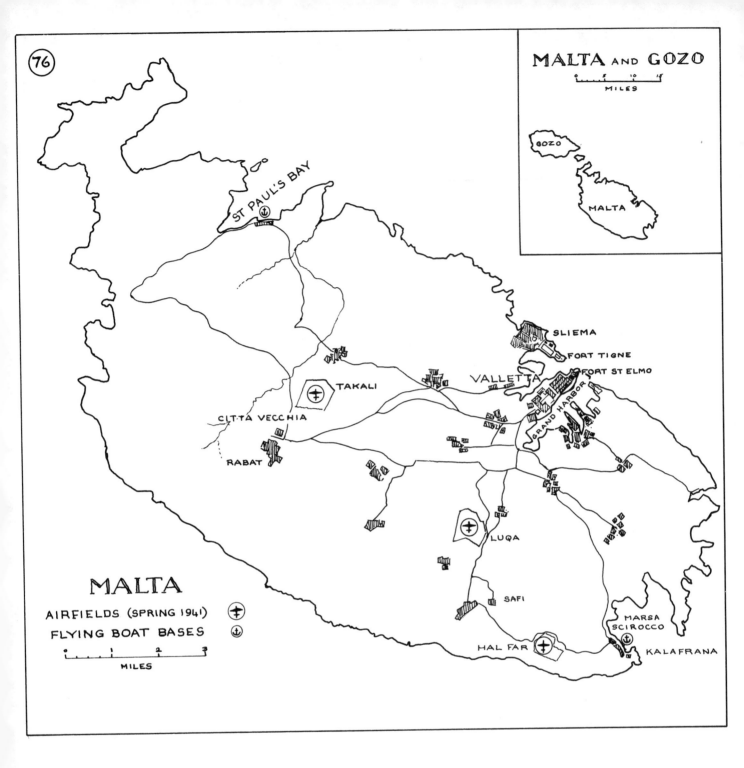

76

MALTA AND GOZO

MILES

GOZO

MALTA

ST PAUL'S BAY

SLIEMA
FORT TIGNE
VALLETTA
FORT ST ELMO
GRAND HARBOR

TAKALI

CITTA VECCHIA

RABAT

LUQA

SAFI

MARSA
SCIROCCO

HAL FAR

KALAFRANA

MALTA

AIRFIELDS (SPRING 1941)
FLYING BOAT BASES

MILES

under it—produced violent reaction by the Axis. So besides the continuous fighting in the desert and the intermittent but often savage encounters at sea, there raged another battle—the battle for Malta. A seesaw, hammer-and-tongs fight this—one whose varying stages had dramatic effect on the struggle in North Africa. When Malta was up, the Axis forces under Rommel staggered. When Malta was on its knees from some particularly hard blow, the Eighth Army was hard pressed too. So it went—month after month—and because of this link between the battered island and the

war in the desert no account of the land campaign can be complete without at least an abbreviated history of the struggle for Malta.

To avoid the inevitable confusion caused by sandwiching accounts of two separate but concurrent campaigns, I have given the Malta story a chapter of its own. The fact that it has been placed at the end of the book in no way reflects on its importance in the winning of the campaign for North Africa.

The island of Malta is some 17 miles long by 9 miles wide—95 square miles. Three miles northwest is the companion island of Gozo (26 square miles). Midway between lies Comino (1 square mile). The islands, mainly limestone, rise in most places steeply from the sea. The fine natural harbors at Valletta had over the years been turned into a major base with docks, yards, and workshops—the only British harbor between the western and eastern entrances to the Mediterranean. In peacetime it was the headquarters of the Mediterranean Fleet. It also was an important air base, with three small airfields and a seaplane base.

Unfortunately, in the years of peace—and economy —little had been done to prepare the island for a possible war with Italy. Nor was this only due to lack of funds. While the Navy was most anxious to retain the base and to make it strong enough to withstand assault, the Army and Air Force were of the opinion that the island would be so vulnerable to overwhelming air attack from Sicily, Libya, and the Italian mainland that it was virtually indefensible. So nothing much was done until it was almost too late to do anything.

For instance, there was the matter of subterranean shelters for submarines. In 1936 it had been proposed that caverns be cut in the soft limestone (of which most of Malta is composed). This fairly obvious and (because the cliffs come sheer down to the water's edge in many places) eminently practical move was endorsed by the Commander-in-Chief of the Mediterranean Fleet and by the governor. However, in July 1937 Chamberlain's cabinet decided not to spend the estimated 300,000 pounds. When the battered 10th Flotilla was withdrawn from the island in April 1942, after suffering several boats sunk or damaged, the Commanding Officer is said to have remarked bitterly that the estimated construction costs were about the price of a single submarine.

It was not until the end of July 1939 that increased anti-aircraft-gun defenses were approved, along with 4 fighter squadrons, but these weapons were still not up to quota by June 1940. Nor, due to commitments at home, were there any fighter aircraft. Under the circumstances the Navy rightly decided that when war came the main portions of the Fleet must be based at Alexandria, and work was accordingly pushed to prepare that port as a major naval base. Needless to say, part of the AA defenses rushed to Alexandria were at the expense of Malta.

Thus when Italy declared war on June 10, 1940, there were only 34 heavy and 8 light anti-aircraft guns, while the air defenses rested on three Sea Gladiators— originally consigned to the carrier *Glorious* and discovered on the docks still in their packing crates. These biplanes (there were 4 but 1 crashed shortly after assembly) were flown by pilots from flying boat units and Air headquarters. The Maltese christened them *Faith, Hope,* and *Charity,* and they duly rose to meet the enemy when Malta received its first air attack early in the morning of June 11. Another attack followed in the afternoon, and by the end of June there had been 36 by day and night, the heaviest by 60 bombers with fighter escort. Hits were made on various dockyard establishments, a submarine in dry dock, and on the floating dock, which sank on June 21.

Seventy civilians were killed in the June raids.

But this was only a sample. Raids were to become part of Malta's way of life. The air-raid sirens were to sound their eerie alarm more than 6,000 times, and before all was over much of the capital and the surrounding villages had been bombed to rubble. A major portion of Malta's 270,000-odd population was centered around Valletta, the capital, and only the heavily built stone houses and virtual absence of wood in construction, coupled with the use of natural caves and shelters dug out of the soft limestone, prevented very heavy casualties. On one occasion nearly 1,000 tons of bombs were dropped on a single objective over a 36-hour period. During one peak period of Axis air activity there were constant alerts day and night for 5 months.

Gloster Gladiator II   Single-seater Fighter

Span: 32′3″. Length: 25′5″. Engine: 840 hp radial. Speed: max. 246 mph at 14,500′. Service ceiling: 32,900′. Armament: two .303 machine guns firing through air screw disc. Two mounted beneath lower wing. Sea Gladiators were merely MKIIs with an arrester hook and catapult points added. Although an anachronism by 1939, the Gladiator saw service in Norway, Finland, Belgium, as well as in Africa and Greece, where it was sometimes pitted against another museum piece, the Fiat CR 42 Falco biplane.

Malta had been referred to as an "unsinkable aircraft carrier anchored off the heel of Italy." Unable to sink the island, the Italian and German air forces did their best to neutralize it and at times all but succeeded. It followed that the efficiency of the island as a base for surface, submarine, and air forces varied as the weight of the enemy attacks waxed and waned. Properly, the account of an action that went on almost without interruption for nearly three years should be interspersed throughout the history of the whole African campaign. To give the story of Malta some cohesion and to avoid too many "meanwhiles," I have written this chapter as a sort of chronology—which in no way does justice to the gallantry of the hard-pressed, often half-starved, islanders and garrison.

1940

June 11: About 5:00 A.M. the air raid sirens sounded in earnest for the first time as 10 planes bombed Hal Far Airfield and the dockyard area. Twenty-five more returned in the afternoon.

June 18: On that date 6 Hurricanes arrived. Two went on to Egypt, but even the addition of 4 modern fighters to the aforementioned *Faith, Hope,* and *Charity,* plus a single Hurricane, which had arrived via Tunis, was a great boost to Malta's air power. The Sea Gladiator pilots had done their duty so well that in the opening days of the war the Italians credited the island with at least 25 fighters.

June 21: This date saw the arrival of 12 Swordfish, the forerunner of numbers of strike aircraft of various types. Continuing raids had damaged the dock area. On this day a submarine was damaged in dock, and a floating dock, hit in previous raids, was finally sunk. Also, the constant bombing made the refueling of the big Sunderland flying boats, used in vital reconnaissance and anti-submarine work, dangerous except during darkness. Operation of the island shore-based planes was also rendered difficult. The airfields were small, and at this time dispersion was difficult.

The war had come to Malta. Seventy civilians died in June. Raids were comparatively light, although there were many alerts. The Maltese, like the Londoners, were beginning to grow used to daily attacks. The islanders learned to ply pick and shovel and to burrow into the rocky soil, one property of which was that, while easy to cut into, the limestone soon hardened upon contact with the air. July passed in this fashion, digging out after raids, digging in in preparation for raids to come. Offensive strikes were carried out. For instance, on July 6, Swordfish from the island (No. 830 Squadron, Fleet Air Arm) bombed hangars and workshops at Catania in Sicily. Three days later, on July 9, 2 convoys for Alexandria that had stopped at Malta from Gibraltar sailed for Egypt under cover of the minor fleet action then in progress off Calabria. Passengers reported 72 raids since the beginning of the war.

August 2: On this date the defenses were augmented (Operation "Hurry") by 12 Hurricanes flown from the carrier *Argus* from a position southwest of Sardinia. Also in August three Glenn Martin Marylands were sent to the island for long-range reconnaissance work. As spare parts for these were scarce, 3 extras were sent to be "cannibalized."

September 2: In Operation "Hats" 2 storeships and an oil tanker arrived from Alexandria, while the battleship *Valiant* and 2 anti-aircraft cruisers (on their way to join the fleet at Alexandria) brought in men and guns, 8 3.7-inch anti-aircraft guns, 10 Bofors 40mms, and 10,000 rounds of 40mm ammunition. This was the first through-passage from Gibraltar to Alexandria attempted since Italy declared war.

September 30: The cruisers *Liverpool* and *Gloucester* came in with 1,200 troops, airmen, and R.A.F. stores. They sailed that night to rejoin the fleet cruising nearby. The air raids were lessening, and during the first half of October there was only a single alert.

October 11: Four storeships arrived from Alexandria heavily escorted by 4 battleships, 2 carriers, 6 cruisers, and 16 destroyers. It was hoped that the Italian fleet might be enticed into action. The Italian battle fleet stayed in port, but that night 3 destroyers were sunk by the cruiser *Ajax*. The cruiser *Liverpool* was damaged by a torpedo-bomber en route back to Alexandria.

By November, Wellington bombers—then the most power R.A.F. bomber in operational use—were staging through Malta to Egypt, and some were stationed on the island. Their arrival gave added power to Malta's slowly growing striking force.

November 9–10: Operation "Coat." Another double play—ships, covered by the western Force H, based at Gibraltar, carried men and stores to Malta, then proceeded on to Egypt while others, convoyed by the Mediterranean Fleet, came in from the East. In this case the battleship *Barham,* 2 cruisers, and 3 destroyers, en route to Alexandria, brought in a battalion of infantry, tankers, and artillerymen, 2,150 men in all. From the East, Admiral Cunningham convoyed 5 storeships in and 4 empties out to Alexandria. Next day Glenn Martin Marylands from the island reconnaissance flights brought in photos that pinpointed the position of the Italian warships at Taranto and made possible the success of the famous strike that partially crippled the enemy fleet on the night of November 11.

November 18: Another attempt to fly Hurricanes to Malta from a carrier. This one ended in disaster. Two flights of 6 planes, each guided by a Skua of Fleet Air Arm, flew off *Argus.* Because enemy forces were reported at sea, the fly-off took place farther west than usual, and because of faulty navigation or failure to use the most economical cruising speed only one Skua and 4 Hurricanes reached the island.

November 19: The cruiser *Newcastle* reached Malta from Gibraltar with airmen, bombs, and stores for the Wellingtons, whose number had been upped to 16.

November 26–27: The "Collar" convoy. This was yet

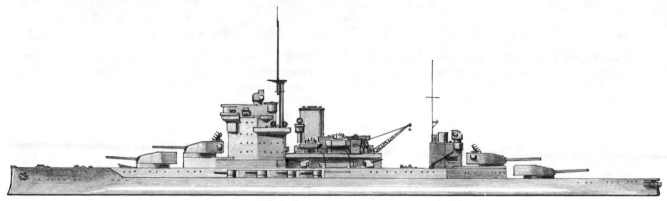

Warspite (Br.) *Queen Elizabeth* Class Battleship (five ships)

Launched 1913.
Displacement: 31,100 tons. LOA: 644'. Beam: 104'. Draft: 31'.
Four screws. 80,000 hp=24 knots.
Armament: eight 15" (4×2), eight 6" (8×1), eight 4" anti-aircraft (4×2), automatics.
Armor: belt 13"–6", deck 3" plus, turrets 11".
Complement: c. 1,124.

another "through" run—two fast merchantmen for Malta escorted partway by Force H and by cruisers carrying R.A.F. personnel for Egypt. Four storeships from the East were under protection of the Mediterranean Fleet. It was a complicated maneuver—with still other supplies and men going to Suda Bay in Crete, empty vessels going back from Malta to Alexandria, and warships being transferred from the eastern Mediterranean to the Atlantic. The Italian squadron was at sea and an indecisive action occurred off Cape Spartivento.

December arrived with Malta in comparatively good shape. Air raids had almost ceased. Ground forces now included 6 battalions of British infantry, plus those of the King's Own Malta Regiment, several batteries of artillery, and a few tanks. Not only were there more planes—bombers, torpedo-bombers, reconnaissance, and fighters—but also facilities for servicing them were being improved, and anti-aircraft defenses were stronger. On the debit side, food was being controlled, and there were severe shortages of other necessities—kerosene among them. There was no wood on the island (generations of goats had seen to that) and coal was bulky and expensive to import. So the Maltese depended largely on kerosene for cooking, lighting, and heating. Malta had never been self-supporting, even with the smaller populations of the past. In recent years it had proved more profitable to plant vineyards than to raise wheat, which could be bought cheaply from Italy. Wheat acreage had dropped from 20,000 acres in 1918 to less than half that in 1940. As with the Italians, pasta figured largely in the Maltese diet. So wheat, a difficult cargo, had to be brought in. And along with wheat and kerosene and other necessities there were stores for the hungry garrison, ammunition for the equally hungry anti-aircraft guns, and, of prime importance, aviation fuel for the growing collection of aircraft.

December 20: As a fitting end to the year, Admiral Cunningham steamed into Grand Harbor in his flagship

Warspite escorting 4 supply ships. He wrote, "As we moved in with our band playing and guard paraded the Barracas and other points of vantage were black with wildly cheering Maltese. Our reception was touchingly overwhelming."

As 1941 opened, things in the eastern Mediterranean were looking up. The Italians were taking a beating in the Western Desert, the offensive that was to drive the Italians out of East Africa had begun, and despite the drain on ships and aircraft entailed by aid to Greece (invaded by the Italians on October 28), the British Navy had been able to retain considerable control over most of the Mediterranean. Malta could well look to the new year with some degree of confidence. But there was a dark cloud on the horizon—a cloud with swastika markings.

As told elsewhere, the German leader had decided to send the Luftwaffe to the support of his hard-pressed colleague. And the easy days were over for Malta.

Another west-to-east convoy (Operation "Excess") was planned in late December with the usual "changing of the guard" near Malta—where the western ships would be met by Cunningham and units of the Mediterranean Fleet, including 2 battleships and a carrier. Under cover of this operation 2 merchantmen were to be run into Malta and empties sent back to Alexandria. Force "H," having "delivered the goods," turned back to Gibraltar. The "goods" were 4 supply ships. One of them, *Essex*, with 4,000 tons of ammunition, 3,000 tons of seed potatoes, and 12 crated Hurricanes, was for Malta, the others for Greece. These went on, escorted by the cruisers *Gloucester* and *Southampton*, which had on January 8 just delivered 500 soldiers and airmen to Malta. Cunningham's main force was now close at hand (less a destroyer crippled by a mine and towed into Malta). The Malta-bound *Essex* reached port late on January 10.

1941

January 10: Several air attacks on Cunningham by

Italian torpedo-bombers had been easily beaten off, but at 1330 radar picked up a strong force of enemy aircraft. Carrier *Illustrious* had just begun to fly off her planes when some 35 Stukas and Ju 88s began a series of fierce and co-ordinated attacks that speedily left the carrier burning fore and aft from 6 bomb hits. Six German aircraft were destroyed by the carrier's Fulmar fighters or by the fleet's anti-aircraft defenses, but the carrier was a wreck and could barely be steered into Valletta Harbor, having been hit by another bomb en route. The convoy and the battleships were undamaged, though heavily attacked, but next day *Gloucester* and *Southampton* were attacked and the latter so badly damaged she had to be sunk. The two cargo vessels had reached Malta from Alexandria under cover of the operation, and 10 empties went out eastbound. All supply ships reached their destinations safely, but naval losses were severe. It was plain that a new force, and one to be reckoned with, had arrived on the scene.

The new force was Fliegerkorps X, formerly stationed in Norway, where many of the pilots had specialized in attacks on shipping. By mid-January the Korps counted 186 aircraft of various types in Sicily alone. (While a Fliegerkorps was normally a unit of a Luftflotte, X was a special force of all types of planes.) The impact of the Luftwaffe's highly trained airmen was soon felt on Malta.

January 12: Despite a successful raid on the airfield at Catania on the night of January 12 and another on January 15, German strength was building up while on Malta there were only 15 Hurricanes serviceable. On January 16 the first heavy attacks on the harbor area began, with *Illustrious* as a prime target. She was slightly damaged by another bomb and *Essex* was also hit, but fortunately her deadly cargo did not explode. Along with 15 of her crew, 7 Maltese stevedores were killed. The rest quit, and the vessel was finally unloaded by soldiers and sailors.

January 18: More heavy attacks, this time on the airfields at Hal Far and Luqa. Six planes were destroyed on the ground, many damaged, and the airfield temporarily knocked out. On the average only some 6 Hurricanes, 3 Fulmars, and a Gladiator could be sent up at any one time, while the raiding planes came over in waves of from 40 to 80.

January 19: The *Illustrious* received more damage but on the evening of January 23 she was able to leave under cover of darkness and foul weather. She reached Alexandria 2 days later, cheered by every ship in harbor. During the attacks on her at Malta 16 German planes were downed by fighters or anti-aircraft fire.

Despite the raids, aircraft of the island's striking force were able to hit back at the enemy. Wellingtons raided the Sicilian fields whenever possible, and on January 27 Swordfish sank a merchantman off Tunisia. At the same time, the Malta submarines took a small but steady toll of the enemy. Despite this, in the period October 1940–January 1941 less than 4 per cent of the cargoes shipped to Africa failed to arrive.

Air strength in January 1941 consisted of one squadron each of Mark I Hurricanes (12 planes), Wellingtons (12), Swordfish (10), Sunderlands (5), and Martin Marylands (4).

There was not much room for enlargement of the 3 fields—Hal Far in the South; Luqa, overlooking Grand Harbor; and Takali, some 3½ miles northwest of Luqa and about in the center of the island. There were 2 landing strips at Safi between Hal Far and Luqa. The flying-boat base was at Kalafrana—near Hal Far—as were the equipment and repair depots. Allowing for dispersion and for aircraft staging through to Egypt, capacity of the fields was about 5 squadrons. Aircraft were dispersed around the perimeter of the fields. Later on, dispersal was better, more elaborate bays were built, and the 3 fields were connected with a maze of taxiways and gravel strips.

The island was so small that there could be no defense in depth. The radar equipment was none too efficient, nor was the radio-telephone communication system. There were no radar-equipped night fighters. There was either a single Hurricane up on patrol, waiting and hoping for the searchlights to pick up a target, or the defense was left to the guns alone.

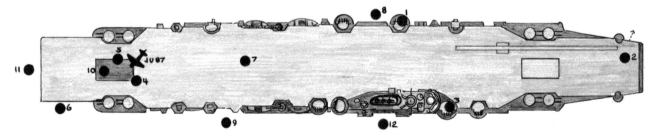

Deck plan of *Illustrious* showing damage sustained January 10, 1941. Hit No. 1 went through the sponson, killing two men and damaging the gun, but failed to explode when it struck the water. A flaming Ju 87 crashed on the edge of the after elevator, adding to the damage. The near misses shown caused underwater damage and many casualties. Eighty-three officers and men were killed, and 100 wounded. Despite the near misses the vessel's watertight integrity was not seriously threatened. Her boiler and engine rooms were undamaged, although smoke and fumes and the intense heat of the fires just above made them almost unbearable.

Ammunition expenditure shows the difference between the intensity of the attacks by the Luftwaffe and the Reggia Aeronautica.

June 1940–mid-January 1941 (Italian)	Heavy AA 9,546	Light AA 1,098
Mid-January 1941–mid-April 1941 (Both)	Heavy AA 21,176	Light AA 18,660

Note the sharp increase in expenditure of light anti-aircraft during the German raids—showing far more low-level attacks.

The Luftwaffe's assault had the desired effect. The Afrika Korps passed over into Tripoli with little interference from the Malta airfields and none from surface craft. The only offensive forces accomplishing anything much were the Malta-based submarines. These, despite restrictions on sinkings, shallow waters, numerous mine fields, and heavily escorted convoys, sank several ships and laid many mines in the enemy home waters.

On February 5, 1941, restrictions on sinking were lifted, and any ships south of 35°46' could be assumed to be enemy transports and sunk on sight. This helped, but during January, February, and March less than 10 per cent of all enemy supplies sent to North Africa failed to reach port.

February 12: This saw the first Messerschmitt 109 fighters over the island. The Me 109 was as good or better than the Hurricane and another headache for the island's few defenders. Fliegerkorps X was growing too, from 243 combat planes in mid-February to 443 at the end of March. But losses were high and the island was beginning to acquire an evil reputation among enemy pilots.

Even so, heavy raids were mounted almost daily. In one, 6 Wellington bombers were destroyed on the ground and 4 more damaged. Also, the mining of the harbors and approaches was stepped up—an added difficulty for the defenders when the few small minesweepers were frequently strafed by daylight and bombed at their anchorage at night.

There was the usual shortage of reconnaissance planes. The big Short Sunderland flying boats were slow, and while they carried an impressive defense armament of 8 .303-caliber machine guns (which prompted the Luftwaffe to nickname them "the porcupine"), they were unsuited for some of the tasks demanded of them. The Martin Marylands were useful but there were never enough—7 at the most, of which only 3 or 4 were operational at any one time. Some Hurricanes were fitted later as photo-reconnaissance planes, but it was still difficult to cover an area from Sardinia and Tunisia in the west to the Adriatic, Ionian, and Aegean seas. Yet it was only by such reconnaissance work, coupled with reports from the ever-watchful submarines, that any co-ordinated attacks on the enemy supply lines could be made.

Few (except veteran airmen) realize the wastage of aircraft in wartime. Besides planes lost in actual combat, the ordinary operational losses—bad landings, bad take-offs, collisions, etc.—were always heavy. Under conditions such as existed on Malta—small fields pitted with craters, under almost constant attack, with swift Me 109s waiting to pounce on aircraft taking off or landing, plus the inevitable damage from bombs and ground strafing—attrition was very high, and keeping the squadrons up to strength was a constant problem.

February 21: Two battalions were brought in on 3 cruisers from Alexandria, bringing the total, exclusive of the King's Own Malta Regiment, to 8.

March 2: Six Hurricanes were flown in from Egypt, followed 12 days later by 6 more. The supply situation was always pressing, and on March 23 a convoy of 4 ships from the east, the first since January, slipped into port under cover of a sweep by the fleet (it was as extra protection for this that the Hurricanes had arrived from Egypt). Even so, the Luftwaffe bombers harried them even in harbor, and two vessels were hit as they berthed. So persistent were the raids that the Wellingtons and Sunderlands were temporarily withdrawn.

March also saw food rationing introduced. The supply of food had previously been controlled, and there had been cuts in many items. Kerosene was also rationed.

April 3: Twelve Hurricane IIs (faster and armed with 12 mgs or 4 20mm cannon) were flown off the carrier *Ark Royal* from a position about 400 miles west of the island. Led by three FAA Skuas, all arrived safely. (During April, May and June, 224 Hurricanes flew to Malta from carriers; 109 stayed on the island, the rest went on to Egypt.)

Despite the efforts of the Malta planes and submarines, supplies were reaching Rommel and the Italians in North Africa in large quantities. Risking the raids and air-dropped mines, on April 11 4 destroyers (14th Destroyer Flotilla) arrived from Alexandria under Captain P. J. Mack to attack enemy shipping. This renewed use of Malta as a base for a naval striking force paid off handsomely. Just before 0200 on April 16 a convoy of 5 merchant vessels (4 German and 1 Italian), guarded by 3 destroyers, was attacked by Mack and his flotilla. In the ensuing melee—at ranges from 2,000 yards down to 50—all 5 supply ships and their escorts were sunk, along with the destroyer *Mohawk*. The action came at a time when there was much pressure from London on the Navy to take drastic action against Rommel's supply routes. It was followed on April 21 by a bombardment of Tripoli by heavy units of the Mediterranean Fleet, supported by raids on the port by Malta-based Wellingtons and Swordfish.

Also on April 21, *Breconshire*, a new, fast (18 knots), 10,000-ton vessel commissioned as a supply ship arrived with gasoline and ammunition. At the same time a convoy of empties made its way eastward.

April 24: The cruiser *Gloucester* arrived to support the striking force—which had found no more convoys but had sunk a lone freighter.

April 27: Twenty-three Hurricanes landed, flown off *Ark Royal;* and on April 28 a cruiser, a minelayer, and 6 destroyers of Captain Lord Louis Mountbatten's 5th Destroyer Flotilla entered the harbor, bringing men and supplies. The 5th Flotilla stayed, relieving the 14th, which sailed for Alexandria with the now-empty *Breconshire.*

May 2: Malta was not to have its strike force for long. On May 2 as the force was entering Grand Harbor one of the destroyers hit a mine and sank, blocking the harbor entrance. *Gloucester* and 2 destroyers were still outside, and they were sent west to join Force "H" at Gibraltar. The three inside stayed until they sailed to support the "Tiger" convoy.

Submarines are not an economical way of transporting stores, but they were occasionally used as supply ships by all major belligerents. Thus on May 15 *Cachalot* arrived from the United Kingdom with 16 tons of special stores. Later *Rorqual, Otus,* and *Osiris* were so employed. It was estimated that at that date the gasoline that could be brought in by a single submarine would keep the Malta planes flying for 3 days.

The "Tiger" convoy referred to above was a daring attempt to run a supply of badly needed tanks and aircraft straight through the Mediterranean to Egypt— thus saving nearly 40 days over the run via the Cape. In the general movement of supporting forces from Alexandria to the central Mediterranean, *Breconshire,* a fast convoy of 4 ships, and a slow convoy of 2 tankers were to be escorted to Malta by various covering forces, which were then to reinforce the "Tiger" convoy for its perilous passage of the narrow central Mediterranean area. One ship of the "Tiger" convoy was mined and sank, taking with her 57 of the 295 tanks and 10 out of 53 Hurricanes. The rest got through safely, as did all the Malta-bound vessels, which docked on May 9.

May 21: Forty-eight Hurricanes were flown off carriers *Furious* and *Ark Royal,* and all but one arrived safely. Reinforcements for the R.A.F. coincided with the withdrawal of Fliegerkorps X—transferred from Sicily to the Balkans as part of Hitler's buildup for "Barbarossa," code name for the invasion of the Soviet Union. From January 10 to the middle of May, 62 German and 15 Italian aircraft had been destroyed over Malta—for the loss of 32 R.A.F. fighters in combat and almost as many destroyed on the ground. The temporary withdrawal of the Luftwaffe ended the first major attempt to neutralize Malta as a military and naval base.

Relief due to lessening of the German air effort was partially offset by heavy naval losses incurred in the withdrawal from Greece (April 24–30) and the un-

successful battle for Crete (May 20–June 1). To meet the needs of these operations the Malta destroyers were withdrawn. Also, as a result of the loss of Crete and Rommel's advance in Libya (El Agheila, March 24; Derna, April 7; Bardia, April 11), German bombers could operate against shipping in the eastern Mediterranean from Crete and Cyrenaica.

June 15: Forty-seven Hurricanes were flown to Malta from *Victorious* and *Ark Royal.* All but 4 arrived.

July 21: Operation "Substance." Six storeships and a troop transport (which grounded at Gibraltar and did not make the voyage) to be convoyed to Malta and 6 empty merchantmen and *Breconshire* to be brought out. The operation was successful. Although cruiser *Manchester* and a destroyer were badly damaged and another destroyer was sunk, the convoy reached Malta on July 24.

The eastern lifeline was, for the moment, closed. But "Substance" showed that a bold move from the west could still reach the island despite attacks by bomb, mine, and torpedo from both submarine and E-boat.

July 26: A heavy attack by Italian "human" torpedoes, explosive motor boats, motor boats, and airplanes. At 0430 human torpedoes tried to blast through the defensive nets. These craft were blown up, along with the leading explosive motor boat. Others were picked up by searchlights and engaged by artillery. Several were sunk by gunfire, others by Hurricanes at first light. Two large motor boats were also sunk, and a motor boat, an explosive motor boat, and a two-man torpedo craft were captured.

August 2: Operation "Style." Two cruisers, the fast minelayer *Manxman,* and 2 destroyers arrived at Malta with supplies and men, as well as reinforcements left at Gibraltar by the grounded transport—1,750 in all.

This brought the number of troops on Malta to more than 22,000, with 112 heavy anti-aircraft guns, 118 light and regular artillery pieces, and coastal guns to the number of 104. There was a supply of military stores adequate for several months. At this time there were some 15 Hurricane Is and 60 Hurricane IIs serviceable.

September: Blenheims were flown in as well as 49 Hurricanes from *Ark Royal* and *Furious.*

During July and August, Malta-based submarines had operated with increased success, and in September a combined attack resulted in the sinking of 2 liners of 19,500 tons each. At the same time the air-strike forces had been built up and were scoring an increasing number of sinkings. Enemy convoys were usually routed from Naples, to the west of Sicily, and through the Narrows, keeping close to the African shore to Tripoli. Others went via the Straits of Messina and east toward Greece before heading south. Once found (which needed regular air surveillance of all main enemy ports), the usual tactic was for daylight attacks by Blenheims and by Swordfish at night. The recon-

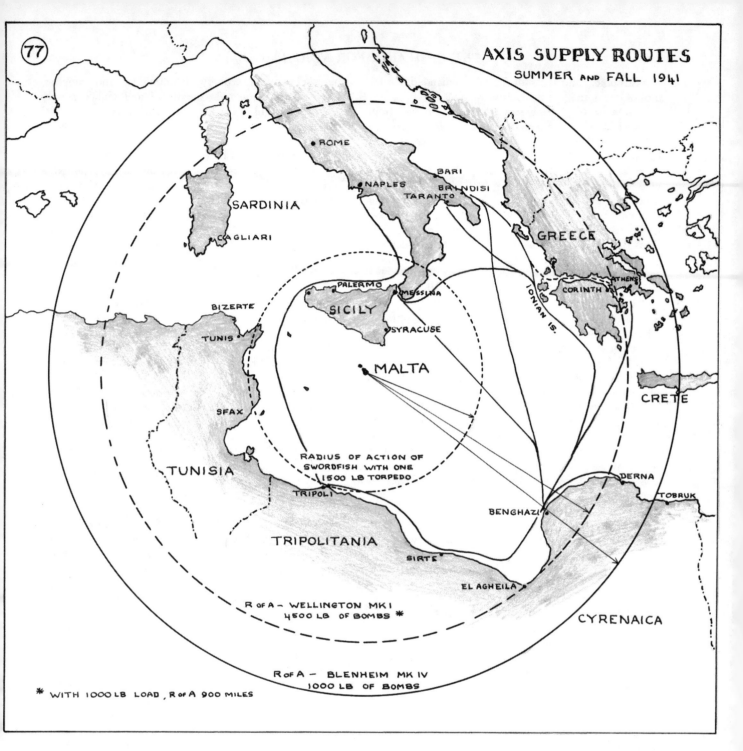

77

AXIS SUPPLY ROUTES
SUMMER AND FALL 1941

SARDINIA

CAGLIARI

ROME

NAPLES

BARI
BRINDISI
TARANTO

GREECE

BIZERTE

TUNIS

PALERMO
MESSINA
SICILY

SYRACUSE

IONIAN IS.

CORINTH

ATHENS

CRETE

MALTA

SFAX

RADIUS OF ACTION OF
SWORDFISH WITH ONE
1500 LB TORPEDO

TUNISIA

DERNA

TOBRUK

TRIPOLI

BENGHAZI

TRIPOLITANIA

SIRTE

EL AGHEILA

R of A — WELLINGTON MK I
4500 LB OF BOMBS ✳

CYRENAICA

R of A — BLENHEIM MK IV
1000 LB OF BOMBS

✳ WITH 1000 LB LOAD, R of A 900 MILES

naissance fell to the Marylands and Wellingtons, usually the former by day and the latter (by now equipped with radar) by night. The Blenheims, attacking as usual at low (sometimes 50 feet) level, suffered heavy losses, but the need to shut off the Axis supply routes, especially with the "Crusader" offensive scheduled for mid-November, was so urgent that the losses had to be accepted.

By the beginning of September, the Malta strike force could count some 7 Marylands, 32 Blenheims, 15 Wellingtons, and 12 Swordfish. During September these were augmented by 2 squadrons of Albacores—faster and with far greater range than the Swordfish. This air effort—along with the arrival in the Mediterranean of the new 630-ton U-class submarines—had considerable impact on the Axis supply forces. For the period January–May 1941, monthly averages of Axis merchant vessels sunk was 6,161 tons by air and 20,358 by submarine. For June–September the averages rose to 23,356 and 37,396, respectively. While these losses were not all due to Malta-based craft, the island must be credited with the lion's share of the score.

In September the Germans described the situation as

"catastrophic," and the staff in Italy demanded the return of strong units of the Luftwaffe to Sicily.

September 19: A single merchantman arrived from the west with a cargo mainly of fodder, after a passage along the African coast in which Spanish, French, and Italian flags were used.

September 24: Operation "Halberd." Admiral Somerville, with a powerful force of 3 battleships, *Ark Royal*, 5 cruisers, and 18 destroyers, left Gibraltar convoying 9 15-knot ships, totaling about 81,000 tons. Some 2,600 troops were embarked on the transports and the warships that would go through to Malta. Despite defending fighter craft from *Ark Royal* a torpedo-bomber scored a hit on the battleship *Nelson*, slowing her down. After the main fleet turned back at the entrance to the Narrows a night torpedo-bomber attack so damaged a merchantman that soldiers and crew were taken off and she was sunk.

September 28: The ships entered harbor, cheered by crowds of Maltese.

October 16: Ark Royal left Gibraltar to fly a squadron of torpedo-bombers to Malta.

October 21: Conditions on Malta had so improved that operation of a surface force from the island was once more possible. Force "K"—2 light cruisers (*Penelope* and *Aurora*) and 2 destroyers—arrived at Malta. This move soon paid off.

November 8: A heavily escorted convoy was reported by a Maryland some 40 miles east of Cape Spartivento. Force "K" sailed and just after midnight made contact with the enemy force (7 merchant ships, with 6 destroyers as close escort, and 2 heavy cruisers and 4 destroyers in support). In a surprise night attack all 7 merchant ships (about 40,000 tons) and a destroyer were sunk. Another destroyer, damaged, was sunk by a submarine later in the day. Force "K" suffered no losses and was back in Malta that afternoon.

November 10: Force "H" left Gibraltar. *Ark Royal* flew off 37 Hurricanes. Thirty-four of these, accompanied by 7 Blenheims, arrived at Malta, but on returning to Gibraltar *Ark Royal* was torpedoed and sank (November 14).

By mid-November there were some 10 U-class submarines at Malta, and these vessels had several successes. Among the more important were the sinking of 2 supply ships of about 13,000 tons (December 13) and the damaging of the battleship *Vittorio Veneto* (December 14). The last was hit in a magazine, with severe damage and heavy loss of life.

November 24: Force "K" sank 2 ships carrying fuel from Greece to Benghazi.

November 29: Force "B"—cruisers *Ajax* and *Neptune* and 2 destroyers—arrived at Malta to reinforce Force "K."

November 29–30: Malta-based Blenheims sank a merchant ship and damaged 2 others.

December 1: Force "K" sank an Italian auxiliary cruiser carrying artillery, ammunition, and supplies, then steamed 400 miles westward and sank a supply ship and a tanker carrying fuel and troops and its escorting destroyer. These sinkings so alarmed the High Command that on December 5 Hitler ordered the return of Fliegerkorps II from the Soviet Union.

December 13: A Wellington from Malta reported 2 cruisers heading for Africa. These vessels were intercepted off Cape Bon by 4 destroyers from Gibraltar, bound for Alexandria. The ships, light cruisers *Alberto di Guissano* and *Alberico da Barbiano* (5,069 tons), with deck cargoes of fuel, were set on fire and sunk.

The enemy losses for October–December 1941, while again not entirely Malta-inflicted, show averages for the three months as 16,680 tons by air attack (down due to unusually bad weather, the demands of the "Crusader" operation, and increasing air attacks on the Malta airfields) and 26,406 by submarine. Losses by surface action (mainly Force "K"), beginning in November, totaled 47,603 tons for November and December.

During the period July–December 1941 (the first major air and naval offensive against the Libyan supply routes), 16.4 per cent of the men and 26.8 per cent of the materiel embarked for North Africa failed to arrive (about 9,500 men and over 130,000 tons of materiel). For November the percentage of materiel lost in transit was 62 per cent!

But the pendulum was about to swing in the other direction. Fliegerkorps II was arriving in Sicily, and German U-boats had entered the Mediterranean in strength (10 ordered to the eastern zone and 15 to the east and west of Gibraltar). By mid-December there were 18 German U-boats in the Mediterranean, with 10 more under orders to proceed there. Their first major victim had been *Ark Royal*. This was followed on November 25 by the sinking of the battleship *Barham* with great loss of life.

December 18: Breconshire arrived with a cargo of fuel oil—under cover of maneuverings of both British and Italian fleets (the so-called First Battle of Sirte).

December 19: Shortly after midnight Force "K" (3 cruisers, 4 destroyers), searching for an enemy convoy near Tripoli, ran into an uncharted Italian mine field. All 3 cruisers were damaged and one later sank, as did one of the destroyers. As if the crippling of Force "K" were not enough, on the same morning underwater mines, placed by 2-man human torpedoes, heavily damaged battleships *Valiant* and *Queen Elizabeth* in Alexandria Harbor. Both were out of action for several months. There were no battleships or carriers to replace these losses. The "battle line" of the eastern Mediterranean Fleet consisted now of 3 light cruisers, while Force "H" was reduced to a battleship, a small carrier, a cruiser, and a few destroyers. Japan was on the rampage; *Repulse* and *Prince of Wales* were on the bottom, and the Navy was stretched almost to the breaking point.

1942

The year 1942 was to be a rough one for everyone, especially Malta! Yet the island had to be maintained as a fighting base at all costs. And, as the *British Official History* says, "All the major operations of the Royal Navy in the Mediterranean in 1942 prior to the Anglo-American landing in November were concerned with taking convoys into Malta."

Convoys were the Italian main concern too. Following up a heavily escorted convoy that left Taranto on December 16, the Italians ran more of these "fleet" convoys—a 6-ship group that arrived at Tripoli on January 5 was covered by 4 battleships, 6 cruisers, and 24 destroyers! At the same time the Malta airfields were subjected to severe bombings, which left many planes destroyed or damaged and the fields temporarily unusable. Even so, strike forces from the island attempted to find the enemy, but very bad weather prevented contact. The widespread submarine net had no success either, and the quantities of tanks, guns, and ammunition carried by this convoy was more than welcome to the once-more-advancing Rommel.

Almost three weeks later, another strongly escorted convoy arrived at Tripoli, minus a 13,000-ton liner torpedoed and disabled by a Beaufort from Malta and later sunk by Albacores from Berka.

Definite intelligence of an attempted sea and airborne assault to capture Malta prompted headquarters to reinforce the garrison still further. On January 8 the fast ship *Glengyle* had been convoyed in from Alexandria and *Breconshire* brought out, and on January 16 four ships left Alexandria carrying men, supplies, "I" tanks, and Bofors guns. One destroyer of the escort was torpedoed the next day. One ship had steering trouble, was sent back, and was sunk by air attack. The rest reached Malta and on January 19 disembarked two thirds of an infantry battalion, 8 tanks, and 20 Bofors guns and their crews as well as 21,000 tons of supplies, despite very heavy German air attacks.

This east-to-west passage was indicative of the reliance placed on air support. The recent advance into Cyrenaica had once more brought the airfields there under British control, and it was from these fields that air support for Malta convoys was flown. For the operation noted above, squadrons of Beaufighters moved from base to base along the coast until the ships were under cover of long-range fighters from Malta. So the seesaw desert battle meant protection or deadly danger for the ships of the Alexandria-to-Malta convoys. Even now the most westerly of the fields were again in German hands, and when on January 26 *Breconshire* again ran into Malta (*Glengyle* and another coming out empty), little air cover could be given.

Despite the fact that by the end of January Rommel had retaken western Cyrenaica, a 3-ship convoy left Alexandria on February 12. The next day one was hit by a bomb and sent into Tobruk. The following day another was bombed and left burning. Force "K" (now reduced to the light cruiser *Penelope* and a few destroyers) met the remaining ship, which was soon disabled by a near miss and had to be sunk. Force "K" returned to Malta empty-handed—although *Breconshire* had slipped out again undamaged. Air attacks were mounting—some 670 tons of bombs in January and over 1,000 tons in February. Soldiers worked alongside Maltese and airmen in filling bomb craters on the runways and building and repairing dispersal pens.

Kerosene for cooking was very scarce. Community feeding was introduced, and soon "victory kitchens" were supplying nearly 200,000 people with hot meals. Many buildings had been destroyed or damaged. Fighter cover was a problem. The available Hurricanes were both outnumbered and outclassed by the Me 109s. This was partially remedied when on March 7 *Eagle*, escorted by Force "H," flew off 15 Spitfires, all of which arrived safely at Malta. Sixteen more were flown in on March 21.

Preparations, including the bombing of enemy airfields in Crete and Cyrenaica, were under way for a convoy, and on March 20 *Breconshire* and 3 other ships left Alexandria with an escort of cruisers and destroyers. On March 22 the escort, under Admiral Vian, had been joined by Force "K" (*Penelope* and a destroyer). An Italian force had been reported leaving Taranto, and Vian made dispositions for action. This, in effect, was designed to interpose divisions of destroyers and cruisers between the convoy (which was soon under air attacks that lasted until dark) and the enemy (battleship *Littorio*, two heavy cruisers, a light cruiser, and 7 destroyers). The British made much use of smoke, which the Italians were understandably reluctant to penetrate. A 25-knot southeast wind aided the British, who were to windward. The Italian attempts to work around to leeward (westward) were foiled by gun and torpedo attacks. Smoke, spray, and rising seas made gunnery very difficult, and few hits were obtained. At sundown the Italians retired. This action, the Second Battle of Sirte, is the model for C. S. Forester's fine book *The Ship*.

So fierce did the gale become that all ships received damage before reaching port. Even the huge *Littorio* had trouble making headway, and 2 Italian destroyers foundered with the loss of all but 7 hands.

Admiral Vian led his ships back to Alexandria, while Force "K" and the convoy headed on for Malta. Despite the bad weather, heavy air attacks on the ships were begun at daylight. Concentrated raids had so damaged the Malta fields that only 42 fighter sorties could be made. Two ships docked, another was sunk 20 miles out, and *Breconshire* was disabled—she was towed into Marsa Scirocco but sank after further damage on March 27. She had made 7 trips to the island.

March 26: Both berthed merchantmen were hit. One, loaded with ammunition, had to be scuttled. The other had all but two holds flooded. Destroyer *Legion*—damaged on March 23—was sunk. Very few of the

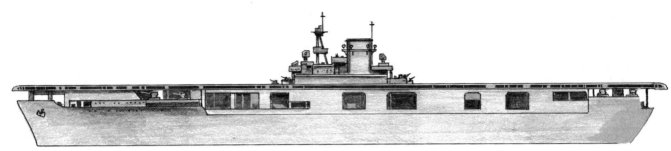

Wasp (U.S.) Aircraft Carrier

Launched April 1939.
Displacement: 14,700 tons. LOA: 739'. Beam: 80¾'. Draft: 20'.
Two screws. 75,000 hp=30 knots.
Armament: eight 5″ anti-aircraft, automatics (40 mm, 20 mm, etc.).
Aircraft: 84.
Complement: 1,800.

many tons of supplies loaded in Egypt were salvaged. Part of the trouble was that the stevedores refused to work during close alerts; troops finished the job, working around the clock. In the future it was decided ships should be berthed in shallow water or beached.

The air assault was now so severe that all surface ships except small ones used for local defense had to leave. *Penelope*, damaged by bombs on March 26, and 3 destroyers undergoing repair remained. The submarines stayed on, widely dispersed, and submerged during the day. One had been damaged past saving and others hit. During the month 4 submarines arrived with gasoline and kerosene.

Malta-based strike forces still managed to operate, although hampered by increasing enemy air attacks. Over 1,000 anti-shipping strikes were flown during the period January–March. They sank or helped sink 8 ships totaling 44,000 tons and damaged others. During the same 3 months the Malta submarines sank 16 merchant ships (75,000 tons), the cruiser *Bande Nere,* and 5 Italian submarines. British losses were 2 submarines by mine, 1 by surface craft, and 1 by bombing in Malta Harbor. Finally the 10th Flotilla was temporarily withdrawn. The Cabinet decision of July 1937 had proved an expensive folly!

Axis policy as to Malta was undecided. Plans had again been formulated for its capture, and Italian troops had begun to train for a sea and airborne attack. On the other hand, if Rommel was successful in the desert there would be no need for what was recognized to be a very costly operation. Certainly, British naval forces were at a dangerously low level. The Mediterranean Fleet had 4 cruisers and 15 destroyers; Force "H" was down to the small carrier *Argus* and a few destroyers, and the submarines (including those at Malta) numbered 25. Opposed to this the Italians could muster 4 battleships, 9 cruisers, 55 destroyers, and 50 submarines, plus 20 German U-boats in the Mediterranean.

Meanwhile, the battering of Malta went on. Between March 24 and April 12 over 2,000 sorties were made against Grand Harbor. An estimated 1,870 tons of

bombs fell, mostly on the dockyards, whose work could only be carried on in the underground shops. Such was the damage that it was difficult to keep open routes for even light vehicles through the piles of rubble.

Civilians and servicemen continued to keep the airfields operational though the damage was severe. By mid-April most of the 31 Spitfires were destroyed and the number of serviceable Hurricanes dropped to as low as 6.

There were 294 alerts in April—some lasting for hours. The anti-aircraft positions were prime targets; the heavy guns fired over 72,000 rounds, and the light over 88,000. Five German and 2 Italian planes were destroyed over the island in April.

Target for many attacks was the damaged cruiser *Penelope*. Working under a rain of bombs, workmen got her patched up enough to sail on April 8. The hundreds of holes in her hull plugged with wood, "H.M.S. Pepperpot," as she was nicknamed, limped into Gibraltar safely, looking, it was said, like a porcupine. In two weeks her anti-aircraft guns had fired 6,500 rounds of 4-inch ammunition.

No attempt could be made to run another convoy into Malta until the fighter defenses had been built up. Of the available British carriers, *Eagle* was in dock, *Argus* too slow and small, and *Victorious* could not accommodate Spitfires in her elevators. So use of a U.S. carrier was requested, and the U.S.S. *Wasp* entered the Mediterranean on the night of April 18–19 with 47 Spitfires aboard. Of these 46 landed safely at Malta. On April 20 German radar in Sicily picked up the flight, and 90 minutes after the first plane landed, heavy air attacks began. During the following three days some 500 tons of bombs were dropped on Luqa and Takali airfields, destroying 17 fighters and damaging 29 others. More had been lost in combat. Left serviceable: 6!

It was partly the seemingly insuperable difficulty of maintaining an adequate fighter force at Malta that decided the Chiefs of Staff not to run a convoy in May. This news was greeted with dismay on the island, but the war was going badly for the Allies. Japan's sun was still rising in the Far East. Vast areas of the Soviet Union were in Nazi hands, and losses in men and materiel had been staggering. The German surface fleet was still powerful enough to threaten the Soviet-bound convoys, while losses from U-boats were rising dramatically—327,357 tons in January, 476,451 in February, and 537,980 in March. Closer to home, the desert war had bogged down again, with Rommel poised on the Gazala–Bir Hacheim line.

It was against this background that Malta's defenders fought their most desperate battle. Over 9,500 sorties were flown against the island during April, and more than 6,700 tons of bombs were dropped. Over 11,000 buildings were destroyed or damaged. Adequate shelters saved a larger death toll; even so, 300 civilians were killed and 330 seriously injured. Three destroyers were sunk in the harbor, as well as 3 submarines, 3 minesweepers, 5 tugs, and the floating crane. Other vessels had been damaged. Loss of so many minesweepers was the deciding factor in the decision to withdraw the 10th Flotilla. Mines were laid in the harbor approaches by fast surface craft, the noise of their engines covered by the incessant racket of the air raids. The few remaining minesweepers, bombed by night and strafed by day, could not cope with the task of keeping the channels swept.

April: The R.A.F. bombers made only 22 sorties and the Fleet Air Arm 11. Reconnaissance planes were down to 3, and by the month's end there were only 2 Albacores and 2 Swordfish operational. Malta had been all but neutralized, and the boost to morale given by the award to the island of the George Cross by the British Sovereign was soon followed by a further reduction in rations, bread being cut to 10½ ounces a day.

At this time too the island lost its popular governor. General Sir William Dobbie, worn out, was replaced by General the Viscount Gort, V.C., on May 7.

May 9: This saw the arrival of another big swarm of Spitfires. Once more President Roosevelt agreed to the use of the U.S.S. *Wasp,* and together with *Eagle* the two ships flew off 64 planes (60 of which reached Malta safely) some 60 miles north of Algiers. This time special landing and handling arrangements were made so that the disaster of April 20 would not be repeated. Each plane as it landed was rushed to a dispersal bay, where it was refueled, serviced, and its long-range tank removed. An account in *The War in the Air* of the arrival of "Screwball" Buerling, soon to become Malta's top fighter ace, describes the frenzied rush of one such landing—his plane hustled up a bumpy track, manhandled into position in a "kind of rabbit burrow formed by heaps of petrol tins filled with sand" and swarmed over by a "crowd of extraordinary-looking individuals, unshaven and dressed in the relics of the uniforms of all three Services." The bewildered Buerling was yanked out of his seat by a waiting pilot. The Bofors were already banging away as the Spitfire taxied out of

the bay, an armorer flat on one wing, frantically screwing down the last machine-gun panel, only rolling off as the plane opened up. Buerling had barely emerged from the bay—"the crowd of madmen had vanished into thin air"—when half a dozen Messerschmitt 109s streaked across the field, guns blazing. As they roared away the first of a swarm of Junker 88s began their dive on the field. For the next few minutes the area was a nightmare of bursting bombs, burning and exploding planes, screaming splinters, and hurtling rock and dust, while a rain of shell fragments and empty cases pattered down from the swirling dogfights taking place in the sky dotted with the black bursts of antiaircraft fire. In ten minutes everything was over, and the surviving planes, many damaged, were coming in, covered by a flight of Hurricanes from the neighboring field.

This incident was typical. In the May 9 flight the landing and dispersal arrangements worked very well; some of the Spitfires were ready for takeoff within 6 minutes of landing, and the new arrivals flew 74 sorties that day.

May 10: The fast minelayer *Welshman* arrived in harbor from Gibraltar with 340 tons of supplies—mostly ammunition. It was to protect her while unloading that the Spitfire delivery had been timed for the previous day. She had masqueraded as a French destroyer and had passed examination by two Ju 88s and a French float plane. Unloading was completed in less than 7 hours, and she sailed again that evening. She had been slightly damaged by 6 near misses, but the Spitfire umbrella broke up the enemy formations and downed several planes.

These reinforcements (17 more Spitfires were flown in from *Eagle* on May 18), coupled with the weakening of Fliegerkorps II by attrition and withdrawals (a bomber and a fighter group to the Soviet Union; 40 dive bombers and 45 fighters to Africa), meant a lessening of the bombing threat (520 tons dropped in May vs. 6,700 tons in April). But Spitfires could not stop convoys, and the lack of strike and reconnaissance planes made the island almost powerless to halt the flow of Axis supplies to North Africa. In April less than 1 per cent of the tonnage of fuel and supplies failed to arrive; in May, less than 7 per cent. Only 13 Axis merchantmen were sunk during April and May—all but 1 by submarines.

Reconnaissance planes were too few, and a request by Admiral Harwood—who had succeeded Admiral Cunningham—for 12 Liberators was turned down by the Admiralty. In consequence, the submarines could seldom be guided onto the enemy convoys. The difficulty of attempting surface-ship operations at the limits of the scant available air cover was pointed out on May 11 when 4 destroyers from Alexandria, attempting to intercept a convoy from Taranto, were repeatedly attacked by bombers and 3 were sunk. Another factor was the imperfect communications between the surface vessels and the small relays of long-range fighter planes.

Three British submarines were lost during April and May. One of these was the famous *Upholder* which, under Lieutenant Commander M. D. Wanklyn, V.C., D.S.O., had sunk 2 destroyers, 2 submarines, and nearly 94,000 tons of merchant shipping. Three German U-boats were also sunk during this period.

Operation "Herkules" (the capture of Malta) was again postponed until the middle of July—by which time Rommel hoped to have taken Tobruk. The assault forces, as planned, included an airborne corps of one German and an Italian parachute division and one Italian airborne division. There were also to be nearly 6 Italian divisions, 2 tank battalions, artillery, etc. The Italian Navy, with the aid of 725 launches and assault boats, 80 landing craft, and other small craft, was to lift the first wave of 8,300 men, tanks, and artillery. Most of Fliegerkorps X would aid Fliegerkorps II, as well as planes from Africa (FliegerFührer Afrika). The main point of attack was to be Marsa Scirocco. The parachute attacks to secure the beachheads were to be in the afternoon, the landings after dark. General Kurt Student's XI Air Corps was to provide 10 Gruppen of Ju 52s and an equal number of 10- and 25-man gliders, plus some 155 Italian transports. As Student said, "It was an impressive force, 5 times as strong as we had against Crete."

The fate of "Herkules" is typical of Hitler's consistent misjudgment of things naval. He was, as he said, "a hero on land but a coward on the sea." At the beginning of June, Student was summoned to Hitler's headquarters and found that the Führer was lukewarm to the plan, to say the least. When Tobruk fell (June 22, 1942) Rommel, flushed with success, demanded and got permission to postpone the Malta operation and drive ahead toward Cairo and Suez. Even Mussolini, who had at first insisted that Malta take precedence over Cairo, agreed to the further postponement of the invasion date. It was put off until September, and by that time it was too late.

By mid-June it became vital to reinforce Malta, although the risks were recognized to be great. Instead of the hoped-for recapture of the Cyrenaican airfields, the battle in the desert had gone against the British forces, and now, as the official history puts it, "Instead of a starving Malta being saved by a victory in the Desert, it required all that the island base could do to help save Egypt."

Two convoys, from east and west, were planned. Strength of the air striking force and reconnaissance units was built up as much as possible. At Malta for reconnaissance work were 6 Baltimores, 4 Wellingtons with ASV (Air-to-Surface-Vessel Radar), and three PRU (Photo Reconnaissance Unit) Spitfires. The strike force was 6 torpedo-carrying Wellingtons and a squadron of Beauforts, with a squadron of Albacores for anti-submarine patrols. Another squadron of Beauforts was available in Egypt as a striking force along with Marylands, ASV Wellingtons, Hudsons, Swordfish, Blenheims, Wellesleys, and Sunderlands for reconnaissance and anti-submarine duty.

To maintain air superiority over Malta, the Spitfire squadrons were reinforced. On June 3 and again on June 9 more Spitfires, 59 in all, were flown off *Eagle*. This brought the total available on the island to 95. A squadron of coastal-type Beaufighters and a flight of night-flying Beaufighters were also flown in. There was enough gasoline (the last brought in by submarine H.M.S. *Olympus* in early May), and *Welshman* was to leave the eastbound convoy at the Narrows and proceed to Malta with more anti-aircraft ammunition, of which the island gunners consumed large amounts.

The eastbound convoy ("Harpoon") was of 6 ships covered as far as the Skerki Channel by battleship *Malaya*, *Eagle* and *Argus* (both old carriers and unable to accommodate as many planes as the modern ones), cruisers *Liverpool*, *Kenya*, and *Charybdis*, and 8 destroyers. Anti-aircraft cruiser *Cairo*, with 5 fleet and 4 Hunt Class destroyers (Force "X"), were to accompany the convoy all the way to Malta, along with 4 fleet minesweepers and 6 minesweeping M.L.s. These last were to reinforce the island's minesweeping flotilla. A tanker, *Brown Ranger*, sailed independently with her own escort; her mission was to refuel the vessels of Force "X" for the return trip.

By June 12 the convoy was inside the Mediterranean, and on the morning of June 14 the expected air attacks began. Italian fighter bombers attacked unsuccessfully, but half an hour later a simultaneous attack by 38 torpedo-bombers and high-level bombers, with 20 fighters, damaged *Liverpool* and sank one of the merchantmen. *Liverpool* was towed back to Gibraltar by a destroyer and screened by another.

The next attack was at 1820. Ten Ju 88s were beaten off by the carrier fighters, as was a heavy attack at 2000 hours by Italian torpedo-bombers and Ju 88s and 87s. Seven FAA fighters were lost as against 17 enemy planes.

At 2100 hours 4 Beaufighters arrived from Malta and, the Skerki Channel reached, the covering force turned west. An Italian surface squadron (2 light cruisers and 5 destroyers) had been sighted leaving Palermo. This squadron engaged Force "X" at 0640 on June 15. For 3 hours Force "X" held the Italians off. Three destroyers, two British and one Italian, were hit and stopped and all the cruisers had been slightly damaged. The Italians were driven off, but in the absence of fighter cover (the first flight of Beaufighters had returned to Malta to refuel), the convoy was dive-bombed, another merchantman was sunk, and the tanker *Kentucky* disabled. A minesweeper took *Kentucky* in tow, and the diminished convoy steamed for Malta at 6 knots.

Long-range Spitfires drove off the next attack, but they too had to leave the convoy, and before the relieving air cover took over, another raid disabled another merchantman. The convoy commander, Captain C. G. Hardy, made the difficult decision to leave the tanker and merchantman and make for Malta with the two remaining ships. Approaching harbor the ships entered an incompletely swept channel and a destroyer was sunk and 2 other destroyers, a minesweeper, and 1 of the 2 remaining merchantmen were damaged. The disabled merchantman and *Kentucky*, which had been left behind, were finished off by Italian surface forces, as was the destroyer *Bedouin*, disabled in the surface action. The other damaged destroyer finally made Gibraltar. "Harpoon" had been costly: 15,000 tons of supplies delivered, against 4 merchantmen and 2 destroyers sunk and a cruiser, 3 destroyers, and a minesweeper damaged. The R.A.F. lost 5 aircraft and the Fleet Air Arm 7. On the credit side, *Welshman* unloaded its cargo of ammunition and departed safely.

Operation "Vigorous" fared even worse. Eleven merchant vessels were in the convoy, escorted by 7 cruisers, an anti-aircraft cruiser, and 26 destroyers. Also present was the old target battleship *Centurion*, disguised as a modern battleship but armed only with a few anti-aircraft guns. There were also 4 corvettes, 4 MTBs, 2 minesweepers, and 2 rescue ships. The convoy sailed from Egypt on June 11. On June 12 a merchantman was damaged by Ju 88s and was sent into Tobruk, and another was unable to keep up and was sent back. By June 14 the MTBs had been sent back because of bad weather and another merchantman proved too slow, was detached, and later sunk by German dive bombers. Two corvettes had engine trouble and were also detached. Up to now (1630 on June 14), most enemy aircraft had been kept away by land-based fighters, but as the convoy passed out of range of British fighters more attacks developed and a merchantman was sunk and another one damaged. The two rescue vessels proceeded to Tobruk with the survivors. At sunset submarine attacks began, as well as attacks by Italian MTBs. A little later, word came that the Italian Fleet (2 Littorio Class battleships, 2 heavy cruisers, 2 light cruisers, and 12 destroyers) was at sea and could be expected to make contact early next morning. This force would be too strong for the convoy escort, and at 0200 the British force turned eastward. At this time a cruiser was torpedoed and damaged by a German MTB, and a destroyer sunk by another. There followed several marches and countermarches by the British as reports of damages by air and submarine to the Italian fleet came in. Actually only the heavy cruiser *Trento* was disabled and later sunk. When Admiral Vian, commanding the operation, realized the Italian force was almost intact, he finally ordered a return to Alexandria. This was accomplished under heavy air and submarine attacks, which sank a cruiser and two destroyers. A Malta-based Wellington had meanwhile torpedoed and damaged *Littorio*, and the Italian Fleet returned to Taranto. So ended the first major attempt to put Malta

back into the war. Of 17 merchantmen in the 2 convoys, 6 had been sunk, 9 turned back, and only 2 arrived. "Vigorous" was the last convoy to attempt the east-to-west route until after the Axis had been driven from Cyrenaica.

During July 2 submarines arrived with gasoline and special stores, and *Welshman* made her third trip on July 16. Also, *Eagle* flew off more Spitfires on July 15 and 21—59 in all.

The first half of July saw increased air activity over the island. Attacks were concentrated on the airfields, and several planes were destroyed and more damaged. But the increased strength of the defense was evident in the returns for the 2 weeks—nearly 1,000 sorties flown, 36 Spitfires lost in combat, but enemy losses amounted to 65 aircraft. The enemy first increased the ratio of fighters to bombers and finally resorted to hit-and-run raids by fighter-bombers. The improved air defense allowed the return of the 10th Submarine Flotilla, ordered back toward the end of the month.

The supply problem in Malta was now acute. The 15,000 tons landed from the "Harpoon" convoy had helped, but it was estimated that to exist, the island needed some 26,000 tons of supplies a month. Rationing was now severe. Bread and flour (the Maltese are a pasta-loving people) made up a great part of their normal diet. Now flour and rice were unobtainable—and the bread ration was 10½ ounces. There was no olive oil—also a staple—and the fat ration was 3½ ounces a week (this was about a third of the British fat ration—and bread and flour were never rationed there). The sugar ration was 7 ounces; as was canned corned beef. There was a great shortage of tobacco, a tiny coffee ration, while meat and fish were seldom obtainable. There was little kerosene—but then there was not much to cook.

Fuel supplies were running low, and it would be impossible to mount a sizable air offensive with the amount of aviation fuel that could be brought in by submarine. There was already a target date—the existence of which (but not, naturally, the date itself) was made known to the Maltese people—when the bread would run out; after that there would be no alternative to surrender.

So the running of another convoy became imperative. The fate not only of Malta, but also very likely Egypt as well, depended on it; for in the Western Desert Rommel and the battered Eighth Army were facing each other, exhausted, at El Alamein. Whoever could build up their forces first would probably win the coming battle. To attempt to cut the Axis supply routes by surface action was out of the question. Ships were too few, and the eastern Mediterranean was ringed by Axis airfields—in Sardinia, Sicily, Greece, Crete, Libya, and part of Egypt. The only hope was Malta—and on August 10 14 large, fast ships, including the 15-knot American-loaned tanker *Ohio*, with 12,000 tons of fuel oil aboard, passed into the Mediterranean.

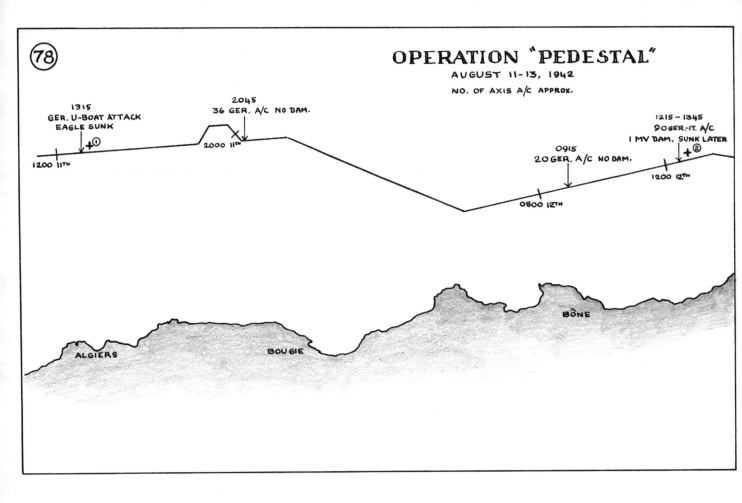

OPERATION "PEDESTAL"

Ships Sunk

1.	H.M.S. *Eagle* (carrier)	Torpedoed
2.	*Devcalion* (MV)	Torpedoed and sunk later
3.	H.M.S. *Foresight* (DD)	Torpedoed and sunk later
4.	H.M.S. *Cairo* (cruiser)	Torpedoed
5.	*Empire Hope* (MV)	Bombed
6.	*Clan Ferguson* (MV)	Bombed
7.	H.M.S. *Manchester* (cruiser)	Torpedoed and sunk later
8.	*Santa Elisa* (MV)	Torpedoed
9.	*Almeria Lykes* (MV)	Torpedoed
10.	*Glenorchy* (MV)	Torpedoed
11.	*Wairangi* (MV)	Torpedoed
12.	*Waimarama* (MV)	Bombed
13.	*Dorset* (MV)	Bombed and sunk later

The escort was formidable—the most powerful ever to accompany a Malta convoy. There were no less than 4 carriers—the modern fleet carriers *Victorious* and *Indomitable* and the veterans *Eagle* and *Furious*—the 2 16-inch-gun battleships *Nelson* and *Rodney*, 6 cruisers, an anti-aircraft cruiser, and 32 destroyers. Two fleet oilers and a tug escorted by 4 corvettes accompanied the fleet, and another tug sailed with the close support group, Force "X." Eight submarines were at sea to watch Italian ports and form an outer screen to the south of Pantelleria. There were some 80 serviceable fighters at Malta at the end of July, but wastage averaged 17 per week, so a reinforcement was to be flown in from *Furious* (Operation "Bellows"), which accomplished, the carrier was to return to Gibraltar.

Strike and reconnaissance units were reinforced on the island, and spoiling raids on Axis airfields were laid on by aircraft from Malta and Liberators from the Middle East.

On Malta arrangements to speed unloading of the awaited ships were perfected. Docking parties were reinforced by men of the armed forces. All available transport was commandeered, and one-way traffic routes were marked—color-cued to the trucks, which were allocated colors according to the stores they carried. Unloading was to be carried on without halt

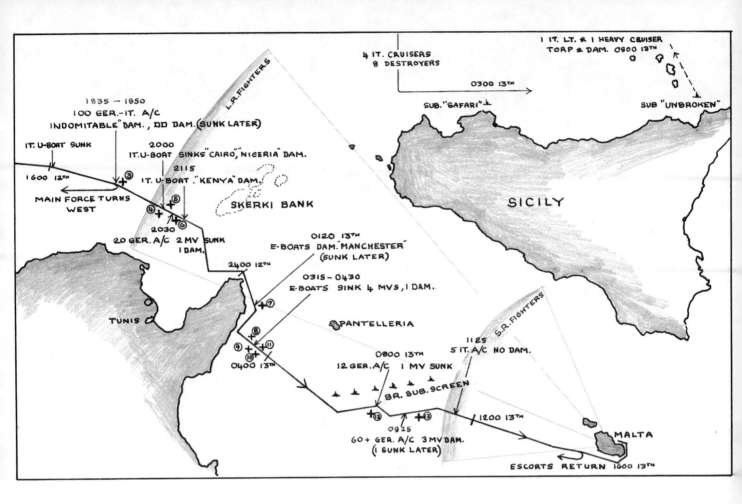

until all cargo was unloaded and rushed to its proper destination.

It was a great effort, this Operation "Pedestal," planned with loving care and calling for close co-operation among units of all 3 Services spread over many thousands of square miles. And as might be expected, the enemy made great efforts to frustrate it. Air and surface squadrons were alerted; the Sicilian and Sardinian fields were crowded with aircraft, and 18 Italian and 3 German U-boats were at sea to intercept (in all, the enemy were to deploy 90 torpedo-bombers, 447 bombers, and 247 fighters).

Soon after daylight on August 11, enemy aircraft began shadowing the convoy, keeping it under almost continuous observation in spite of the carriers' fighters. *Furious* began flying off her 38 planes at noon. At 1315 4 towering plumes of water rose in rapid succession along *Eagle*'s port side as torpedoes from *U-73* struck home. In 3 minutes she had listed 45 degrees, planes and men sliding into the sea. Five minutes later she had gone, taking a quarter of the fleet's air cover with her. *Furious* resumed flying off her Spitfire—36 of which landed at Malta—and turned for Gibraltar. En route one of her escorting destroyers rammed and sank the Italian submarine *Dagabur*.

At dusk the first of the expected air attacks came—a torpedo and bombing attack by 36 Ju 88s and Heinkel 111s. Sirens screamed as the ships heeled to emergency turns, and every gun that would bear spat fire. Great columns of smoke and spray sprang up around the ships, and white torpedo tracks streaked the water. Tracer rose lazily like clouds of sparks, and a furious barrage from the large anti-aircraft guns flashed and smoked overhead. It was over as suddenly as it began. No ships had been hit, and at least three attacking aircraft had been shot down.

Dawn brought radar reports of snooping aircraft, and just after 0900 the fighter cover broke up a formation of Ju 88s, claiming 8 certain victories and 3 probables. The morning passed with several submarine contacts, and the vessels reverberated to the boom of depth charges.

At noon came a major raid from the Sardinian fields. Some 72 Italian torpedo-bombers attacked, aided by fighter bombers. Clawed at by the FAA fighters and unnerved by the dense barrage put up by the escort, the bombers dropped their torpedoes far short of the convoy. But an almost simultaneous attack by 20 Ju 87s badly damaged a merchantman, which was later attacked again and sunk. Fighters had downed 9 of the attackers and ships' anti-aircraft 2 more. Later in the afternoon, after many asdic contacts, destroyers forced

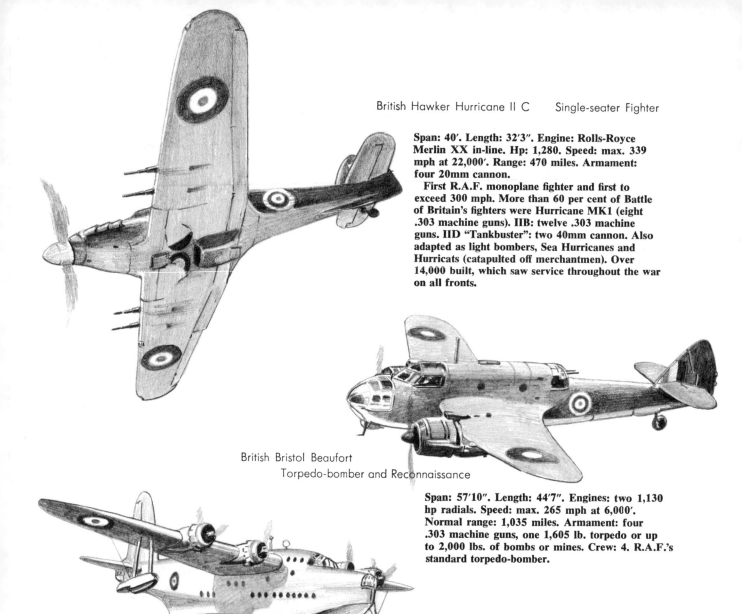

British Hawker Hurricane II C   Single-seater Fighter

Span: 40′. Length: 32′3″. Engine: Rolls-Royce Merlin XX in-line. Hp: 1,280. Speed: max. 339 mph at 22,000′. Range: 470 miles. Armament: four 20mm cannon.

 First R.A.F. monoplane fighter and first to exceed 300 mph. More than 60 per cent of Battle of Britain's fighters were Hurricane MK1 (eight .303 machine guns). IIB: twelve .303 machine guns. IID "Tankbuster": two 40mm cannon. Also adapted as light bombers, Sea Hurricanes and Hurricats (catapulted off merchantmen). Over 14,000 built, which saw service throughout the war on all fronts.

British Bristol Beaufort
Torpedo-bomber and Reconnaissance

Span: 57′10″. Length: 44′7″. Engines: two 1,130 hp radials. Speed: max. 265 mph at 6,000′. Normal range: 1,035 miles. Armament: four .303 machine guns, one 1,605 lb. torpedo or up to 2,000 lbs. of bombs or mines. Crew: 4. R.A.F.'s standard torpedo-bomber.

British Sunderland Flying Boat MKI—Short Brothers, Ltd.

Long-range Reconnaissance and Anti-submarine Patrol
Span: 112′9½″. Length: 85′3½″. Engines: four 1,010 hp radials. Speed: max. 210 mph at 6,500′. Normal range: c. 2,000 miles. Armament: eight .303 machine guns—two in power turret in bow, two port and starboard, and four in tail turret. Also carried over two tons of bombs or depth charges. Crew: 10.

the Italian submarine *Cobalto* to the surface, and *Ithuriel* rammed and sank her. The destroyer's damaged bow forced her to return to Gibraltar.

At 1835, as the fleet neared the Skerki Channel, the next big attack began, from the nearby Sicilian fields. A combined torpedo and bomb attack fatally damaged the destroyer *Foresight* and set huge fires fore and aft on *Indomitable*. Surrounded by bomb splashes and wreathed in smoke and flame the carrier, her speed reduced to 13 knots, fell astern, her guns and those of several supporting vessels desperately fighting off her attackers. Admiral Syfret, commanding the main Force "Z," now turned back. The "Narrows," where capital ships could not be risked, was only an hour's steaming away. With only 25 per cent of his fighter force still remaining and a crippled carrier to escort, he decided

that further cover was not practicable. At 1900 Force "Z" turned back toward Gibraltar—leaving Admiral Burrough's Force "X," cruisers *Kenya, Nigeria,* and *Manchester,* and anti-aircraft cruiser *Cairo* with destroyers to escort the 13 merchantmen.

At 2000, as the convoy was changing from 4 columns to 2 preparatory to entering the Narrows, Italian submarines *Axum* and *Dessie* attacked almost simultaneously. *Nigeria* (flagship), *Cairo,* and tanker *Ohio* were all hit within a few minutes of one another. *Nigeria* turned back to Gibraltar with an escort (Admiral Burrough transferring his flag to destroyer *Ashanti*). *Cairo* had to be sunk, and *Ohio* was finally able to proceed. While the harassed destroyers were trying to restore some order to the convoy it was attacked by a formation of German bombers and torpedo-

British Vickers Wellington II   Medium Bomber and Reconnaissance

Span: 86′2″. Length: 61′. Engines: two 1,145 hp in-line Rolls-Royce Merlins (other marks with various radial engines). Range: 2,200 miles. Armament: six .303 machine guns—two in bow turret, two in tail turret, and one port and starboard amidships. Bomb load: 4,500 lbs. Crew: 6. The Wellington frame was built on the crisscross lattice (geodetic) principle, fabric-covered, and proved capable not only of carrying great loads but also of absorbing much punishment.

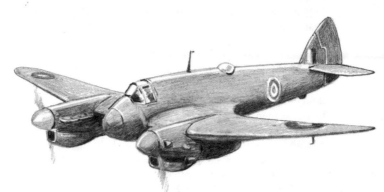

British Bristol Beaufighter MKII   Night Fighter and Anti-shipping Strike

Span: 57′10″. Length: 41′4″. Engines: two 1,280 hp in-line Merlin XX. Rolls-Royce. Speed: max. 323 mph at 15,000′. Max. range: 1,470 miles. Armament: four 20mm cannon in nose, six .303 machine guns in wings. Crew: 2.
Other marks used radial engines of various horsepowers. Experiments using torpedoes resulted in the Torbeau, a fast and deadly torpedo-bomber.

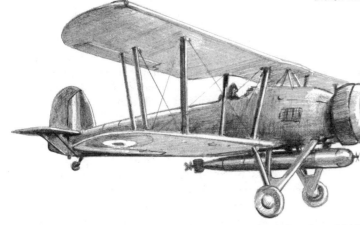

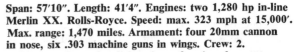

British Fairey Swordfish
Torpedo-bomber and Reconnaissance

Span: 45′6″. Length: 35′8″. Hp: 690. Speed: max. 138 mph at 5,000′. Normal range: 546 miles. Armament: two .303 machine guns, one 18″ (1,610 lb.) torpedo. Crew: 2 or 3.

bombers. Long-range fighter planes from Malta were on hand, but the carefully planned fighter-direction controls were installed in only two ships—*Nigeria* and *Cairo!* In the gathering dusk, ships fired on British fighters and there was general confusion. *Empire Hope* had been hit by a bomb and sunk; *Clan Ferguson* was torpedoed and blew apart with a blast that could be heard on the Tunisian coast, and a torpedo also struck and stopped *Brisbane Star*.

A little later, lookouts on *Kenya* spotted a surfaced submarine. As the cruiser swung toward the sub (Italian *Alagi*), one of a spread of 4 torpedoes tore off part of the cruiser's bow. Still able to steam at fair speed, she continued with the convoy, which was by now considerably strung out. Cape Bon was passed by midnight, and some 40 minutes later the first of many

MTB attacks began. *Manchester* was hit and so much damaged that she was scuttled. Four merchantmen were sunk. Still the battered remnants of the convoy steamed on, 4 ships now, with *Ohio* and *Brisbane Star* limping along behind.

During the night cruiser *Charybdis* and 2 destroyers, sent back from Force "Z," joined Force "X."

With first light the danger of more MTB attacks was ended, but at 0800 the inevitable air attacks commenced. Despite long-range air cover from Malta, *Waimarama* was hit and exploded; an enemy bomber crashed on board *Ohio*, and near misses damaged her engines; *Dorset* was hit and stopped; and *Rochester Castle* was set on fire.

The last attack, at about 1130, was beaten off. Malta was now some 80 miles away, and the main body of the convoy—*Port Chalmers, Melbourne Star,* and damaged *Rochester Castle*—were now under short-range Spitfire cover. They entered port at 0600 on August 13. *Brisbane Star,* after hugging the Tunisian coast, made port on August 14. Despite repeated air attacks, attempts were made to tow the helpless *Ohio* and *Dorset.* At 1900 both were hit again and *Dorset* sunk. After a great struggle *Ohio* (twice she was temporarily abandoned) was brought into port the next day, partly burned, her hull holed by bombs and a torpedo, her upperwork covered with debris. Almost awash, her back nearly broken, with a destroyer lashed on either side of her, she was eased into shallow water; and as her precious cargo was pumped out and the seawater came in, she settled gently on the bottom.

So ended Operation "Pedestal." Forty-seven thousand tons of supplies had been brought in. Nine merchantmen out of 14 had gone down, along with a carrier, 2 cruisers, and a destroyer, while another carrier and 2 more cruisers were damaged. Eighteen aircraft had been lost—as well as those that went down with *Eagle.* It was a high price.

An Italian squadron had been at sea, but in view of reports of strong forces on Malta's airfields they did not attack. Before they returned to base 2 cruisers were torpedoed by British submarine *P-42.* Both reached port but never came back into service.

The wastage of fighter planes called for a further reinforcement, and on August 17 *Furious* flew off 29 more Spitfires.

The slackening of the German air offensive (due in part to the reinforcements of fighters) in turn allowed an increase in the effectiveness of the island's air-reconnaissance and strike forces. Coupled with the return of the 10th Submarine Flotilla, this meant more pressure on the Axis supply routes. In July over 90,000 tons of military cargo and fuel had been landed in Africa, and only 6 per cent lost en route. In August this dropped to some 51,000 tons with a 33 per cent loss.

Submarines had a good month, accounting for 7 out of the 12 ships (of over 500 tons) sunk. Besides routine patrols and occasional supply runs, submarines laid mine fields, landed Commando raiding parties and undercover agents, and made many gun attacks on enemy objectives—coastal railways in Sicily and southern Italy being favorite targets. Considerable Axis military traffic was carried in small coasters, some of them sail, especially in the Aegean. Gun attacks destroyed many such vessels (most were not worth the expenditure of a torpedo), which do not figure in the overall tonnage loss reports—but which nevertheless represented considerable loss in men and materiel.

"Pedestal" had given Malta a new lease on life, but only for a time. The island was still on starvation rations. In terms of calories (average for adult male workers, 1,690; for women and children, 1,500), the islander's diet—as any weight-watching American knows—will sustain life but will result in rapid loss of weight and, ultimately, bodily efficiency. Some relief would be found by the decision in August to begin to slaughter the island's remaining livestock—and special foodstuffs, in small quantities, could be run in by the fast minelayers *Welshman* and *Manxman.* But another convoy must be sent, and the success of this effort was dependent to a great extent on the result of the impending Battle of El Alamein and, to a lesser degree perhaps, the landings in North Africa ("Torch") that were planned for early November.

The success of the Eighth Army in the great battle that began on October 23 and Rommel's subsequent retreat (begun on November 2) meant that pressure from the Cyrenaican fields would be greatly lessened; so a convoy ("Stoneage") was planned for mid-November. In the meantime, submarines made 4 trips in October carrying aviation fuel, diesel and lubricating oil, torpedoes, and special foodstuffs, with 2 more in early November. On November 12, *Manxman* arrived from Alexandria with 350 tons of powdered milk, dried cereal, and preserved meat. On November 18 *Welshman* reached Malta from the west with a similar cargo. The same ship made a run to Haifa for much-needed torpedoes for the Malta submarines.

These runs were made in defiance of the increasing air attacks—the "October Blitz." Regretting perhaps the decision to defer the elimination of Malta until the victorious drive to Suez and stung by the increasing losses to their convoys (an average of 22 per cent of cargo tonnage lost in the period June–September 1942), the enemy made a final effort to neutralize Malta.

The stepped-up bombing was met this time by a far larger and more effective defending force—at the beginning 113 Spitfires and 11 Beaufighters, although there was a shortage of pilots. Now radar could pick up enemy aircraft as they formed up over their bases, and raids were usually met at sea. The success of the defenders was evidenced by the increasing ratio of enemy fighters to bombers. On October 11, when the heavy attacks began, some 150 fighters might escort 80 Ju 88s. Four days later, the ratio might be as high as 100 fighters to 15 bombers. By October 18 losses were such that Ju 88s were no longer used—Me 109 fighter-bombers being used instead. By the ninth day it was evident that the effort had failed, and heavy raids ceased. Due to the large proportion of fighters to regular bombers—although the enemy flew nearly 2,400 sorties—only some 440 tons of bombs were dropped. German losses were 9 fighters and 35 bombers; their Italian allies probably lost nearly as many. The defenders lost 30 Spitfires in the air (17 pilots survived) and a Spitfire and a Beaufighter on the ground—this last an indication of the effectiveness of the defense. The striking force was able to carry out attacks on every night that enemy vessels came within range.

This was the last major air assault on the island. There were numerous hit-and-run raids, attacks by

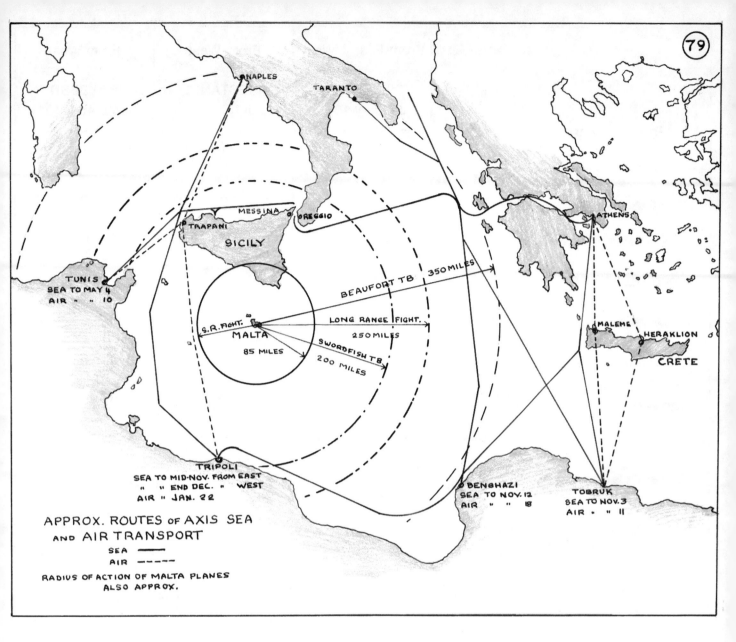

NAPLES
TARANTO
MESSINA
REGGIO
TRAPANI
SICILY
TUNIS
SEA TO MAY 4
AIR " " 10
BEAUFORT TB   350 MILES
S.R. FIGHT.
MALTA
LONG RANGE FIGHT.
85 MILES
250 MILES
SWORDFISH TB
200 MILES
ATHENS
MALEME
HERAKLION
CRETE
TRIPOLI
SEA TO MID-NOV. FROM EAST
"   " END DEC. " WEST
AIR " JAN. 22
BENGHAZI
SEA TO NOV.12
AIR " " 18
TOBRUK
SEA TO NOV.3
AIR " " 11

APPROX. ROUTES OF AXIS SEA
AND AIR TRANSPORT
SEA ————
AIR - - - - -
RADIUS OF ACTION OF MALTA PLANES
ALSO APPROX.

fighter-bombers, and a 40-bomber raid on Luqa on the night of December 18, which destroyed 4 Spitfires and 9 Wellingtons on the ground. But Malta's ordeal by air was about over.

Axis losses in September ran to some 20 per cent of cargoes loaded for Africa. In October this jumped to 44 per cent—at a time when the battle for the Western Desert was approaching its climax. Fuel in Rommel's army was particularly scarce, and the sinking of 6 ships loaded with fuel and ammunition in 7 days (October 26–November 1) was a severe blow. It should be pointed out again that these losses were not all inflicted by Malta-based units. But the co-ordination among commands was such that a ship sunk, for instance, off Tobruk by aircraft based in Egypt, had probably been first reported and shadowed by reconnaissance planes from Malta, and then damaged by a Malta-based sub-marine.

By now Rommel was in full retreat, and the compar-atively safe Axis supply route—under cover of the Cre-tan airfields—from Greece and the Adriatic to Cyre-naica was a thing of the past. The last Axis convoy arrived in Tobruk on November 3, and the town fell 10 days later. The last ships sailed into Benghazi on No-vember 12, and British troops entered on November 19. Tripoli was once more the main source of supply for the Axis in Libya. Tobruk had been out of range of Malta's Wellingtons, but Tripoli and the routes to it could be reached even by the obsolescent Swordfish. In the meantime, the main Axis supply route had sud-denly shifted even farther westward. The "Torch" landing had been successful, but the inevitable difficul-ties plus delays in wringing some degree of co-opera-tion from the generally pro-Vichy French had given the time for the Germans to land troops and planes in Tunisia (German bombers landed at El Aouïna on November 9). The main supply route now would be across the far shorter Sicilian Channel. While

Naval Forces Employed	From East & West 'EXCESS' January 1941			From West 'SUBSTANCE' July 1941			From West 'HALBERD' September 1941		
	No.	Sunk	Dmgd.	No.	Sunk	Dmgd.	No.	Sunk	Dmgd.
Capital Ships	4	0	0	2	0	0	3	0	1
Carriers	2	0	1	1	0	0	1	0	0
Cruisers	8	1	1	5	0	1	5	0	0
A.A. Ships	1	0	0	0	0	0	0	0	0
Destroyers	23	0	1	18	1	1	18	0	0
Minesweepers & Corvettes	4	0	0	0	0	0	1	0	0
Submarines*	3	0	0	8	0	0	9	0	0
Transports & Merchant Ships	6 (3 for Greece)	0	0	6	0	0	9	1	0
Number of Merchant Ships and Transports which arv. Malta	3			6			8		

*Deployed to intercept Italian Naval Forces

CONVOY OPERATIONS

this passage appeared at first glance to be one that could be easily cut, the route to Tunis was short, only 130 sea miles from Trapani, which meant that much of the distance could be covered in darkness. It also ran through very dangerous waters, confined and heavily mined (see map) with numerous alert surface patrols and aircraft, many of which were fitted with ASV.

Because of this, the British submarines were mainly deployed north of Sicily and off Naples and other likely ports. The Italian Navy, under threat of bombing (a heavy raid on Naples on December 4 sank a cruiser and badly damaged 2 more and 4 destroyers), withdrew most of its heavy units to La Spezia. Others went from Messina to Maddalena or Taranto. To add to its troubles, the Italian Fleet was chronically short of fuel.

Submarine sinkings in November were disappointing, partly for the reason given above, partly because at the beginning of the month many boats were involved in the "Torch" operation—deployed to meet the Italian Fleet (which did not put in an appearance). Only 4 ships, totaling 6,517 tons, were sunk. Aircraft did bet-

ter—12 ships, totaling 42,649 tons. And while no ships were lost in November on the run to Tunis, overall cargo losses amounted to 26 per cent of tonnage shipped.

It was obvious that the task of cutting the enemy supply line would fall mainly on the Allied air forces, and in this Malta was to play an increasingly important part.

Preparations for "Stoneage" were going ahead and measures were taken to ensure complete co-operation between the Royal Navy and the R.A.F. from Egypt and Cyrenaica and Malta. U. S. Liberators would also co-operate (the sailing date was to be held up until after the recapture of the Tobruk airfields). Four ships were to be convoyed; the escort was 5 cruisers and 17 destroyers. Strong anti-submarine patrols were flown, and shore-based fighters covered the convoy during daylight hours. The convoy entered the Mediterranean from the Canal late on November 16. On November 18 a small force of Ju 88s attacked but were driven off. At 1800 a torpedo-bomber attack badly damaged cruiser

From East 'M.W. 10' March, 1942			From West 'HARPOON' June, 1942			From East 'VIGOROUS' June, 1942			From West 'PEDESTAL' August, 1942			From East 'STONEAGE' November, 1942		
No.	Sunk	Dmgd.	No.	Sunk	Dmgd.	No.	Sunk	Dmgd.	No.	Sunk	Dmgd.	No.	Sunk	Dmgd.
0	0	0	1	0	0	0	0	0	2	0	0	0	0	0
0	0	0	2	0	0	0	0	0	4*	1	1	0	0	0
4	0	3	3	0	1	7	1	2	6	1	2	5	0	1
1	0	0	1	0	1	1	0	0	1	1	0	0	0	0
18	3	2	18	2	3	26	3	0	31	1	0	17	0	0
0	0	0	4	0	1	6	0	1	4	0	0	0	0	0
5	1	0	4	0	0	9	0	0	8	0	0	0	0	0
4	1	0	6	4	0	11	2	2	14	9	3	4	0	0
3 (All sunk after arv.)			2			0			5			4		

TO MALTA, 1941-1942

*FURIOUS flew off 38 Spitfires and returned to Gibraltar

Arethusa, which limped back to Alexandria with 155 dead. A later attack on the convoy was without effect. With the dawn came the Malta air cover, and by 1500 hours on November 20 the convoy was safely in Malta. Besides adequate air cover the operation was marked by the improvement in communications between ships and aircraft due to use of the VHF radio-telephone apparatus. The ships were unloaded in record time with little interference from enemy air attacks.

On December 5 another convoy ("Portcullis")—5 ships and a tanker—arrived with no opposition. On December 11, 13, 21, and January 2, ships in pairs, picked up off Benghazi by escorts from Malta, ran into Malta without incident. The siege was over.

In the beginning, "Torch" command's strike force consisted of only a few Swordfish based on Algiers— 450 miles from the Axis supply route. This would soon be remedied, but in the meantime the Malta planes would have to do what they could. This meant reinforcing the Malta squadrons, despite shortage of aviation fuel and crowded fields.

At the end of November there were on Malta 4½ squadrons of single-engine fighters (mostly Spitfires), 3 of Beaufighters (including 1 of night fighters), 1 of photographic and reconnaissance, 3 of torpedo-bombers (Beauforts, Albacores, and Swordfish), and 2 of Wellington medium bombers. These were reinforced during December, among these reinforcements being the first of the island's Mosquito squadrons.

More submarines arrived, also some MTBs. On November 27 Force "K" was reconstituted—3 cruisers and 4 destroyers. Another squadron, Force "Q"—3 cruisers and 2 destroyers—was based at Bône on November 30. This latter force had an immediate success (December 1–2) sinking an entire convoy, 3 merchant vessels, a transport, and a destroyer of the escort. There were no British casualties during the action, but a destroyer was sunk by a torpedo-bomber off Bône at dawn.

There were further minor successes, but because of the massacre of December 1–2 Axis night sailings were greatly curtailed and day passages substituted, with

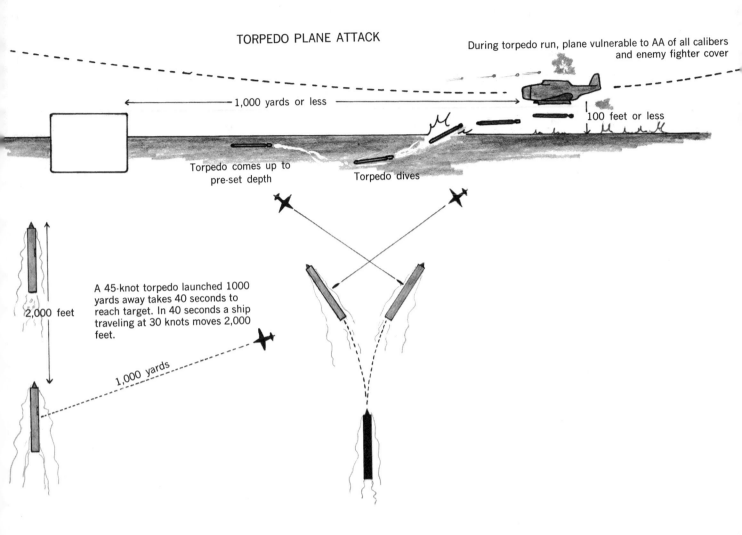

TORPEDO PLANE ATTACK

During torpedo run, plane vulnerable to AA of all calibers and enemy fighter cover

← 1,000 yards or less →

100 feet or less

Torpedo comes up to pre-set depth

Torpedo dives

2,000 feet

A 45-knot torpedo launched 1000 yards away takes 40 seconds to reach target. In 40 seconds a ship traveling at 30 knots moves 2,000 feet.

1,000 yards

strong air escort. This held true until new Italian mine fields (see map 49) hampered surface attacks from the west. British submarines sank several ships during December, and the FAA from Malta sank 5 ships and shared in 3 others, while Malta-based Wellingtons dropped more than 500 tons of bombs on Tunisian ports. Some 23 per cent of Axis cargoes for Tunisia were lost during December.

Recognizing the difficulties of surface transport, the Axis had begun large-scale supply and transport operations by air—using Me 323s, BV 222s, FW 200s, Ju 90s and 290s, as well as a variety of smaller aircraft, both German and Italian. In November 1942, transport of German supplies and men by air to Tunisia amounted to 581 tons and 15,273 men. In December this rose to 3,503 tons and 18,162 men. The figures for January, February, March, and April 1943 were 4,047 tons and 14,257 men; 4,953 tons and 12,893 men; 7,651 tons and 11,756 men; 4,327 tons and 8,388 men, respectively. These do not include Italian supplies or personnel carried.

The effort at once drew the attention of the Allied fliers, and from that point until the end of the African campaign increasing emphasis was placed on the disruption of this air traffic both by attacking the enemy flights and by bombing their fields.

During December the Malta aircraft destroyed at least 17 enemy transport planes, some 17 bombers, 8 plus fighters and 3 flying boats. In addition to the normal reconnaissance or attack missions, more and more mine-laying operations were called for, magnetic mines being laid off all strategic enemy ports.

In December 52 per cent of cargo sent to Libya and 23 per cent shipped to Tunisia was lost. In October, November, and December a total of 66 ships (of over 500 tons)—tonnage 202,258—and some 50 smaller vessels—tonnage 9,000—were sunk. Of the larger ships 30 were sunk by air, 25 by submarine.

Malta continued to be of prime importance, both as a base of submarine and surface forces and for the ever-increasing air effort. Movements of Axis shipping were under close surveillance by PRU Spitfires from the island, while the striking-force aircraft were in almost constant operation—torpedo-bombers, fighter-bombers, Wellingtons, Mosquitoes, and Beaufighters. Besides attacks on shipping, ground targets in Sicily and the southern tip of Italy were attacked daily—sorties being flown against railways, ground convoys, factories, power stations, and, of course, airfields.

1943

Tripoli was captured on January 23, 1943, and the battle for Italian North Africa was almost over. The fighting now centered in Tunisia, where the Axis had succeeded in building up strong forces. The Malta story now merges almost completely with the history of the Allied efforts to strangle the Axis in Tunisia—and due to the close interrelation of forces, the part the Malta-based ships and aircraft played is hard to distinguish from those of other commands. The whole offensive comprised such divergent activities as massive bomber raids on Italian ports to the launching by Malta-based submarines of the first British human-torpedo craft (chariots) to be used in the Mediterranean.

The Allied air-sea offensive covered not only the Tunis–Sicily–Sardinia triangle but in fact struck whenever worthwhile targets presented themselves. The submarine forces were deployed mainly off the Italian ports and on the more distant supply routes (the west coast of Italy and the north coast of Sicily were good hunting grounds), as the following figures show. Of 17 ships sunk by submarines in January, 6 were supplying Tunisia; in February, of 19, only 4 were on the Tunis supply route. Italy had already lost over 1.3 million tons of merchant shipping out of some 2 million tons available in June 1940. A considerable additional tonnage had been acquired by seizure or purchase (French ships seized when Axis troops moved into the Occupied Zone amounted to some 875,000 tons), and some ships had been built, but shipping was very scarce.

Besides the North African supply routes there was a constant movement of shipping along the coasts of Italy itself and Dalmatia; between the mainland and Sicily, Sardinia, and Corsica; and the islands of the Dodecanese, Greece, and Crete. Much of this latter commerce was carried in small vessels, but numbers of these too had been sunk (273 to the end of 1942). To the above losses must be added the considerable number of ships unavailable because of war damage, normal overhauls, etc.

Inevitably losses inflicted in any one area were soon felt in another. Axis ships of over 500 tons sunk from all causes in January 1943 totaled 34, and in February, 30—in all, 212,661 tons. In the same period about 85 smaller vessels went down—some 7,000 tons. Twenty-three per cent of cargo shipped to Tunisia was lost on the way. At the same time the enemy's naval forces were suffering severe losses. In the period November 1942 through February 1943 4 cruisers, 5 destroyers, 13 submarines, 5 torpedo boats, and many smaller escort vessels were sunk.

The restocking of Malta continued. Two convoys arrived in January and 2 in February. Between them they carried some 83,000 tons of general supplies, 16,000 tons of oil, 6,000 tons of aviation fuel, and 4,000 tons of kerosene. Despite numbers of Axis bombers on the fields of Sicily, Greece, and Crete, no merchant ships of over 500 tons were lost by air attack in the central or eastern Mediterranean during those 2 months. Submarines did better, and *U-617* torpedoed and sank the famous *Welshman* on February 1. Besides her regular mine-laying duties, *Welshman* had made 5 unescorted dashes into Malta in the times when supplies were measured in hundreds of tons instead of thousands.

Although there was little chance of surface attack by the ships of the battered and fuel-starved ships of the Italian Navy, striking forces were always in readiness. As the victorious Eighth Army advanced westward, naval co-operation squadrons followed, until the sea routes were covered from the Tunisian border to the Levant. There were a few submarine attacks on the Alexandria-to-Tripoli supply route, but during March and April only 4 supply vessels, none of them large, were sunk en route—all by the same submarine, *U-593*. A few ships were bombed in Tripoli Harbor, in spite of strong anti-aircraft-gun defenses and fighter protection. In one raid a British destroyer was damaged by a novel Italian device—a circling torpedo. This was dropped by a parachute, which released when the torpedo hit the water. The rudders were turned automatically at intervals, steering the torpedo in a pattern of circles some 200 feet in diameter until it either hit something or its fuel ran out. As they ran on the surface they proved easy to destroy by automatic-weapons fire.

This account of Malta and the battle of the convoys ends with the final capitulation of the Axis forces in North Africa on May 13. The last months had seen a desperate attempt by the Axis forces to run men and supplies into Tunisia—both by sea and by air. The smaller vessels of the Italian Navy made voyage after voyage on the "Death Route," convoying supply vessels whose chances of making port became ever slimmer as the weeks went by.

After the convoy disaster of December 1–2 nearly all Axis troops were ferried over to Tunisia (usually from Pozzuoli) on destroyers. The number of these ferry trips can be estimated from the fact that over 51,000 troops were transported—mostly by destroyers or destroyer escorts, which could carry only some 300 men at a time and no heavy equipment. All vessels on this route—and they included even diesel-powered sailing and fishing craft—ran the gauntlet of surface, submarine, and air attack and mines, and they did it time after time. Nor were they safe in port. Raids on harbors in Sicily, southern Italy, and Tunisia increased in

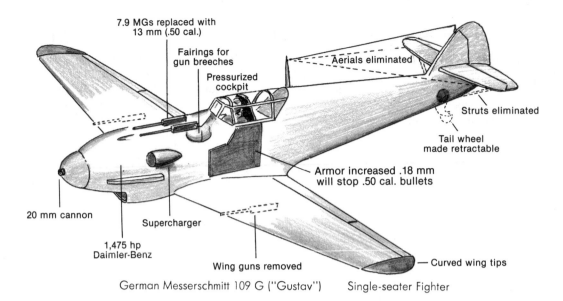

7.9 MGs replaced with
13 mm (.50 cal.)

Fairings for
gun breeches

Pressurized
cockpit

Aerials eliminated

Struts eliminated

Tail wheel
made retractable

Armor increased .18 mm
will stop .50 cal. bullets

20 mm cannon

Supercharger

1,475 hp
Daimler-Benz

Wing guns removed

Curved wing tips

German Messerschmitt 109 G ("Gustav")   Single-seater Fighter

**Span: 32′8½″. Length: 29′4″. Engine: 1,475 hp in-line. Speed: max. 400 mph at 22,000′.
Armament: one 20mm cannon firing through spinner, two 13mm machine guns.**
**Standard Luftwaffe fighter in the first part of World War II was the 109 E. Underwent
several changes of engine and armament. The Me 109 was first produced in 1936 and
manufacture continued until the war's end. Over 33,000 are believed to have been built. Ranks
with the Supermarine Spitfire as one of the war's "greats."**

ferocity as more heavy bombers became available to the Allied commanders. All the target ports were hard hit. Palermo was nearly wrecked and Naples and Messina suffered great damage, while heavy bombers from the United Kingdom attacked the northern ports. In April more tonnage was sunk by aircraft in harbor than was sunk at sea.

The hazards of the "Death Route" were such that it was only by the devotion of the crews of the merchantmen and escorts that cargoes got through at all. Admiral Cunningham wrote, "It was always a surprise to me that the Italian seamen continued to operate their ships in the face of the dangers that beset them."

In March and April Axis losses were almost double those of the previous months, reaching 41.5 per cent of cargoes shipped. Nor was the fury of the assault confined to the sea. By the end of March a daily average of some 200 transport aircraft, Ju 52s, Ju 90s, Ju 290s, and Me 323s (these last capable of carrying over 21,000 pounds of freight or 130 troops) were flying between the mainland, Sicily or Sardinia, and North Africa. The majority of these flights began at Naples and either used the western Sicilian fields as staging points or flew straight through to Tunisia. They were heavily escorted, and it was not until Allied air forces had been assembled in great strength that a serious attempt could be made to completely disrupt this traffic.

A plan ("Flax") calling for concentrated bombing of the terminal and staging fields and large-scale fighter sweeps of the Sicilian Narrows was put into action April 5. At least 30 enemy transports and several fighters were destroyed that day alone. U. S. Lightnings accounted for many of the losses, and on one especially successful sweep they shot down 32 Ju 52s out

of a flight of 100 as well as some of their fighter escort. On April 22, Spitfires and Kittyhawks sent 16 of the giant Me 323s—each carrying 10 tons of gasoline—blazing into the sea, as well as 2 large Italian transports. This was the end of large-scale day-transport traffic. Göring, enraged, forbade all transport flights to Africa, but a few days later Kesselring's protest wrung a resumption of night flights. In effect the sorties fell from 24-hour totals of from 100–250 to 60–70.

The results of the combined sea-air attacks were impressive and effectively sealed the doom of the enemy forces in Tunisia. The tonnage of ships lost during March, April, and May climbed to 340,438 tons. Of these, aircraft accounted for 211,647 tons, submarines 86,097 tons, and surface craft only 11,053 tons. In addition, 31,641 tons were shared, lost to mines or other causes. On top of this, losses in barges, Siebel ferries, landing craft, and other small vessels were also heavy, estimated at some 25,000 tons. In the 13 days in May before the surrender only 3,000 tons of cargo were offloaded in Tunisia. On May 26—just over 2 years since Operation "Tiger"—the first through convoy reached Alexandria from the west.

The cost of the battle for Malta was a heavy one. A total of 1,436 civilians had been killed and 3,415 wounded and some 37,000 buildings destroyed or damaged. In addition, many servicemen had died in defense of the island. Losses of planes ran into the hundreds. From the beginning of January 1941 ("Excess") to August 1942 ("Pedestal"), 79 supply ships sailed for Malta—either from Gibraltar or Alexandria. Of these, 46 arrived—unloading a total of some 330,000 tons. Twenty-three were sunk; the remainder were turned back. To the above tonnage must be added that delivered by minelayers *Welshman* and *Manxman* and by submarine. Warships lost in the various convoy operations included an aircraft carrier, 3 cruisers, an anti-aircraft cruiser, and 11 destroyers sunk, and a battleship, 2 carriers, 12 cruisers, an anti-aircraft cruiser, and 6 destroyers damaged.

The cost to the enemy was far greater; for while it is estimated that over 1,000 German and Italian aircraft were shot down or damaged in the 3-year assault on the island and large formations involved and so unavailable for operations elsewhere, the true value of the "unsinkable carrier" can only be assessed in terms of enemy ships sunk or damaged and the immense quantities of war materiel sent to the bottom.

The struggle to supply the Axis forces in Libya cost 342 merchant vessels—totaling some 1.3 million tons and loaded with over 313,000 tons of cargo. Troop movements fared better, and of 211,719 Italian and German troops who sailed for Libya only 14,393 (6.8 per cent) were on vessels that went down, and a number of these were rescued. Naval losses were also high.

Units lost while engaged in missions connected with the Libyan convoys totaled 4 cruisers, 14 destroyers, 12 destroyer escorts, 10 submarines, and 47 smaller units.

The efforts to supply Tunisia (November 12, 1942–May 13, 1943) cost 243 vessels of all types, with 242 more damaged. Of 408,447 tons of cargo loaded in Italy, 114,365 tons (28 per cent) were lost. Of 72,616 troops embarked, 5,118 (7 per cent) were missing. Twelve destroyers and 11 destroyer escorts were lost—as well as many smaller units. To these must be added those shot down in transport planes, as well as the not inconsiderable tonnage lost in cargo aircraft.

While the great portion of the losses in the Tunisian supply operations were inflicted by forces other than those based on Malta, the island must be credited with the major role in the strangling of the Libyan supply route.

As Rommel wrote, "Malta . . . has the lives of many thousands of German and Italian soldiers on its conscience."

TONNAGE LANDED BY AXIS SHIPPING IN NORTH AFRICA

	(FUEL AND SUPPLIES)	% LOST
June 10, 1940–September	148,817	none
October–January 1941	197,742	3.5%
February	79,183	1.3%
March	95,753	9
April	81,472	8
May	69,331	8
June	125,076	6
July	62,700	19.5
August	83,956	12.6
September	67,513	28
October	73,614	20.2
November	29,843	62
December	39,092	18
January 1942	66,170	none
February and March	106,553	9
April	150,389	1
May	86,439	7.2
June	32,327	22
July	91,491	6
August	51,655	33
September	77,526	20
October	45,698	44
November	63,736	26
	30,309 (Tunisia)	0
December	6,151	52
	58,763 (Tunisia)	23
January 1943	69,908 ⎞	
February	59,016 ⎠ (Tunisia)	23
March	43,125 ⎞	
April	29,233 ⎠ (Tunisia)	41.5
May 13	3,728 (Tunisia)	77

APPENDIXES

Alexander, Gen. The Hon. Sir Harold (Br.)—C in C Middle East, Aug. '42–Feb. '43; later commanding Eighteenth Army Group

Allen, Maj. Gen. Terry de la M. (U.S.)—CO 1st Inf. Div.

Anderson, Lt. Gen. Sir Kenneth A. N. (Br.)—CO First Army

Arena, Brig. Gen. Francesco (It.)—CO Ariete Div.

Arnim, Gen. Jurgen von (Ger.)—CO PzAOK5 from Mar. '43 of Army Group Afrika

Auchinleck, Gen. Sir Claude (Br.)—C in C Middle East. Relieved Aug. '42

Auphan, Rear-Adm. Paul (Fr.)—Minister of Marine

Barré, Lt. Gen. G. (Fr.)—CO troops in Tunisia

Bastico, Marshal Ettore (It.)—CO Italian Armed Forces in N. Africa to Feb. '43

Bayerlein, Maj. Gen. Fritz (Ger.)—COS D.A.K.; later of Ger. It. Panzerarmee, later Ger. COS AOK1

Bennett, Rear-Adm. Andrew C. (U.S.)—CO U. S. Naval Operating Bases, Oran Area

Bèthouart, Maj. Gen. Emile (Fr.)—CO Casablanca Div.

Boissau, Gen. Robert (Fr.)—CO Oran Div.

Boisson, Gen. Pierre (Fr.)—Gov. Fr. West Africa

Bradley, Maj. Gen. Omar N. (U. S.)—Eisenhower's rep. at front; later Lt. Gen. CO U. S. II Corps

Briggs, Maj. Gen. R. (Br.)—CO Br. 1st Arm. Div.

Broich, Maj. Gen. Freiherr Fritz von (Ger.)—CO Div. von Broich, later of 10th Panzer Div.

Brooke, Gen. Sir Alan (Br.)—Chief of Imperial General Staff

Buelowius, Maj. Gen. Karl (Ger.)—Chief Eng. Ger.-It. Panzerarmee, later of Army Group Afrika; temporarily CO D.A.K. Assault Group and von Manteuffel Div.

Burckhardt, Lt. Gen. (Ger.)—CO 19th Flak Div., Panzergruppe Afrika

Burrough, Vice-Adm. Sir Harold (Br.)—Eastern Naval Task Force (Algiers)

Caffey, Col. Benjamin F., Jr. (U.S.)—CO U. S. 39th Combat Team and 1st Cmdo. (Br.) (Algiers)

Cass, Brig. E. E. (Br.)—CO 11th Inf. Brigade Group (Algiers)

Cavallero, Marshal Ugo (It.)—COS It. Armed Forces

Châtel, M. Yves (Fr.)—Gov. Gen. of Algeria

Clark, Lt. Gen. Mark W. (U.S.)—Deputy Allied C in C

Clutterbuck, Maj. Gen. W. E. (Br.)—CO 1st Br. Inf. Div.

Coningham, Air Vice-Marshal Sir Arthur (Br.)—AOC Western Desert Air Force

Copland-Griffith, Brig. F. A. V. (Br.)—CO 1st Guards Brigade

Crocker, Lt. Gen. Sir John T. (Br.)—CO Br. IX Corps

Cunningham, Adm. of the Fleet Sir Andrew (Br.)—Nov. '42, Naval Cmdr., Expeditionary Force; Feb. '43, C in C Medit.

Darlan, Admiral Jean François (Fr.)—C in C French Armed Forces

Davidson, Rear-Adm. Lyal A. (U.S.)—Cmdr. Southern Attack Group

De Gaulle, General Charles (Fr.)—Leader of Free French

Derrien, Rear-Adm. Edmond (Fr.)—Naval CO, Bizerte

Dobbie, Lt. Gen. Sir William (Br.)—Gov. of Malta to May 1942

Dody, Maj. Gen. André (Fr.)—CO Meknès Div., CO North Morocco Sector

Doolittle, Maj. Gen. James H., U.S.A.A.F. (U.S.)—CO Western Air Command to Feb. '43, then CO Northwest African Strategic Air Force

Drake, Col. Thomas D. (U.S.)—168th RCT

Dunphie, Brig. Charles A. L. (Br.)—26th Arm. Brigade

Durgin, Cmdr. E. R., U.S.N. (U.S.)—Control and Fire Support DDs, Center Attack Group (Fedala)

Eddy, Maj. Gen. Manton S. (U.S.)—CO U. S. 9th Inf. Div.

Eisenhower, Lt. Gen. Dwight D. (U.S.)—Allied C in C, No. Afr. Theater

Emmett, Capt. Robert R. M., U.S.N. (U.S.)—Cmdr. Center Attack Group (Fedala)

Estéva, Vice-Adm. Jean Pierre (Fr.)—Resident Gen. of Tunisia

Evelegh, Maj. Gen. V. (Br.)—CO Br. 78th Div.

Ferla, Brig. Gen. Francesco la (It.)—CO Trieste Motorized Div.

Fischer, Lt. Gen. Wolfgang (Ger.)—CO 10th Panzer Div.

Franco, Gen. Francisco (Sp.)—Span. Dictator

Fredendall, Lt. Gen. Lloyd R. (U.S.)—Cmdr., Center Task Force, U. S. II Corps; relieved by Patton, Mar. '43

Freyberg, Lt. Gen. Sir Bernard, V.C. (Br.)—CO N.Z. Div., XXX Corps, Eighth Army

Gardiner, Lt. Col. Henry E. (U.S.)—CO 2nd Bn., 13th Arm. Rgt.

Gatehouse, Maj. Gen. A. H. (Br.)—CO 10th Br. Arm. Div.

Giffen, Rear-Adm. Robert C., U.S.N. (U.S.)—Cmdr. TG 34.1 Covering Group, Task Force 34

Giraud, General Henri (Fr.)—Nov. 13, '42, CO French Forces, North Africa

Gloria, Maj. Gen. Alessandro (It.)—CO Bologna Div.

Göring, Field Marshal Hermann (Ger.)—Head of Hitler's Luftwaffe

Gore, Lt. Col. A. C. (Br.)—CO 10th Bn. Royal Buffs; CO "Gore" Force at Kasserine

Gort, General the Viscount, V.C. (Br.)—Replaced Dobbie as Gov. of Malta, May '42

Gott, Lt. Gen. W. H. E. (Br.)—CO XIII Corps; chosen CO Eighth Army; killed Aug. '42

Gray, Capt. Augustine H., U.S.N. (U.S.)—CO Northern Attack Group Transports TG 34.8 (Mehdia)

Greer, Col. F. V. (U.S.)—CO 18th Combat Team, "Z" Beach Green (Oran)

Hamilton, Maj. P. M. (U.S.)—Emissary to French H.Q., Port Lyautey

Harding, Maj. Gen. A. F. (Br.)—CO 7th Arm. Div., XIII Corps, Eighth Army

Hardy, Capt. C. C., R.N. (Br.)—Cmdr. convoy to Malta ("Harpoon") June '42

Harmon, Maj. Gen. Ernest N. (U.S.)—CO U. S. 2nd Arm. Div., Cmdr. Sub-Task Force "Blackstone" at Safi; later CO 1st Arm. Div.

Hartman, Capt. C. C., U.S.N. (U.S.)—Control Fire Support DDs, Southern Attack Group TG 34.10 (Safi)

Harwood, Adm. Sir Henry (Br.)—C in C Medit. (May '42–Feb. '43)

Hawkesworth, Maj. Gen. J. L. I. (Br.)—CO 4th Br. Inf. Div.

Heffernan, Capt. John B., U.S.N. (U.S.)—Screening DDs Center Attack Group TG 34.9 (Fedala)

Henri-Martin, Maj. Gen. (Fr.)—CO Safi-Mogador sector

Hewitt, Rear-Adm. H. Kent (U.S.)—CO Western Naval Task Force

Hightower, Lt. Col. Louis V. (U.S.)—CO 3rd Bn., U. S. 1st Arm. Rgt. (Sidi Bou Zid)

Hopkins, Harry (U.S.)—Personal adviser to President Roosevelt

Horrocks, Lt. Gen. B. G. (Br.)—CO XIII Corps, Eighth Army

Hughes, Maj. Gen. I. T. P. (Br.)—CO 44th Div., XIII Corps, Eighth Army

Jodl, Lt. Gen. Alfred (Ger.)—Chief of Op. Staff, OKW

Juin, Gen. Alphonse (Fr.)—C in C Fr. Military Forces, N. Africa

Keightley, Maj. Gen. Sir Charles (Br.)—CO Br. 6th Arm. Div.

Kelly, Rear-Adm. Monroe, U.S.N. (U.S.)—CO Northern Attack Group TG 34.8 (Mehdia)

Kern, Col. William B. (U.S.)—CO 1st. Bn., U. S. 6th Arm. Inf.

Kesselring, Field Marshal Albert (Ger.)—C in C South and CO Luftflotte 2

King, Adm. Ernest J., U.S.N. (U.S.)—Chief of Naval Operations

Kisch, Brig. F. K. (Br.)—School of Mine Clearance, Eighth Army

Knight, Edgeway (U.S.)—U. S. Vice-Consul, Oran

Koeltz, Lt. Gen. Louis-Marie (Fr.)—Cmdr. Algiers region, later Fr. XIX Corps

Koenig, Brig. Gen. M. P. (Fr.)—1st Fighting French Brigade Group

Krause, Maj. Gen. Fritz (Ger.)—Art. Cmdr. Ger.-It. Panzerarmee; later 334th Div.

Laborde, Adm. Jean de (Fr.)—CO French Fleet, Toulon

Lafond, Rear-Adm. Gervais de (Fr.)—Cmdr. 2nd Light Squadron, Casablanca

Lahoulle, Gen. (Fr.)—CO French Air Forces in Morocco

Lang, Col. Rudolph (Ger.)—CO 69th Panzer Grenadier Rgt.; Cmdr. Battle Group Lang

Lascroux, Gen. George (Fr.) C in C Moroccan Troops

Laval, Pierre (Fr.)—Chief of Government under Pétain

Leclerc, Gen. Jean (Fr.)—French Forces, Equatorial Africa; "L" Force, Eighth Army

Leese, Lt. Gen. Sir Oliver (Br.)—XXX Corps, Eighth Army

Liebenstein, Maj. Gen. Freiherr Kurt von (Ger.)—CO 164th Light Div.; CO D.A.K. Jan.–Feb. '43

Lloyd, Air Vice-Marshal Sir Hugh (Br.)—CO Northwest African Coastal Air Force

Loerzer, Gen. Bruno (Ger.)—Cmdr. Fliegerkorps II until Mar. '43

Lorenzelli, Gen. Dante (It.)—Superga Div.

Lumsden, Lt. Gen. H. (Br.)—CO Br. 1st Arm. Div., then CO X Corps, Eighth Army Aug.–Dec. '42

Mack, Capt. P. J., R.N. (Br.)—CO 14th Destroyer Flotilla (Malta)

Madeira, Cmdr. D. L., U.S.N. (U.S.)—CO Screen DDs, Northern Attack Group TG 34.8 (Mehdia)

Manteuffel, Maj. Gen. Hasso von (Ger.)—Cmdr. Division Manteuffel

Maraist, Col. Robert V. (U.S.)—CO CC "D," 1st Armored Div. (Maknassy)

Marshall, Gen. George C. (U.S.)—COS, U.S.A.

Martin, Maj. Gen. Henri (Fr.)—Commanding Gen. at Marrakech

Masina, Brig. Gen. (It.)—CO Trento Division

Mast, Maj. Gen. Charles (Fr.)—CO Algerian Div.

Mathenet, Brig. Gen. Maurice (Fr.)—Moroccan Div. CO at Meknès then Port Lyautey; later with Allied forces in Tunisia

McCarley, Major Percy De W., Jr. (U.S.)—CO 1st Bn. Landing Team, 60th RCT (Mehdia)

McGinness, Lt. Col. John R. (U.S.)—CO CC "B" (at Medjez el Bab)

McNabb, Brig. C. V. (Br.)—COS First Army

McQuillin, Brig. Gen. Raymond E. (U.S.)—CO CC "A," U. S. 1st Arm. Div. (Sidi Bou Zid)

McWhorter, Rear-Adm. Ernest D., U.S.N. (U.S.)—CO Air Group (TG 34.2)

Messe, Gen. Giovanni (It.)—Cmdr. AOK1, promoted marshal, May 12, '43

Michelier, Vice-Adm. François (Fr.)—CO French Naval Forces Morocco; CO Naval Forces, Casablanca Area

Monsabert, Brig. Gen. A. J. de (Fr.)—Cmdr. Blida Area; later CO Corps Franc d'Afrique

Montgomery, Gen. Sir Bernard Law (Br.)—CO Eighth Army

Moon, Capt. D. P., U.S.N. (U.S.)—Cmdr. DD Screen, Western Naval Task Force

Morshead, Lt. Gen. Sir Leslie (Br.)—CO 9th Australian Div., XXX Corps, Eighth Army

Mountbatten, Capt. Lord Louis, R.N. (Br.)—5th Destroyer Flotilla; later Vice-Adm., Chief of Combined Operations

Murphy, Robert D. (U.S.)—U. S. Consul General in Algiers

Navarrini, Lt. Gen. Enea (It.)—Italian XXI Corps

Nebba, Lt. Gen. Edoardo (It.)—Italian X Corps

Nehring, Gen. Walther (Ger.)—CO D.A.K., June–Aug. '42; later CO XC Corps, Tunisia

Nichols, Maj. Gen. J. S. (Br.)—CO 50th Div., XIII Corps, Eighth Army

Nicholson, Brig. C. G. G. (Br.)—2nd in command, Br. 6th Armored Div.

Noguès, Gen. Auguste Paul (Fr.)—Resident Gen., Morocco

O'Daniel, Col. John W. (U.S.)—CO 168th Combat Team (Algiers)

Oliver, Brig. Gen. Lunsford A. E. (U.S.)—CO CC "B," U. S. 1st Arm. Div. (Oran)

Patton, Maj. Gen. George S. (U.S.)—CO Western Assault Force; later Lt. Gen. CO U. S. II Corps

Petit, Col. Charles (Fr.)—CO Port Lyautey

Pétain, Marshal Henri Philippe (Fr.)—Chief of State, Vichy Govt.

Phillips, Capt. Wallace B., U.S.N. (U.S.)—CO Transports, Southern Attack Group (Safi)

Pienaar, Maj. Gen. D. H. (S.A.)—CO 1st S. African Div., XXX Corps, Eighth Army

Raff, Col. E. D. (U.S.)—CO 2nd Bn./509th U. S. Parachute Rgt.

Ramcke, Maj. Gen. Bernhard (Ger.)—CO Ramcke Para. Brigade, D.A.K.

Ramsey, Vice-Adm. Sir Bertram (Br.)—Deputy Naval Cmdr., Expedit. Force ("Torch")

Randow, Maj. Gen. Heinz von (Ger.)—CO 21st Panzer Div., D.A.K.

Ravenstein, Maj. Gen. Johann von (Ger.)—CO 21st Panzer Div.; captured Nov. '41

Ritchie, Lt. Gen. N. M. (Br.)—CO Eighth Army Nov. '41–June '42

Robinett, Col. Paul McD. (U.S.)—CO Arm. Task Force Green (Oran); later Brig. Gen. CC "B," U. S. 1st Arm. Div.

Robison, Cmdr. H. C., U.S.N. (U.S.)—DD Screen, Southern Attack Group (Safi)

Rommel, Field Marshal Erwin (Ger.)—CO Panzergruppe Afrika; later CO Ger.-It. Panzerarmee Afrika; later CO Army Group Afrika

Roosevelt, Brig. Gen. Theodore (U.S.)—CO 26th RCT, 1st Inf. Div. (Oran)

Ryder, Maj. Gen. Charles W. (U.S.)—CO U. S. 34th Inf. Div.; Cmdr. Eastern Assault Force (Algiers)

Scattaglia, Brig. Gen. N. (It.)—CO Italian Pavia Div.

Smith, Maj. Gen. Walter Bedell (U.S.)—COS to Eisenhower

Somerville, Vice-Adm. Sir James F., R.N. (Br.)—Flag Officer Force "H" to Jan. '42

Sponeck, Maj. Gen. Theodor Graf von (Ger.)—CO 90th Light Division, D.A.K.

Stack, Col. Robert I. (U.S.)—CO CC "C," 1st Arm. Div.

Stark, Col. Alexander N., Jr. (U.S.)—CO 26th Inf. Rgt.—"Stark Force"

Stephanis, Lt. Gen. Giuseppe de (It.)—Italian XX Corps

Student, Gen. Kurt (Ger.)—CO Fliegerkorps XI

Stumme, Gen. Georg (Ger.)—Acting CO Ger-It. Panzerarmee Sept.–Oct. '42; died El Alamein

Syfret, Vice-Adm. Sir Neville (Br.)—Flag Officer Force "H," Jan. '42

Tedder, Air Chief Marshal Sir Arthur (Br.)—AOC in C

Thoma, Lt. Gen. Ritter von (Ger.)—CO D.A.K.; took command Panzerarmee after Stumme

Tostain, Col. Paul (Fr.)—COS Oran Div.

Trevor, Lt. Col. T. H. (Br.)—CO 1st Commando (Algiers)

Troubridge, Rear-Admiral T. H., R.N. (Br.)—Center Naval Task Force (Oran)

Truscott, Brig. Gen. Lucian K. (U.S.)—CO Force "Z," "Goalpost," Northern Attack Group (Mehdia)

Tuck, S. Pinkney (U.S.)—U. S. Chargé d'Affaires at Vichy

Tuker, Maj. Gen. F. I. S. (Br.)—CO 4th Indian Div.

Turner, Lt. Col. V. B. (Br.)—CO 2nd Rifle Brigade; CO at "Snipe"

Vaerst, Maj. Gen. Gustav von (Ger.)—CO 15th Panzer Div.; later Gen. PzAOK5 (after von Arnim)

Vian, Rear-Adm. Sir Phillip L., R.N. (Br.)—CO 15th Cruiser Sqdn. convoys to Malta

Ward, Maj. Gen. Orlando (U.S.)—CO U. S. 1st Arm. Div.

Waters, Lt. Col. John K. (U.S.)—CO 1st Arm. Rgt. "Lessouda Force" (Sidi Bou Zid)

Wellborn, Capt. Charles, Jr., U.S.N. (U.S.)—CO Air Group Screen, Northern Attack Group TG 34.8 (Mehdia)

Welsh, Air Marshal Sir William (Br.)—AOC Eastern Air Command

Welvert, Gen. Joseph Edouard (Fr.)—CO Constantine Div.

Westphal, Maj. Gen. Siegfried (Ger.)—Chief Ops. Branch, H.Q. C in C South

Wimberley, Maj. Gen. D. N. (Br.)—CO 51st (Highland) Div.

Ziegler, Lt. Gen. Heinz (Ger.)—COS PzAOK5; Acting CO D.A.K. Feb.–Mar. '43

II. OPERATIONAL CODE NAMES

"ACROBAT"—Plan for advance from Cynenaica into Tripolitania after "Crusader."

"BARBAROSSA"—Hitler's invasion of the Soviet Union

"CRUSADER"—British offensive in Western Desert, November 1941

"EILBOTE" (Express Messenger)—PzAOK5 operation in northern Tunisia, January 1943

"FLAX"—Allied air operation against air supply line from Italy

"FRÜHLINGSWIND" (Spring Breeze)—PzAOK5 operation, central Tunisia, February 1943

"GYMNAST"—Plan for British landing in French North Africa after "Acrobat."

"HERKULES"—Plan for capture of Malta, 1942

"LIGHTFOOT"—First phase, Battle of El Alamein—October 1942

"OCHSENKOPF" (Bull's Head)—PzAOK5 operation in northern Tunisia, February–March 1943

"RESERVIST"—Quick seizure of vital points in Oran

"ROUND UP"—Proposed cross-Channel invasion of France in 1943

"SATIN"—Planned Allied attack toward Sfax, December 1942—abandoned

"SLEDGEHAMMER"—Proposed superraid cross-Channel, 1942

"STRIKE"—Final phase, attack on Tunis and Bizerte, May 1943

"SUPERCHARGE"—(a) Final phase, Battle of El Alamein, October–November 1942 (b) British attack at Tebaga Gap, March 1943

"SUPERGYMNAST"—Plan for Anglo-American landing in French North Africa (became "Torch")

"TERMINAL"—Operation in harbor at Algiers, November 8, 1942

"TORCH"—Allied landings in North Africa, November 1942

"VULCAN"—Eighteenth Army Group offensive in Tunisia, April–May 1943

BIBLIOGRAPHY

Alexander, Field Marshal Earl. *The Memoirs of Field-Marshal Earl Alexander of Tunis 1940–1945*. London: Cassel, 1963.

The Army Air Force in World War II. V-4 Airforce Historical Division. Chicago: University of Chicago Press, 1950.

Barnett, Correlli. *The Desert Generals*. New York: Viking Press, 1972.

Bishop, Edward. *Mosquito. Wooden Wonder*. New York: Ballantine Books, 1971.

———. *Wellington Bomber*. New York: Ballantine Books, 1974.

Blumenson, Martin. *Kasserine Pass*. Boston: Houghton Mifflin, 1967.

Bradley, Omar N. *A Soldier's Story*. New York: Henry Holt & Co., 1951.

Bragadin, Commander Marc Antonio, Italian Navy (ret.). *The Italian Navy in World War II*. Annapolis, Md.: U. S. Naval Institute, 1957.

Carell, Paul. *Foxes of the Desert*. New York: E. P. Dutton, 1961.

Chatterton, E. Keble. *The Royal Navy*. London: Hutchinson & Co. Ltd.

Churchill, Winston. *The Second World War*. 6 vols. Boston: Houghton Mifflin, 1948–53.

Crisp, Robert, D.S.O., M.C. *Brazen Chariots*. New York: W. W. Norton & Co., 1961.

Crow, Duncan. *British and Commonwealth Armoured Formations (1919–46)*. Windsor, England: Profile Publications Ltd., 1971.

———. *Armoured Fighting Vehicles in Profile*. 4 vols. Garden City, N.Y.: Doubleday & Co., 1971.

Cunningham, *A Sailor's Odyssey: The Autobiography of Admiral of the Fleet Viscount Cunningham of Hynd Hope*. New York: E. P. Dutton, 1951.

Douglas, Keith. *Alamein to Zem Zem*. New York: Chillmark Press, 1966.

Duncan, Nigel, Maj. Gen. *79th Armoured Division*. Windsor, England: Profile Publications Ltd., 1972.

Eisenhower, Dwight D. *Crusade in Europe*. Garden City, N.Y.: Doubleday & Co., 1948.

Fahey, James C. *Ships and Aircraft of the U. S. Fleet*. New York: Ships & Aircraft, 1945.

Gander, Terry, and Chamberlain, Peter. *Weapons of the Third Reich*. New York: Doubleday & Co., 1978.

Gosset, Renée Pierre-. *Conspiracy in Algiers, 1942–1943*. Translated by Mary Hecksher. New York: Nation, 1945.

Green, William. *Fighters (War Planes of the Second World War)*. 2 vols. Garden City, N.Y.: Doubleday & Co., 1967.

———. *Famous Bombers of the Second World War*. 2 vols. Garden City, N.Y.: Doubleday & Co., 1967.

———. *Famous Fighters of the Second World War*. 2 vols. Garden City, N.Y.: Hanover House, 1960.

———. *Flying Boats*. Garden City, N.Y.: Doubleday & Co., 1962.

Heckstall-Smith, Anthony, D.S.C. *Tobruk*. New York: W. W. Norton & Co., 1959.

History of the Second World War: The Mediterranean and Middle East. 4 vols. London: Her Majesty's Stationery Office, 1954–66.

Hogg, Ian. *Grenades and Mortars*. New York: Ballantine Books, 1974.

———. *The Guns 1939–45*. New York: Ballantine Books, 1970.

Holmes, Richard. *Bir Hakim*. New York: Ballantine Books, 1971.

Howard, Michael. *The Mediterranean Strategy in the Second World War*. New York: Praeger, 1968.

Jablonski, David. *The Desert Warriors*. New York: Lancer Books, 1972.

Jablonski, Edward. *Flying Fortress*. Garden City, N.Y.: Doubleday & Co., 1965.

Jackson, W. G. F. *Alexander of Tunis (as Military Commander)*. New York: Dodd, Mead & Co., 1971.

Johnson, J. E. *Full Circle—The Tactics of Air Fighting 1914–1964*. New York: Ballantine Books, 1964.

Jones, Vincent. *Operation Torch: Anglo-American Invasion of North Africa*. New York: Ballantine Books, 1972.

Kafka, Roger, and Pepperburg, Roy L. *Warships of the World*. New York: Cornell Maritime Press, 1946.

Killen, John. *A History of the Luftwaffe*. Garden City, N.Y.: Doubleday & Co., 1967.

Kirk, John, and Young, Robert, Jr. *Great Weapons of World War II*. New York: Bonanza Books, 1961.

Landsborough, Gordon. *Tobruk Commando*. New York: Avon Pub., 1958.

Low, Sampson. *Jane's Fighting Ships, 1936*. London: Marston & Co. Ltd.

———. *Jane's Fighting Ships, 1941*. New York: The Macmillan Company, 1941.

Lyall, Gavin. *The War in the Air—The Royal Air Force in World War II*. New York: William Morrow & Co., 1970.

Macksey, Major K. J., M.C. *Afrika Korps*. New York: Ballantine Books, 1968.

———. *Beda Fomm—The Classic Victory*. New York: Ballantine Books, 1971.

Majdalany, Fred. *The Battle of Alamein*. Philadelphia: J. B. Lippincott, 1965.

Montgomery, Field Marshal the Viscount, K.G., G.C.B., D.S.O. *El Alamein to the River Sangro*. New York: E. P. Dutton & Co., 1949.

Moorehead, Alan. *The March to Tunis*. New York: Harper & Row, 1965.

———. *Don't Blame the Generals*. New York: Harper & Row, 1943.

Mordal, Jacques, and Auphan, Rear Admiral Paul, French Navy (ret.). *The French Navy in World War II*. Annapolis, Md.: U. S. Naval Institute, 1959.

Munson, Kenneth. *Aircraft of World War II*. Garden City, N.Y.: Doubleday & Co., 1968.

Ogorkiewicz, R. M. *Design and Development of Fighting Vehicles*. Garden City, N.Y.: Doubleday & Co., 1968.

Orgill, Douglas. *German Armor*. New York: Random House, 1974.

Potter, E. B., and Nimitz, Fleet Admiral Chester W., U.S.N., eds. *The Great Sea War*. Englewood Cliffs, N.J.: Prentice-Hall, 1960.

Price, Alfred. *Luftwaffe*. New York: Ballantine Books, 1969.

The Rommel Papers. New York: Harcourt, Brace & Co., 1953.

Roskill, Captain S. W., D.S.C., R.N. *The War at Sea*. 2 vols. London: Her Majesty's Stationery Office, 1954.

Ruge, Vice-Admiral Friedrich. *Der Seekrieg*. Annapolis, Md.: U. S. Naval Institute, 1957.

Schofield, Vice-Admiral B. B., C.B., C.B.E. *The Attack on Taranto*. Annapolis, Md.: U. S. Naval Institute, 1973.

Senger und Etterlin, Dr. F. M. von. *German Tanks of World War II*. New York: Galahad Books, 1969.

Shankland, Peter, and Hunter, Anthony. *Malta Convoy.*
New York: Ives Washburn, 1961.

Sibley, Roger, and Fry, Michael. *Rommel.* New York: Random House, 1974.

Silverstone, Paul H. *U. S. Warships of World War II.* Garden City, N.Y.: Doubleday & Co., 1970.

Smith, W. H. B. *Small Arms of the World.* Harrisburg, Pa.: Military Service Publishing Co., 1943.

Stock, James W. *Tobruk—The Siege.* New York: Ballantine Books, 1973.

Swinson, Arthur. *The Raiders: Desert Strike Force.* New York: Ballantine Books, 1968.

Tantum, W. H. IV, and Hoffschmidt, E. J. *Navy Uniforms, Insignia & Warships of World War II.* Old Greenwich, Conn.: We, Inc., 1968.

Tedder, *With Prejudice* (the World War II Memoirs of Marshal of the Royal Air Force Lord Tedder, Deputy Supreme Commander of the Allied Expeditionary Force). Boston: Little, Brown and Co., 1966.

Thompson, R. W. *Montgomery.* New York: Random House, 1974.

Thursfield, Rear Admiral H. G. *Brassey Naval Annual, 1942.* London: William Clowes, 1942.

———. *Brassey Naval Annual, 1945.* New York: The Macmillan Company, 1945.

The U. S. Army in World War II: Mediterranean Theater of Operation. Office of the Chief of Military History, 1957 Department of the Army, Washington, D.C.

Vader, John. *Spitfire.* New York: Ballantine Books, 1969.

Wagner, Ray. *American Combat Planes.* Garden City, N.Y.: Doubleday & Co., 1968.

Warlimont, Walter. *Inside Hitler's Headquarters.* Translated by R. H. Barry. New York: Praeger, 1964.

Warships in Profile. Vol. 1. Garden City, N.Y.: Doubleday & Co., 1970.

Young, Desmond. *Rommel: The Desert Fox.* New York: Harper & Bros., 1950.

INDEX